Addison-Wesley
Small-Scale Chemistry
Laboratory Manual

• •

Teacher's Edition

Edward L. Waterman

Stephen Thompson

▲▼

Addison-Wesley Publishing Company
Menlo Park, California • Reading, Massachusetts • New York
Don Mills, Ontario • Wokingham, England • Amsterdam
Bonn • Paris • Milan • Madrid • Sydney • Singapore
Tokyo • Seoul • Taipei • Mexico City • San Juan

Contents of the Teacher's Edition

● ●

Cover photographs
Paul Silverman/Fundamental Photographs; Joel Gordon (background)

ISBN 0-201-86168-2

4 5 6 7 8 9 10-ML-98 97 96

What Is Small-Scale Chemistry?

Addison-Wesley's *Small-Scale Chemistry Laboratory Manual* is designed to provide a complete laboratory program for a full-year course in first-year high school chemistry. Small-scale chemistry employs inexpensive, and for the most part, locally available plastic equipment, such as soda straws, cups, disposable pipets, and file protectors, to carry out surprisingly sophisticated and diverse chemical investigations on a small scale. Rather than using conventional glassware, such as beakers and test tubes, students perform qualitative experiments on hydrophobic plastic surfaces. Students also build, calibrate, and use quantitative instruments, such as balances, digital burets, spectroscopes, and pH meters.

This *Small-Scale Chemistry Laboratory Manual* contains both qualitative and quantitative studies of each of the major classes of chemical reactions as well as studies of chemical principles commonly covered in high school chemistry. Literally hundreds of chemical reactions are covered, including acid–base, precipitation, oxidation–reduction, organic, and biomolecule reactions. Those chemical reactions and principles are applied to solving many problems related to consumer and environmental chemistry.

Small-scale chemistry is designed to put the learning of chemistry into the hands of students. Students learn to do real experiments rather than just following recipes. Students participate in creative problem solving, invention, analytical thinking, effective writing, and descriptive chemistry while following the content of a standard high school chemistry curriculum.

Small-scale chemistry is designed to create a laboratory-based instructional chemistry program that fosters student creativity, invention, and problem solving. Small-scale was not developed simply to do better what traditional laboratory environments try to do. Small-scale does not, for example, miniaturize traditional experiments. Forty-seven original small-scale experiments focus students' attention on concepts, thought processes, and invention. Students are given the freedom to design their own lab apparatus and procedures. Small-scale creates an environment where students make original discoveries, accumulate new knowledge, and participate in creating methods for investigating the chemical world.

Finally, small-scale chemistry solves some of the most burdensome problems of conventional chemistry laboratories. Historically, traditional labs have been designed around conventional pieces of equipment such as beakers, flasks, and Bunsen burners. By their very nature, these apparatus, developed in the nineteenth century, dictate experimental methodology, the types of experiments that can be performed, the time constraints, and the physical scale of experiments. By redefining the philosophy, the equipment, and the practice of the instructional chemistry laboratory, small-scale solves the problems of costly equipment and chemicals, safety and teacher liability, time constraints, class size, chemical waste disposal, and related environmental concerns.

Why Use Small-Scale Chemistry?

Small-scale chemistry is relatively safe. Small-scale builds in safety at the design stage of an experiment rather than consigning teachers to try to control hazards at the execution stage. Hazardous reagents and procedures were eliminated before the experiments were designed. For example, solution concentrations are usually about $0.2M$ or less, and concentrations never exceed $1.0M$. Plastic thin-stemmed pipets, originally designed for biomedical research, serve both as liquid-storage vessels and transfer devices. Each pipet delivers only about 20 microliters of dilute solution. The potential for major accidents in traditional labs is replaced by minor inconveniences in small-scale labs.

Small-scale chemistry is time-efficient. Set up is made easy for the teacher and the student. The experimental format does not rely on lengthy written instructions. Instead, the directions are easy to read and follow. Experimental results are immediate and obvious, and the time students take to set up, manipulate, and clean equipment is minimal. Teachers are available to spend their valuable time and energy interacting with students during the laboratory. The simplicity of the experiments also enhances learning outcomes. The simple organization under the reaction surface helps students accurately record, compare, and correlate their data. Students focus on what's happening rather than on what to do. The teacher decides and chooses which learning outcomes are best for the class.

Small-scale chemistry labs have less environmental impact than do conventional chemistry labs. Cleanup with a paper towel takes seconds, and the minute quantities of chemicals can be disposed of safely, usually in the waste bin. As many school districts trim budgets and tighten regulations on the use and disposal of school-laboratory chemicals, small-scale offers immediate solutions. The small amounts of common, relatively safe chemicals employed never become a waste-management problem.

Small-scale chemistry is a lab-based program that can be used as the central focus of a high school chemistry course. Teachers can build the conventional content around the lab where it seems to fit. For example, students write and balance only those chemical equations for reactions that they have carried out in lab. Quantitative concepts, such as stoichiometry, are well suited for lab-centered teaching. Thus teachers can bring the content of chemistry into the laboratory. Through small-scale, students can and do learn much more chemistry than they can through conventional labs. In addition, they learn to be creative and inventive with chemistry; to be good problem solvers; and to communicate effectively.

Why use small-scale? It is relatively safe, time-efficient, easy to set up, and environmentally sound. Small-scale enhances learning outcomes, provides for lab-practical evaluations, and teaches chemistry through direct, hands-on experience. Most important, small-scale creates an environment where students can do serious science. It is an environment where the teacher does not already know all the answers but forms partnerships with the students to devise methods of finding answers. Small-scale actively engages students in the processes of creativity and invention. Finally, small-scale teaches students and teachers to ask questions but not to be satisfied with the answers.

Teacher's Guide to Safety with Small-Scale Chemistry

Handling chemicals of any kind in a high school lab setting always poses significant safety concerns. Though small-scale quantities and techniques are far safer than those used in conventional chemistry labs, and the experiments in this book were carefully constructed with safety in mind, some safety issues remain. The following suggestions should help minimize risk in your small-scale laboratory.

One of the largest potential problems is that students might use small-scale pipets as squirt guns. This misuse cannot be tolerated and requires immediate action on your part at the first sign of such a problem. To show your resolve to curtail this behavior, consider removing from the laboratory area any student who uses small-scale pipets in unauthorized ways.

Hold students accountable not only for what they learn in the lab, but also for their behavior while learning it. Consider periodically giving students a safety grade based on how safe their behavior is in the laboratory. You may also want to give an "environmental" grade based on how environmentally sound their cleaning methods are. Be sure to stress cleaning the small-scale reaction surface in a way that the solutions touch only the paper towel and not the student's hands. Make available a container of liquid soap at every lab table, and insist that students wash their hands thoroughly when they finish cleaning up.

Solutions used in this book never exceed $1.0M$ and are usually $0.1M$ or $0.2M$. Do not let students handle chemical solutions greater than $1.0M$. Always dilute concentrated acids yourself, by slowly and carefully adding them to water. In small-scale it is unnecessary for high school students to conduct this very dangerous procedure. You may want to make up stock solutions of $3.0M$ acids and use these to prepare $1.0M$ solutions as you need them. This practice minimizes your own exposure to concentrated acids.

Keep your chemical storage area secure from students. Do not store chemicals alphabetically. Store chemicals by an approved method.

The National Electrical Code now requires that ground-fault-circuit-interrupter (GFCI) receptacles be installed in homes where an electrical outlet is within six feet of a kitchen or bathroom sink. Consider having your school install ground-fault-protected receptacles wherever electrical outlets are within six feet of a laboratory sink. This will greatly reduce the risk of death by electrocution if a student happens to come into simultaneous contact with a grounded metal plumbing fixture or a concrete floor and an electrical appliance such as a hot plate or light fixture. Be sure to inspect your electrical appliances on a regular basis, and replace faulty cords and equipment immediately.

Bunsen burners, alcohol burners, or open flames of any kind are not appropriate for small-scale because they provide sources of heat that are far too intense for small-scale quantities. Use hot plates only on their lowest settings for heating small-scale quantities. Keep in mind too that most commercial hot plates are not designed for small-scale quantities. They can become excessively hot! If you do not have access to low-temperature hot plates, the evaporations required in some of the experiments can be done overnight at room temperature.

Always model good safety practices for your students. Wear safety glasses when it is appropriate. If you do not have a sterilization procedure for safety glasses, consider requiring students to purchase and maintain their own safety glasses. This greatly reduces the risk of students transmitting skin diseases and eye infections.

How to Set Up and Run a Small-Scale Chemistry Laboratory

Efficient organization on the part of the teacher is a key to running a successful small-scale chemistry lab program. Here are some suggestions for the set-up and day-to-day operations of a small-scale laboratory.

1. Assemble the following list of basic equipment. The quantities here assume you plan to convert your laboratory to small-scale chemistry entirely and further, that you will teach five to six sections of chemistry per day, with 24 students per section. You will need to adjust the numbers if you plan to use fewer small-scale labs your first year to augment your traditional program.

   4 boxes of thin-stemmed plastic disposable pipets (500 per box), to store and deliver liquids.

   50 plastic reagent bottles (250 mL), to store prepared solutions.

   10 plastic reagent bottles (1.0 L), to store prepared solutions.

   60 plastic screw-capped specimen jars (60 mL), to fill pipets.

   60 plastic cups (12 ounce), to store sets of pipets.

   120 plastic pill vials (30–60 mL), to store and dispense solid reagents.

   1 plastic "egg crate" light panel (2 feet × 4 feet, cut) to hold pipets for easy access.

   48 small-scale reaction surfaces (file protectors or overhead projection transparencies), to mix chemicals qualitatively.

   24 well plates (1 × 12), to calibrate pipets.

   12 pairs of scissors, to construct instruments.

   12 office hole punches (1/4-inch), to construct instruments.

   6 standard staplers, to construct instruments.

   150 plastic cups (1-ounce), for titrations and balance pans.

   150 plastic cups (3 1/2 ounce), for titrations and chromatography.

2. Prepare the reagent solutions on the Master Solutions. Store each reagent solution in an appropriately sized plastic reagent bottle. Label each bottle with the concentration, the chemical formula of the contents, the number of grams of solute per volume of solution, and the date of preparation (e.g. $1M$ NaCl, 14.6 g per 250 mL, Jan. 20, 1996). When a reagent bottle is empty, simply make a new solution from the labeled directions and change the date. You do not have to make all the solutions at once; prepare the necessary solutions only for the first lab. Then as the year goes on you can add solutions as you need them. By the end of your first year of small-scale chemistry you will have a complete set that will need only occasional maintenance. Once a small-scale lab is setup, a teacher in charge of 5 sections of 24 students each should count on replenishing about 10 to 15 solutions a year.

3. Store each reagent bottle in a dedicated place. The storage area should be secure from students but easily accessible by a teacher during a laboratory period. The prepared solutions and solids in this book require approximately 36 feet of shelf space.

4. For a classroom of 24 students, prepare and label 15 small-scale pipets and one 60 mL screw-capped plastic specimen jar (reagent-filling container) for each of the solutions listed on the Master Solutions List. Fill each set of pipets and store them stem-up in a labeled 12-ounce plastic cup on the shelf along with the reagent bottle and plastic specimen jar. To save time, you may want to spend a few minutes in class having students pull pipets and tape labels on them. Use a computer to make labels or print the number of labels you need before you cut them out and tape them to the pipets.

5. Cut the egg-crate plastic light panel into small sections to use as pipet racks. Wear your safety glasses and use a hacksaw. This is

a job you have to do only once. Cut sections that are three squares by ten squares, that will hold as many as 30 pipets.

6. When it is time to set up a lab, place one pipet of each of the reagents needed in the lab in 12 small-scale pipet racks. Distribute the reagent sets to your lab tables. Two students can share a set of reagents even if they are doing the lab individually. Leave three pipets of each solution in reserve in your storage area. Alternatively, you may want to set out the 12-ounce storage cups with sets of pipets in them. Let students be responsible for obtaining their own racks of pipets at the beginning of the lab and returning them at the end.

7. Fill empty pipets as students call your attention to them. Because students often need only one or two drops of each reagent, many pipets will not need filling until after several sections of students have done the lab. You may want to set out selected reagent bottles of chemicals of which students will need larger quantities, and teach them how to fill their own pipets, as described in "Safe and Efficient Techniques for Using Small-Scale Equipment" on page 8.

8. When the lab is finished, return the pipets to their storage cups. You may want to leave one or two sets out for another day or two to accommodate students who were absent during the lab.

9. For a classroom of 24 students, prepare and label plastic pill vials (30–60 mL) for each solid on the Master Solids list. Punch small holes in the lids and cover them with tape. To use the vials, students can remove the tape and carefully shake out the desired quantity. Store the solids in the plastic pill vials with the openings taped. You can store each set in a large plastic cup or in a standard plastic ice-cube tray.

How to Use This Book

Addison-Wesley's *Small-Scale Chemistry Laboratory Manual* is designed to be used in a variety of ways. Each experiment includes a reference to an appropriate section of the textbook, a set of Objectives, an Introduction, an Experimental Page or Experimental Procedure, an Experimental Data section, a Questions for Analysis section, and a Now It's Your Turn section.

The Experimental Page is designed to give students the instructions they need to carry out the basic experiment. In most of the qualitative labs and some of the quantitative labs, students place the Experimental Page under a plastic small-scale reaction surface and do the experiment on top of the page, following the directions that show through the plastic. Often the Experimental Page is marked with black X's where students are to place drops of solutions. These X's provide both black and white backgrounds against which students can observe reaction mixtures. In the labs where the Experimental Page is not used under a small-scale reaction surface, the heading Experimental Procedure indicates this difference.

The Experimental Data section follows the Experimental Page. Here students record their data as they do the experiment. You may choose to have students write their experimental results directly into a lab notebook. In this case they would use the printed Experimental Data table(s) as an example and construct a similar table(s) in their notebooks.

The Questions for Analysis section allows students to think about and write about the main points of each experiment. You may want to have students work on these questions as they do the lab so that they can answer each question in context with the chemistry they see in front of them. Also, the questions can be assigned as homework, or you can ask students to answer them in their laboratory notebooks for future reference.

The Now It's Your Turn section suggests some extended experiments that ask students to apply what they learned in the basic experiment. Specific instructions are not always given; students are left to decide for themselves what to do based on what they have learned in the basic experiment. Depending on the time you want to spend and the depth at which you want to cover the material, you may want to assign one item or all the items in this section. Some of the Now It's Your Turn items could be used for lab-practical exams. Students will often suggest other experiments to try. Be open to their ideas and let them try other experiments that you consider to be appropriate and safe.

Evaluation of Student Learning through Small-Scale Chemistry

The following list provides some suggestions for how you could evaluate what your students learn from doing small-scale chemistry laboratories.

1. **Lab notebook:** Rather than having students write lab reports or hand in data sheets, you may want to have them keep a laboratory notebook. The lab notebook is a real-time, permanent, hand-written record of all of a student's laboratory experiences, including dates, titles, experimental procedures, data, conclusions, and further research and investigations. Pick the lab notebooks up periodically, and grade them for completeness rather than for specific details. With only a quick glance you can verify that a student has kept his work up to date. You may be less interested in format than in how well students can use their own lab records to solve problems. In this case, look for signs of creativity, invention, problem solving, and good thought processes. Tell students beforehand what you are looking for. You may want to give extra credit for evidence of creativity or invention. For example, students might discover interesting new questions or ways to solve problems, or a student might choose to write the lab procedure in cartoon format.

2. **Open-lab-notebook tests:** To check for details and understanding, you may want to give students regular lab tests and allow them to use their own hand-written notes to answer the questions. Try to balance the range of questions from knowledge-level questions to those that evaluate comprehension, analysis, synthesis, evaluation, and creativity. Students soon learn that to score well on these exams, they must not only bring to class a well-written lab book, but they must be able to use it to interpret their results and to suggest new questions and experiments.

3. **Closed-lab-notebook tests:** Some skills learned in lab need to be internalized by any student of chemistry. Use closed-book tests to evaluate how well students have learned these skills. For example, test students' abilities to write and balance equations.

4. **Laboratory-practical exams:** Small-scale chemistry lends itself well to the direct hands-on evaluation of problem solving using both qualitative and quantitative analysis. Variations of the unknowns in Small-Scale Experiments 20 and 21 provide good examples. Quantitative titrations of unknowns in Small-Scale Experiments 11 and 12 provide others. The various items in the Now It's Your Turn sections provide still other possibilities for lab-practical exams.

5. **Writing essays:** Consider having students write short essays on their conclusions of various labs. Try to assign essays that bring creativity and original thought out of students. For example, upon measuring vitamin C in various fruit juices in Small-Scale Experiment 45, you might assign this: "Write a letter to the editor of the local newspaper telling him of your findings and recommendations," or "Write to Linus Pauling explaining your results, and ask him for additional information on vitamin C," or "Write Linus Pauling's reply."

Master Materials List

The following lists give all chemicals necessary to do all the experiments in Addison-Wesley's *Small-Scale Chemistry Laboratory Manual*. The first is an alphabetical list of chemical solutions. Indicator solutions follow in a separate alphabetical list. The last two lists are the Master Solids List and the Master Household Products List.

Master Solutions List

The most efficient way to organize your small-scale lab is to make up the appropriate aqueous solutions and use and replace them as needed. Store each solution in a plastic reagent bottle. Depending on the labs you do, some solutions will have to be replaced several times during the year, and others will last the entire year. Most solutions are $0.1M$ or $0.2M$. In no case is any solution in greater concentration than $1.0M$. Also, in no case are there two different concentrations of the same chemical. For example, all the experiments that use sodium hydroxide use $0.5M$ NaOH. All salts are anhydrous unless the hydrated formula is given.

Label each reagent bottle with the chemical formula, the concentration, the number of grams of solute per volume of solution, and the date. When the bottle is empty, simply replenish it by following the directions on the label, and change the date. When making dilute acid solutions from concentrated acids, remember always to add acid to water slowly and carefully. **Be sure to make up all solutions with the quantities given to a volume of 250 mL, unless one liter or 50 mL is specified.**

Chemical	Quantity	Concentration	Experiments
ethanoic acid, CH_3COOH	Use commercial vinegar	$0.8M$ (5%)	8, 9, 11, 12, 15, 19, 31, 32, 33, 34, 40
aluminum chloride hexahydrate, $AlCl_3 \cdot 6H_2O$	12.1 g	$0.2M$	19, 24, 30, 39, 42
ammonia, NH_3	67 mL conc. in 1.0 L	$1.0M$	1, 8, 9, 19, 20, 21, 23, 26, 31, 32, 33, 38, 41, 42
ammonium chloride, NH_4Cl	13.4 g	$1.0M$	6, 15, 24, 31, 33
boric acid, H_3BO_3	7.8 g	$0.5M$	28, 31
calcium chloride, $CaCl_2$	14.2 g	$0.5M$	1, 6, 10, 12, 19, 20, 21, 24, 30, 39, 41, 42
calcium hydroxide, $Ca(OH)_2$	1.0 g, then filter	saturated	6, 9, 31
citric acid, $C_6H_8O_7$	9.6 g	$0.2M$	28, 31
copper(II) sulfate pentahydrate, $CuSO_4 \cdot 5H_2O$	12.5 g	$0.2M$	1, 6, 10, 19, 20, 21, 24, 26, 30, 34, 35, 36, 37, 38, 41, 46
ethylenediamine tetraacetic acid, EDTA, disodium salt, dihydrate	0.744 g in 1.0 L	$0.002M$	19
hydrochloric acid, HCl	82 mL of $12M$ in 1.0 L	$1.0M$	1, 8, 9, 12, 15, 16, 19, 20, 21, 23, 25, 26, 31, 32, 33, 34, 36, 38, 41, 46
hydrogen peroxide, H_2O_2	Use commercial	3%	15, 19, 25, 27, 41
iron(III) chloride, hexahydrate, $FeCl_3 \cdot 6H_2O$	6.8 g in 250 mL of $0.1M$ NaCl	$0.1M$	6, 10, 19, 20, 21, 24, 27, 36, 41
iron(II) sulfate, $FeSO_4$	3.8 g in 50 mL $1.0M$ H_2SO_4, enough water to make 250 mL		35

Chemical	Quantity	Concentration	Experiments
lead(II) nitrate, $Pb(NO_3)_2$	16.6 g	0.2M	1, 6, 10, 12, 20, 21, 24, 25, 26, 30, 37, 39, 41, 42
magnesium sulfate, $MgSO_4$	6.0 g	0.2M	6, 24, 34, 37, 39, 42
nitric acid, HNO_3	63 mL 15.8M in 1.0 L	1.0M	8, 9, 11, 12, 15, 16, 19, 20, 21, 26, 31, 32, 34, 39
phosphoric acid, H_3PO_4	67.5 mL 14.8M in 1.0 L	1.0M	8, 16, 19, 28, 32, 33, 34
potassium bromide, KBr	6.0 g	0.2M	6, 38, 41
potassium chloride, KCl	7.5 g	0.4M	30, 33, 38, 41
potassium dichromate, $K_2Cr_2O_7$	7.3 g	0.1M	36
potassium fluoride, KF	5.8 g	0.4M	6, 41
potassium hydroxide, KOH	2.8 g	0.2M	9, 19, 23, 39, 47
potassium iodate, KIO_3	5.35 g	0.1M	25, 36, 41, 44, 45
potassium iodide, KI	4.2 g	0.1M	1, 6, 10, 15, 20, 21, 24, 25, 33, 36, 38, 40, 41, 44, 45, 46
potassium permanganate, $KMnO_4$	0.16 g in 50 mL 1.0M H_2SO_4	0.02M	15, 36
potassium thiocyanate, KSCN	2.4 g	0.1M	26, 39
silver nitrate, $AgNO_3$	2.1 g	0.05M	1, 6, 10, 12, 20, 21, 24, 26, 30, 35, 37, 39, 41, 42
sodium ethanoate, CH_3COONa	10.3 g	0.5M	6, 8, 31, 33
sodium carbonate, Na_2CO_3	26.3 g	1.0M	1, 6, 8, 10, 12, 16, 19, 20, 21, 24, 26, 30
sodium chloride, NaCl	58.5 g in 1.0 L	0.10M	6, 10, 22, 24, 42
sodium dihydrogen phosphate, NaH_2PO_4	17.2 g	0.50M	6, 8, 31, 33
sodium hydrogen carbonate, $NaHCO_3$	21 g	1.0M	1, 6, 8, 15, 16, 19, 25, 30, 31, 33, 42
sodium hydrogen phosphate, Na_2HPO_4	7.1 g	0.2M	6, 8, 31
sodium hydrogen sulfate $NaHSO_4$	34.5 g	1.0M	1, 8, 19, 31
sodium hydrogen sulfite, $NaHSO_3$	2.6 g	0.1M	8, 15, 31, 36
sodium hydroxide, NaOH	20.0 g in 1.0 L	0.5M	1, 6, 8, 10, 11, 12, 15, 19, 20, 21, 24, 26, 32, 33, 39, 46
sodium hypochlorite, NaOCl	Dilute 50 mL household bleach with 200 mL water.	1.0%	1, 15, 25, 36, 40 41, 46
sodium nitrate, $NaNO_3$	4.26 g	0.2M	24, 37, 38
sodium nitrite, $NaNO_2$	6.9 g	0.4M	6, 15, 31, 36
sodium phosphate, dodecahydrate, $Na_3PO_4 \cdot 12H_2O$	9.5 g	0.1M	6, 8, 10, 19, 20, 21, 24, 27, 31

Chemical	Quantity	Concentration	Experiments
sodium sulfate, Na_2SO_4	7.1 g	0.2M	10, 24, 38
sodium thiosulfate pentahydrate, $Na_2S_2O_3 \cdot 5H_2O$	24.8 g	0.1M	25, 26, 36, 40, 41
starch	Dilute 50 mL liquid household starch with 200 mL water.	20%	1, 15, 36, 38, 40, 41, 44, 45, 46
sulfuric acid, H_2SO_4	56 mL 18M in 1.0 L	1.0M	8, 9, 11, 12, 15, 16, 19, 20, 21, 25, 31, 34
tin(IV) chloride pentahydrate, $SnCl_4 \cdot 5H_2O$	17.6 g	0.2M	6, 30, 42
zinc chloride, $ZnCl_2$	6.8 g	0.2M	19, 24, 30, 35, 37, 39, 42

Master Indicator Solutions List

Indicator	Quantity	Concentration	Experiments
alizarine yellow R, AYR	50 mg	0.02%	8, 28, 29
blue dye	15 drops blue food coloring		
bromcresol green, BCG*	100 mg in 14.3 mL 0.01M NaOH	0.04%	8, 29
bromphenol blue, BPB*	100 mg in 14.9 mL 0.01M NaOH	0.04%	8, 9, 12, 15, 23, 26, 29, 30, 31, 38, 41
bromthymol blue, BTB*†	100 mg in 16.0 mL 0.01M NaOH	0.04%	8, 9, 29
FD&C blue #1‡	50 mg in 50 mL water	0.1%	1, 22
FD&C blue #2	50 mg in 50 mL water	0.1%	22
FD&C green #3	50 mg in 50 mL water	0.1%	22
FD&C red #3	50 mg in 50 mL water	0.1%	22
FD&C red #40	50 mg in 50 mL water	0.1%	22
FD&C yellow #5	50 mg in 50 mL water	0.1%	22
FD&C yellow #6	50 mg in 50 mL water	0.1%	22
meta cresol purple, MCP*	100 mg in 26.2 mL 0.01M NaOH	0.04%	8, 29
methyl orange, MO	125 mg	0.05%	8, 29
methyl red, MR	50 mg in 250 mL 70% 2-propanol	0.02%	8, 9, 11, 29
phenolphthalein, phen	250 mg in 250 mL 70% 2-propanol	0.10%	1, 8, 9, 11, 12, 15, 29, 47
Sudan III	50 mg in 50 mL rubbing alcohol	0.1%	46
thymol blue, TB*	100 mg in 21.5 mL 0.01M NaOH	0.04%	8, 29
universal indicator, UI	See formulation directions for UI in the Teaching Suggestions for Small-Scale Experiment 28.		12, 28, 29, 31, 32, 33

*If this indicator is available as the sodium salt, dissolve directly in 250 mL of deionized or distilled water.
†The final solution of bromthymol blue should be green. If it is yellow, add 0.01M NaOH drop by drop with stirring until it is green. If it is blue, add 0.01M HCl drop by drop with stirring until it is green.
‡FD&C dyes are used in consumer products as colorants and are certified by the FDA. The set used in this text is available from Rainbow Colors, 286 Baxter St., Tolland, CT 06084.

Master Solids List

Fill six 30 to 60 mL plastic pill vials with each solid. Use a 1/4-inch office hole punch to make a hole in each plastic lid. Cover the hole with plastic tape. Label each vial and store each set of six in plastic ice cube trays. When a laboratory calls for a solid, distribute the set of six vials among 24 students.

Solid	Experiments
aluminum (foil), Al	34, 38
ammonium chloride, NH_4Cl	23, 25
calcium carbonate, $CaCO_3$ (granular)	16, 25
calcium chloride, $CaCl_2$	23, 27
chalk	7
copper, Cu	34, 35, 37
eriochrome black-T, Ero-T*	19
fluorite	7
glass marble	7
hematite	7
iron, Fe (granular)	34, 35
lead, Pb	37
magnesium, Mg (turnings)	25, 31, 34, 35, 37, 47
polystyrene peanut	7
potassium chloride, KCl	23
silver, Ag	35, 37
sodium carbonate, Na_2CO_3	23
sodium chloride, NaCl (rock salt)	23, 27
sodium chloride, NaCl (table salt)	7, 19, 22, 23
sodium hydrogen carbonate, $NaHCO_3$	27
sucrose, $C_{12}H_{22}O_{11}$	7, 23, 46
sulfur, S	7
zinc, Zn (granular)	25, 34, 37

* Mix 0.1 g of eriochrome black-T with 100 g of sodium chloride (table salt), thoroughly.

Master Household Products List

Obtain one container of each of the following household products. Store liquids in their original containers. When a laboratory calls for a household product, place it where it is accessible to students working in the lab.

Household Product	Experiments
ammonia	8, 9, 28
antacid (tablets)	8, 9, 16, 23, 28, 33
aspirin	8, 28, 33
baking powder	8, 16, 23, 28, 33
baking soda	1, 8, 16, 28, 33
beans, dry	1, 5, 46
bleach, liquid containing NaOCl	1, 8, 15, 25, 36, 40, 41, 46
cabbage juice	8, 28, 29, 40
cola	8, 23, 28, 46
copper polish	34, 35
cream of tartar	8, 16, 28, 33
grape juice	8, 28, 29, 40
glass cleaner, liquid	1, 8, 28, 33
laundry detergent, powdered	1, 8, 28
lemon juice	8, 9, 28
milk, powdered	8, 28, 46
orange juice, canned, frozen, fresh	8, 22, 28, 45
oven cleaner (Bicarbonate based. Do not use products containing lye.)	1, 8, 16, 28
peas, dry	1, 5, 46
pens, colored fiber-tipped	1, 28, 40
popcorn, dry unpopped	1, 5, 46
rubbing alcohol, 70% 2-propanol	22, 23, 29
rubbing alcohol, 70% ethanol	22, 23, 29
salt, iodized	1
salt, noniodized	1, 22, 23, 27, 28
sidewalk de-icer ($CaCl_2$ or KCl)	1, 27

Household Product	Experiments
silver polish	34, 35
soft-drink mixes, dry (Kool-Aid)	1, 8, 22, 28, 40
starch, liquid	1, 15, 28, 36, 38, 40, 41, 46
toilet-bowl cleaner containing HCl	1, 8, 11, 12, 28, 34
toilet-bowl cleaner containing NaHSO$_4$	1, 8, 23, 28, 34
vinegar	8, 9, 11, 28, 34
vitamin C tablets (100 mg)	8, 28, 44

Master Equipment List

All equipment quantities in the Teaching Suggestions for each experiment are given per student unless otherwise indicated. The Common Equipment, mentioned in the Teaching Suggestions, is to be shared among students.

Equipment	Experiments
acid resin ion exchanger	19
adhesive label	2, 3, 4, 17
alcohol thermometer	14
atomic emission tubes and sources	18
boxes, various shapes and sizes	17
candle	18
chromatography paper	22
clothespins	13
colored construction paper	18
colored plastic light filters	18
conductivity/electrolysis apparatus	23, 31, 38
cotton swab	9, 11
diffraction grating	17
dimes	4, 37
electronic balance (optional)	3, 7, 12, 13, 14, 19, 44, 45
filter paper disks (9 cm)	37
glass slide	9, 16, 23, 34, 41, 46
graph paper, tenth inch	2

Equipment	Experiments
nails, galvanized and iron	17
nickels	3, 4, 37
paper clips, jumbo	2
paper clips, standard	2, 3, 13
paper, various kinds	22
paper towels, brands with price tags	13
pennies	3, 4, 37
pennies, set of 10 from 1978–1987	4
pin, extra-long (1 1/4 inch)	2
plastic cup, 1-ounce	2, 11, 12, 14, 25, 26, 27, 32, 33, 40, 44, 45, 47
plastic cup, 3 1/2-ounce	2, 5, 13, 41
plastic cup, clear	15, 18, 22
plastic light rod (clear plastic picnic knife)	17
plastic spoon	7, 27
polystyrene coffee cup	14
poster board	13, 17, 22
rubber bands	17
ruler	17
silverware	35
small-scale pipet	1, 4, 6, 8, 9, 10, 16, 20, 21, 24, 26, 28, 29, 30, 31, 32, 39, 41, 42
small-scale pipet rack	1
small-scale reaction surface	1, 6, 8, 9, 10, 15, 16, 20, 21, 23, 24, 25, 26, 27, 28, 29, 30, 31, 32, 33, 34, 35, 36, 37, 38, 39, 40, 41, 42, 44, 46
soda straws, long and short	2, 3, 26
toothpicks	46
typing paper	22, 46
washers, zinc plated	35
well plate, 1 × 12	11, 40
wood blocks, drilled	2
zipper-locking plastic bag	3, 43

Common Equipment	Experiments
batteries (dry cells), various, 4 each	37
brass or steel wire, 24-gauge, 1 spool	2, 3
cellophane tape, 6 rolls	2, 17
colored marking pens, 12 sets	22
hot plates, 6	9, 16, 23, 34, 46
model sets, 12 as follows: 6 one-inch polystyrene spheres 12 pop beads 3 black pipe cleaners (30 cm × 3 mm) 3 white pipe cleaners (30 cm × 3 mm)	43
office hole punches, 1/4-inch, 6	2, 3, 13
scissors, 12 pairs	2, 3, 13, 17, 22, 37, 46
standard staples	3
standard weights, 5 mg	2
staplers, 6	3, 22
teacher-built spectroscope	17
thread, 1 spool	2
volt meters, 12	37
watches or clocks, 12	47

A Study of Chemical Changes

Text Section 1.7

Estimated Class Time: One to three 50-minute periods, depending on how many household products are used in Now It's Your Turn.
Estimated Teacher Preparation Time: 20 minutes, after stock solutions are prepared.

Overview

Students mix solutions and observe a variety of macroscopic chemical changes (color, texture, precipitation, etc.). Students learn to recognize distinctive changes and to use them to identify specific chemicals in household products.

Materials

Small-scale pipets of the following solutions:

sodium hydrogen carbonate	hydrochloric acid
FD&C Blue No. 1	sodium hypochlorite
potassium iodide	lead(II) nitrate
calcium chloride	sodium hydrogen sulfate
sodium carbonate	phenolphthalein
sodium hydroxide	silver nitrate
ammonia	copper(II) sulfate
starch	

Household Products:

Baking soda, iodized table salt, bread, cereal, crackers, potato chips, or similar foods containing starch, automatic dishwashing liquid containing NaOCl.

Equipment (per student throughout book unless otherwise specified)

Small-scale pipet racks, Experimental Page, small-scale reaction surface, empty pipets for stirring.

Teaching Suggestions

This lab, designed for the first week of school, allows students to become familiar with the use of basic small-scale equipment and to do qualitative analysis on real samples very early in the course.

Provide each student with an Experimental Page to be placed under the reaction surface. You can use file protectors, overhead transparencies, or plastic wrap for the reaction surface. Tell students that the black X's on the Experimental Page serve as contrasting backgrounds for viewing the reactions in the drops of aqueous solutions. Tell them to view their mixtures against both the white and black backgrounds the X's provide. All students should perform the experiments on the Experimental Page and answer the Questions for Analysis.

Emphasize the importance of making good observations and using them to solve problems. Students should not be concerned with specific chemical details like names, formulas, and reactions. The intent here is to convince students that chemical observations can be useful to them in exploring their world.

You may want to emphasize the importance of designing experiments. Even on the first day of chemistry class, students can design their own experiments. You may want to assign only a portion of Now It's Your Turn depending on the time you have and the household products available. Place the household products in their original containers in a reagent area common to students. Students should sample them using clean soda straws. Solids are sampled by making small-scale spatulas as described in "Safe and Efficient Small-Scale Techniques," and liquids are sampled by dipping the tip of a clean soda straw into the liquid, holding a finger over the other end and removing a drop to be placed on the reaction surface.

Good lab-practical problems include having students distinguish between iodized and non-iodized salt and between carbonate-based and noncarbonate-based laundry detergents.

Design and Construction of a Small-Scale Balance

Text Section 2.1

Estimated Class Time: Two 50-minute periods.
Estimated Teacher Preparation Time: 20 minutes, after materials are organized.

Overview

Students learn that weighing is the fundamental method of measuring mass. Students practice invention by designing and constructing their own milligram balances, which they use to investigate macroscopic matter.

Equipment

6 soda straws, 1 extra-long pin (1 1/4-inch), 2 paper clips, 1 adhesive label, 1 drilled wood block, 4 square centimeters of tenth inch graph paper, 1 plastic cup (1-ounce or 3 1/2-ounce).

Common Equipment

1 spool of thread, 1 spool of wire, six 1/4-inch office hole punches, 12 pairs of scissors, 6 rolls of cellophane tape, 36 longer soda straws, standard 5 mg weights.

Teaching Suggestions

To prepare for the lab you need to drill balance bases made from square pieces of 1 × 4's or 2 × 4's. Drill 1/4-inch holes half way through the wood at the places marked on the diagram below. Each hole should be 3/4 inch from the center.

If the soda straws do not fit snugly in the holes, wrap tape around the ends of the straws. Purchase extra-long straws and plastic cups from a restaurant-supply store or a membership warehouse store. You can buy extra long pins (1 1/4 inch) from a fabric store.

Using the Introduction, go over the basic principles of an operating balance, especially sensitivity, capacity, and the critical parts of a balance, with the students. Then let them begin to build the basic balance as given in Figure 2.1. As they build it, encourage them to invent and create as they try to improve the major features: a light beam, a frictionless fulcrum, and square angles. Some students will build only the basic balance, but others will make innovations that you will want to share with the rest of the class.

Most students need to be reminded that a freely swinging beam is most important. If students build the basic balance shown in Figure 2.1, they will have a functional instrument that will serve them well if the beam swings freely and without friction.

The pencil holes that hold the pin fulcrum should be made so the head of the pin slips through them easily. After mounting the beam-fulcrum assembly, gently press the posts together to keep the pin from falling out. Do not squeeze so tightly that the ends of the pin touch the insides of the straws. The aim here is to get the beam to swing freely without having the pin fall out.

Some students will choose to build high balances with long pointers so that a small movement in the beam will produce a large movement of the pointer. Discuss with them the trade-off between structural stability problems of high balances versus the greater sensitivity they produce. Students will solve these problems if they are given the time and encouragement to do so. Other students will think they have a better way to design the superstructure and spend their time being creative with it. A few students will want to work on building a better beam-fulcrum assembly. Still other students may want to try a magnetic levitation of the beam by simple electromagnets or permanent magnets. The possibilities for invention are many.

Small-Scale Experiment 3 **Design and Construction of a Set of Standardized Weights**

Text Section 2.9

Estimated Class Time: One or two 50-minute periods, depending on how much time you allow for invention.
Estimated Teacher Preparation Time: 20 minutes, after purchase of materials.

Overview

Students learn about calibration and make weight sets to use with their balances. Invention is the key!

Equipment

Half-page of graph paper that is divided into one-tenth-inch squares, standard paper clip, jumbo paper clip, zipper-locking plastic sandwich bag, penny, nickel.

Common Equipment

6 staplers with standard staples, six 1/4-inch office hole punches, 36 soda straws, *1 spool of 24-gauge brass or steel wire, 36 small adhesive labels, 12 pairs of scissors.

*Equipment for Now It's Your Turn.

Teaching Suggestions

Standard staples are 33 mg each, one square inch of standard 20-pound paper weighs 50 mg, and 1/4-inch disks punched from soda straws are 5 mg each. Photocopied graph paper that is divided in tenths of inches works well, but you can make your own by drawing a grid of square inches on a standard 8 1/2 × 11 piece of paper and photocopying it. Because staples are more precisely made than paper, students do best if they use more staples and less paper. Students who make the following weight set will get good results.

5 mg to 30 mg: Use the appropriate number of 1/4-inch soda straw disks.

50 mg: 1 square inch of photocopied graph paper.

100 mg: 2 square inches of photocopied graph paper.

300 mg: 2 square inches of photocopied graph paper + 6 staples.

Weights of 500 mg and larger will not be exactly 500 mg or 1000 mg, but their exact weight can be determined by using the smaller weights. Here are some approximations:

500 mg: One standard paper clip with an adhesive label (1/2" × 3/4")

1500 mg: One jumbo paper clip with an adhesive label (1/2" × 3/4")

2550 mg: One penny (post-1982) with an adhesive label (1/2" × 3/4")

5050 mg: One nickel with an adhesive label (1/2" × 3/4")

If there is an accurate milligram balance in the lab, allow students to check their smaller weights (50–300 mg) against the accurate balance and make the necessary corrections by adding pieces of adhesive labels or cutting off corners. Then they can use the small weights with their small-scale balance to calibrate the larger weights. If an accurate balance is not available, experience has shown that if students are careful, their smaller weights (50–300 mg) are rarely in error by more than a few milligrams. Emphasize the importance of recycling all the materials students do not use.

Given the time and encouragement, students can invent many different kinds of weights.

Highly reproducible, small objects make the most reliable weights. Stainless-steel or brass wire (28-gauge) can be weighed on an analytical or electronic milligram balance and the length of wire needed to make a certain weight can be calculated. The same method works with a soda straw, measuring the straw and cutting an appropriate length. If you have an accurate balance in the lab, students can have fun exploring the precision of all kinds of objects to see which are suitable to use as reliable weights.

Weighing Activities for a Small-Scale Balance

• •

Text Section 3.3

Estimated Class Time: One or two 50-minute periods, depending on how much time you allow for Now It's Your Turn.
Estimated Teacher Preparation Time: 20 minutes, after purchase of materials.

Overview

Students use their balances to solve a variety of problems associated with matter at the macroscopic level.

Equipment

Penny, nickel, dime, and enough adhesive labels to attach to them; small-scale balance; small-scale pipet filled with water; *a set of ten pennies representing each year from 1978 to 1987.

Teaching Suggestions

This is a good opportunity for students to practice using their balances, test the accuracies of their weights, and solve any problems. If the percent error exceeds 5%, have the student adjust the fulcrum for a frictionless, freely swinging beam, and try again. Students can also check and adjust their weights on an analytical or milligram balance.

Label 48 pennies and weigh each on an accurate balance before class so students can know the "accurate" weight. Do not tell them the accurate weight until they have determined the weight using their balances. The experiment is a

*Equipment for Now It's Your Turn.

good blind test of their balances and weights. Once they consistently get the "right" answer, they grow confident in the accuracies of their own balances. Post-1982 pennies weigh about 2550 mg with an adhesive label (1/2" × 3/4"). Nickels weigh about 5050 mg with labels, and dimes weigh about 2250 mg.

Most small-scale pipets deliver around 50 drops per mL (1000 mg) of water. All pipets are different, however, and they often vary ±10 drops per mL. The angle and the air bubble affect the results.

For item 1 of Now It's Your Turn, make up sets of ten pennies: one each for the dates 1978 through 1987. Place each set of ten pennies in a zipper-locking bag and label it for easy identification. Some of the 1982 pennies are copper and some are zinc, so students will get varying answers, depending on what sets they have.

Suggest that they solve this problem by making more weights or by using a larger counterweight on the balance. This approach increases the capacity of the balance. (Remind students that it also results in a heavier beam, which reduces the sensitivity of the balance; there are always trade-offs when designing experiments.) Alternatively, you may want to suggest that they weigh a portion of their vegium, say half, and then multiply the result by two (or a fifth and multiply by five). The beans are of various sizes, so if a student weighs just one bean and multiplies by the number of beans to get the total weight of beans, a significant error might result. Emphasize that it is important to weigh a large enough sample to get a good estimation of the average weight of a bean.

Although the calculations and concepts are the same for each student, each sample will be slightly different and will yield a slightly different atomic mass. You may want to pursue number 2 of Now It's Your Turn with your students. Emphasize the importance of sampling techniques and the size of samples. Larger samples give more homogeneous results. Relate this to the number of atoms in even a very small mass, and students should get the idea that it's easier to obtain more consistent samples of atoms than of vegium.

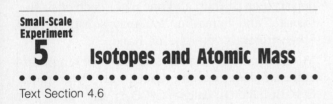

Small-Scale Experiment 5

Isotopes and Atomic Mass

Text Section 4.6

Estimated Class Time: One 50-minute period.
Estimated Teacher Preparation Time: 15 minutes.

Overview

Students weigh sample mixtures of peas, beans, and corn and use their data to calculate the average weight of all the particles. They relate this to the concept of atomic weight.

Equipment

A sample of vegium in a plastic cup, balance.

Teaching Suggestions

For a class of 24 students, thoroughly mix 1-pound bags each of: dried kidney or pinto beans, dried split peas, and unpopped popcorn. Mass-produce enough samples for your class by dipping out a level 1-ounce plastic cup full of vegium, and place each sample in a 3 1/2-ounce plastic cup to distribute to each student.

When students weigh the various kinds of vegium particles, they will encounter some technical problems. For example, the sample of beans might be too large to weigh on their balances.

Small-Scale Experiment 6

Chemical Names and Formulas

Text Sections 5.10, 5.11

Estimated Class Time: One 50-minute period.
Estimated Teacher Preparation Time: 30 minutes.

Overview

Students observe small-scale samples of ionic compounds and learn to name them and to write their formulas. Students use aqueous solutions to synthesize new compounds and explore their names and formulas. Students learn that chemical formulas are symbolic representations of submicroscopic matter.

Materials (per pair of students)

Small-scale reaction surface where 1 drop of each of the following solutions has been allowed to evaporate in its place as indicated on the Experimental Page:

potassium iodide	ammonium chloride
sodium chloride	sodium phosphate
magnesium sulfate	calcium hydroxide
copper(II) sulfate	tin(IV) chloride
sodium hydrogen carbonate	potassium bromide
	calcium chloride
silver nitrate	iron(III) chloride
sodium nitrite	sodium hydrogen phosphate
potassium fluoride	
sodium carbonate	sodium dihydrogen phosphate
lead(II) nitrate	
*iron(III) chloride	*silver nitrate
*potassium iodide	*lead(II) nitrate
*sodium hydroxide	*copper(II) sulfate
*sodium carbonate	*magnesium sulfate
sodium ethanoate	

Equipment

Dry pipet, clean small-scale reaction surface.

Teaching Suggestions

The day before the lab (or an hour before), place 1 drop of each indicated compound on a small-scale reaction surface on top of the Experimental Page and allow the water to evaporate. Make up one reaction surface for each pair of students. Keep these sets to use from class to class throughout the day. Alternatively, have students do this at the beginning of the period. As they name the compounds and write the formulas, the solutions will evaporate and the solid compounds will appear. In this case, have students clean the file protector as usual.

This lab is designed to get students to name and write formulas of compounds they are likely to encounter in the rest of the course. As a start, suggest to students that they memorize the names and formulas of a few monatomic and polyatomic ions. They can master the system of naming and writing formulas without becoming overloaded with information.

Now It's Your Turn provides an excellent pre-chemical-reaction exercise. Tell students that these kinds of chemical reactions and their products will be studied in Chapter 7.

*Materials for Now It's Your Turn.

Small-Scale Experiment 7 — Weighing: A Means of Counting

Text Section 6.4

Estimated Class Time: One 50-minute period.
Estimated Teacher Preparation Time: 15 minutes.

Overview

Students weigh common chemicals and calculate moles, molecules and atoms from their data. Students also weigh common objects and investigate their quantitative compositions using the chemical quantities of mass, moles, and atoms.

Materials (per student)

Solids: one teaspoon of sucrose, one teaspoon of sodium chloride, a piece of chalk, a glass slide, a polystyrene peanut, and one piece each of sulfur, fluorite, and hematite. You may substitute any other minerals you have on hand.

*A nickel coin, and pieces of the following mineral samples: gypsum, $CaSO_4 \cdot 2H_2O$; graphite, C; barite, $BaSO_4$; calcite, $CaCO_3$; pyrite, FeS_2; and galena, PbS_2.

Equipment

Balance, plastic spoons.

Teaching Suggestions

Assign as many or as few of the weighings as time permits. The calculations are given to the students in dimensional-analysis form, so they can focus on the fact that the experimental data (the weighings) are the keys to counting atoms. Students can learn how to construct their own solutions to problems using dimensional analysis from the text.

A possible lab-practical problem would be to give students objects of known composition, with weights known only to the teacher, and have the students weigh them and calculate chemical quantities.

Make classroom sets of materials and place them in zipper-locking plastic bags. One set of materials should consist of one piece each of sulfur, fluorite, and hematite; a piece of chalk;

a marble; a polystyrene peanut; and a plastic spoon. Sugar and salt can be placed in containers on the lab benches. You can substitute other minerals.

Small-Scale Experiment 8
Chemical Equations

Text Section 7.2

Estimated Class Time: One 50-minute period.
Estimated Teacher Preparation Time: 20 minutes, after stock solutions are prepared.

Overview

Students observe color changes in indicators and learn how to write single-replacement chemical equations to describe them. Students classify solutions as acids or bases based on the color changes.

Materials

Small-scale pipets of the following solutions:

sodium hydrogen carbonate	*bromcresol green
	*phenol red
phosphoric acid	ethanoic acid
sodium hydroxide	sodium dihydrogen phosphate
hydrochloric acid	
sodium hydrogen phosphate	nitric acid
	sodium carbonate
sodium hydrogen sulfate	sodium phosphate
	ammonia
sulfuric acid	bromthymol blue
sodium hydrogen sulfite	phenolphthalein
	*alizarine yellow R
bromphenyl blue	*thymol blue
sodium ethanoate	*meta cresol purple
*methyl red	

Household Products: Baking soda, vinegar, cola, ammonia cleaner, laundry detergent, grape juice, cabbage juice, food dyes, flower petals, vegetable juices, fabric dyes, and water-soluble pen inks.

Equipment

Empty pipet for stirring, small-scale reaction surface.

*Materials for Now It's Your Turn.

Teaching Suggestions

Small-Scale Experiments 8, 9, 11, and 12 use acid–base concepts to illustrate both qualitative and quantitative properties of chemical reactions. Acid–base reactions were chosen because of their simplicity, the colorful chemistry they produce in the presence of indicators, and the availability and low toxicity of the reagents. Small-Scale Experiment 8 uses simple acid–base reactions and the color changes they impart to indicators to introduce simple chemical reactions and the chemical equations that represent them. Small-Scale Experiment 9 uses acid–base neutralization reactions as examples of how chemical equations are balanced. Small-Scale Experiments 11 and 12 also use neutralization reactions and titrations of acids and bases to apply the mole concept in the laboratory. All four of these laboratory investigations are equally well suited to be taught with Chapters 19 and 20 of the textbook. As a consequence, you may want to leave these labs for later in your course or refer to them during your students' formal study of acids and bases in Chapters 19 and 20.

Small-Scale Experiment 9
Balancing Chemical Equations

Text Section 7.4

Estimated Class Time: One 50-minute period.
Estimated Teacher Preparation Time: 20 minutes, after stock solutions are prepared.

Overview

Students carry out reactions between acids and bases and use indicators to detect the reactions. Students learn to balance the chemical equations that describe the reactions. Students learn to recognize chemical equations as symbolic interpretations of submicroscopic chemical reactions.

Materials

Small-scale pipets of the following solutions:

phosphoric acid	ethanoic acid
hydrochloric acid	*phenolphthalein
nitric acid	*methyl red
sulfuric acid	sodium hydroxide

potassium hydroxide   bromthymol blue
calcium hydroxide   *bromphenyl blue
ammonia

*Household Products: Vinegar, lemon juice, ammonia cleaner, antacid tablets.

Equipment

Small-scale reaction surface, glass slide, cotton swab, empty pipet for stirring.

Common Equipment

6 hot plates.

Teaching Suggestions

Emphasize to students that the given examples reveal a pattern for how to balance the equations. Stress that the coefficients they use indicate the number of formula units and the number of moles of each reactant and product.

The chemical equations the students balance are more concrete to them when they can see or smell evidence of chemical change beyond the indicator changes. Point out that a salt is formed in each reaction and that when students evaporate mixtures they can see the salts. Extinction of the ammonia smell by HCl brings meaning to the word *neutralization*.

Small-Scale Experiment 10 — Precipitation in Double-Replacement Reactions

Text Section 7.9

Estimated Class Time: One 50-minute period.
Estimated Teacher Preparation Time: 20 minutes, after stock solutions are prepared.

Overview

Students carry out precipitation reactions of silver and lead salts and learn to write double-replacement equations to describe them.

Materials

Small-scale pipets of the following solutions:

lead(II) nitrate   sodium hydroxide
potassium iodide   sodium sulfate

*Materials for Now It's Your Turn.

sodium carbonate   iron(III) chloride
calcium chloride   sodium phosphate
silver nitrate   copper(II) sulfate
sodium chloride

Equipment

Empty pipet for stirring, small-scale reaction surface.

Teaching Suggestions

Be sure to encourage students to write the equations while they carry out the chemical reactions and while the results are still in front of them. Students receive a lot of practice writing and balancing real equations for reactions that they actually carry out in lab. Writing equations is a more concrete activity this way.

Stress the fact that a chemical equation is a shorthand method to describe a chemical reaction and that to master chemistry, students need to master this chemical language. Also stress that for now, the identity of the precipitates is given. A later lab (Small-Scale Experiment 24) will give students some empirical evidence for predicting which mixtures will form precipitates and what the identities of the precipitates are.

As a lab practical, give students unlabeled small-scale pipets of some or all of the reagents along the horizontal of Table 10.1. Ask them to identify the unknowns by mixing them with silver nitrate and/or lead nitrate. Have them write correct chemical equations for any reactions they observe.

Students will probably not be able to write the equations for the reactions of $FeCl_3$ with KI and Na_2CO_3 or of $CuSO_4$ with KI. You may want to write these equations for students and have students balance the equations.

Small-Scale Experiment 11 — Titration: Determining How Much Acid Is in a Solution

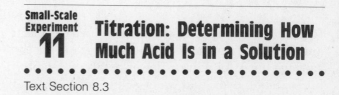

Text Section 8.3

Estimated Class Time: Two 50-minute periods.
Estimated Teacher Preparation Time: 20 minutes, after stock solutions are prepared.

Overview

Students use the technique of titration to measure the concentration of various acids in solution. Students learn to calibrate small-scale pipets and analyze errors associated with quantitative determinations.

Materials

Small-scale pipets of the following solutions:

hydrochloric acid   ethanoic acid

nitric acid   phenolphthalein

sulfuric acid   sodium hydroxide

*Household Products: Vinegar and toilet-bowl cleaner (containing HCl).

Equipment

Plastic cup, 1 × 12 well plate, cotton swabs.

Teaching Suggestions

This experiment is set up in a way that not only gives students procedures to follow but also allows them to invent procedures and concepts as they go along. For example, students invent their own methods for calibrating small-scale pipets. Most students prefer to expel the air bubble first and count drops while holding the pipet vertically. It does not matter what criteria the students use to define a full well as long as the students are consistent.

Point out the difference between qualitative and quantitative analysis in this lab. In a lab-practical exam, you may want to have each student identify three unknown acids. He or she might also titrate each and calculate the molar concentration of each.

Give students the algorithm (in the Experimental Data section) for calculating the molarity of the acid, and let them work with it before you explain it. Once they have used the equation, they are ready to understand where it comes from and why it works.

Students are challenged to analyze their errors and make necessary adjustments in procedures and the experimental design to minimize error. As a result, students learn about the limitations of experimental designs. For example, the difference in the end point and the equivalence point is as much as one drop. Therefore, a larger number of drops for a sample size will make the relative error smaller. Point out that larger sample

*Materials for Now It's Your Turn.

sizes also produce diminishing returns as the errors from other factors come into play. There is no right or wrong answer. Students must trust their own results on the basis of precision rather than comparing them to some "known" value.

Finally, students learn to apply what they have learned to real samples of household products with real problems (highly colored, high concentration).

Small-Scale Experiment 12 — Weight Titrations: Measuring Molar Concentrations

• •

Text Section 8.5

Estimated Class Time: One 50-minute period.
Estimated Teacher Preparation Time: 20 minutes, after stock solutions are prepared.

Overview

Students use balances to carry out weight titrations of acids and bases.

Materials

Small-scale pipets of the following solutions:

sodium hydroxide   hydrochloric acid

phenolphthalein   nitric acid

ethanoic acid   sulfuric acid

*universal indicator   *bromthymol blue

*silver nitrate   *lead(II) nitrate

*calcium chloride   *sodium carbonate

*Household Products: Vinegar and toilet-bowl cleaner (containing HCl).

Equipment

Balance, plastic cup.

Teaching Suggestions

Emphasize that weighing samples can be more accurate than counting drops because sample sizes are larger and relative errors are smaller. Students should use two small-scale balance pans, one for the titrations and one for weighing the NaOH pipets. As in Small-Scale Experiment 11, point out that the stoichiometry of the $NaOH/H_2SO_4$ reaction is 2:1, so the equation used to calculate the molarity of the acid must have a factor of 2 in the denominator.

Small-Scale Experiment 13
Absorption of Water by Paper Towels: A Consumer Lab

Text Section 9.4

Estimated Class Time: One 50-minute period.
Estimated Teacher Preparation Time: 20 minutes, once materials are purchased.

Overview

Students investigate questions like "What does it mean to be wet? Which paper towel is best? What is the best buy?" Students find that there are quantitative answers for consumers.

Equipment (per 24 students)

Several brands of paper towels, one roll each with their labels, including price tag; twelve 5 cm × 10 cm cards, balance, 24 plastic cups, 50 clothespins, water, 24 soda straws.

Common Equipment

12 pairs of scissors, six 1/4-inch office hole punches.

Teaching Suggestions

Cut a classroom set of 5 cm × 10 cm posterboard templates to save students' time measuring. Students use them to trace out equal-size pieces of paper towels. These are the same templates you will use for Small-Scale Experiment 22.

One roll of each brand of paper towels is more than sufficient for many sections of 24 students. The day before the experiment, suggest to students that they bring from home two or three sheets of paper towels along with their labels. This gives the students ownership in the experiment.

Encourage students to invent different ways to test wet strength. For example, they could stack pennies on a stretched wet towel. In Part C, be sure students use 1 × 10 cm strips of towels.

Small-Scale Experiment 14
Heat of Fusion of Ice

Text Section 10.7

Estimated Class Time: Less than one 50-minute period.
Estimated Teacher Preparation Time: 10 minutes.

Overview

Students use the technique of calorimetry to measure the heat of fusion of ice.

Materials

hot water from the tap
crushed ice

Equipment

Alcohol thermometer, one ounce plastic cup, polystyrene coffee cup, balance.

Teaching Suggestions

Discuss with students the importance of heat losses to the surroundings and their relationship to errors. Point out that larger samples of hot water and ice will probably involve greater heat losses to the environment. The sample data given for Trial 3 in Table 14.2 is good evidence that larger samples produce greater errors. (Compare Trials 1 and 2 with Trial 3.) The ideal final temperature to achieve is room temperature (about 25°C).

Emphasize that melting ice absorbs much more heat than simply changing the temperature of liquid water. It requires only one calorie to change the temperature of one gram of liquid water by one Celsius degree and 80 calories to melt one gram of ice. Ice cools drinks by melting, not by changing temperature.

Small-Scale Experiment 15
Synthesis and Qualitative Analysis of Gases

Text Section 11.1

Estimated Class Time: One 50-minute period.
Estimated Teacher Preparation Time: 20 minutes, once materials are purchased.

Overview

Students carry out chemical reactions that produce important commonplace gases. Students identify the gases using indicators.

Materials

Small-scale pipets of the following solutions:

sodium hydrogen sulfite	potassium permanganate
sodium nitrite	sodium hypochlorite

sodium hydroxide

potassium iodide

*ethanoic acid

*sulfuric acid

hydrochloric acid

sodium hydrogen
  carbonate

hydrogen peroxide

ammonium chloride

bromthymol blue

starch

*nitric acid

*phenolphthalein

Equipment

2 clear plastic cups, small-scale reaction surface.

Teaching Suggestions

Because stray gases from other experiments can affect results, tell students to do only two of the experiments on the Experimental Page at a time. Remind the students of the importance of cleaning the cup between experiments with a dry paper towel to absorb stray gases. Emphasize that the reactions do not happen all at once and that they have to watch patiently for several minutes for some of the indicators to change.

Use freshly prepared solutions of $NaHSO_3$ (4.1 g in 250 mL), $NaNO_2$ (6.9 g in 250 mL), and $KMnO_4$ (a few grains in 100 mL of $0.1M$ H_2SO_4). The $NaHSO_3$ and $NaNO_2$ solutions degas over time, and the $KMnO_4$ solution forms an insoluble brown MnO_2 precipitate over time.

The word equations in the Questions for Analysis section are designed to give students valuable experience writing and balancing chemical equations. Point out the relationships between the equations they write and the observations they made in Table 15.1.

The six unknowns in Now It's Your Turn provide a good lab-practical exam. For convenience, label the unknown pipets with numbers and keep a key of the identities. You might want to use the other Now It's Your Turn items as lab practicals.

Small-Scale Experiment 16

Reactions of Carbonates that Produce Carbon Dioxide

• •

Text Section 11.8

Estimated Class Time: One 50-minute period.
Estimated Teacher Preparation Time: 20 minutes, once materials are purchased.

*Materials for Now It's Your Turn.

Overview

Students study double-replacement and decomposition reactions and learn to write their chemical equations.

Materials

Small-scale pipets of the following solutions:

hydrochloric acid

sulfuric acid

sodium hydrogen
  carbonate

sodium carbonate

phosphoric acid

nitric acid

ethanoic acid

bromthymol blue

Solids: Calcium carbonate, sodium hydrogen carbonate, *limestone, *marble.

*Household Products: Antacid tablets, chalk, egg shells, sea shells, baking soda, baking powder, cream of tartar.

Equipment

Dry pipet for stirring, small-scale reaction surface, glass slide.

Common Equipment

6 hot plates.

Teaching Suggestions

This lab asks students to write and balance chemical equations by examining the pattern followed by given equations. Emphasize that CO_2 and H_2O are always products of reactions of acids and carbonates. Also stress that all these reactions are double-replacement reactions followed by decomposition. The H_2CO_3 formed in the double-replacement reaction is not stable in aqueous solution, and decomposes to CO_2 and H_2O. Assign students to write the number of equations you think is practical.

As an alternative to using hot plates, consider allowing the drops on the glass slide to evaporate overnight. Do not use Bunsen burners or other sources of flame to evaporate the droplets. Flames produce far too much heat for small-scale quantities.

Item 4 of Now It's Your Turn provides a good lab practical. Have students identify which materials contain carbonates.

Small-Scale Experiment 17
Design and Construction of a Quantitative Spectroscope

Text Section 12.6

Estimated Class Time: One 50-minute period.
Estimated Teacher Preparation Time: 20 minutes, once materials are purchased.

Overview

Students build their own small-scale spectroscopes. Students use them to study the interaction of light with matter.

Equipment

Precut 28 × 23.7 cm poster board, diffraction grating, adhesive label, plastic light rod, 3 rubber bands.

Common Equipment (per 6 students)

1 teacher-built spectroscope, 1 roll of tape, 3 pairs of scissors, 3 rulers, three 2-cm guide strips, 3 nails. *Various boxes like shoe boxes, cereal boxes, safety-glasses boxes, toothpaste boxes, pizza boxes, etc.

Teaching Suggestions

Build a few spectroscopes (without diffraction gratings) as examples, and have them available in the lab as students work through the Experimental Page. This exercise will help the students understand how to build their own spectroscopes.

The poster board should be a dark color. Black, dark blue, red, or green work equally well. You will need four or five 22 × 28 inches (56 cm × 71 cm) standard poster boards for a class of 24 students. To save time and waste, you can precut each standard board to make six equal 23.7 × 28 cm pieces.

Precut with a paper cutter several 2 × 28 cm guide strips for students to use to trace their borders. This saves them the time of measuring.

Precut the diffraction grating material into 1 × 2 cm rectangles with the diffraction lines parallel to the 2 cm side. An 8 1/2 × 11 inch piece of diffraction grating material will make about 270 gratings.

*Equipment for Now It's Your Turn.

The plastic light rods can be made from clear plastic drink stirrers or clear plastic picnic knives. Score each light rod by placing it over the template or a piece of tenth-inch graph paper and carefully making straight parallel scratches every 1/10 inch.

Boxes are good alternatives to poster board. Shoe boxes, safety-glasses boxes, cracker boxes, cereal boxes, and pizza boxes work well. Experiment with sizes and designs.

Small-Scale Experiment 18
Visible Spectra and the Nature of Light and Color

Text Section 12.6

Estimated Class Time: One or two 50-minute periods, depending on how much of the Now It's Your Turn you assign.
Estimated Teacher Preparation Time: 20 minutes, once materials are purchased.

Overview

Using their spectroscopes, students find that there is important chemical information linked to light. They examine emission, reflection, transmission, and absorption.

Equipment (per 24 students)

Small-scale spectroscope, 4 to 6 fluorescent and incandescent light sources. *4 candles, *4 sets of colored plastic filters (red, green, blue, and yellow), *1 set of food dye (red, green, blue, and yellow), *16 clear plastic cups, *4 pieces of colored construction paper (red, blue, green, and yellow), *3 to 4 atomic emission tubes and sources.

Teaching Suggestions

For light sources, students can use overhead incandescent or fluorescent lights. They can use the incandescent light in an overhead projector if you cover it with white paper and do not let students look directly into it. They can even use its reflection off a white screen.

For reflectance spectra, tape various colors of construction paper to a wall or screen, and shine an overhead projector on them. If students use colored plastic films for absorption, have them cover only half the slit with the colored film so they can simultaneously compare a white light spectrum with an absorption spectrum. Place a drop of food dye in a clear plastic cup, add some water, set it in front of a light source; and students can explore the absorption spectra of various colored solutions.

You can set up one or more discharge tubes around the room for students to examine. Hydrogen, neon, and mercury work well. You may also wish to demonstrate flame tests to students. **Caution:** *Do not let students use Bunsen burners!*

Small-Scale Experiment 19 — Hard and Soft Water

Text Sections 13.A, 17.B

Estimated Class Time: Two 50-minute periods.
Estimated Teacher Preparation Time: 30 minutes.

Overview

Students titrate various water samples for hardness and learn how to soften water.

Materials

Small-scale pipets of the following solutions:

ethylenediamine tetraacetic acid	ammonia/ammonium chloride
deionized water	various water samples
*hydrochloric acid	*potassium hydroxide
*bromthymol blue	

Solids: Eriochrome black T indicator.

Equipment

Balance, extra small-scale balance pan.

Common Equipment

*Acid resin ion exchanger.

Teaching Suggestions

The end point of this titration is difficult for students to see. As they titrate, the color gradually changes from wine-red through reddish-blue to blue. Tell the students to adjust the amount of Ero-T until they see the change from wine-red to blue with the last drop.

Make the Ero-T indicator by mixing 0.1 g Ero-T with 100 g solid NaCl. Place in plastic-topped vials, and punch holes in the plastic tops so each vial functions like a salt shaker.

If you do not want to collect real water samples, you can make hard water. To prepare a stock solution of 1000 ppm $CaCO_3$, dissolve 1.22 g $CaCl_2$ in 1100 mL of deionized water. Add 5 drops of $0.2M$ $MgSO_4$ solution. Proportions for solutions of varying hardness are shown in the table below. Place the hard water in small-scale pipets labeled "water sample 1," etc. Prepare the buffer by dissolving 9.2 g NH_4Cl and 67 mL concentrated NH_3 in 1 L of deionized water.

Small-Scale Experiment 20 — Reactions of Aqueous Ionic Compounds

Text Section 14.4

Estimated Class Time: One or two 50-minute periods.
Estimated Teacher Preparation Time: 20 minutes, once solutions are prepared.

Overview

Students carry out many mixings of ionic compounds and learn to organize large amounts of information in ways that will help them to solve problems logically.

Materials

Small-scale pipets of the following solutions:

ammonia	hydrochloric acid
sodium carbonate	silver nitrate

To make a $CaCO_3$ solution of:	400 ppm	300 ppm	200 ppm	100 ppm	50 ppm
take this much stock solution:	400 mL	300 mL	200 mL	100 mL	50 mL
and dilute with deionized water:	600 mL	700 mL	800 mL	900 mL	950 mL
to a total volume of:	1000 mL	1000 mL	1000 mL	1000 mL	1000 mL

*Materials and equipment for Now It's Your Turn.

sodium hydroxide	sulfuric acid
sodium phosphate	nitric acid
copper(II) sulfate	potassium iodide
lead(II) nitrate	iron(III) chloride
calcium chloride	

Equipment

Small-scale reaction surface, empty pipet for stirring.

Teaching Suggestions

Set up one set of chemicals for each two students. They can share chemicals and still do their own work.

To save time, consider having students draw data tables like Table 20.1 in their notebooks as homework the day before the lab. Emphasize to students the right way to use and read Table 20.1. The most common mistake with students is to make their mixings in the wrong places, and they are often off by just one line. Having them do all the lead nitrate reactions first is often enough to get them started correctly.

Have students play the games on the smaller grids in the Now It's Your Turn until they become proficient at using chemical reactions to identify unknown chemicals. These types of exercises provide good lab practical exams. The equation writing provides review and practice in writing equations for precipitation reactions and for the reactions of acids with carbonates.

Small-Scale Experiment 21

Identification of Eight Unknown Solutions

· ·

Text Section 14.5

Estimated Class Time: One 50-minute period.
Estimated Teacher Preparation Time: 20 minutes, once solutions are prepared.

Overview

Students use what they learned in Small-Scale Experiment 20 to work out the identities of unknown solutions by various methods.

Materials

Small-scale pipets of the following solutions:

| ammonia | hydrochloric acid |
| sodium carbonate | silver nitrate |

sodium hydroxide	sulfuric acid
sodium phosphate	nitric acid
copper(II) sulfate	potassium iodide
lead(II) nitrate	iron(III) chloride
calcium chloride	

Eight small-scale pipets of unknown solutions labeled with different numbers per student.

Equipment

Small-scale reaction surface, empty pipet for stirring.

Teaching Suggestions

Prepare 15 small-scale pipets of each of the 13 solutions in Small-Scale Experiment 20. Label each of these 195 pipets with a number, and record the numbers on a master list for your reference for refilling, grading, and helping students identify their unknowns. For a class of 24 students, use the 195 pipets to make up 24 sets of eight different unknowns ($24 \times 8 = 192$ pipets). Place each set of eight in a plastic cup, to be handed out to students. Any combination of solutions is solvable using known solutions as probes. Time may permit for them to do more than one combination.

Keep in mind that for a given set of unknowns to be identifiable by the approach used in Now It's Your Turn (no known chemicals can be used), it must contain eight distinctly different chemicals. Furthermore, the acids are distinguished from each other only if each is accompanied by a specific solution. An unknown set containing sulfuric acid must also contain calcium chloride; hydrochloric acid must be accompanied by silver nitrate; and nitric acid must have lead nitrate with it.

Consider coding the unknowns by assigning each of the 13 solutions with a number between 3 and 16. Use a four-digit number for each unknown. The sum of the middle two digits identifies the unknown. For example, assign calcium chloride the number 3. The following numbers, then, identify an unknown as calcium chloride: 1123, 8301, 4215, and 9031. (The middle two digits in each case add to three.) If you use a code, don't tell students that it even exists. It is surprising how easily students break any code, once they know one exists!

Once you have the original 24 sets made up, you can keep them labeled for several years. All you need to do is refill them and mix and match the numbers to make a large number of unknown sets.

Small-Scale Experiment
22 Paper Chromatography
• •
Text Section 15.11

Estimated Class Time: One or two 50-minute periods.
Estimated Teacher Preparation Time: 20 minutes.

Overview

Students learn about paper chromatography and use it to separate and identify dyes in inks.

Equipment (per 24 students)

24 template cards, 48 pieces of chromatography paper, 6 pieces of typing paper, 48 clear plastic cups, 6 small bottles of solvent (0.1% NaCl in water), 6 sets of FD&C dyes in 1 × 12 well strips. *Various other papers like coffee filters and tablet paper, various solvents like rubbing alcohol, various colored food, candy, soft drinks, and food colors.

Common Equipment

12 sets of colored marking pens, 12 pairs of scissors, 6 staplers.

Teaching Suggestions

To make 0.1% aqueous sodium chloride solution, dissolve one gram NaCl in one liter of water. Rubbing alcohol (70% isopropyl alcohol) straight from the bottle works well also, but it takes three to five times as long to elute a chromatogram. The aqueous solvent needs no cover cup.

Prepare a classroom set (12 to 24) 10 cm × 5 cm template cards from poster board marked exactly like the one in Figure 22.1. Students simply trace the card on chromatography paper, then cut out and mark the paper. Consider using a paper cutter to cut strips of chromatography paper 5 cm wide. This saves even more time and paper.

*Equipment for Now It's Your Turn.

Make a 0.1% solution of each FD&C dye (50 mg of dye in 50 mL of water) and store it in a small plastic dropping bottle. Make up six sets of dyes for student use in 1 × 8 or 1 × 12 well strips. Tape each to a 3 × 5 index card, and label each dye by writing its identity next to its well. Replenish the wells periodically by dropping in the correct dyes. Consider making up sets of soft drink, food color, and other samples in this way.

Remind students to use typing paper triangles and not chromatography paper when spotting dyes. Plastic and wood toothpicks also work for spotting samples, but they are more expensive.

For a lab practical, consider mixing several dyes and having the students identify the components of the mixture. Alternatively, you can select some colors of a brand of pens that students have not analyzed and have them identify the dyes.

Small-Scale Experiment
23 Electrolytes
• •
Text Section 16.8

Estimated Class Time: One 50-minute period.
Estimated Teacher Preparation Time: 20 minutes, once conductivity devices are constructed.

Overview

Students discover that matter is electrical. They investigate the conductivity of aqueous solutions and draw conclusions about electrolytes and nonelectrolytes.

Materials

Small-scale pipets of the following solutions:

calcium chloride	hydrogen peroxide
sodium hydrogen sulfate	iron(III) chloride
	copper(II) sulfate
sodium hydroxide	aluminum chloride
sodium phosphate	zinc chloride
sodium hydrogen carbonate	sodium carbonate
	ethanol
water	methanol
2-propanol	

Solids:

sodium chloride	potassium chloride
potassium iodide	calcium chloride
sodium carbonate	sucrose
*hydrochloric acid	*ethanoic acid
*nitric acid	*ammonia
*sulfuric acid	*potassium hydroxide
*phosphoric acid	

*Household Products: Soda pop, orange juice, pickle brine, coffee, seltzer tablets, solid toilet-bowl cleaner, baking powder, plaster of Paris.

Equipment

Small-scale reaction surface, conductivity apparatus, glass slide.

Common Equipment

6 hot plates.

Teaching Suggestions

Make a classroom set of electrolysis/conductivity devices (see lab Figure 23.1). The materials needed are: 9-volt battery, 9-volt battery clip, small light-emitting diode (any color), 330-ohm 1/4-watt resistor, 4 micro clips (for 0.042-inch holes), 1 × 4 inch piece of pre-punched perfboard (0.042-inch-hole diameter, 0.100 × 0.100 spacing), 1/2 inch of fabric adhesive or similar fastener, 2 nickel-plated sewing pins.

Cut the perfboard from 6 × 8 inch or larger pieces using a hacksaw or band saw. Place the micro clips and other components in the locations shown in the diagram, and solder the components together with a soldering iron. Fix the battery in place with the fabric adhesive or a similar fastener. The exact arrangement is not critical. The wire leads should be about 1/2 cm apart and extend about 1 to 2 cm from the edge of the perfboard. The light-emitting diode (LED) is polarized, so be sure to connect the positive (red) lead of the battery clip to the positive (long) lead of the LED, and the negative (black) lead of the battery clip to the negative (short) lead of the LED.

Remind students to keep the hot plates on a low setting. As an alternative to a hot plate, try a heat gun or a hair dryer on a low setting, or consider having students store their glass slides overnight at room temperature. **Caution:** *Do not*

*Materials for Now It's Your Turn.

use Bunsen burners, as they are dangerous and produce far too much heat to be appropriate for a small-scale experiment.

This is a great place to introduce net ionic equations. Consider reviewing the chemical reactions studied so far in terms of net ionic equations. Small-Scale Experiment 24 then naturally follows.

24 Solubility Rules

Text Section 17.1

Estimated Class Time: One 50-minute period.
Estimated Teacher Preparation Time: 20 minutes.

Overview

Students investigate precipitation reactions and correlate large amounts of data to generalize about solubility rules.

Materials

Small-scale pipets of the following solutions:

aluminum chloride	lead(II) nitrate
ammonium chloride	silver nitrate
sodium chloride	magnesium sulfate
calcium chloride	sodium sulfate
copper(II) sulfate	potassium iodide
iron(III) chloride	zinc chloride
sodium carbonate	sodium hydroxide
sodium phosphate	sodium chloride
sodium nitrate	sodium sulfate

Equipment

Empty pipet for stirring, small-scale reaction surface.

Teaching Suggestions

Students can derive general solubility rules easily from this colorful experiment. You may want to break this experiment into two shorter sessions and discuss the results with students as they proceed. Point out to students that the Experimental Page is set up to allow them to readily find the right reagents (the complete formula is given) and to easily write the net ionic equations. Emphasize that all of the 2+ cations will yield similar net ionic equations, as will all the 1+ cations and 3+ cations.

Factors Affecting the Rate of a Chemical Reaction

Small-Scale Experiment 25

Text Section 18.2

Estimated Class Time: One 50-minute period.
Estimated Teacher Preparation Time: 15 minutes.

Overview

Students study the effects of concentration, temperature, and surface area on the rates of chemical reactions.

Materials

Small-scale pipets of the following solutions:

hydrochloric acid
water
*lead nitrate
*sulfuric acid
sodium hydrogen carbonate
*potassium iodide
*calcium chloride

Solids: Magnesium, calcium carbonate.

Equipment

Small-scale reaction surface, ice, hot water, 2 plastic cups.

Teaching Suggestions

Magnesium turnings and split-pea-size $CaCO_3$ chips work well. Use plastic jars or large plastic vials to serve as recycling containers. Wash the recycled magnesium turnings and calcium carbonate chips with water and dry them. They can be used again for another lab.

Hot water from the tap is sufficient. Have students equilibrate their pipets in both ice water and hot water long enough to see a difference.

You may have to review the chemical equations with students, especially the reaction of magnesium with acid, since they have not seen it

*Materials and equipment for Now It's Your Turn.

before. Clean Mg works best. Use steel wool to clean Mg ribbon. Clean turnings by dipping briefly in $1M$ HCl, wash with water and dry thoroughly.

Le Châtelier's Principle and Chemical Equilibrium

Small-Scale Experiment 26

Text Section 18.4

Estimated Class Time: One 50-minute period.
Estimated Teacher Preparation Time: 15 minutes.

Overview

Students investigate chemical systems at equilibrium by disturbing the equilibria and then explaining the observable changes in terms of Le Châtelier's Principle.

Materials

Small-scale pipets of the following solutions:

hydrochloric acid
lead(II) nitrate
nitric acid
sodium hydroxide
copper(II) sulfate
potassium iodide
*phenolphthalein
*methyl red
*thymol blue
*potassium thiocyanate
sodium carbonate
bromthymol blue
silver nitrate
ammonia
sodium phosphate
sodium thiosulfate
*bromphenyl blue
*alizarine yellow R
*iron(III) chloride

Equipment

Small-scale reaction surface, empty pipet for stirring, plastic cup, *small (4-inch) piece of soda straws.

Teaching Suggestions

Be sure to remind students to stir each mixture thoroughly; stirring is critical. Use small pieces of soda straws to separate the $FeCl_3$/KSCN mixture in Now It's Your Turn. Simply place the end of the straw into the mixture and drag it across the reaction surface. Some of the mixture will move, while the bulk of it will stay behind. Suggest that students invent efficient ways to move liquids from place to place on the reaction surface without contamination.

A Small-Scale Colorimetric pH Meter

Text Section 19.4

Estimated Class Time: One 50-minute period.
Estimated Teacher Preparation Time: 45 minutes to make up fresh buffer solutions.

Overview

Students build a colorimetric pH meter and measure the pHs of various laboratory and household chemicals.

Materials

Small-scale pipets of the following solutions:

universal indicator

buffer solutions, pH 1–12

Household Products: Baking soda, vinegar, window cleaner, baking powder, lemon juice, tea, a cola soft drink, laundry detergent, milk, orange juice, *red cabbage or juice, *flower petals, *grape or berry juice, *common indicators.

Equipment

Small-scale reaction surface, empty pipet for stirring.

Teaching Suggestions

To make up the universal indicator solution add the following to 1000 mL of water:

150 mg phenolphthalein (disodium salt)

150 mg bromthymol blue (sodium salt)

113 mg methyl orange (sodium salt)

225 mg alizarine yellow R (sodium salt)

75 mg bromcresol green (sodium salt)

150 mg meta cresol purple

Store indefinitely in a plastic bottle. This amount should last two or three years, assuming 125 students a year.

Make the following stock solutions and prepare fresh buffer solutions each year from these stock solutions:

Solution A: Dissolve 0.5 g thymol, 14.9 g boric acid (H_3BO_3), and 12.6 g citric acid ($C_6H_8O_7$) in 1200 mL deionized or distilled water.

Small-Scale Experiment **27** Energy Change and Solution Formation

Text Section 18.7

Estimated Class Time: One 50-minute period.
Estimated Teacher Preparation Time: 20 minutes.

Overview

Students investigate energy changes associated with the solution process and relate them to exothermic and endothermic reactions.

Materials

Solids:

rock salt, sodium chloride

ammonium chloride

calcium chloride

crushed ice

*potassium chloride

*sodium carbonate

*sodium hydrogen carbonate

*sodium phosphate

Equipment

Plastic spoon, four 1-ounce plastic cups, alcohol thermometer, small-scale reaction surface.

Teaching Suggestions

Use only small alcohol based thermometers (6-inch glass alcohol thermometers work well). **Caution:** *Never use mercury thermometers for teaching labs. Mercury is an insidious poison and breakage with the loss of mercury is a continuing risk.* Consider donating your mercury thermometers in good condition to a research lab or trading them for alcohol-based thermometers.

Remind students to treat glass thermometers carefully. (This is one of the few labs that requires *any* glass equipment.) For best results, students may stir the contents of the plastic cup gently with a thermometer.

*Materials for Now It's Your Turn.

Solution B: Dissolve 0.5 g thymol and 45.6 g sodium phosphate (Na_3PO_4) in 1200 mL of water.

Prepare the buffer solutions, pH 1–12 by mixing the stock solutions according to the following table: (Use 1.0M phosphoric acid for pH 1.)

pH	mL of Solution A	mL of Solution B
2	195	5
3	176	24
4	155	45
5	134	66
6	118	82
7	99	101
8	85	115
9	69	131
10	54	146
11	44	156
12	17	183

Be sure students add the buffer to the universal indicator and not vice versa. This helps to stir the indicator into the buffer. Students should then stir with an empty pipet. Each integer pH should have a unique and distinguishing color. If not, tell students to add more buffer.

Have students sample solid household products by using soda straw spatulas. Have them sample liquid products by inserting the end of a straw one to two cm into the liquid and withdrawing it while they hold a finger on the other end. A student can then immediately place a few drops on his or her reaction surface.

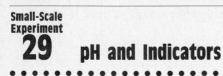

Small-Scale
Experiment
29   pH and Indicators

Text Section 19.4

Estimated Class Time: One 50-minute period.
Estimated Teacher Preparation Time: 20 minutes.

Overview

Students investigate the pH at which various indicators change and estimate their pK_as.

Materials

Small-scale pipets of the following solutions:

universal indicator   bromphenol blue
bromthymol blue   thymol blue

*Materials for Now It's Your Turn.

buffer solutions,   phenolphthalein
    pH 1–12   methyl red

*Any other common indicators in the laboratory.

Equipment

Small-scale reaction surface, empty pipet for stirring.

Teaching Suggestions

You can use any or all the indicators listed here, depending on what you have on hand. The main point is to let students explore the acid–base properties of different indicators and relate them to weak acids and bases.

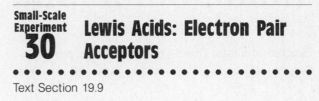

Small-Scale
Experiment
30   Lewis Acids: Electron Pair Acceptors

Text Section 19.9

Estimated Class Time: One 50-minute period.
Estimated Teacher Preparation Time: 15 minutes.

Overview

Students study the acidic properties of common metal cations in solution.

Materials

Small-scale pipets of the following solutions:

bromthymol blue   universal indicator
sodium hydrogen   sodium chloride
    carbonate   silver nitrate
tin(IV) chloride   calcium chloride
copper(II) sulfate   zinc chloride
lead(II) nitrate   potassium chloride
iron(III) chloride   *sodium carbonate
aluminum chloride
*buffer solutions,
    pH 1–12

Equipment

Small-scale reaction surface, empty pipet for stirring.

Teaching Suggestions

Remind students that the color of the universal indicator follows the visible spectrum. It is red to orange to yellow for acidic solutions, green for neutral solutions, and blue to violet for basic solutions. The redder the indicator, the more acidic the solution. A good rule of thumb is to remember that the colors of the visible spectrum, ROY G BIV, stand for the pHs 1, 3, 5, 7, 9, 11, and 12, respectively. With this tool, students don't need to measure the integer pH of each solution. Rather they can compare the relative acidities of the solutions. Alternatively, students can set up their pH meters to find the integer pHs.

Small-Scale Experiment 31 Strong and Weak Acids and Bases

Text Section 19.10

Estimated Class Time: One 50-minute period.
Estimated Teacher Preparation Time: 20 minutes.

Overview

Students carry out tests to distinguish between strong and weak acids and bases. Students learn to write hydrogen-ion-transfer equations to enhance their understanding of Brønsted-Lowry theory.

Materials

Small-scale pipets of the following solutions:

sodium hydrogen
    sulfate
sodium hydrogen
    carbonate
sodium hydroxide
sodium dihydrogen
    phosphate
sodium hydrogen
    phosphate
calcium hydroxide
ethanoic acid
sodium carbonate
sodium hydrogen
    sulfite
sodium phosphate
*Solids: Magnesium.

boric acid
citric acid
sodium ethanoate
hydrochloric acid
bromthymol blue
nitric acid
sulfuric acid
ammonium chloride
ammonia
universal indicator
potassium hydroxide
*buffer solutions,
    pH 1–12

*Materials for Now It's Your Turn.

Equipment (per 24 students)

24 small-scale reaction surfaces, 12 conductivity devices, 24 empty pipets for stirring.

Teaching Suggestions

Remind students of the single-replacement equations they wrote in Small-Scale Experiment 8. Part B of this experiment is essentially the same thing except now the universal indicator helps students to refine their concept of acids and bases in terms of their strengths. Remind students that they can approximate the pH of any solution from the color it imparts to universal indicator. The following rule of thumb is helpful. The colors of the visible spectrum, ROY G BIV, when imparted to universal indicator approximately correlate with the pHs 1, 3, 5, 7, 9, 11, and 12 respectively. Alternately, students can set up the same pH meter with the universal indicator and buffers from Small-Scale Experiment 29. Remind students to clean the leads of the conductivity apparatus before each test.

Small-Scale Experiment 32 Titration Curves

Text Section 20.2

Estimated Class Time: One 50-minute period.
Estimated Teacher Preparation Time: 15 minutes.

Overview

Students carry out titrations of strong and weak acids and bases. Students observe how the pH changes with added titrant and plot their data.

Materials

Small-scale pipets of the following solutions:

buffer solutions,
    pH 1–12
*sulfuric acid
*phosphoric acid
sodium hydroxide
ethanoic acid

*ammonia
*nitric acid
universal indicator
hydrochloric acid
*sodium carbonate

Equipment

Plastic cup, small-scale reaction surface, empty pipet for stirring.

Teaching Suggestions

The initial experiment on the reaction surface is designed to get students to visualize each step of the entire titration simultaneously. Be sure to have students stir each mixture thoroughly. Depending on how carefully they add the drops, they will get varying results. Some will see a distinct pH jump between two drops, while others will have an intermediate drop between the pH inflection. A few students who have been less careful adding drops will see a sharp increase, followed by a decrease and then another increase as the pH jumps. Once the students have visualized the effect, they should do all the rest of the titrations in a cup, as described in Step 3.

Small-Scale Experiment

33 Buffers

Text Section 20.6

Estimated Class Time: One 50-minute period.
Estimated Teacher Preparation Time: 15 minutes.

Overview

Students make various buffer solutions and test them for pH and buffer capacity.

Materials

Small-scale pipets of the following solutions:

sodium hydroxide	hydrochloric acid
ethanoic acid	sodium ethanoate
ammonia	ammonium chloride
sodium carbonate	sodium hydrogen carbonate
phosphoric acid	
sodium chloride	sodium dihydrogen phosphate
potassium iodide	
water	sodium nitrate
buffer solutions, pH 1–12	sodium sulfate
	universal indicator

*Household Products: Seltzer tablets, baking soda, baking powder, cream of tartar, aspirin, vitamin C.

*Materials for Now It's Your Turn.

Equipment

3 plastic cups, small-scale reaction surface.

Teaching Suggestions

This experiment becomes more meaningful if students can make buffers from common household products. A solution of an effervescent tablet is an especially good buffer. Others include solutions of baking powder and mixtures of baking soda and cream of tartar or citric acid. Make these items available for student experimentation.

Small-Scale Experiment

34 Reactions of Acids with Metals

Text Section 20.2

Estimated Class Time: One 50-minute period.
Estimated Teacher Preparation Time: 20 minutes.

Overview

Students react metals with acids and learn about oxidation–reduction reactions and how to write equations to describe these reactions.

Materials

Small-scale pipets of the following solutions:

hydrochloric acid	nitric acid
sulfuric acid	phosphoric acid
ethanoic acid	copper(II) sulfate
*sodium hydroxide	*potassium hydroxide

Solids: zinc, magnesium, iron, copper.

*Household Products: Damaged post-1982 pennies, toilet-bowl cleaners, vinegar, copper polish, silver polish.

Equipment (per 24 students)

24 small-scale reaction surfaces, 24 glass slides.

Common Equipment

6 hot plates.

Teaching Suggestions

Use hot plates only on their lowest settings. As an alternative, try a hair dryer or allowing the mixtures to evaporate overnight. **Caution:** *Do not use Bunsen burners because they produce far more heat than is safe for small-scale experiments.*

Use magnesium turnings or cut Mg ribbon into enough 0.5 cm pieces. Set up recycling containers where students will deposit their pieces of metal. Wash the pieces of metal with water and dry them. You can use recycled metal in future labs. As an alternative to pure zinc and iron samples, try using galvanized nails (Zn) and standard staples (Fe) from a stapler. Be sure to tell students that galvanized nails are only coated with zinc and staples are really made of steel, an alloy of iron. Look for other common metal alternatives.

Have the students study the example equations given in the Questions for Analysis, and use the pattern to write the others. The copper(II) sulfate reactions are designed to introduce students to half-reactions, which will be covered more thoroughly in the next experiment.

Small-Scale Experiment 35 Determination of an Activity Series

Text Section 21.5

Estimated Class Time: One 50-minute period.
Estimated Teacher Preparation Time: 20 minutes.

Overview

Students learn that metals and metal ions in aqueous solution have different tendencies to gain and lose electrons. Students construct an activity series from experimental data.

Materials

Small-scale pipets of the following solutions:

silver nitrate	copper(II) sulfate
iron(II) sulfate	magnesium sulfate
zinc chloride	

Solids: zinc, magnesium, iron, copper, silver.

*Household Products: Copper polish, silver polish.

Equipment

Small-scale reaction surface, *galvanized nails, pennies, staples, zinc-plated washers.

*Materials and equipment for Now It's Your Turn.

Teaching Suggestions

As in the last lab, look for alternatives to pure-metal pieces like staples (Fe) and galvanized nails (Zn). Because silver does not react, consider using reusable silver coins or pieces of old plated silverware. Set up recycling containers for all the metals. Students should wash and dry each metal thoroughly after use.

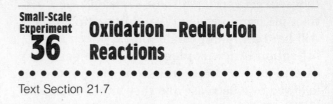

Small-Scale Experiment 36 Oxidation–Reduction Reactions

Text Section 21.7

Estimated Class Time: One 50-minute period.
Estimated Teacher Preparation Time: 20 minutes.

Overview

Students explore the redox reactions of common ions in solution and learn to write and balance their half-reactions and equations. Students recognize common oxidizing and reducing agents.

Materials

Small-scale pipets of the following solutions:

potassium iodide	sodium hypochlorite
potassium permanganate	potassium iodate
hydrogen peroxide	sodium hydrogen sulfite
sodium nitrite	potassium dichromate
copper(II) sulfate	iron(III) chloride
hydrochloric acid	starch solution
sodium hydrogen sulfate	*sodium thiosulfate

Equipment

Small-scale reaction surface.

Teaching Suggestions

The Experimental Page gives students the reactants and products of each redox equation in ionic form. From these, students can determine oxidation numbers and write half-reactions for each oxidation and reduction. You may want to have your students balance only the half-reactions or add them to write the entire equation as described in Section 20.7.

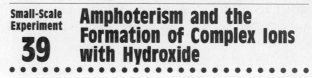

Small-Scale Experiment 37
Small-Scale Voltaic Cells

Text Section 22.3

Estimated Class Time: One 50-minute period.
Estimated Teacher Preparation Time: 20 minutes.

Overview

Students explore the nature of the voltaic cell and then make and test many variations.

Materials

Small-scale pipets of the following solutions:

silver nitrate	copper(II) sulfate
magnesium sulfate	lead(II) nitrate
zinc chloride	sodium nitrate

Solids: silver, copper, magnesium, lead, zinc.

Equipment (per 24 students)

24 small-scale reaction surfaces, 24 filter paper disks (9 cm), *dimes, nickels, nails, galvanized nails, washers.

Common Equipment

12 pairs of scissors, 12 volt meters, 4 each of various commercial batteries (dry cells).

Teaching Suggestions

Have students practice using the volt meters on different batteries of each type: carbon, heavy-duty carbon, alkaline, and rechargeable. You may want to have students bring batteries from home. "Dead" batteries work fine, as they usually still have measurable voltages. Steps 1 and 2 are designed to allow students to get an idea of the concept before they do the more complicated Step 3.

*Materials and equipment for Now It's Your Turn.

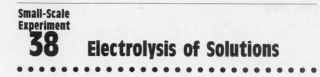

Small-Scale Experiment 38
Electrolysis of Solutions

Text Section 22.9

Estimated Class Time: One 50-minute period.
Estimated Teacher Preparation Time: 20 minutes.

Overview

Students apply electric current to solutions and study the chemistry that results.

Materials

Small-scale pipets of the following solutions:

water	sodium chloride
bromthymol blue	potassium bromide
starch	*ammonia
sodium sulfate	copper(II) sulfate
potassium iodide	*sodium nitrate

Equipment (per 24 students)

24 small-scale reaction surfaces, 12 electrolysis devices.

Teaching Suggestions

Use the conductivity/electrolysis device constructed for Small-Scale Experiment 23. As an alternative, tape a short wire to each end of a standard 1.5-volt battery and use the two leads as an electrolysis device. **Caution:** *Do not use a 110-volt AC source because of the great potential for hazardous electrical shock!*

Small-Scale Experiment 39
Amphoterism and the Formation of Complex Ions with Hydroxide

Text Section 23.3

Estimated Class Time: Less than one 50-minute period.
Estimated Teacher Preparation Time: 20 minutes.

Overview

Students learn that amphoteric substances act as both acids and bases. Students explore the phenomenon and probe the chemistry of amphoteric cations.

Materials

Small-scale pipets of the following solutions:

copper(II) sulfate	sodium hydroxide
silver nitrate	nitric acid
aluminum chloride	lead(II) nitrate
zinc chloride	calcium chloride
iron(III) chloride	magnesium sulfate
potassium hydroxide	*potassium
*sodium thiosulfate	thiocyanate

Equipment

Small-scale reaction surfaces, empty pipet for stirring.

Teaching Suggestions

This lab might be used to encourage students to design their own experiments. Consider asking the students to mix one drop each of $AlCl_3$ and KOH to form $Al(OH)_3(s)$ three times. Then, as on the Experimental Page, have them add excess NaOH to one precipitate and excess HNO_3 to another. Explain the results as in the introduction and then give them these directions:

"Your assignment is to devise and perform a series of experiments to determine which of the insoluble hydroxides are amphoteric. Make a list of the amphoteric hydroxides. Check your results with your instructor and obtain the formulas of the complex ions that are formed. Write net ionic equations to describe the reactions of both acid and base with the amphoteric hydroxides you observe."

Estimated Class Time: One 50-minute period.
Estimated Teacher Preparation Time: 20 minutes.

Overview

Students use the chemistry of several nonmetal compounds to determine quantitatively the amount of sodium hypochlorite and other oxidizing agents in household products like bleach.

Materials

Small-scale pipets of the following solutions:

sodium hypochlorite	potassium iodide
ethanoic acid	household bleach
starch	(diluted, 20 mL bleach
*FD&C dyes	+ 80 mL H_2O)
sodium thiosulfate	

*Household Products: Colored marker pens, automatic-dishwashing liquid, powdered cleansers.

Equipment

Small-scale reaction surface, plastic cup, 1×12 well plates.

Teaching Suggestions

Part A of the Experimental Procedure is designed to help students understand the complicated chemistry of the titration and the end point. You can have students do the titration by calibrating their burets using well strips, as described in Part B of the Experimental Procedure. Alternatively, consider having them calibrate a buret using a balance or doing a weight titration, as described in Now It's Your Turn and in Small-Scale Experiment 12.

*Materials for Now It's Your Turn.

Make up fresh NaOCl solution by diluting 20 mL of household bleach with 80 mL of water. Use this solution for the NaOCl and for the household bleach solution the students titrate. Explain that the dilution factor used in the calculation is due to the fact that the bleach was diluted by one fifth before students titrated it. **Caution:** *Do not use full-strength household bleach: It is noxious and irritating to the skin, eyes, and nose.*

41 Halogen Ions in Solution

Text Section 23.7

Estimated Class Time: One 50-minute period.
Estimated Teacher Preparation Time: 20 minutes, once materials are purchased.

Overview

Students investigate the aqueous reactions of the halides and learn to identify them by their different chemical properties.

Materials

Small-scale pipets of the following solutions:

calcium chloride	potassium fluoride
lead(II) nitrate	potassium chloride
silver nitrate	potassium bromide
sodium hypochlorite	potassium iodide
ammonia	sodium thiosulfate
starch	bromthymol blue
hydrochloric acid	copper(II) sulfate
FD&C blue #1, blue dye	hydrogen peroxide
iron(III) chloride	

*Household Products: Baby oil.

Equipment

Empty pipet for stirring, small-scale reaction surface, 3 1/2-ounce clear plastic cup, *glass slide.

*Materials and equipment for Now It's Your Turn.

Teaching Suggestions

Emphasize that the reactions students observe are typical of the halide anions written across the top of the Experimental Page and the cations of the compounds written down the left side (except hypochlorite, OCl^-). Therefore, the precipitates all contain a halide ion.

Be sure to use freshly prepared NaOCl (20 mL household bleach + 80 mL water) because an old solution will give poor results. The bromine produced in the NaOCl + KBr reaction is sometimes slow to form. Tell students to be patient.

Remind students that Step 2 requires the reaction surface to be very clean and free of stray gases.

You may want to have students use net ionic equations in this lab, as they are easier to write than the balanced equations that include all of the spectator ions.

42 Formation of Complex Ions with Ammonia

Text Section 23.10

Estimated Class Time: Less than one 50-minute period.
Estimated Teacher Preparation Time: 20 minutes.

Overview

Students search for metal cations that form complex ions with ammonia.

Materials

Small-scale pipets of the following solutions:

copper(II) sulfate	magnesium sulfate
silver nitrate	sodium chloride
aluminum chloride	tin(IV) chloride
zinc chloride	*sodium hydroxide
iron(III) chloride	sodium hydrogen
ammonia	carbonate
lead(II) nitrate	*sodium phosphate
calcium chloride	

Equipment

Small-scale reaction surface, empty pipet for stirring.

Teaching Suggestions

Be sure to make up a fresh solution of ammonia. As with Small-Scale Experiment 39, consider using this lab to encourage your students to devise their own procedures and methods of organizing data. Rather than using the organization printed in this book, consider having the students find out what happens to copper(II) sulfate when they add a drop of sodium hydrogen carbonate followed by several drops of ammonia. Explain the result as in the introduction and then give them these directions:

"Your assignment during the remainder of this lab is to devise an experiment that will detect the formation of complex ions with ammonia by adding excess ammonia to various carbonate precipitates. The cations you will use all formed carbonate precipitates in Small-Scale Experiment 24. Devise the experiment and record your observations in a logical fashion. Check your results with your instructor and obtain the formulas of the complex ions. Make a list of the cations that do form complex ions with ammonia and another list of those that do not. Write net ionic equations to describe their formation and designate their colors."

Small-Scale Experiment 43 Molecular Structure of Hydrocarbons

Text Section 24.5

Estimated Class Time: One 50-minute period.
Estimated Teacher Preparation Time: 10 minutes.

Overview

Students use pipe cleaners, pop beads, and polystyrene spheres to construct models of hydrocarbons. Students invent other ways to accurately depict structures.

Common Equipment

12 rulers, 12 pairs of scissors, 12 zipper-locking bags containing model sets consisting of: six

*Materials for Now It's Your Turn.

1-inch polystyrene spheres, 12 pop beads, 3 black and 3 white pipe cleaners (30 cm $\times$ 3 mm).

Teaching Suggestions

Keep student sets of pipe cleaners in zipper-locking plastic bags for reuse. Have extra pipe cleaners for students to replace in their sets as needed. Each carbon-hydrogen bond is represented by a 2-cm piece of pipe cleaner, so consider having students cut all the white pipe cleaners into 2-cm pieces before they begin. Each carbon-carbon bond is represented by a 5-cm piece of black pipe cleaner, so students can also cut these to 5-cm lengths before they begin. For the line-angle models in Now It's Your Turn, students will need several 4-cm pieces of white pipe cleaner and black pipe cleaners cut in lengths of multiples of 5 cm.

Small-Scale Experiment 44 Vitamin C in Tablets

Text Section 25.10

Estimated Class Time: One 50-minute period.
Estimated Teacher Preparation Time: 20 minutes.

Overview

Students measure the amount of the important organic compound, vitamin C, in various vitamin tablets.

Materials

Small-scale pipets of the following solutions:

0.1M potassium iodate	starch
ascorbic acid (vitamin C)	potassium iodide
	hydrochloric acid

Household Products: 48 vitamin C tablets (100 mg), *vitamin C tablets (250 mg, 500 mg, or 1000 mg).

Equipment

Plastic cup, small-scale reaction surface, balance.

Teaching Suggestions

Be sure to put away any 0.1M KIO$_3$ pipets at the end of this lab so students do not use them by mistake in Small-Scale Experiment 45.

Part A of the Experimental Procedure is designed to help students to understand the chemistry of the titration and the end point. Students can do the weight titration given in the procedure, or they can calibrate their pipets using a 12-well plate or the balance and then count drops.

Make a fresh vitamin C solution for Part A. Dissolve 3.5 g of ascorbic acid in 100 mL water.

You will need two 100-mg vitamin C tablets per student. If 100-mg tablets are not available, students can use 250- or 500-mg tablets. These larger tablets will make counting drops tedious because of the large amount of KIO_3 needed for the titration. It is better to do a weight titration for larger amounts of vitamin C. Alternatively, students can weigh a tablet, crush it, and then weigh and titrate only a portion of it and make the correction in their calculations. For example, if a tablet weighs 300 mg and a student titrates a 100-mg portion of the tablet, the student needs to multiply the experimental result by three to obtain the amount of vitamin C in the whole tablet.

Small-Scale Experiment
45   Vitamin C in Drinks
. . . .

Text Section 25.10

Estimated Class Time: One 50-minute period.
Estimated Teacher Preparation Time: 20 minutes.

Overview

Students try to find the answer to the question, "What's the best source of vitamin C?" by titrating various drinks for vitamin C.

Materials

Small-scale pipets of the following solutions:

0.01M potassium iodate   potassium iodide
hydrochloric acid   starch

Household Products: Various samples of fruit juices and fruit drinks, *powdered fruit drinks, *fresh vegetables.

Equipment

Plastic cup, balance.

*Materials for Now It's Your Turn.

Teaching Suggestions

The potassium iodate solution in this experiment is 0.01M (one tenth the concentration of the KIO_3 used in Small-Scale Experiment 44) because of the low concentration of vitamin C normally found in fruit drinks and juices. Be sure not to have the students use the 0.1M solution you prepared for Small-Scale Experiment 44.

Prepare the 0.01M KIO_3 by diluting 50 mL of 0.1M KIO_3 stock solution to 500 mL total. Label a classroom set of small-scale pipets with a different color to distinguish them from the more concentrated KIO_3 solution that you will use in Small-Scale Experiment 44.

Remind students that they do not have to weigh exactly 5000 mg of juice as given in the procedure, but they do have to know how much juice they weigh. For example, if a student's nickel weighs 5080 mg, then he or she will weigh 5080 mg of juice and use 5080 mg as the weight of juice in the calculation.

Small-Scale Experiment
46   Reactions of Biomolecules
. . . .

Text Section 25.13

Estimated Class Time: One 50-minute period.
Estimated Teacher Preparation Time: 20 minutes.

Overview

Students explore the chemical reactions typical of the various classifications of foods: fats, carbohydrates, and proteins.

Materials

Small-scale pipets of the following solutions:

potassium iodide	*hydrochloric acid
starch	sodium hypochlorite
copper(II) sulfate	sodium hydroxide
Sudan III	water
*Benedict's solution	*galactose

Small samples of various foods, including: dry cereal, milk, powdered milk, pasta, sugar, potato chips, crackers, peanut butter, margarine, corn oil, yeast, gelatin, and flour.

Equipment (per 24 students)

24 small-scale reaction surfaces, 150 toothpicks, 6 sheets of white typing paper, *24 glass slides.

Common Equipment

12 pairs of scissors, *6 hot plates.

Teaching Suggestions

A day or two before the lab, hand out zipper-locking bags and assign students to bring in various foods. This makes the lab more interesting. Just in case, you may want to take a few bags home to your own kitchen and supply the lab with what you need. Once in the lab, students can use toothpicks or small pieces of soda straw to sample messy foods like peanut butter and margarine. To sample liquid foods, dip a clean soda straw into the liquid, hold your finger over the end to capture a few drops, and release the drops onto the reaction surface.

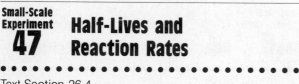

Small-Scale Experiment 47

Half-Lives and Reaction Rates

Text Section 26.4

Estimated Class Time: One 50-minute period.
Estimated Teacher Preparation Time: 20 minutes.

Overview

Students study the rate of a first-order chemical reaction and plot their data to obtain the half-life and order of the reaction. Students relate what they learn to the process of nuclear decay.

Materials

Small-scale pipets of the following solutions:

hydrochloric acid   potassium hydroxide
phenolphthalein   water

Solids: magnesium ribbon, *calcium carbonate.

Equipment (per 24 students)

Twenty-four 1-ounce plastic cups.

Common Equipment

12 watches or clocks.

Teaching Suggestions

Emphasize that although this is a chemical reaction, the same principle of half-life applies to nuclear decay. Nuclear decay simply occurs by first-order kinetics, as do many chemical reactions.

Each student needs a 2- or 3-cm piece of Mg ribbon. Students should be sure to stop the reaction on time by washing the magnesium thoroughly. Be sure the wash water (and the remaining acid) goes into the cup to be titrated. Also, be sure students dissolve the tarnish from the magnesium and dry it before they begin the experiment. Stirring by moving the magnesium to dislodge the bubbles is critical. Keep the magnesium submerged to a constant depth. If the reaction is too fast, try diluting the 1.0M HCl to 0.8M (80 mL HCl + 20 mL water).

*Materials and equipment for Now It's Your Turn.

Addison-Wesley
Small-Scale Chemistry
Laboratory Manual

● ●

Edward L. Waterman

Stephen Thompson

▲▲
▲

Addison-Wesley Publishing Company
Menlo Park, California • Reading, Massachusetts • New York
Don Mills, Ontario • Wokingham, England • Amsterdam
Bonn • Paris • Milan • Madrid • Sydney • Singapore
Tokyo • Seoul • Taipei • Mexico City • San Juan

Acknowledgments

Many people contributed ideas and resources during the development and writing of this small-scale laboratory manual. Mrs. Jackie Resseguie prepared solutions, organized equipment and provided other logistical support during the early stages of the experimental design. Peter Markow created the original formulation of the Thompson-Markow universal indicator and designed the first prototype of the small-scale balance which has since been modified and refined over the past decade by chemistry students at Rocky Mountain High School. These same students provided uncounted suggestions about the manuscript and numerous modifications of the experiments as they worked through them over the years. Bill Cook and Karen Dixon were enthusiastic cheerleaders at the appropriate moments. John Knight and Nicki Miller provided thoughts and insights as they worked through the experiments with their own students. The US West Foundation and the Hach Scientific Foundation provided resources to make the most of the time spent preparing the manuscript. Finally, a special thanks goes to Mrs. Kathryn C. Hach for her unparalleled love for and commitment to laboratory chemistry and the students who study it.

Cover photographs

Paul Silverman/Fundamental Photographs; Joel Gordon (background)

ISBN 0-201-86167-4

4 5 6 7 8 9 10-ML-98 97 96

Contents

● ●

©Addison-Wesley Publishing Company, Inc.

To the Student

Can you imagine learning how to play a musical instrument, paint a picture, or play a game by reading about it in a book? Books can give you valuable information when you are learning music, art, and sports, but to master any of these you have to practice and think about what you are doing as you are doing it.

The same is true of chemistry. The only way to really learn chemistry is to do chemistry. Chemistry is not a body of knowledge that exists in some textbook. Like music, art, and sports, it is something you do. To learn chemistry, you have to do lab work; you have to practice interacting with matter; you have to learn how to ask questions about matter, how to interpret the answers, and how to use this information to solve problems. Textbooks can be as valuable to chemistry students as they are to music students. But to learn the art of chemistry you have to participate in it.

This book is about practicing, or doing, chemistry. The idea is to put chemistry into your hands so you can explore chemistry for yourself. This book is designed to help you interact with matter, to interpret what you see, to solve problems, and to become inventive and creative. The labs are designed to help you to ask questions, to help you find ways to answer your questions, and to help you contribute your original ideas and discoveries to chemistry.

Practice chemistry yourself. Your participation will take patience. You will have to observe, concentrate, think about what you are doing, learn the rules, and apply the rules in original ways. If you do, you will discover that doing chemistry can be a lot of fun!

Small-Scale Laboratory Safety

The chemistry laboratory is a unique place where you will have the opportunity to investigate a variety of different chemical and physical phenomena. The experiments and procedures in this book have been carefully designed and written to minimize risk and provide for your personal safety. However, safety is also your responsibility. At all times your behavior is expected to be consistent with a safe laboratory. Here are some rules that are essential in promoting safety in the laboratory. You are responsible to know them and follow them at all times.

1. Wear safety glasses at all times when working in the laboratory or near someone else who is working in the laboratory. Safety glasses are designed to protect your eyes from injury due to chemicals and other foreign substances. To minimize the possibility of transmitting eye and skin disease, it's best to purchase and care for your own safety glasses. Do not loan them to another person. While working in the lab, do not rub your eyes because chemicals are easily transferred from your hands to your eyes.

2. Recognize that all laboratory procedures involve some degree of risk. Take steps to reduce the risk for yourself and for your neighbors. Read and listen to all directions carefully. When in doubt, ask your instructor.

3. Use full small-scale pipets only for the carefully controlled delivery of liquids, one drop at a time. Protect yourself and your neighbors by always using small-scale pipets correctly.

4. Minimize danger, waste, extra work, and cleanup by always using minimum amounts of chemicals to perform experiments.

5. Conduct only the assigned experiments, and do them only when a teacher is present and has given you permission to work.

6. Dispose of chemicals in a way that protects you, your neighbors, and your environment. Always follow your instructor's cleanup and disposal directions.

7. Know the location of the fire extinguisher, the emergency shower, the eye wash, the fire blanket, and the emergency exits. Know how and when to use each.

8. Consider all chemicals to be toxic. *Never* taste any laboratory chemical, including the many food products you will study in the laboratory. Consider these items to be contaminated with unknown chemicals. Keep all food and drink out of the laboratory. Do not eat, drink, or chew gum in the laboratory. Wash your hands thoroughly with soap and water before leaving the laboratory.

9. Report any accident, no matter how minor, to your instructor.

10. Recognize that electrical appliances pose an electrical-shock hazard, especially in the presence of water. Keep electrical appliances away from sinks and faucets. Take care not to spill water or other liquids in the vicinity of an electrical appliance. If you do, stand back, notify your instructor, and warn other students in the area.

11. Do not handle heated glass or broken glass. In case of breakage, notify your instructor and your neighbors. Sweep up broken glass with a brush and pan provided by your instructor. Do not use chipped or cracked glassware. Discard it according to your instructor's directions.

12. Protect your clothing and hair from chemicals and sources of heat. Tie back long hair and roll up loose sleeves when working in the laboratory. Avoid wearing bulky or loose-fitting clothing. Remove dangling jewelry.

13. Wear closed-toed shoes in the laboratory at all times.

14. Help facilitate a quick exit from the classroom by keeping classroom furniture away from escape routes and walkways. Keep your work area orderly and free of personal belongings like coats and backpacks.

15. Safety begins and continues with a clean laboratory. Report chemical spills immediately to your instructor. Clean up spills according to your instructor's directions. Warn other students about the identity and location of spilled chemicals. Clean up thoroughly every time you finish your laboratory work.

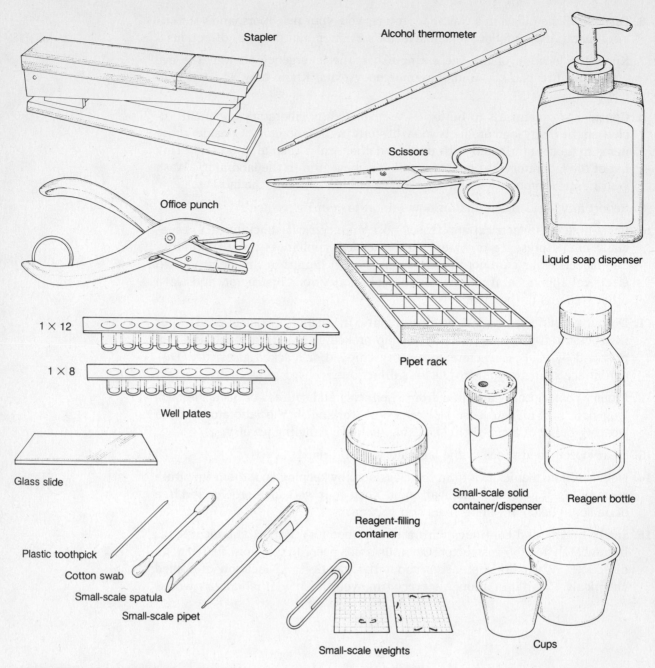

Stapler

Alcohol thermometer

Scissors

Liquid soap dispenser

Office punch

Pipet rack

1 × 12

1 × 8

Well plates

Glass slide

Small-scale solid container/dispenser

Reagent bottle

Reagent-filling container

Plastic toothpick

Cotton swab

Small-scale spatula

Small-scale pipet

Small-scale weights

Cups

Small-Scale Equipment

Cotton Swab: cotton and plastic; used to clean well plates, reaction surfaces.

Cups: plastic, 1-ounce and $3\frac{1}{2}$-ounces; used for titrations, balance pans, chromatography.

Glass Slide: only glass equipment in small-scale; may be heated; used for evaporations.

Hot Plate: low-temperature capability, used for evaporations.

Liquid Soap Dispenser: plastic, used to wash hands after every laboratory.

Office Hole Punch, $\frac{1}{4}$-inch: metal; used to punch holes in straws for construction of apparatus.

Pipet Rack: plastic; used to arrange and hold pipets for easy access.

Reagent Bottle: plastic; used to store solutions.

Reagent-Filling Container: plastic; used to fill pipets.

Safety Glasses: plastic; must be worn at all times while working in the laboratory.

Scissors: metal; used to cut paper and plastic for construction of instruments.

Small-Scale Balance: student-built; used for quantitative chemistry.

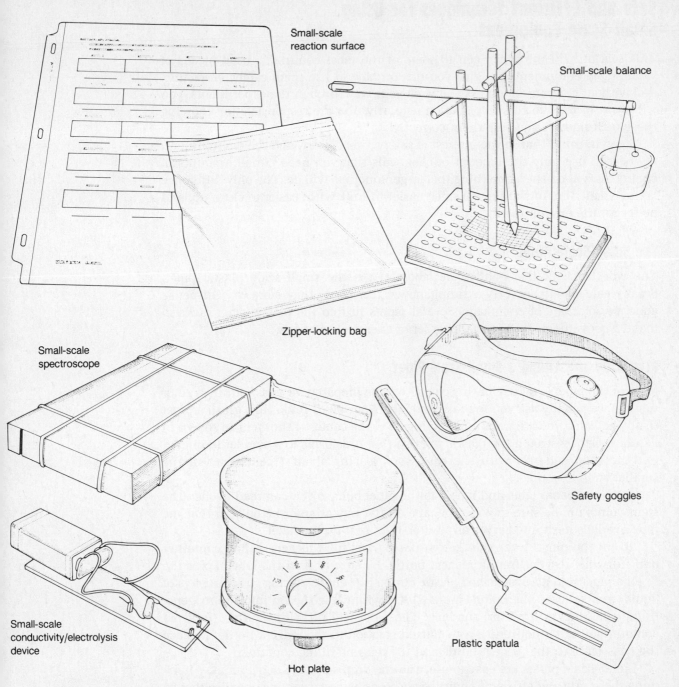

Small-scale reaction surface

Small-scale balance

Zipper-locking bag

Small-scale spectroscope

Safety goggles

Small-scale conductivity/electrolysis device

Hot plate

Plastic spatula

Small-Scale Conductivity/Electrolysis Device: teacher- or student-built; used to measure conductivity and to electrolyze solutions.

Small-Scale Pipet: plastic; used to store and deliver liquids.

Small-Scale Reaction Surface: plastic; used to mix chemicals qualitatively.

Small-Scale Solid Container/Dispenser: plastic; used to store and dispense solids.

Small-Scale Spatula: student-built; used to sample solids.

Small-Scale Spectroscope: student-built; used for analysis of light.

Small-Scale Weights: student-built; used with balance to measure mass.

Spatula: plastic; used to retrieve hot glass slides from hot plate.

Stapler: metal and plastic; used in making weights, chromatography, dispensing steel samples.

Thermometer: glass; alcohol type; used to measure temperature.

Toothpick: plastic; used to stir liquids in well plates.

Well Plates: plastic; common sizes are 1×12 and 1×8; used for quantitative work.

Zipper-Locking Bag: plastic; used to store weights and transfer dry-food samples.

Safe and Efficient Techniques for Using Small-Scale Equipment

This section will introduce you to some of the most commonly used pieces of small-scale equipment and give you tips on how to use them safely, efficiently, and without contamination. As you work your way through the experiments, you will want to refer to this information regularly. You are responsible for knowing these techniques and using them correctly!

Keep in mind that in the interest of safety, time, effort, and the environment, it's best to use only the amount of chemicals that you need. Small amounts of chemicals will do the same thing that larger amounts will do. The only difference is that small amounts are much safer, easier to work with, easier to clean up, and better for the environment.

The Small-Scale Pipet

The workhorse of the small-scale laboratory is the small-scale plastic pipet. Small-scale pipets serve two simultaneous functions: they store *and* dispense aqueous solutions of chemicals. Several pipets fit into the plastic pipet racks to make a convenient, readily available set of chemical solutions.

Preparing and Filling a Small-Scale Pipet

Most of the pipets you use in this course will be prepared for you. Your instructor might occasionally ask you to make and label your own. To do this, grasp a pipet firmly between your thumbs and forefingers at the center of the stem as shown in Figure I. Gently stretch the plastic stem so that it deforms to a smaller diameter. Cut the stem squarely with sharp scissors, leaving about 1 centimeter of the smaller stem as a tip.

Cut out a paper label and tape it to the pipet bulb so you can read it when the stem points up. Be sure to wrap the tape all the way around the bulb so that the tape overlaps itself and serves as a water-tight seal for the label.

To fill the pipet, wear your safety glasses and fill a reagent-filling container half full with reagent from a reagent bottle. Be sure to read the label! Point the tip of a pipet into an overturned plastic cup to prevent scattering stray droplets of liquid, and squeeze the bulb (Figure II). Now immerse the tip into the reagent-filling container and release the bulb. The pipet will fill with solution. To avoid contamination, do not return any unused solution to the reagent bottle. Replace the caps on both the reagent bottle and the reagent-filling container.

Small-scale pipets are easy to use, and the drop size they deliver makes handling them safe and efficient. They deliver drops having a volume of only about 20 microliters (20 millionths of a liter, or about 20 millionths of a quart). These small quantities of chemicals are also easier to clean up and present only a minimal environmental waste problem.

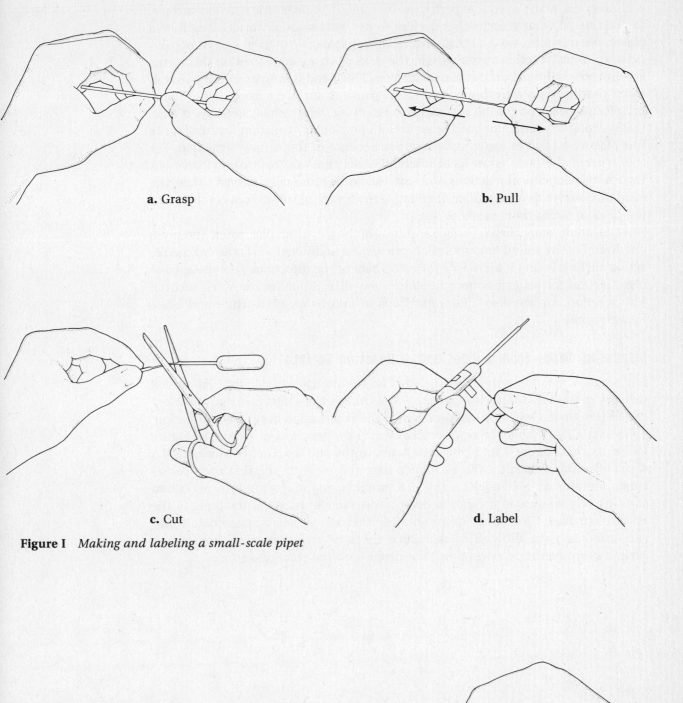

a. Grasp

b. Pull

c. Cut

d. Label

Figure I *Making and labeling a small-scale pipet*

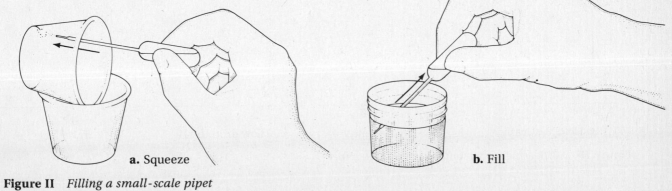

a. Squeeze

b. Fill

Figure II *Filling a small-scale pipet*

Safe and Efficient Techniques for Using Small-Scale Equipment   **9**

The Small-Scale Reaction Surface

Rather than using conventional glassware like glass test tubes and beakers, you will carry out many of your experiments on a small-scale plastic reaction surface. Depending on what your teacher decides to use, this reaction surface might be a plastic file protector, an overhead projection transparency, or even a piece of plastic wrap. Your "reaction vessel" will be the drop of an aqueous solution that forms a hemispherical bead on the plastic surface. This bead is similar to the beads of water that form on a freshly waxed car. Because of surface tension, water naturally forms beads on plastic surfaces or on car wax. Water molecules have a relatively strong attraction for each other and no particular attraction for substances like plastic. A bead of water stays together because of this strong attraction. For this reason, the bead is an ideal reaction vessel that you can use to carry out thousands of chemical reactions on a small scale. Because of its curved shape, the bead also serves as a magnifier. It enlarges the image of substances contained in the bead, making them easier to see.

The small-scale plastic surface encourages the use of smaller, safer, and more environmentally sound amounts of chemicals. An additional advantage of the reaction surface is that it allows for the placement of the directions and any special organization for an experiment in plain view, directly under the work surface. The reaction surface also allows for drops to appear on both white and black backgrounds.

Dispensing Drops from a Pipet onto a Reaction Surface

Full small-scale pipets are to be used only for the storage and carefully controlled delivery of liquids. Delivering one drop at a time is the safest and most efficient use of the pipet. One-drop delivery is also the best way to avoid contamination. To deliver a drop, hold the pipet vertically over the reaction surface as in Figure III, so its tip is about 1 to 2 centimeters above the surface. Gently squeeze off a drop, allowing it to fall a short distance onto the surface. The first drop sometimes contains an air bubble; if this is a problem, you may want to expel it into the sink or a waste cup before you begin. Never touch the tip of the pipet to the reaction surface. "Touching" drops onto the reaction surface causes contamination and makes it difficult to reproduce drops of the same size. Remember: Always *drop* the drops, never touch the drops onto the reaction surface.

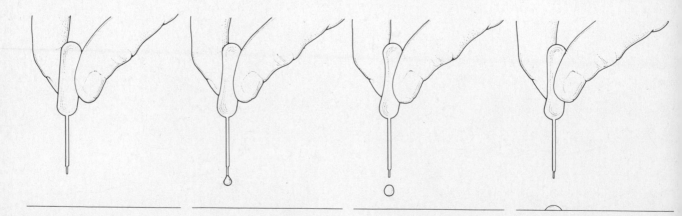

a. Hold vertically   **b.** Squeeze gently   **c.** Allow drop to fall   **d.** Perfect

Figure III *Delivering a drop with a small-scale pipet*

   ©Addison-Wesley Publishing Company, Inc.

Stirring without Contamination

You can stir a hemispherical droplet on a reaction surface by gently blowing air from an empty pipet onto the droplet as in Figure IV, "air stirring." Aim the tip of an empty pipet at the droplet while holding it 2 to 3 centimeters away. Gently squeeze the bulb repeatedly. Moving air from the empty bulb will stir the contents of the droplet. Be sure not to touch the tip of the stirring pipet to the droplet as this will result in contamination, or the droplet might be absorbed into the stirring pipet. Both outcomes are undesirable.

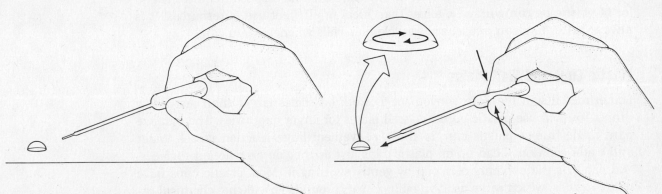

a. Aim tip of empty pipet 2 to 3 cm away   **b.** Squeeze bulb gently; moving air stirs drop

Figure IV *Stirring a drop by blowing air from an empty small-scale pipet*

To correct errors on small parts of the reaction surface, simply absorb small amounts of any undesired material onto a cotton swab or onto the edge of a rolled paper towel as shown in Figure V.

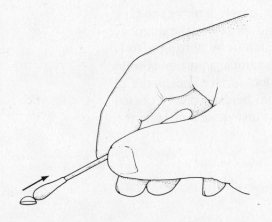

a. With a cotton swab   **b.** With the edge of a rolled paper towel

Figure V *Correcting a mistake*

Cleaning the Small-Scale Reaction Surface

You can clean the small-scale reaction surface more quickly and easily than conventional glassware. To clean the entire reaction surface, absorb the liquids onto a paper towel and dispose the towel in a solid-waste bin. Then wipe the surface with a damp paper towel. Finally, dry the surface with another paper towel. Take care that the chemical solutions touch only the paper towel and not your hands.

Disposal of paper towels is preferable to rinsing the chemicals down the drain because the paper towels eventually end up in landfills as solid waste. By contrast, liquid waste dumped down the drain ends up in sewage-treatment plants and can be introduced into rivers or lakes. Solid waste, while a mounting international problem, is much easier to control and to dispose of than liquid waste. Keeping solid waste to a minimum and disposing of it properly helps reduce environmental problems.

Plastic wrap as a reaction surface has the advantage that it does not need to be cleaned. When you are finished with it, simply fold it up carefully so that it contains all the chemicals you used, and dispose of it in the solid-waste bin. The disadvantage of plastic wrap is that its one time use and disposal requires that a lot of plastic be thrown away, a less than ideal or efficient use of resources! It is always better to clean, reuse, and recycle materials whenever you can.

Plastic Cups and Well Plates

Sometimes it will be more convenient to work on scales larger than just a few drops. You will use plastic cups and well plates for larger quantities. The balance pan, made from a plastic cup, is also a convenient large-reaction vessel. Water and water solutions bead up on plastic cups just as they do on reaction surfaces. You can stir the contents of a cup by gently swirling it. Most plastic cups have white insides, which serve as ideal built-in backgrounds for viewing chemical reactions. To clean a cup, rinse it with water, shake the water out, and dry it with a paper towel. To clean a well plate, flood it with water, and scrub the wells with a cotton swab. Shake the water out and dry the wells with a clean cotton swab. When you clean plastic cups and well plates, take care not to get the chemicals on your hands.

Dispensing Solids

To dispense solids into a cup or onto a reaction surface, simply remove the tape covering the hole in the top of the plastic vial and gently shake out the quantity you need. Alternatively, you can make a small-scale spatula by cutting a soda straw at an angle as shown in Figure VI. Use the straw to sample a portion of solid directly from the container. Your instructor will have lots of bits and pieces of recycled straws on hand for this purpose. Once a straw has been used with chemicals, do not use it again. Dispose of it according to your instructor's directions.

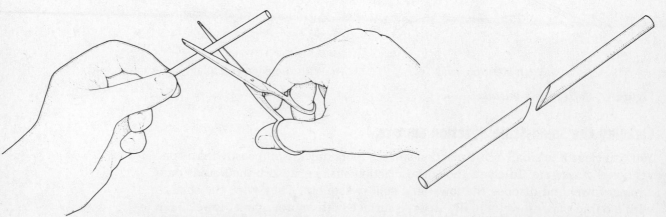

a. Cut at an angle   **b.** Two small-scale spatulas

Figure VI   *Making a small-scale spatula from a soda straw*

The Safe Use of Glass Slides and Hot Plates

The glass microscope slide is one of the few pieces of glassware you will use in small-scale experiments. Before you use a glass slide, check to see that it is free of cracks and chips. Replace any broken slide with a new one. If you break a glass slide, notify your teacher. Sweep up the glass with a brush and pan. Never handle broken glass with your fingers!

From time to time it will be necessary to heat liquid droplets. The best way to heat droplets is to dispense them onto a glass slide and heat the slide on a hot plate. Because small-scale quantities require very little heat, usually the lowest setting on the hot plate is sufficient. Even so, keep in mind that the hot plate is hot, and so is the glass slide. A hot glass slide can burn you, and it will break if you drop it! Remove the hot slide using a plastic spatula. Even though the glass slide does not look hot, do not touch it until you have allowed it to cool on the lab bench. Do not place a hot slide on a plastic reaction surface; the thin plastic reaction surface will melt!

Keep in mind that hot plates are electrical appliances. To avoid electrical shock, keep them away from sinks, water faucets, and other sources of water.

Measuring Mass on a Small-Scale Balance

Early in this course you will construct your own small-scale balance. You will have the option of using it in a variety of experiments throughout the course to measure mass. Before you begin any weighing, check to see that the balance beam swings freely, without friction and interference. Use your small-scale balance to measure mass in the following ways:

1. To measure the mass of a solid object:

   a. Place the solid object in the pan.

   b. Adjust the beam and/or the counterweight so the beam rests in the horizontal position as indicated by the pointer. To check for accuracy, tap the beam gently so it oscillates back and forth without friction or interference and comes to rest in the horizontal position.

   c. Replace the object with known weights until the beam again returns to the horizontal position, oscillating freely and without interference.

2. To measure the mass of a specified amount of a liquid:

   a. Place a known mass equal in size to the mass of the liquid you wish to measure in the pan.

   b. Adjust the beam and/or the counterweight so the beam rests in the horizontal position as indicated by the pointer. To check for accuracy, tap the beam gently so it oscillates back and forth without friction or interference and comes to rest in the horizontal position.

   c. Remove the known weight and use a small-scale pipet to deliver, drop by drop, enough liquid to return the beam to the horizontal position, oscillating freely and without interference.

3. To calibrate a small-scale pipet:

   a. Place a 1000-mg mass in the pan.

   b. Adjust the beam and/or the counterweight so the beam rests in the horizontal position as indicated by the pointer. To check for accuracy, tap the beam gently so it oscillates back and forth without friction or interference and comes to rest in the horizontal position.

c. Remove the 1000-mg weight, and count from a small-scale pipet the number of drops needed to return the beam to the horizontal position. Divide 1000 by the number of drops to obtain the volume of a drop in microliters.

4. To measure the volume of a liquid delivered by a pipet:

a. Place a small-scale pipet full of the liquid you wish to deliver in the pan.

b. Adjust the beam and/or the counterweight so the beam rests in the horizontal position as indicated by the pointer. To check for accuracy, tap the beam gently so it oscillates back and forth without friction or interference and comes to rest in the horizontal position.

c. Deliver the required amount of liquid from the small-scale pipet to another container. Place the small-scale pipet back into the pan, and add enough known masses to return the beam to the horizontal position. The sum of the added masses is equal to the mass of the liquid you delivered to the container.

Measuring Mass on an Electronic Balance

As an alternative to the small-scale balance, your teacher may make an electronic balance available to you. Before proceeding with any weighing activity, push the tare control on the balance and wait for the digital display to stabilize at zero. Take care not to lean on the balance table or cause air currents to circulate about the balance. Place a clean, dry cup on the balance, push the tare control and wait for the digital display to stabilize at zero.

1. To measure the mass of a solid object:

a. Place the solid object in the cup and wait for the digital display to stabilize before you read the mass.

2. To measure the mass of a specified amount of liquid:

a. Remove the cup from the balance and carefully deliver liquid to the cup from a full small-scale pipet. A full pipet is approximately 4 g. Half a pipet is approximately 2 g.

b. Replace the cup on the balance pan and wait until the digital display stabilizes to read the mass. Keep in mind that for all the experiments you need not use the exact quantities of liquids specified. However, you do need to know what quantities you use.

3. To calibrate a small-scale pipet:

a. Remove the cup from the balance and holding a full small-scale pipet vertically, carefully deliver exactly 50 drops to the cup.

b. Replace the cup on the balance pan and wait for the digital display to stabilize before you read the mass. Divide the mass in milligrams by 50 to obtain the mass of a single drop in mg.

4. To measure the volume of a liquid delivered by a pipet:

a. Place a full small-scale pipet of the liquid you wish to deliver in the pan.

b. Deliver the required amount of liquid from the pipet to another container. Place the pipet back into the cup and wait for the digital display to stabilize before you read the weight.

Name _____

Safety Contract

I have read in the Addison-Wesley *Small-Scale Chemistry Laboratory Manual* the pages that describe laboratory safety, laboratory hazards, and safe laboratory techniques. I have asked questions about any section that is unclear to me.

I agree to behave in a way that always promotes a safe laboratory environment for myself and my classmates. I agree to use chemicals and to clean them up in a way that protects myself, my classmates, and my environment.

I agree to wear safety glasses at all times during chemistry laboratory experiments and whenever my teacher thinks it is appropriate.

_____
Signature

_____
Date

A Study of Chemical Changes

Text Section 1.7

Objectives

- **Observe** and **record** chemical changes involving chemicals found in common consumer products.

- **Design** and **carry out** experiments to identify chemicals in consumer products.

- **Demonstrate** the use of the names and formulas of common chemical compounds.

Introduction

Chemistry is a science that investigates changes in matter. Chemical reactions are the changes matter undergoes. The changes you can observe are called "macroscopic changes." Often these changes, such as color changes, the formation of a solid, or the formation of gas bubbles, are visible. Thus, though we can not see the atoms and molecules reacting, we can see indications that chemical changes have taken place.

Different atoms and molecules often react in different ways. Chemistry attempts to explain macroscopic changes in terms of the behavior of atoms and molecules, that is, on the submicroscopic level. You can use these different reactions to detect the presence of specific kinds of chemicals in mixtures.

Purpose

In this lab you will study some reactions of common chemicals contained in consumer products. You will observe the notable macroscopic changes these chemicals undergo. In later labs you will interpret these macroscopic changes in terms of submicroscopic changes, the behavior of atoms and molecules. As the name implies, submicroscopic changes are changes we cannot see, even with a microscope. The essence of understanding chemistry is to infer from macroscopic changes the submicroscopic behavior of atoms and molecules.

Safety

- Wear your safety glasses.
- Use full small-scale pipets only for the carefully controlled delivery of liquids.

Materials

Small-scale pipets of the following solutions:

sodium hydrogen carbonate (NaHCO$_3$)

FD&C blue No. 1 (blue dye)

potassium iodide (KI)

calcium chloride (CaCl$_2$)

sodium carbonate (Na$_2$CO$_3$)

sodium hydroxide (NaOH)

ammonia (NH$_3$)

hydrochloric acid (HCl)

sodium hypochlorite (NaOCl)

lead(II) nitrate (Pb(NO$_3$)$_2$)

sodium hydrogen sulfate (NaHSO$_4$)

phenolphthalein (phen)

silver nitrate (AgNO$_3$)

copper(II) sulfate (CuSO$_4$)

starch

Equipment

small-scale reaction surface

empty pipet for stirring

Experimental Page

Use small-scale pipets to put 2 drops of each chemical on the X's in the indicated spaces below. For background contrast, view the drops on black and white backgrounds provided by the X's. Stir each mixture by blowing air through an empty pipet. Record what you see in Table 1.1.

a. **X** $NaHCO_3$
+
HCl

b. **X** HCl
+
blue dye

c. **X** blue dye
+
NaOCl   Now add 1 drop of HCl.

d. **X** NaOCl
+
KI   Now add 1 drop of starch.

e. **X** KI
+
$Pb(NO_3)_2$

f. **X** $Pb(NO_3)_2$
+
$CaCl_2$

g. **X** $CaCl_2$ Be patient!
+   Some chemical
$NaHSO_4$ reactions are slow!

h. **X** $NaHSO_4$
+
Na_2CO_3

i. **X** Na_2CO_3
+
phen

j. **X** phen
+
NaOH

k. **X** NaOH
+
$AgNO_3$

l. **X** $AgNO_3$ Absorb this mixture onto
+   a scrap of paper, expose it to
NH_3 sunlight, and tape it to your
data table.

m. **X** NH_3
+
$CuSO_4$

n. **X** $CuSO_4$
+
$NaHCO_3$

Place this side of the Experimental Page facedown. Use the other side under your small-scale reaction surface.

Experimental Data

Record your results in Table 1.1 or a table like it in your notebook.

Table 1.1   Experimental Mixings

a.	bubbles	$NaHCO_3$ + HCl	h.	bubbles	$NaHSO_4$ + Na_2CO_3
b.	green	HCl + blue dye	i.	bright pink	Na_2CO_3 + phen
c.	yellow then colorless	blue dye + NaOCl and then HCl	j.	bright pink	phen + NaOH
d.	yellow then black	NaOCl + KI and then starch	k.	brown ppt.	NaOH + $AgNO_3$
e.	bright yellow ppt.	KI + $Pb(NO_3)_2$	l.	wht ppt. Brown paper*	$AgNO_3$ + NH_3
f.	white milky ppt.	$Pb(NO_3)_2$ + $CaCl_2$	m.	light blue ppt.	NH_3 + $CuSO_4$
g.	slow white ppt.	$CaCl_2$ + $NaHSO_4$	n.	light blue ppt.	$CuSO_4$ + $NaHCO_3$

*This fleeting, faint precipitate might be seen only to the most observant students. The paper turns brown only after several hours or upon exposure to intense light or sunlight.

Cleaning Up

Avoid contamination by cleaning up in a way that protects you and your environment. Carefully clean the small-scale reaction surface by absorbing the contents onto a paper towel, wipe it with a damp paper towel, and dry it. Dispose of the paper towels in the waste bin. Wash your hands thoroughly with soap and water.

Questions for Analysis

Use what you learned in this lab to answer the following questions.

1. Sodium hydrogen carbonate is baking soda, $NaHCO_3$. When HCl is added to $NaHCO_3$, carbon dioxide bubbles are formed. Do you know the chemical formula of carbon dioxide? In what consumer product is the gas commonly found?

CO_2. Carbonated drinks.

---

2. Which of the other mixings form bubbles?

$NaHSO_4 + Na_2CO_3$.

---

3. What do you think the gas is that results from the mixing in Question 2?

Carbon dioxide.

---

4. The body uses hydrochloric acid, HCl, to help digest food. Where in the body is hydrochloric acid found? What color does blue food dye turn when HCl is added?

The stomach. Green.

---

5. Sodium hypochlorite, NaOCl, is a common ingredient in household bleaches and cleansers. What happened to the color of blue dye when both HCl and NaOCl are added?

It becomes colorless.

---

6. Potassium iodide, KI, is the source of iodine in iodized salt. What color is the KI + NaOCl mixture? What color does starch change to in the presence of KI and NaOCl?

Yellow-brown. Black.

---

7. A precipitate is a solid that separates upon mixing solutions. Which reaction produced a very bright yellow precipitate?

e. $KI + Pb(NO_3)_2$.

---

8. Which other mixings produced precipitates? Describe their colors and textures with words like milky, cloudy, and grainy.

f. white; g. white; k. brown; l. brown paper; m. light blue; n. light blue.

---

9. Which mixture produced a precipitate that was very slow to form?

g. $CaCl_2 + NaHSO_4$.

---

10. Which solutions produced a distinctive "muddy" brown precipitate?

k. $AgNO_3 + NaOH$.

---

11. Observe the scrap of paper you used to absorb the $AgNO_3 + NH_3$ mixture. What evidence do you see that indicates that silver compounds are light-sensitive?

Light caused the damp swab to turn brown over time.

---

12. Review your results and list at least three different kinds of changes that indicate that a chemical reaction is occurring.

Bubbles, precipitates, and color changes.

13. Describe any other notable observations you made.

The descriptions students write here, especially adjectives, are varied and

original.

Now It's Your Turn!

1. What two compounds turn phenolphthalein pink in the original experiment? What others do this? Experiment and find out!

Na_2CO_3 and NaOH. Mixing each of the other 13 chemicals with phen will

reveal that NH_3 and $NaHCO_3$ turn pink as well.

2. What happens when you add ammonia, NH_3, to copper(II) sulfate, $CuSO_4$? Does the result depend on the amount of ammonia you add? Try adding several drops of NH_3 to just 1 drop of $CuSO_4$. Then try adding several drops of $CuSO_4$. Record your observations.

A small amount of NH_3 makes a light-blue precipitate. Excess NH_3 turns

the solution clear royal blue. Excess $CuSO_4$ brings back the light-blue

precipitate.

3. Sodium hydrogen carbonate, $NaHCO_3$, forms gas bubbles when hydrochloric acid, HCl, is added.

a. Suppose a label of a household product says it contains sodium hydrogen carbonate (also called bicarbonate of soda or baking soda). How would you test this material to indicate the presence of sodium hydrogen carbonate, $NaHCO_3$?

Add a drop of HCl to a small amount of baking soda or other sample. Expect

bubbles if the material contains $NaHCO_3$.

b. Try your procedure with various household products whose labels say they contain $NaHCO_3$. Record your results.

Na_2CO_3 also produces bubbles with HCl.

c. Find out if any of the other chemicals you used in this experiment form gas bubbles with hydrochloric acid. Based on your results, describe any limitations this experiment might have.

A positive CO_2 test does not distinguish between $NaHCO_3$ and Na_2CO_3.

4. Many foods contain starch. You know that starch turns black in the presence of potassium iodide, KI, and sodium hypochlorite, NaOCl. Try adding KI and NaOCl to various foods to confirm the presence or absence of starch. Explain what you do, what you observe, and what it means.

Add one drop of KI and one drop of NaOCl to various foods like cereal,

bread, crackers, and potato chips. A black color indicates the presence

of starch.

5. Potassium iodide, KI, turns black when sodium hypochlorite, NaOCl, and starch are added. The label on a package of iodized table salt says that it contains potassium iodide, KI. Tell what you would do to confirm this. Try it and record your results. Does your procedure work with non-iodized salt? Explain.

Add 1 drop of starch to the edge of a conical pile of table salt so only a

portion is wet. Then add 1 drop of NaOCl to the wet portion. As the pile

absorbs the extra liquid, a black line forms and disappears, moving

with the solvent into the dry portion. (This is tricky, but with some

creative experimentation the results are obvious and gratifying!)

6. Many household products like automatic dishwashing liquid contain sodium hypochlorite, NaOCl. Design an experiment to confirm the presence or absence of NaOCl in automatic dishwashing liquid and other household chemicals. Add one drop of starch and one drop of KI to the household chemical which lists NaOCl as an ingredient. A black color confirms the presence of NaOCl. Note: Do not use full strength household bleach. Dilute 50 mL of household bleach with 200 mL of water.

Teacher's Note: Hypochlorite ion oxidizes iodide ion to iodine:
$2H^+ + OCl^- + 2I^- \rightarrow I_2 + Cl^- + H_2O$. **Starch turns black in the presence of iodine:** I_2 + **starch** $\rightarrow$ **blue-black starch-iodine complex.**

2 Design and Construction of a Small-Scale Balance

Text Section 2.1

Objectives

- **Design** and **build** a balance that is capable of accurately weighing 10 grams and is sensitive to 5 milligrams.
- **Explain** the relationship between the structure and function of each part of a balance.
- **Troubleshoot** the balance, and make modifications and innovations to make it work better.

Introduction

A *balance* is an instrument used to measure mass. Because it is often the most accurate instrument in the laboratory, you commonly use the balance to calibrate other instruments, such as burets and pipets, that are used to measure volume. The balance operates much like a see-saw because it consists of a *beam* that pivots on a central *fulcrum* as shown in Figure 2.1. A *balance pan* hangs from one end of the beam, and a *counterweight* is attached to the other end. You use a *substitution balance* to determine mass by comparing the weight of an unknown object to the weights of known objects. You place a substance of unknown weight in the pan and adjust the mechanism so the beam balances. You then remove the unknown substance and substitute known weights until the beam balances again. The weight of the unknown substance is equal to the amount of known weights you used to restore the beam to the balanced position.

Sensitivity refers to the smallest weight a balance can measure accurately. Whenever you add weight to the pan, the balance beam moves. You express the sensitivity of the balance as the amount of change in the position of the beam when a known quantity of weight is added. Sensitivity can be measured by the *distance* the beam moves or the *angle* through which the beam moves per unit weight. The smaller the weights you want to measure accurately, the more sensitive your balance must be. If the balance is too sensitive, it will move with even the slightest air currents and will be difficult to use.

The *capacity* of a balance is the maximum amount of weight that can be accurately determined by the balance. Very sensitive balances generally have small capacities. With larger-capacity balances, you sacrifice sensitivity. You want a balance to be just sensitive enough to do the job in a convenient way. You design a balance to make the best compromise among sensitivity, capacity, and ease of use.

The *principal* moving part of the balance is the *beam*. The beam's mass, length, and flexibility affect the sensitivity of the balance. The longer, lighter, and more rigid the beam, the more sensitive the balance will be. However, the longer the beam, the heavier it is. In designing your beam, find a compromise between the extremes of length and mass, and yet design it to remain rigid under maximum loads. Very sensitive balances have the advantage of measuring the masses of very small objects accurately. Unfortunately, they cannot weigh heavy objects because the long light beam required for high sensitivity is usually too flexible to carry large loads. Balances designed to weigh larger objects must use rigid beams, which are usually very heavy. Thus, sensitivity is sacrificed for capacity and vice versa. In short, the same balance cannot be used to weigh both a truck and a feather. Designers of balances must make compromises and design balances that meet specific objectives. You want your balance to be sensitive to 5 milligrams and have a capacity of about 10 grams.

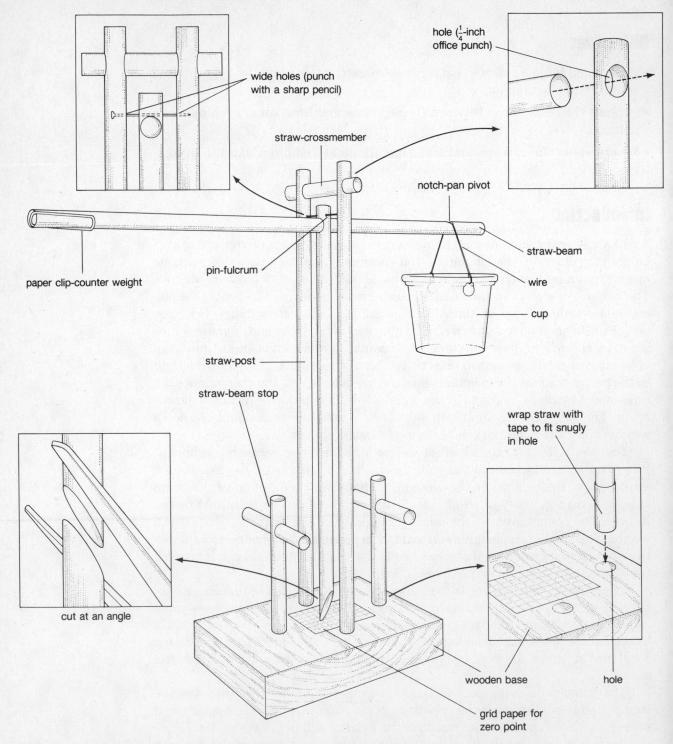

Figure 2.1 *Construction of a small-scale balance*

The most critical part of the balance is the *fulcrum,* the part on which the beam pivots. For maximum sensitivity, the fulcrum should be nearly friction-free. You should locate it above and at right angles to the beam, and as close to the beam's center of mass as possible. The beam will swing freely back and forth only if the center of mass of the beam is *below* the fulcrum. The beam will not be stable if the center of gravity is above the fulcrum.

A highly visible *pointer* readily determines the horizontal position of the beam. The balance is most sensitive when the beam is exactly horizontal. The pointer should be attached rigidly and at right angles to the beam and the fulcrum. When the beam is horizontal, the pointer will be vertical.

The *zero point* is the point indicated by the pointer when the beam is horizontal. In order to know the horizontal position reliably, the zero point must not move from one weighing to another.

The *balance posts* and *crossmember* make up the superstructure that gives support and stability to the balance and does not interfere with its operation. The balance posts must be anchored and rigid because if they move, the zero point moves. Build the posts perpendicular to the base, then center the zero point in a fixed position between the posts. With a sharp pencil, make holes in the straw posts to provide nearly frictionless surfaces to support the fulcrum. The taller the posts and the longer the pointer, the easier it is to see a small movement in the beam. However, very tall posts are sometimes not rigid enough to support the weight of the instrument.

The *pan pivot* suspends the pan from the beam. Like the fulcrum, it must be sturdy, nearly frictionless, and at right angles to the beam. The pan pivot must not move back and forth along the beam.

The *balance pan* holds the known weights and the objects you want to weigh. The balance pan should be sturdy and lightweight to keep the beam's center of mass close to the fulcrum.

The *beam stops* hit the pointer and allow the beam to move only through a small arc. By preventing excessive motion of the balance beam, they protect the vital moving parts of the balance and shorten the time the beam takes to come to the horizontal position. The sensitivity of a good balance is such that even the slightest touch will cause the balance beam, without beam stops, to rotate and the pan to swing wildly. When trying to make an accurate weighing, this situation is inconvenient at best and disastrous at worst.

The *counterweight* offsets the weight in the pan. A friction-tight but easily moved counterweight serves as a convenient adjustment device for leveling the beam. Make it light to keep the total weight of the beam assembly low.

Summary of principal parts of a balance and their functions:

- A *balance* is an instrument used to measure mass.

- The *beam* is the principal moving part. The beam also affects sensitivity. For maximum sensitivity, it should be lightweight, rigid, and long.

- The *fulcrum* is the critical pivot point for the beam. The position and friction of the fulcrum affect accuracy and sensitivity. The fulcrum should be frictionless at the posts, friction-tight at the pointer, close to the beam's center of mass and just above it, and at right angles to the beam and the posts.

- The *counterweight* moves to offset the weight in the pan. The counterweight is light and friction-tight but easily moved.

- *Sensitivity* refers to the smallest weight a balance can measure accurately.

- The *capacity* of a balance is the maximum amount of weight that can be accurately determined by the balance.

- The *pointer* points to the zero point when the beam is horizontal. The pointer should be long, visible, and at right angles to the beam.
- The *zero point* shows when the beam is horizontal. The zero point is positioned so the pointer points to it when the beam is horizontal.
- The *posts* support the weight of the balance. They should be sturdy, friction-tight, and out of the way of moving parts.
- The *crossmember* keeps the balance rigid and square. The crossmember is friction-tight and at right angles to the posts.
- The *pan pivot* is the critical point upon which the pan rests. The pan pivot is frictionless at the beam, at right angles to the beam, and foolproof so the pan does not fall off.
- The *beam stops* keep the beam from swinging wildly. The beam stops are sturdy and out of the way of moving parts.

Purpose

In this lab you will design and construct a balance out of common objects such as soda straws, pins, tape, wood blocks, wire, and plastic cups. For optimal use in small-scale chemistry, your balance should be sensitive to 5 milligrams and have a capacity of 10 grams. Your balance should be sturdy and foolproof so it can make many accurate weighings in very short times with little trouble. You should build your balance with careful consideration of features that make it function accurately and reliably. The preceding paragraphs provided information about the working parts of a balance. Reread them and refer to these criteria as you design and build your balance.

Safety

- Behave in a way that is consistent with a safe laboratory.

Equipment

6 soda straws
1 extra long pin (1-1/4 inch)
2 paper clips
1 adhesive label
thread
wire
1/4-inch office hole punches

1 pre-drilled wood block
4 square centimeters of graph paper
1 plastic cup
scissors
cellophane tape
longer soda straws
standard 5 mg weights

Experimental Procedure

Use the following template to assemble the proper pieces for constructing your small-scale balance. Use the template to cut the soda straws to the appropriate lengths. Use a 1/4-inch office hole punch to make holes where indicated. Use a sharp pencil to make holes in the posts for the fulcrum. Assemble the parts as shown in the template and in Figure 2.1.

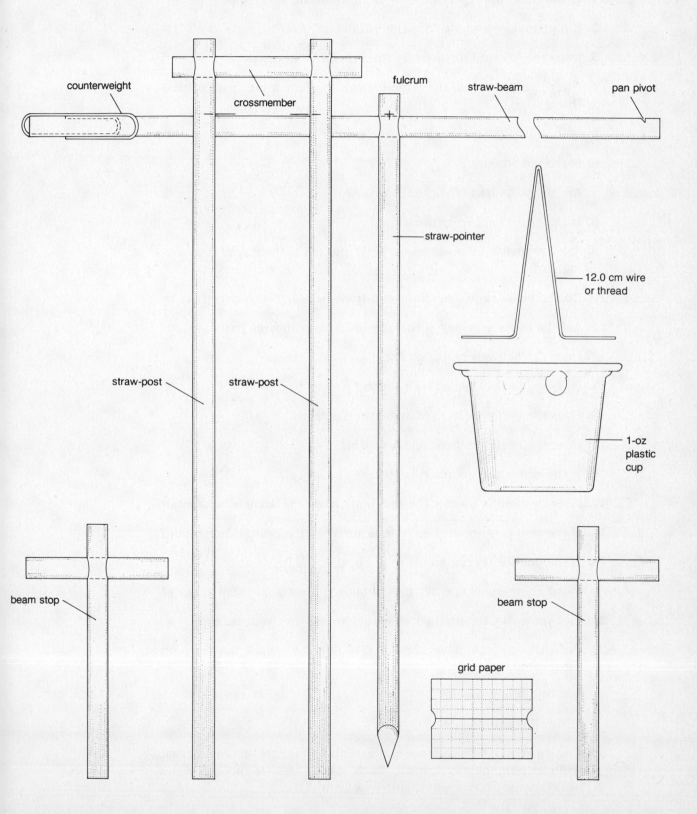

Experimental Data

As you assemble your balance according to the template on the Experimental Page, check it and make adjustments and/or modifications until the answer to each of the following questions is "yes."

_____ **1.** Is the fulcrum perpendicular to both the beam and the pointer?

_____ **2.** It it just *above* and *touching* the beam?

_____ **3.** Does the fulcrum rotate freely from the holes in the post?

_____ **4.** Are the holes round and large enough to allow a pin head to pass through?

_____ **5.** Is the fulcrum friction-tight at the pointer?

_____ **6.** Is the pin straight?

_____ **7.** Are the posts friction-tight at the base?

_____ **8.** Is the crossmember friction-tight?

_____ **9.** Are the posts and crossmember rigid and out of the way of the moving parts?

_____ **10.** Do the beam stops keep the beam from swinging excessively?

_____ **11.** Are the beam stops out of the way of all other moving parts?

_____ **12.** Does the pan stay on consistently?

_____ **13.** Is the pan easily loaded with weight?

_____ **14.** Does the pan pivot at right angles to the beam?

_____ **15.** Does the beam not bend under weight?

_____ **16.** Is the end of the pointer easy to see?

_____ **17.** Does the pointer point at the zero point when the beam is horizontal?

_____ **18.** Is the zero point positioned to indicate when the beam is horizontal?

_____ **19.** Is the pointer at right angles to the beam?

_____ **20.** Is the counterweight easily moved but friction-tight to stay in place?

_____ **21.** Can you easily fix anything that goes wrong with your balance?

_____ **22.** Does the pointer move when a 15-milligram weight is placed on the pan?

_____   A 10-milligram weight?

_____   A 5-milligram weight?

_____   The *sensitivity* of the balance is the minimum weight on the pan that will cause the pointer to move. Each of the three weights cause the beam to move how many graph-paper units?

Cleaning Up

Please clean up at the end of the period. Recycle all the materials you do not use. Dispose of unusable scraps in the waste bin. Label your balance with your name, and store it as directed by your teacher.

You may want to store balances on shelves or in cabinets.

Questions for Analysis

Use what you learned in this lab to answer the following questions.

1. How does a substitution balance work? Does it measure mass or weight? Explain. Make a rough sketch of your balance and label all the parts.

A substitution balance is used to measure mass by comparing weights of

known objects with those of unknown objects. An object of unknown mass

is placed in the pan. The beam is balanced. The object is removed and

substituted with known masses until the beam is again balanced. Because

the gravitational force of each object is the same, it is cancelled out, giving

a good approximation of mass.

Design and Construction of a Small-Scale Balance

2. What is sensitivity? What is capacity?

The smallest weight the balance can accurately measure. The maximum

amount of weight that can be determined accurately by the balance.

3. What critical part of a balance most affects its sensitivity? Give three important criteria for this critical part.

The fulcrum. Frictionless at the posts, friction-tight at the pointer, and

perpendicular to the beam and the posts.

4. Name another part of a balance that also affects its sensitivity.

The beam.

5. At what position is the beam most sensitive?

Horizontal.

6. What is the function of the pointer? Of the zero point?

Both indicate when the beam is horizontal.

7. Why is it important for the balance posts and crossmember to be well-anchored and rigid?

They keep the angles square and the zero point fixed.

8. What aspects of your balance are most important?

A frictionless fulcrum and a free-swinging beam.

9. What other criterion besides sensitivity must be considered when creating a balance beam?

Capacity.

10. Explain how each of the following materials would affect the *sensitivity* and *capacity* of your balance if each material was used for the beam. Give the advantages and disadvantages of each: **a.** a solid steel rod, **b.** a hollow aluminum tube, and **c.** a wood dowel.

a. decreased sensitivity, increased capacity; b. decreased sensitivity,

increased capacity; c. decreased sensitivity, increased capacity.

11. The sensitivity of a balance increases with increasing length and decreasing mass of the beam. Why is the ideal case of having an infinitely long beam of zero mass not possible?

The longer the beam, the heavier it must be.

12. How many graph-paper units did the pointer move upon addition of a 10-mg weight? Explain how you might make your balance even more sensitive.

Typically about one. Make the beam lighter or longer.

13. Why is it important to have the holes in which the fulcrum rest at exactly the same height? If they are not at the same height, how might you be able to fix them without remaking one or both the posts?

To keep the fulcrum perpendicular to the posts. Cut off the bottom of the

longer one.

14. If the fulcrum pin were placed at a 45-degree angle to the beam, how would this affect the function and sensitivity of your balance?

The beam assembly would hit other parts of the balance. Sensitivity would

decrease because the angle through which it moves would be less per unit

mass.

Now It's Your Turn!

1. Why must the fulcrum be placed *above the beam?* What will happen to a balance beam set in motion if the fulcrum is below it? (To answer these questions, see what happens when you place the fulcrum below the beam. Go ahead; you can always move it back!)

Gravity will restore the beam to the horizontal position only if the fulcrum

is above the beam.

2. Design a longer beam for your balance. Use a 1/4-inch wood dowel, an aluminum tube, and an extra-long soda straw, or try to put together one or more soda straws. What are some of the advantages and disadvantages of your longer beam?

3. Design a better way to hold your balance up. Redesign the posts into a more rigid superstructure. Try building a triangular or a rectangular superstructure.

4. A taller balance will be more sensitive because the movement of a long pointer will be easier to detect for a small weight. Try modifying your balance so that it is very tall.

5. Try redesigning the beam-fulcrum assembly. You might consider using permanent magnets to suspend the beam-fulcrum.

3 Design and Construction of a Set of Standardized Weights

Text Section 2.9

Objectives

- **Distinguish** between mass and weight.
- **Construct** a set of weights to use with a small-scale balance.
- **Weigh** objects accurately using your weights.

Introduction

Now that you've built a balance, you can use it to measure mass. To do so, you must first make a set of known weights to use with your balance for comparison with unknown weights. But before you make the weights, let's clarify a few things about how mass is different from weight.

Mass is the quantity of matter in an object. *Weight,* on the other hand, is the gravitational force of attraction exerted between the mass of an object and its surroundings, principally the earth. The weight of an object on Earth will differ slightly depending on its geographical location. Because the gravitational field is weaker at the equator than at the poles, the same object will weigh less in Mexico City than in Anchorage, Alaska. The gravitational pull also decreases with higher elevation. An object will weigh slightly less in Denver, "the mile-high city," than in New York, which is at sea level.

In chemistry you are always interested in the determination of mass because you do not want the results to depend on where you are. You can readily determine mass by comparing the weight of an unknown object to the weights of known objects through the use of a *balance,* a device used to compare weights. Since gravity will affect both known and unknown objects to exactly the same extent, the effect of gravity will cancel, and a measure of mass will result.

It is important to note that the distinction between mass and weight in chemistry is not commonly observed. For example, determining the mass of an object is called *weighing.* Known masses that are used to compare unknown masses are called *weights.* Hereafter, we will use the terms *mass* and *weight* synonymously, but strictly speaking, we are referring to *mass.*

To weigh things accurately, your small-scale balance is used with a set of weights. The set of weights must be calibrated, that is, compared to accurately known weights. Calibration is usually done with a balance more sensitive and accurate than your small-scale balance. Once calibrated, this known set of weights will become your set of standardized weights.

The number and sizes of standardized weights in a set should be such that any combination of weight can be added within the sensitivity and capacity of the balance. Your balance has a sensitivity of 5 mg and a capacity of about 10 g (10 000 mg). Thus, you need to build a set of weights that can combine to provide any number of milligrams between 5 mg and 10 000 mg in intervals of 5 milligrams.

Design and Construction of a Set of Standardized Weights   **35**

Purpose

In this lab you will take advantage of small objects that can be uniformly reproduced to make a set of standardized weights. Common objects like staples, soda straws, graph paper, and wire all have reproducible weights for equal-sized pieces. The plastic "disks" punched from super-jumbo soda straws all weigh exactly 5 mg. Standard staples all weigh 33 mg, and graph paper, if cut precisely, can produce very uniform small weights. Large objects are not as uniformly produced, but they can be standardized by weighing them and labeling them with their milligram values.

Safety

■ Behave in a way that is consistent with a safe laboratory.

Equipment

1/2 page of graph paper
1 standard paper clip
1 jumbo paper clip
1 zipper-locking plastic sandwich bag
1 penny
1 nickel
staplers with standard staples
1/4-inch office hole punches
soda straws
adhesive labels
scissors

Experimental Procedure

Use the information below to design a set of weights, and then make them with the available materials. Where you can, write the weight value and your name on each weight. Place them in a labeled zipper-locking sandwich bag for storage.

Weights with the following milligram values will enable you to weigh any object between 5 mg and 10 000 mg. Your set of weights will probably not be ideal; that is, some of the values will not be exactly the values listed below.

5 mg	10 mg	20 mg	30 mg
50 mg	100 mg	200 mg	300 mg
500 mg	1000 mg	2500 mg	5000 mg

1. One 1/4-inch plastic disk cut from a soda straw weighs 5 mg. Make enough plastic disks to weigh things between 5 and 45 mg.

2. Design and make weights from 50 to 500 mg, using the following information:
   1 square inch of graph paper (cut very carefully) weighs 50 mg.
   1 standard staple weighs 33 mg.
   Keep in mind that the staples tend to be more precise than the graph paper, and the weights need to be within only a few (2 to 3) milligrams of the ideal values.

3. Make the following larger weights, and then use your small-scale balance and your smaller weights to determine their masses.

      1 standard paper clip with an adhesive label attached.
      1 jumbo paper clip with an adhesive label attached.
      1 penny with an adhesive label attached.
      1 nickel with an adhesive label attached.

To use your balance to determine the mass of a larger weight, follow these steps:

  a. Place the larger weight in the pan, and slide the beam and/or the counter-weight back and forth so the pointer indicates the beam is horizontal.

  b. Remove the larger weight from the pan, and replace it with smaller weights until the pointer again indicates the beam is horizontal.

  c. The weight of the larger weight is the sum of the small weights in the pan.

  d. Write this milligram value on the label of the larger weight.

4. If your lab has a precision or analytical balance, use it to check the weights of your larger weights, following the directions of your teacher. Also, in the next lab you will do some experiments to find out how good your weights really are!

Experimental Data

1. Draw a picture of each standardized weight you make, tell what it is made from, and label it with its milligram value.

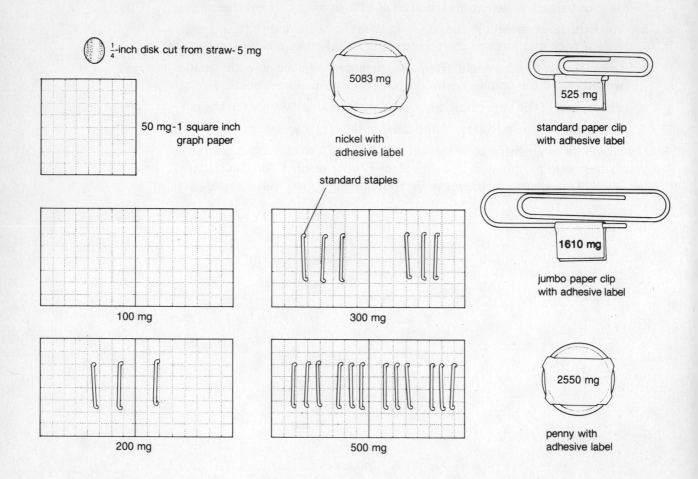

$\frac{1}{4}$-inch disk cut from straw- 5 mg

50 mg-1 square inch graph paper

5083 mg

nickel with adhesive label

525 mg

standard paper clip with adhesive label

standard staples

100 mg

300 mg

1610 mg

jumbo paper clip with adhesive label

200 mg

500 mg

2550 mg

penny with adhesive label

Cleaning Up

Please recycle all the materials you do not use. Dispose of unusable scraps in the waste bin. Store your labeled weights as directed by your teacher.

Questions for Analysis

Use what you learned in this lab to answer the following questions.

1. Distinguish between the terms *mass* and *weight*. Why do we often use them interchangeably?

   A mass is a quantity of matter. Weight is the force of gravity acting on that

   mass. You usually encounter various weights in the same gravitational

   field on Earth.

2. What is the mass of an object in outer space, where there is no gravitational field? What is its weight?

   The same as anywhere. Zero.

3. Will the mass of an object be the same on Earth as it is on the moon? Explain.

Yes. An object, assuming no gains or losses, will always have the same

quantity of matter.

4. Is the weight of an object the same on Earth as it is on the moon? Explain.

No. The moon's gravitational field is different from Earth's gravitational

field.

5. Would your balance work equally well on the moon as it does on Earth? Explain. Would the result of each weighing be the same? Explain.

Yes. The moon's gravity would act on both the known and unknown

weights and thus be canceled out in the same way Earth's gravity is

canceled out.

6. Would your balance work equally well in the absence of a gravitational field, say, in outer space? Explain.

No. The balance needs gravity to restore the beam to the horizontal position.

7. Explain what we mean by the *sensitivity* and *capacity* of a balance.

Sensitivity is the smallest mass and capacity is the largest mass that a

balance will weigh accurately.

8. Your balance is sensitive to 5 mg, and its capacity is about 10 g, or 10 000 mg. Are the weights you made sufficient to measure any unknown weight up to 10 000 mg to a sensitivity of 5 mg?

Yes, if their sum is at least 10 000 mg and any combination will sum to any

number between 5 and 10 000 that is divisible by 5.

9. The mass of a carbon atom is about 2.0×10^{-23} g. Discuss the major problems associated with determining the mass of a carbon atom by using a balance of the design you have constructed.

Such a small mass would require a beam of unusual sensitivity. It would

have to be extremely light and very long, so light that almost no mass

could be used for its construction and so long that a lot of mass must be

used. The length and mass requirements are mutually exclusive.

10. If you weigh an object in Panama and again in Canada on the same balance, will you get the same value for its weight? Explain.

Yes, even though the gravitational fields vary slightly from equator to pole,

they both cancel.

11. Which of the following would be useful in studying the small differences in gravitational field in various locations: a balance or a spring scale that measures weight? Explain.

A spring scale measures weight, the force of Earth's gravitational field.

Now It's Your Turn!

1. Can you devise another way to make small-scale weights? If your laboratory has a precision or analytical balance, you may want to use it to investigate the weights of various common objects to see if you can devise a better set of standardized weights.

2. If your lab does have a very sensitive balance, you can make larger weights from a standardized spool of brass or steel wire. Since wire is very uniform, its length is proportional to its weight. All you need to know is how much a certain length of wire weighs, and you can make any size weight you want by measuring the appropriate length. Notice that you are basing mass on the fundamental quantity of length. By using a very sensitive and accurate analytical balance, you can determine what the mass of one meter of any wire is. From this you can calculate what length of wire must be cut to make a weight of any desired quantity. Typical results might look something like this:

One meter (100 cm) of wire weighs 936.8 mg, so:

to make a wire of this *weight* (mg)	cut a wire to this *length* (cm)
500.0	53.4
300.0	32.0
200.0	21.3
100.0	10.7
50.0	5.34
30.0	3.20
20.0	2.13
10.0	1.07
5.0	0.534

Each spool of wire is slightly different in weight, so each must be calibrated and a table of weights made accordingly. Also, the smaller weights (100 mg and smaller) are often difficult to store and handle so it is less convenient to make them from wire.

Beginning with the largest weight measure, cut the indicated length of wire by stretching it along a meter stick, smoothing out any bends and kinks as you go. Keep in mind that wire is ductile; it will become longer if stretched too hard. The trick is to smooth out the bends and kinks while handling the wire gently.

To store the larger wire weights, you can wrap the wire in a tight coil around a nail and poke one end into a straw on the beam stop. You should mark each one to distinguish it from other weights.

4 Weighing Activities for a Small-Scale Balance

Text Section 3.3

Objectives

- **Determine** accurate weights of various objects by using a small-scale balance.
- **Calibrate** a pipet by weighing drops.

Introduction

How accurate are your weights? How well does your balance work? Will it help you get the right answers? What is a "right answer," anyway? Now that you've spent so much time building your balance and weights, what kinds of problems can you solve with them?

Purpose

In this lab you will explore a few of these questions. You will begin by tuning your balance and set of weights by using them to weigh objects of known mass. You will compare your results to the known values to evaluate how good your balance is. Then you will make any necessary adjustments and explore ways you can use your balance to investigate matter, answer questions, and solve problems.

The first thing you will do is weigh a penny and compare it to its known weight. If your result is not close, you will make the necessary adjustments to your balance and/or weights and try again until you can consistently weigh known objects to a high degree of accuracy. Then you can rely on your balance and use it to find unknown masses.

Safety

- Behave in a way that is consistent with a safe laboratory.

Equipment

various objects to weigh, like pennies, nickels, and dimes
adhesive labels
small-scale balance
small-scale pipet filled with water

Experimental Procedure

Part A. Weighing Pennies

1. Place a small adhesive label on a penny and weigh the penny as follows. Record your results in Table 4.1.

   a. Place the penny in the balance pan, and move the beam and the counter-weight until the pointer indicates the beam is horizontal.

   b. Remove the penny and substitute weights until the pointer is again zeroed. If you go too far, do not be afraid to remove a larger weight and replace it with a smaller one.

   c. When you think the beam is horizontal, tap the beam gently and allow it to make a few oscillations before coming to rest. This avoids a false rest point due to friction at the fulcrum.

   d. The weight of the penny in milligrams is the sum of the weights in the pan. Calculate the *absolute error* and *percent relative error* of the penny weighed on your small-scale balance compared to the same penny weighed on an electronic balance as follows: (Assume that the electronic weight is the actual or theoretical weight.)

   $$\text{absolute error} = |\text{small-scale weight} - \text{electronic weight}|$$

   $$\% \text{ relative error} = \frac{|\text{small-scale weight} - \text{electronic weight}|}{\text{electronic weight}} \times 100$$

2. Weigh a second penny (with a label) and calculate its percent relative error. Record your results in Table 4.1. If the absolute error in the case of either penny is greater than about 10 mg, and the percent relative error is greater than about 0.5%, work with your balance and your weights to determine the cause. Obtain another penny, and repeat Part A until you can weigh a penny to within a 0.5% error. Label this penny with your name and its weight in milligrams, and keep it as a standard weight. Hints: The most common problem is friction at the fulcrum. Adjust your balance so the beam assembly moves freely. Also ask your instructor to weigh your larger weights for you to determine if they are accurate.

Part B. Weighing Experiments

3. Weigh a nickel and calculate its absolute, relative, and percent error. Record your results in Table 4.1. Label your nickel as you labeled your penny, and keep it as a standard weight.

4. Weigh a dime and calculate its absolute, relative, and percent error. Record your results in Table 4.1.

5. Design an experiment to find the weight in milligrams of 1 drop of water. Record your results in Table 4.2. Count the number of drops it takes to equal a certain weight. (Any weight will do!) Divide that weight by the number of drops to get the weight of a drop. Repeat the experiment with various sizes of weights to see how consistent you can be. Try 100, 300, 500, and 1000 mg weights.

6. Design an experiment to determine if the size of drops varies with the angle at which they are delivered. Record your results in Table 4.3. Use a 1000 mg weight. Try vertical (90°), horizontal (0°), and halfway between (45°).

Experimental Data

Record your results in Tables 4.1, 4.2, and 4.3 or tables like them in your notebook.

Table 4.1   Weighing Coinage

Object	Small-Scale Weight (mg)	Electronic Weight (mg)	Absolute Error (mg)	Percent Error
penny #1	2560	2550	10	0.39%
penny #2	3110	3125	15	0.48%
nickel	5025	5015	10	0.20%
dime	2220	2212	8	0.36%

Table 4.2   Weighing a Drop of Water

Weight (mg)	Number of Drops	Weight of Drop (mg)
100	4	25
300	15	20
500	24	21
1000	48	21

Table 4.3   Checking Drop Angle

Drop Angle	Number of Drops	Weight of Drop (mg)
vertical (90°)	48	21
horizontal (0°)	36	28
halfway (45°)	40	25

Cleaning Up

Please recycle all the materials you do not use. Store your balance and weights according to your teacher's directions.

Questions for Analysis

Use what you learned in this lab to answer the following questions.

1. Discuss some major sources of error if a weighing has a percent relative error of greater than about 0.5%.

   Friction at the fulcrum. Inaccurate counting of weights. Inaccurate larger

   weights.

2. If your weighings exceed about 0.5% relative error, what changes might you make to get better results?

   Adjust the fulcrum so that it is friction-free. Check the accuracy of the

   weights on an analytical balance.

3. How many milligrams does 1 drop of water weigh?

   Approximately 20 to 25, depending on the small-scale pipet.

4. How many grams does 1 drop of water weigh? (1000 mg = 1 g.)

   $$x \text{ g} = 1 \text{ drop} \times \frac{\text{mg wt. of drops}}{\text{no. of drops}} \times \frac{1 \text{ g}}{1000 \text{ mg}} = \textbf{0.020 to 0.025 g}$$

5. If you use a larger weight to determine the size of a drop, will you get a more or less accurate result than with a smaller weight? Explain.

   More accurate. A larger weight requires more drops, so the error is smaller.

6. What angle for holding the pipet is best? Explain. Why is it important to expel the air bubble before you begin the experiment?

   The best angle is vertical (90°) because it's easiest to control. It's important

   to expel the air bubble because the drop containing the air bubble contains

   less water than the others.

7. What is the volume in cm³ of 1 drop? The density of water is 1.00 g/cm³. This means that 1 gram of water occupies a volume of 1 cubic centimeter. Thus, if we measure weight, we can calculate volume as a function of weight. That is, if we weigh a certain amount of water, we will know its volume.

   $$x \text{ cm}^3 = 1 \text{ drop} \times \frac{\text{no. of grams}}{1 \text{ drop}} \times \frac{1 \text{ cm}^3}{1 \text{ g}} = \textbf{0.020 to 0.025 cm}^3$$

   Calculate the volume of a single drop in mL. (1 mL = 1 cm³.) What is the volume of a drop in microliters, mL? (1000 mL = 1 mL.)

   0.020 mL. 20 mL.

8. What is the density of water in units of mg per cm³? (1 gram = 1000 mg.) Express the density in units of mg per mL.

   1000 mg/cm³. 1 mg/mL.

Now It's Your Turn!

1. Recently, the United States government changed the composition of the American penny, which had remained essentially the same for nearly 120 years. Older pennies are made of an alloy consisting of 95% copper and 5% zinc. The newer penny's copper coating comprises only 2.4% of its total weight. This copper-coated zinc slug looks just like its copper ancestor, but it is easily distinguished by its different weight. Because the density of zinc is less than that of copper, the newer pennies are lighter than the older ones.

   Obtain a set of ten pennies dated 1978–1987 from your teacher. Use your balance to determine in which year the penny's composition changed. Hint: If you're clever, you don't have to find the exact milligram weight of each penny. Record in your lab notebook the date and any weight data you have for each penny.

   Please do not break up the set. Return the entire set to your teacher when you finish.

   Place any of the pennies in the balance pan, and slide the beam so that the

   pointer is at zero. Without adjusting the balance systematically, replace

   each penny with another one, noting which are about the same weight and

   which are heavier or lighter than the first penny.

   a. In the year the penny's composition was changed, some of the pennies were made of copper and some of zinc. In what year was the change made? How do you know? On what property do you base your answer?

   1982. Pre-1982 pennies are heavier than post-1982 pennies. Copper is more

   dense than zinc.

   b. Calculate the average weight of a copper penny and the average weight of a zinc penny. (density Zn = 7.14 g/cm³; density Cu = 8.92 g/cm³.) How are these densities consistent with the relative weights of the two kinds of pennies?

   Copper is more dense than zinc, so copper pennies will weigh more than

   zinc pennies.

   c. Using the average weights of the zinc and copper pennies and the percentage of copper and zinc in each kind of penny, calculate the actual worth of each kind of penny in terms of zinc and copper prices. You'll need to get the current cost per pound of copper and of zinc from your teacher. A copper penny is 95% copper and 5% zinc:

$$\text{wt. (mg)} \times \frac{95 \text{ mg Cu}}{100 \text{ mg penny}} \times \frac{1 \text{ g Cu}}{1000 \text{ mg Cu}} \times \frac{1 \text{ pound Cu}}{454 \text{ g Cu}} \times \frac{\text{cost(\$) Cu}}{\text{pound of Cu}} = \$ \text{ Cu}$$

$$\text{wt. (mg)} \times \frac{5 \text{ mg Zn}}{100 \text{ mg penny}} \times \frac{1 \text{ g Zn}}{1000 \text{ mg Zn}} \times \frac{1 \text{ pound Zn}}{454 \text{ g Zn}} \times \frac{\text{cost (\$) Zn}}{\text{pound of Zn}} = \$ \text{ Zn}$$

A zinc penny is 2.4% copper and 97.6% zinc:

$$\text{wt. (mg)} \times \frac{2.4 \text{ mg Cu}}{100 \text{ mg penny}} \times \frac{1 \text{ g Cu}}{1000 \text{ mg Cu}} \times \frac{1 \text{ pound Cu}}{454 \text{ g Cu}} \times \frac{\text{cost (\$) Cu}}{\text{pound of Cu}} = \text{\$ Cu}$$

$$\text{wt. (mg)} \times \frac{97.6 \text{ mg Zn}}{100 \text{ mg penny}} \times \frac{1 \text{ g Zn}}{100 \text{ mg Zn}} \times \frac{1 \text{ pound Zn}}{454 \text{ g Zn}} \times \frac{\text{cost (\$) Zn}}{\text{pound of Zn}} = \text{\$ Zn}$$

d. Any coin that is composed of metals worth less than the face value of the coin is called a subsidiary coin. Which of the two kinds of pennies is a subsidiary coin?

Any penny whose total Cu and Zn value is less than $0.01 is a subsidiary coin.

2. Devise a way to weigh a Sunday edition of a major newspaper by using your balance. Weigh the Sunday edition.

Tear out 1 page, weigh it, and multiply by the total number of pages.

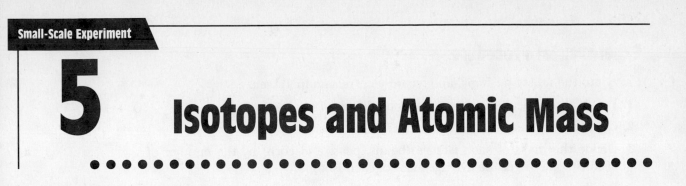

5 Isotopes and Atomic Mass

Text Section 4.6

Objectives

- **Determine** the average weights of each isotope of the fictitious element vegium.
- **Determine** the relative abundances of isotopes of vegium.
- **Calculate** from experimental data the atomic mass of vegium.

Introduction

Isotopes are atoms of the same atomic number having different masses due to different numbers of neutrons. The atomic mass of an element is the weighted average of the masses of the isotopes of that element. The weighted average takes into account both the mass and relative abundance of each isotope as it occurs in nature. The relative abundances and masses of small atomic particles are measured in the laboratory by an instrument called a mass spectrometer. The mass spectrometer separates particles by mass and measures the mass and relative abundance of each. From these data a weighted average is calculated to determine the atomic mass of the element.

Purpose

In this lab you will carry out experiments and perform the necessary calculations to determine the atomic mass of the fictitious element vegium. The three different isotopes of vegium are beanium, peaium and cornium. As in real elements, these isotopes are collections of particles having different masses. Your job will be to obtain a sample of vegium and determine the relative abundance of each isotope and the mass of each type of particle. From this data you will calculate the weighted average mass, or atomic mass, of vegium. Unlike real isotopes, the individual isotopic particles of vegium differ slightly in mass, so you will determine the average mass of each type of isotopic particle. Then you can calculate the weighted average mass, or "atomic mass," of vegium.

Safety

- Behave in way that is consistent with a safe laboratory environment.

Equipment

a sample of vegium in a plastic cup
balance

Experimental Procedure

Carry out the following steps, and record your results in Table 5.1.

1. Weigh all the beans, all the peas, and all the corn.

2. Count all the beans, all the peas, and all the corn.

3. Divide the mass of each isotope (beans, peas, and corn) by the number of each isotope to get the average mass of each isotope.

4. Divide the number of each isotope, the total number of particles, and multiply by 100 to get the percent abundance of each isotope.

5. Divide the percent abundance from Step 4 by 100 to get the relative abundance of each isotope.

6. Multiply the relative abundance from Step 5 by the average mass of each isotope to get the relative weight of each isotope.

7. Add the relative weights to get the average mass of all particles in vegium, the "atomic mass." Note: When you weigh the various isotopes of vegium, you may encounter some problems. For example, the sample of beans might be too large to weigh on your small-scale balance. You might solve this problem by making more weights or by using a larger counterweight on your small-scale balance. This approach increases the capacity of your small-scale balance. Keep in mind that it also results in a heavier beam, which reduces the sensitivity of your small-scale balance. Alternatively, you might weigh a portion of your vegetables, say half, and then multiply your result by two (or a fifth and multiply by five). The beans are of various sizes, so if you weigh just one bean and multiply by the number of beans to get the total weight of beans, a significant error might result. Weigh a large enough sample so you get a good estimation of the average weight of a bean.

Experimental Data

Record your results in Table 5.1 or a table like it in your notebook.

Table 5.1   "Atomic Mass" of Vegium

	Beans	Peas	Corn	Total
1. Mass of each isotope	6766	7451	10 151	24 368
2. Number of each isotope	22	115	104	241
3. Average mass of each	308	64.8	97.6	470.4
4. Percent of each	9.1	47.7	43.2	100
5. Relative Abundance	0.091	0.447	0.432	1.0
6. Relative Weight	27.9	31.1	42.0	101

Cleaning Up

Place the entire sample of vegium back in the plastic cup. Make sure that none of the particles are in the sink or on the floor.

Questions for Analysis

Use what you learned in this lab to answer the following questions.

1. Which of your data in Table 5.1 must be measured and which can be calculated?

   The data for the individual vegetables in Steps 1 and 2 are measured; the

   rest are calculated.

2. In all except Step 3 in Table 5.1, the numbers in the "Total" column can be obtained by adding the numbers across each row. Step 3 is an exception because it does not take into account the fact that there are different numbers of each kind of particle. Rather than add across, calculate this number in the same way you calculated the other numbers in row 3.

   Divide the total weight of all the particles by the total number of particles.

3. What is the difference between percent and relative abundance?

   Relative abundance is percent divided by 100.

4. What is the result when you total the individual percentages? The individual relative abundances?

   100.   1.

5. The percentage of each vegetable tells you how many of each kind of vegetable there are in every 100 particles. What does relative abundance tell you?

The decimal fraction of each kind of vegetable out of one total.

6. Compare the total values for Steps 3 and 6 on Table 5.1.

They are equal.

7. Why can't atomic masses be calculated the way the total for row 3 is calculated?

A mass spectrometer yields only information about the masses of atomic

particles and their relative abundances. It does not count each individual

particle, nor does it measure their total mass as you did.

8. Explain any differences between the atomic mass of your vegium sample and that of your neighbor. Explain why the difference would be smaller if larger samples were used.

The samples are probably similar but not exactly the same. Differences are

largely due to errors in sampling. Not all the samples are the same. The larger

the sample, the smaller the expected error due to sampling procedures.

Now It's Your Turn!

1. Do the experiments to determine the atomic weight of a second sample of vegium. How does it compare to the first? Why?

It's similar but not exactly the same because of sampling errors.

2. Select three beans from your sample—the largest, the smallest, and one bean that appears to be average in size. Determine the mass of each of the three. Compute the average mass of the largest and smallest, and compare this average to the mass of the "average" bean and to the average mass of beans you determined in Step 2 on Table 5.1. Which average mass do you think is most reliable? Why?

The one in Table 5.1 because it relies on a larger sample. Small errors in

individual beans cancel out in larger samples.

Small-Scale Experiment

6 Chemical Names and Formulas

Text Sections 5.10 and 5.11

Objectives

- **Write** the chemical names and formulas of common chemical compounds.
- **Describe** the colors and textures of common ionic compounds.
- **Synthesize** chemical compounds, and write their names and formulas.

Introduction

Chemical substances are described not only by unique names but also by chemical formulas. A chemical name will describe a unique chemical formula and a chemical formula will have a unique chemical name. We use this language to communicate about chemistry.

All ions, of which some substances are made, have unique chemical names. The names and formulas of common monatomic and polyatomic anions and cations are listed below.

Name	Formula	Name	Formula
fluoride	F^-	oxide	O^{2-}
chloride	Cl^-	sulfide	S^{2-}
bromide	Br^-	sulfate	SO_4^{2-}
iodide	I^-	carbonate	CO_3^{2-}
acetate	CH_3COO^-	hydrogen phosphate	HPO_4^{2-}
nitrate	NO_3^-	phosphate	PO_4^{3-}
nitrite	NO_2^-		
hydroxide	OH^-		
hydrogen carbonate	HCO_3^-		
dihydrogen phosphate	$H_2PO_4^-$		
sodium	Na^+	magnesium	Mg^{2+}
potassium	K^+	calcium	Ca^{2+}
copper(I)	Cu^+	copper(II)	Cu^{2+}
ammonium	NH_4^+	iron(II)	Fe^{2+}
		iron(III)	Fe^{3+}
		lead(II)	Pb^{2+}
		lead(IV)	Pb^{4+}
		tin(II)	Sn^{2+}
		tin(IV)	Sn^{4+}

Most transition metals and the representative elements tin and lead form two or more cations. To distinguish different cations of the same element, a Roman numeral is used in the name to indicate the numerical value of the charge.

Cations and anions combine in a ratio that makes all ionic compounds electrically neutral. Formulas for ionic compounds are written so that the positive charge contributed by the cations exactly balances the negative charge contributed by the anions. For example, the formula for the ionic compound formed from Na^+ cations and O^{2-} anions is Na_2O. The formula for the cation is always written first. The subscript, 2, refers to two Na^1 ions that exactly balance the 2^- charge on one O^{2-} ion. To name an ionic compound, state the name of the cation and the name of the anion. Don't forget to use a Roman numeral to specify the numerical value of the positive charge of those atoms that form more than one cation. Some examples of formulas and names of ionic compounds are listed below.

Na_2O	sodium oxide	$CaSO_4$	calcium sulfate
KF	potassium fluoride	NH_4Br	ammonium bromide
FeS	iron(II) sulfide	$Cu_3(PO_4)_2$	copper(II) phosphate
$FeCl_3$	iron(III) chloride	$Pb(OH)_2$	lead(II) hydroxide

Purpose

In this lab you will observe and describe the colors and textures of various ionic compounds. Either the names or formulas of these compounds will be given. If the name is given, you will write its formula, and if the formula is given, you will write its name.

Safety

- Wear your safety glasses.
- Use full small-scale pipets only for the carefully controlled delivery of liquids.

Equipment

empty pipet for stirring
small-scale reaction surface with dried solid ionic compounds

Name _____ Class _____ Date _____

Experimental Page

1. Observe the solid compounds below. Write the color and any other descriptive information. If the name is given, write the formula. If the formula is given, write the name. Record your results in Table 6.1.

potassium iodide	sodium chloride	magnesium sulfate	copper(II) sulfate

$NaHCO_3$	$AgNO_3$	$NaNO_2$	KF

sodium carbonate	lead(II) nitrate	sodium acetate	ammonium chloride

sodium phosphate	calcium hydroxide	tin(IV) chloride	potassium bromide

$CaCl_2$	$FeCl_3$	Na_2HPO_4	NaH_2PO_4

Place this side of the Experimental Page facedown. Use the other side under your small-scale reaction surface.

Experimental Data

Record your results in Table 6.1 or a table like it in your notebook.

Table 6.1   Names and Formulas of Ionic Solids

potassium iodide	sodium chloride	magnesium sulfate	copper(II) sulfate
white	white	white	blue
KI	**NaCl**	**MgSO$_4$**	**CuSO$_4$**
NaHCO$_3$	AgNO$_3$	NaNO$_2$	KF
white	brown	light yellow	white
sodium hydrogen carbonate	**silver nitrate**	**sodium nitrite**	**potassium fluoride**
sodium carbonate	lead(II) nitrate	sodium ethanoate	ammonium chloride
white	white	white	white
Na$_2$CO$_3$	**Pb(NO$_3$)$_2$**	**CH$_3$COONa**	**NH$_4$Cl**
sodium phosphate	calcium hydroxide	tin(IV) chloride	potassium bromide
white	white	white	white
Na$_3$PO$_4$	**Ca(OH)$_2$**	**SnCl$_4$**	**KBr**
CaCl$_2$	FeCl$_3$	Na$_2$HPO$_4$	NaH$_2$PO$_4$
white	yellow	white	white
calcium chloride	**iron(III) chloride**	**sodium hydrogen phosphate**	**sodium dihydrogen phosphate**

Cleaning Up

Avoid contamination by cleaning up in a way that protects you and your environment. When you have finished answering the questions, return the small-scale reaction surface with its solid ionic compounds in place to your instructor.

Questions for Analysis

Use what you learned in this lab to answer the following questions.

1. Write the formulas (with charges) and names of all the cations represented in this experiment.

   K^+, potassium; Na^+, sodium; Mg^{2+}, magnesium; Cu^{2+}, copper(II); Ag^+, silver;

   Pb^{2+}, lead(II); NH_4^+, ammonium; Ca^{2+}, calcium; Sn^{4+}, tin(IV); Fe^{3+}, iron(III).

2. Write the formulas (with charges) and names of all the anions represented in this experiment.

   I^-, iodide; Cl^-, chloride; SO_4^{2-}, sulfate; NO_3^-, nitrate; NO_2^-, nitrite; PO_4^{3-},

   phosphate; OH^-, hydroxide; Br^-, bromide; HCO_3^-, hydrogen carbonate;

   HPO_4^{2-}, hydrogen phosphate; $H_2PO_4^-$, dihydrogen phosphate; F^-, fluoride;

   $CH_3COO_2^-$, acetate.

3. Write some simple rules for naming an ionic compound.

   Name the cation. Name the anion.

4. When is it appropriate to use Roman numerals in naming compounds?

   When the cation has more then one possible ionic charge.

5. What does a numerical subscript following an element in a chemical formula mean?

   It multiplies the element immediately preceding it.

6. What does a numerical subscript following a set of parentheses in a chemical formula mean?

   It multiplies all the elements enclosed by the parentheses.

7. Write some simple rules for writing the formula for an ionic compound.

   Write the cation first and the anion last. Use subscripts to indicate the

   number of cations and anions in a way the makes the total of the positive

   and negative charges add to zero. Use parentheses to multiply polyatomic

   ions by subscripts.

Name _____ Class _____ Date _____

Now It's Your Turn!

1. a. Place 1 drop of each solution in the indicated spaces below. Stir by blowing air from a dry pipet.

b. Combine the ions to write the formulas of the chemical compounds that are produced by the mixings. Name each compound.

c. What happened with each mixing? Make a table describing your results. Write the formula and name of each compound produced by the mixings.

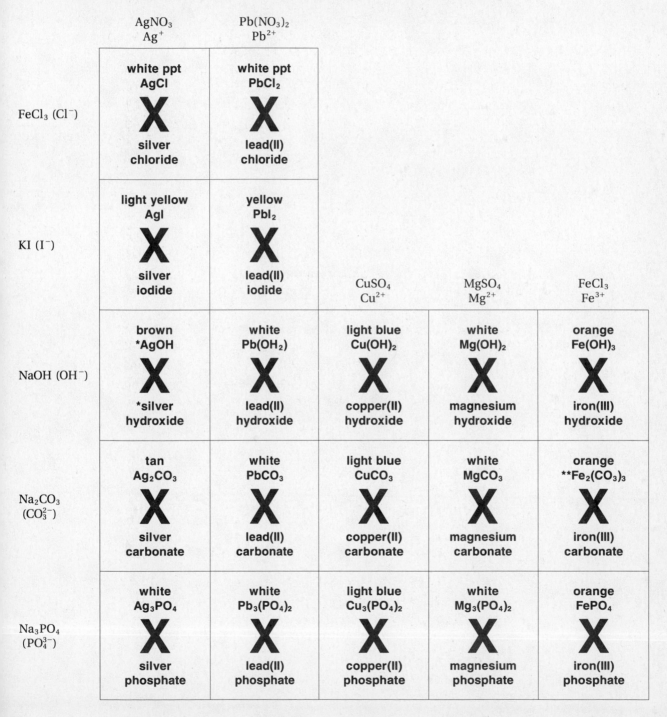

* This brown precipitate is really silver oxide, Ag_2O: $2Ag^+ + 2OH^- \rightarrow Ag_2O + HOH$.

** Because of the acidity of Fe^{3+}, iron(III) carbonate does not exist. This is probably an amorphous iron(III) hydroxy carbonate.

7 Weighing: A Means of Counting

Text Section 6.4

Objectives

- **Measure** masses of common compounds, objects, and minerals.
- **Calculate** moles and atoms from experimental masses.

Introduction

You can often measure how much of something you have by counting individual objects. For example, you can count the number of pennies you have in your pocket or the number of pencils you have in your locker. You learned in Chapter 6 that in chemistry there is a name for a number of atoms, ions, or molecules. One mole of a substance is equal to 6.02×10^{23} atoms, ions, or molecules of that substance. You also learned that you can "count" the number of moles in a substance by weighing the substance.

Purpose

In this lab you will measure the masses of samples of various common compounds like water, salt, and sugar. You will use your results as a means of counting the atoms, ions, and molecules in your samples. You will extend your technique to common objects that you can consider to be pure substances, like glass marbles, pieces of chalk, and polystyrene peanuts. Finally, you will measure the masses of various mineral samples and use your results to find the number of atoms in each.

Safety

- Behave in a way that is consistent with a safe laboratory.

Materials

Solids: Sucrose ($C_{12}H_{22}O_{11}$), sodium chloride (NaCl), chalk ($CaCO_3$), glass slides, polystyrene peanuts, sulfur, fluorite, hematite, or other common minerals specified by your teacher.

Equipment

balance   plastic spoons

Experimental Procedure

1. Weigh one level teaspoon of sodium chloride, NaCl. Record its mass in Table 7.1. Repeat for one level teaspoon of water and one of sucrose, $C_{12}H_{22}O_{11}$.

2. Weigh a glass slide, and record its mass in Table 7.2. Repeat for a piece of chalk and a polystyrene peanut.

3. Weigh a piece of sulfur, and record its mass in Table 7.3. Repeat for a piece of fluorite and a piece of hematite.

Experimental Data

Record your results in Tables 7.1, 7.2, and 7.3 or tables like them in your notebook.

Table 7.1   Counting Particles in Common Substances

Formula	Name	Mass in mg	Molar mass	Moles in 1 teaspoon	Moles of each element	Atoms of each element
NaCl	sodium chloride	5090	58.5	0.0087	0.087 Na 0.087 Cl	5.2×10^{22} Na 5.2×10^{22} Cl
H_2O	water	4300	18	0.24	0.24 O 0.48 H	1.4×10^{23} O 2.8×10^{23} H
$C_{12}H_{22}O_{11}$	sucrose	3990	342	0.012	0.14 C 0.26 H 0.13 O	8.4×10^{22} C 1.6×10^{23} H 7.8×10^{22} O

Table 7.2   Counting Particles in Common Items

Formula	Name	Mass in mg	Molar mass	Moles in 1 sample	Moles of each element	Atoms of each element
SiO_2	glass slide	5020	60*	0.084	0.084 Si 0.17 O	5.1×10^{22} Si 1.0×10^{23} O
$CaCO_3$	chalk	9680	100**	0.097	0.097 Ca 0.0897 C 0.29 O	5.8×10^{22} Ca 5.8×10^{22} C 1.8×10^{23} O
$(-CHCH_2-)_n$ $\mid$ C_6H_5	polystyrene peanut	55	104***	5.3×10^{-4}	4.3×10^{-3} C 3.7×10^{-3} H	2.6×10^{21} C 2.2×10^{21} H

* assuming the slide is pure SiO_2
** assuming the chalk is pure $CaCO_3$
*** per unit molecule

Table 7.3   Counting Particles in Minerals

Formula	Mineral name	Mass in mg	Molar mass	Moles	Moles of each element	Atoms of each element
S	sulfur	485	32	0.015	0.015	9.1×10^{21}
CaF_2	fluorite	890	78	0.011	0.011 Ca 0.022 F	6.9×10^{21} Ca 1.4×10^{22} F
Fe_2O_3	hematite	2545	160	0.016	0.032 Fe 0.048 O	1.9×10^{22} Fe 2.9×10^{22} O

Cleaning Up

Avoid contamination by cleaning up in a way that protects you and your environment. Return all the materials to their proper places. Sweep up and dispose of any spilled salt or sugar. Wash your hands thoroughly with soap and water.

Questions for Analysis

Use what you learned in this lab to answer the following questions.

1. Calculate the number of moles of one level teaspoon of NaCl. Repeat for all the other compounds in Tables 7.1, 7.2, and 7.3.

$$x \text{ mol NaCl} = \text{wt. in mg NaCl} \times \frac{1 \text{ g}}{1000 \text{ mg}} \times \frac{1 \text{ mol}}{58.5 \text{ g}} = \text{mol NaCl.}$$

2. Calculate the moles of each element in H_2O. Repeat for all the other compounds in Tables 7.1, 7.2, and 7.3.

$$x \text{ mol H} = \text{mol HOH} \times \frac{2 \text{ mol H}}{1 \text{ mol HOH}} = \text{mol H}$$

$$x \text{ mol O} = \text{mol HOH} \times \frac{1 \text{ mol O}}{1 \text{ mol HOH}} = \text{mol O}$$

3. Calculate the atoms of each element in H_2O. Repeat for all the other compounds in Tables 7.1, 7.2, and 7.3.

$$x \text{ atoms H} = \text{mol H} \times \frac{6.02 \times 10^{23} \text{ atoms}}{1 \text{ mol H}} = \text{atoms H}$$

4. In Step 1, you measured equal volumes of three different compounds. Which of the three compounds has the greatest number of moles in one teaspoon?
Water.

5. Which of the three compounds in Step 1 has the greatest total number of atoms?
Water.

6. Why can we use the technique of measuring volume as a means of counting?
Once we know the mass of a unit volume, we can use volume to determine mass and mass to determine moles.

Now It's Your Turn!

1. Design an experiment that will determine the number of atoms of calcium, carbon, and oxygen it takes to write your name on the chalkboard with a piece of chalk. Assume chalk is 100 percent calcium carbonate, $CaCO_3$.

   Weigh a piece of chalk, write your name, and weigh the piece again. The

   difference is the mass of $CaCO_3$ needed to write your name.

2. A nickel coin is a mixture of metals called an alloy. It consists of 75 percent copper and 25 percent nickel. Design an experiment to find out how many nickel atoms there are in one 5-cent piece.

   Weigh the nickel in grams, and do the following calculation.

   $$x \text{ atoms } = \text{ grams of coin} \times \frac{25 \text{ g Ni}}{100 \text{ g coin}} \times \frac{1 \text{ mol Ni}}{58.7 \text{ g}} \times \frac{6.02 \times 10^{23} \text{ atoms}}{\text{mol}}$$

3. A common mineral used in wallboard and plaster of Paris is gypsum, $CaSO_4 \cdot 2H_2O$. Gypsum is an example of a hydrate. A hydrate is a compound that has water molecules incorporated into its crystal structure. The chemical formula of gypsum indicates that there are two water molecules for every calcium and sulfate ion within the crystal structure of gypsum. These water molecules are called water of hydration. Design an experiment to determine the number of water molecules in a sample of gypsum.

   Weigh the gypsum and do the following calculation.

   $$x \text{ water molecules } = \text{ grams gypsum} \times \frac{1 \text{ mol}}{172 \text{ g}} \times \frac{2 \text{ mol } H_2O}{1 \text{ mol gypsum}} \times \frac{6.02 \times 10^{23} \text{ molecule}}{1 \text{ mol}}$$

4. Determine the number of atoms in various samples of other minerals like graphite, C; barite, $BaSO_4$; Calcite, $CaCO_3$; pyrite, FeS_2; and galena, PbS_2.

   Use the same method as in Step 3.

8 Chemical Equations

••

Text Section 7.2

For your course planning, you may not want to use this lab until Chapter 19.

Objectives

- **Classify** solutions as acids and bases.
- **Describe** chemical phenomena by writing chemical equations.
- **Identify** household products as acidic, basic, or neutral, on the basis of their reactions with indicators.
- **Investigate** the behavior of other synthetic and natural indicators in the presence of acids and bases.

Introduction

All chemical reactions involve changes in substances. These changes are often visible, and you call them macroscopic changes. Macroscopic changes can help you to classify chemical reactions. For example, in Small-Scale Experiment 1, the macroscopic changes you observed included the formation of precipitates, color changes, and the production of bubbles. The chemical reactions in Small-Scale Experiment 1 may be classified based on the macroscopic changes you observed.

To understand chemistry you must make many careful macroscopic observations and learn to infer from them the submicroscopic interactions of atoms and molecules. When chemical reactions occur, changes take place in individual atoms and molecules that cause the macroscopic changes you observe. A fundamental activity of chemistry is to try to find out what happens at the submicroscopic level.

To help you connect macroscopic changes and submicroscopic changes, chemical equations are used to represent symbolically what happens to atoms, ions, and molecules in chemical reactions. You learned in Section 7.2 that a chemical equation consists of an arrow separating the chemical formulas of the reactants (on the left) and the chemical formulas of products (on the right).

reactants → products

Acids and bases are classified on the basis of their chemical properties. (Acids and bases are discussed more fully in Chapter 19.) Acids are recognized as a group of chemical compounds that have similar macroscopic chemical properties. They were originally classified on the basis of their sour taste (the word *acid* is derived from the Latin word for *sour*.) Further work showed that acids had other common properties, among them the ability to cause vegetable dyes to change colors and the ability to dissolve a wide variety of substances. Bases have a bitter taste and the ability to destroy or *neutralize* the properties of acids.

Chemical Equations **63**

The fact that different acids show similar characteristic macroscopic chemical properties suggests that they are somehow related on the submicroscopic level. Similarly, bases must be related to each other.

The macroscopic changes associated with acids and bases are seen in changes in indicators. An indicator signals the occurrence of a chemical reaction by changing colors. You have already used phenolphthalein, a common synthetic acid–base indicator. Recall that it turned from colorless to bright pink in the presence of sodium hydroxide, a base. Other indicators exhibit other distinct color changes, signaling the occurrence of a chemical reaction.

Purpose

In this lab you will mix various solutions of acids and bases with an indicator and observe the macroscopic color changes that occur. You will classify solutions as acids or bases based on the color change they impart to the indicator, bromthymol blue, BTB. That is, you will classify solutions according to their macroscopic behavior. (Acids turn BTB yellow, and bases turn BTB blue.) Then you will repeat the experiment twice with two different indicators—phenolphthalein, phen, and bromphenol blue, BPB.

Finally, you will interpret your results in terms of submicroscopic properties, the behavior of atoms and molecules. You will learn how to express these unseen submicroscopic properties in a symbolic language of chemical formulas and equations. For example, one common submicroscopic property of acids is that they produce H_3O^+ ions in water. This can be explained by the following chemical equation:

$$HCl + H_2O \rightarrow H_3O^+ + Cl^-$$

The acid, HCl, transfers an H^+ ion to the water molecule to form H_3O^+.

Safety

- Wear your safety glasses.
- Use full small-scale pipets only for the carefully controlled delivery of liquids.

Materials

Small-scale pipets of the following solutions:

sodium hydrogen carbonate ($NaHCO_3$)
phosphoric acid (H_3PO_4)
sodium hydroxide (NaOH)
hydrochloric acid (HCl)
sodium hydrogen phosphate
   (Na_2HPO_4)
sodium hydrogen sulfate ($NaHSO_4$)
sulfuric acid (H_2SO_4)
sodium hydrogen sulfite ($NaHSO_3$)
bromphenyl blue (BPB)

ethanoic acid (CH_3COOH)
sodium dihydrogen phosphate
   (NaH_2PO_4)
nitric acid (HNO_3)
sodium carbonate (Na_2CO_3)
sodium phosphate (Na_3PO_4)
ammonia (NH_3)
bromthymol blue (BTB)
phenolphthalein (phen)
sodium ethanoate (CH_3COONa)

Equipment

empty pipet for stirring
small-scale reaction surface

Experimental Page

1. Mix 1 drop of BTB with 1 drop of each of the indicated solutions. Record the color change in Table 8.1.

	1 drop BTB		1 drop BTB		1 drop BTB
1 drop		1 drop		1 drop	
a. NaHCO₃		**f.** CH₃COONa		**k.** H₃PO₃	
b. CH₃COOH		**g.** NaOH		**l.** NaH₂PO₄	
c. HCl		**h.** HNO₃		**m.** Na₂HPO₄	
d. Na₂CO₃		**i.** NaHSO₄		**n.** Na₃PO₄	
e. H₂SO₄		**j.** NH₃		**o.** NaHSO₃	

2. Repeat Step 1, using phenolphthalein, phen, in place of BTB as the indicator. Record the color change in Table 8.1.

3. Repeat Step 1, using bromphenyl blue, BPB, as the indicator. Record the color change in Table 8.1.

Place this side of the Experimental Page facedown. Use the other side under your small-scale reaction surface.

Experimental Data

Record your results in Table 8.1 or a table like it in your notebook.

Table 8.1 Macroscopic and Submicroscopic Changes

a. BTB NaHCO$_3$ phen BPB	blue pink blue	**f.** CH$_3$COONa	blue pink blue	**k.** H$_3$PO$_3$	yellow colorless yellow
b. BTB CH$_3$COOH phen BPB	yellow colorless yellow	**g.** NaOH	blue pink blue	**l.** NaH$_2$PO$_4$	yellow colorless yellow
c. BTB HCl phen BPB	yellow colorless yellow	**h.** HNO$_3$	yellow colorless yellow	**m.** Na$_2$HPO$_4$	blue pink blue
d. BTB Na$_2$CO$_3$ phen BPB	blue pink blue	**i.** NaHSO$_4$	yellow colorless yellow	**n.** Na$_3$PO$_4$	blue pink blue
e. BTB H$_2$SO$_4$ phen BPB	yellow colorless yellow	**j.** NH$_3$	blue pink blue	**o.** NaHSO$_3$	yellow colorless yellow

Cleaning Up

Avoid contamination by cleaning up in a way that protects you and your environment. Carefully clean the reaction surface by absorbing the contents onto a paper
towel, rinse the reaction surface with a damp paper towel, and dry it. Dispose of
the paper towels in the waste bin.

Questions for Analysis

Use what you learned in this lab to answer the following questions.

1. Define an acid and a base in terms of the color each turns BTB.

   An acid turns BTB yellow. A base turns BTB blue.

2. Name each acid and base you classified in this experiment. (See text Sections 5.7 and 5.13.)

   a. sodium hydrogen carbonate   **f. sodium acetate**   **k. phosphoric acid**

   b. acetic acid   **g. sodium hydroxide**   **l. sodium dihydrogen phosphate**

   c. hydrochloric acid   **h. nitric acid**   **m. sodium hydrogen phosphate**

   d. sodium carbonate   **i. sodium hydrogen sulfate**   **n. sodium phosphate**

   e. sulfuric acid   **j. ammonia**   **o. sodium hydrogen sulfite**

3. What is the common feature of the formula of each acid?

Each contains the H^+ ion.

4. What is an indicator? What purpose does it serve in this lab?

An indicator signals the occurrence of a chemical reaction—in this case,

reactions of acids and bases in water.

5. On a macroscopic level, your observations are that all acids turn BTB yellow. The common explanation on the submicroscopic level is that an acid produces H_3O^+ ions in water solution. Such submicroscopic interactions are described by the following symbolic representations, called chemical equations:
b. $CH_3COOH + H_2O \rightarrow H_3O^+ + CH_3COO^-$
c. $HCl + H_2O \rightarrow H_3O^+ + Cl^-$
i. $HSO_4^- + H_2O \rightarrow H_3O^+ + SO_4^{2-}$
Notice that in all three examples, a hydrogen ion, H^+, moves from the acid to a water molecule. Notice also that in **i**, you can take away the Na^+ ion before you write the equation. Write hydrogen-ion-transfer chemical equations, like the examples above, that describe the reactions of the other acids with water. Remember that whenever BTB turns yellow, one product is always H_3O^+.

e. $H_2SO_4 + H_2O \rightarrow H_3O^+ + HSO_4^-$

h. $HNO_3 + H_2O \rightarrow H_3O^+ + NO_3^-$

k. $H_3PO_4 + H_2O \rightarrow H_3O^+ + H_2PO_4^-$

l. $H_2PO_4^- + H_2O \rightarrow H_3O^+ + HPO_4^{2-}$

o. $HSO_3^- + H_2O \rightarrow H_3O^+ + SO_3^{2-}$

6. On a macroscopic level, a base turns BTB blue. The common explanation on the submicroscopic level is that a base produces OH^- ions in solution. Chemical equations to describe these interactions can be written like the ones below:
a. $HCO_3^- + HOH \rightarrow H_2CO_3 + OH^-$
j. $NH_3 + HOH \rightarrow NH_4^+ + OH^-$
Notice that in each case a base accepts a hydrogen ion, H^+, from a water molecule that forms a hydroxide ion, OH^-. Write hydrogen-ion-transfer chemical equations like the ones above to describe the reactions of the other bases with water. Every time you see BTB turn blue, one product is OH^-.

d. $CO_3^{2-} + HOH \rightarrow HCO_3^- + OH^-$

f. $CH_3COO^- + HOH \rightarrow CH_3COOH + OH^-$

g. $OH^- + HOH \rightarrow HOH + OH^-$

m. $HPO_4^{2-} + HOH \rightarrow H_2PO_4^- + OH^-$

n. $PO_4^{3-} + HOH \rightarrow HPO_4^{2-} + OH^-$

7. Define an acid and a base in terms of what ions they produce in solution.

An acid produces H_3O^+ in solution. A base produces OH^- in solution.

8. What macroscopic changes did you find when you used phen and BPB to classify solutions as acids and bases?

Phen turned pink in base but remained colorless in acid. BPB turned yellow

in acid but remained blue in base.

Now It's Your Turn!

1. Use BTB to classify several household products as acids or bases. Read the product labels to determine as best you can (name or formula) which acids or bases they contain. Organize your data into a concise table. While you're at it, test water from the tap.

2. BTB, BPB, and phen are only a few of many synthetic acid–base indicators. Design some experiments that use other indicators to classify the solutions you used in this lab as acids or bases. Tell what you did and make a table of your results. You may use any of the following synthetic indicators or any that your instructor provides:

methyl red, MR   alizarin yellow R, AYR
bromcresol green, BCG   thymol blue, TB
phenol red, PR   meta cresol purple, MCP

Hint: One such experiment might use methyl red, MR, to test both NaOH and HCl. You can then report the color of the indicator in each solution, draw a conclusion about the color the indicator changes in acid and base, and test your hypothesis by using other acids and bases. Finally, you can organize your results into a concise table. Cite advantages and disadvantages of using other indicators to classify acids and bases.

3. Many common substances also act as acid–base indicators. Design and carry out an experiment to use some or all of these to classify solutions as acids or bases. Tell what you do and make a table of your results. Try several of the following: grape juice, cabbage juice, food dyes, flower petals, vegetable juices, fabric dyes, and water-soluble pen inks. Can you think of anything else to try?

9 Balancing Chemical Equations

Text Section 7.4

For your course planning, you may not want to use this lab until Chapter 19.

Objectives

- **Probe** the occurrence of neutralization reactions by using an acid–base indicator.
- **Balance** chemical equations that describe reactions between acids and bases.
- **Test** other means to detect neutralization reactions.

Introduction

In Small-Scale Experiment 8 you saw that acids and bases can be distinguished by the color changes they induce in indicators. For example, bromthymol blue is yellow in acid solution and blue in basic solution.

On the submicroscopic level, acids produce H_3O^+ ions in solution, and bases produce OH^- ions in solution. Acids and bases also react with each other in what is called a *neutralization reaction*. In general, an acid and a hydroxide base react to produce a salt and water. A salt is any ionic compound produced by a neutralization reaction. For example, the reaction of hydrochloric acid, HCl, with sodium hydroxide, NaOH, produces sodium chloride, NaCl, and water. The chemical equation that represents this neutralization reaction is written as follows:

$$HCl + NaOH \rightarrow NaCl + HOH$$

$$acid + base \rightarrow salt + water$$

Two more examples of neutralization reactions follow here:

$$H_2SO_4 + 2NaOH \rightarrow Na_2SO_4 + 2HOH$$

$$acid + base \rightarrow salt + water$$

$$H_3PO_4 + 3KOH \rightarrow K_3PO_4 + 3HOH$$

$$acid + base \rightarrow salt + water$$

Notice that each equation is balanced; there are the same number of each kind of atom on both sides of the equation. Notice also that these neutralization reactions are examples of double-replacement reactions (Section 7.9), which involve an exchange of positive ions between two compounds. In the examples above, a potassium or sodium ion is exchanged with a hydrogen ion.

Purpose

In this lab you will use bromthymol blue, as well as other probes, to examine neutralization reactions more closely and learn to balance the chemical equations that describe them. An indicator is usually necessary to detect acid–base neutralization reactions because often the reaction is invisible without an indicator. The reason is that often both the reactants and the products of neutralization reactions are colorless solutions. You can use an acid–base indicator such as BTB to detect a neutralization reaction.

Safety

- Wear your safety glasses.
- Use full small-scale pipets only for the carefully controlled delivery of liquids.

Materials

Small-scale pipets of the following solutions:

phosphoric acid (H_3PO_4)   sodium hydroxide (NaOH)
hydrochloric acid (HCl)   potassium hydroxide (KOH)
nitric acid (HNO_3)   calcium hydroxide ($Ca(OH)_2$)
sulfuric acid (H_2SO_4)   ammonia (NH_3)
ethanoic acid (CH_3COOH)   bromthymol blue (BTB)

Equipment

small-scale reaction surface
glass slide
cotton swab
hot plate
empty pipet for stirring

Experimental Page

1. Add 1 drop of BTB to each square. Then add 1 drop of base and finally 2 drops of acid. Record in Table 9.1 the initial color, the color after addition of base, and the color after addition of acid.

Bases	Strong Acids			Weak Acids	
	HCl	HNO_3	H_2SO_4	CH_3COOH	H_3PO_4
NaOH	a	b	c	d	e
KOH	f	g	h	i	j
$Ca(OH)_2$	k	l	m	n	o
NH_3 (NH_4OH)	p	q	r	s	t

2. Add 1 drop of NaOH to 2 drops of HCl. Record your observation.

3. Predict what will happen if you add a few drops of base to each yellow mixture on the small-scale reaction surface. Try it and find out! Record your observations.

4. Mix 1 drop of each indicated solution on a glass slide as shown below, and evaporate on a low-temperature hot plate. **Caution:** *The glass will be hot. Handle with a plastic spatula.* Record what you observe.

NaOH	NaOH	KOH	NH_3
+	+	+	+
HCl	HNO_3	H_2SO_4	CH_3COOH

5. Place 1 drop of ammonia, NH_3 (also NH_4OH), on one end of a clean cotton swab. CAREFULLY note its odor. **Caution:** *Both NH_3 and HCl can have strong odors. Avoid prolonged inhalation of fumes from these solutions.* Now place 2 drops of hydrochloric acid, HCl, on your reaction surface, and absorb this acid onto the cotton swab containing the ammonia. Note and record its odor.

Place this side of the Experimental Page facedown. Use the other side under your small-scale reaction surface.

Experimental Data

1. Record your results in Table 9.1 or a table like it in your notebook.

Table 9.1   Reactions of Acids and Bases

Bases	Strong Acids			Weak Acids	
	HCl	HNO$_3$	H$_2$SO$_4$	CH$_3$COOH	H$_3$PO$_4$
NaOH	Green to blue	with base, then	yellow with acid	for all reactions.	
KOH					
Ca(OH)$_2$					
NH$_3$ (NH$_4$OH)					

2. What do you observe when you mix an acid and base without BTB as an indicator? Why is the indicator necessary to detect these reactions?

No change. The reactants and products are both colorless.

3. What happened when you added a few drops of base to each yellow mixture?

They turned blue again.

4. What did you observe when you evaporated the mixtures on a hot plate?

White solid salts appeared.

5. What happened to the ammonia odor from the cotton swab when you added HCl?

The odor disappeared.

Cleaning Up

Avoid contamination by cleaning up in a way that protects you, your neighbors, and your environment. Carefully clean the small-scale reaction surface by absorbing the contents onto a paper towel (not onto your hands). Rinse the reaction surface with a damp paper towel and dry it. Dispose of the paper towels in the waste bin. Clean the glass slide, rinse it thoroughly with water, and dry it with a paper towel. Wash your hands thoroughly with soap and water.

Name _____ Class _____ Date _____

Questions for Analysis

Use what you learned in this lab to answer the following questions.

1. Why is the indicator necessary to detect these reactions?

These reactions have colorless reactants and colorless products.

2. Besides indicators, what other ways are there to detect neutralization?

Evaporation and odor.

3. What is the chemical formula for ethanoic acid? What is its common name?

CH_3COOH. Vinegar.

4. The complete chemical equations for reactions **a–e** on the Experimental Page are listed below. Balance each equation by placing the proper coefficient in front of each chemical formula so that each side of the equation has the same number of atoms of each element.

a. **1** $NaOH$ + **1** HCl → **1** $NaCl$ + **1** HOH

b. **1** $NaOH$ + **1** HNO_3 → **1** $NaNO_3$ + **1** HOH

c. **2** $NaOH$ + **1** H_2SO_4 → **1** Na_2SO_4 + **2** HOH

d. **1** $NaOH$ + **1** CH_3COOH → **1** CH_3COONa + **1** HOH

e. **3** $NaOH$ + **1** H_3PO_4 → **1** Na_3PO_4 + **3** HOH

5. Write down the chemical formulas for the reactants for reactions **f–j** on the Experimental Page. Now write an arrow and the formulas of the products. Finally, balance each chemical equation you write. (Hint: Equations **f–j** will look just like equations **a–e**, except K replaces Na.)

f. **1** KOH + **1** HCl → **1** KCl + **1** HOH

g. **1** KOH + **1** HNO_3 → **1** KNO_3 + **1** HOH

h. **2** KOH + **1** H_2SO_4 → **1** K_2SO_4 + **2** HOH

i. **1** KOH + **1** CH_3COOH → **1** CH_3COOK + **1** HOH

j. **3** KOH + **1** H_3PO_4 → **1** K_3PO_4 + **3** HOH

6. Balance equations **k–o**, below.

k. **1** $Ca(OH)_2$ + **2** HCl → **1** $CaCl_2$ + **2** HOH

l. **1** $Ca(OH)_2$ + **2** HNO_3 → **1** $Ca(NO_3)_2$ + **2** HOH

m. **1** $Ca(OH)_2$ + **1** H_2SO_4 → **1** $CaSO_4$ + **2** HOH

n. **1** $Ca(OH)_2$ + **1** $2CH_3COOH$ → **1** $(CH_3COO)_2Ca$ + **2** HOH

o. **3** $Ca(OH)_2$ + **2** H_3PO_4 → **1** $Ca_3(PO_4)_2$ + **6** HOH

7. Ammonia is a base and reacts with water to produce ammonium ion and hydroxide ion:

$$NH_3 + HOH \rightarrow NH_4^+ + OH^-$$

Often the formula for aqueous ammonia is written as if it were ammonium hydroxide, NH_4OH. Balance equations **p–t** below.

p.   __1__ NH_4OH + __1__ $HCl \rightarrow$ __1__ NH_4Cl + __1__ HOH

q.   __1__ NH_4OH + __1__ $HNO_3 \rightarrow$ __1__ NH_4NO_3 + __1__ HOH

r.   __2__ NH_4OH + __1__ $H_2SO_4 \rightarrow$ __1__ $(NH_4)_2SO_4$ + __2__ HOH

s.   __1__ NH_4OH + __1__ $CH_3COOH \rightarrow$ __1__ CH_3COONH_4 + __1__ HOH

t.   __3__ NH_4OH + __1__ $H_3PO_4 \rightarrow$ __1__ $(NH_4)_3PO_4$ + __3__ HOH

8. Define neutralization. Write a chemical equation to illustrate your answer.

A reaction between an acid and a base that usually produces a salt and

water. HCl + NaOH $\rightarrow$ HOH + NaCl.

9. Define a salt. Write the chemical formulas for examples from this experiment.

Any ionic compound that is the result of a neutralization reaction. NaCl,

$NaNO_3$, Na_2SO_4, KCl, KNO_3, K_2SO_4, CH_3COONa, Na_3PO_4, K_3PO_4, NH_4Cl, etc.

10. What is a double-replacement reaction? How is a double replacement reaction different from a single-replacement reaction?

A reaction in which reactants switch cations and anions. Only one reactant

swaps in a single-replacement.

11. Give two ways of expressing the formula for water. In this lab, did water act as an acid or a base? Explain.

HOH and H_2O. Neither. BTB remains green in pure water.

12. Upon evaporation of the NaOH + HCl reaction, what is the name and chemical formula of the white solid that remains? Write a chemical equation to explain your answer.

Sodium chloride, NaCl. HCl + NaOH $\rightarrow$ HOH + NaCl.

13. What happened to the ammonia odor when you added HCl to it? Write a chemical equation to explain your answer.

The odor disappeared because ammonia is neutralized by acid.

NH_4OH + HCl $\rightarrow$ NH_4Cl + HOH.

Now It's Your Turn!

1. Design an experiment using several different indicators to detect neutralization reactions. Write down what you do, what happens, and what it means. Design a concise data table to summarize your results.

Do the same experiment with other indicators like phenolphthalein,

bromphenyl blue, and methyl red.

2. Design an experiment to see if you can neutralize the ammonia odor with acids other than hydrochloric acid.

Repeat Step 5 and use other acids in place of HCl.

3. Describe a procedure you would use to neutralize the ammonia smell in household ammonia or glass cleaner. Try it in the lab! Can a similar procedure be used to neutralize the smell of vinegar, CH_3COOH? Try it in the lab! Does your procedure work to neutralize the smell of other acids like lemon juice?

Absorb a drop of ammonia onto a swab, and add a drop or two of acid

(vinegar or lemon juice) until the ammonia smell is gone. A base like NaOH

will neutralize vinegar and lemon juice.

4. Antacids are so named because they are designed to neutralize stomach acid (HCl). Design some experiments using indicators to show that antacids really do neutralize acids. Use acids other than just HCl. Write down each experiment you do, what happens, and what it means.

Add a drop of BTB to a drop of acid, then add a few grains of crushed

antacid tablet. The BTB will turn from yellow to blue.

10 Precipitation in Double-Replacement Reactions

Text Section 7.9

Objectives

- **Observe** precipitation reactions by mixing aqueous solutions of cations and anions.
- **Write** and balance complete chemical equations to describe precipitation reactions.

Introduction

In chemistry, the term precipitation does not refer to meteorological phenomena such as rain or snow. Rather, precipitation occurs in solution when two chemicals react to form a product that is insoluble in water and falls out of solution like rain or snow. A precipitate is a solid substance that separates from solution during a chemical reaction. A precipitate can be identified by the cloudy, milky, gelatinous, or grainy appearance it gives to the mixture. The solid might even settle to the bottom of the container.

A barium sulfate precipitate can be produced by the reaction of barium chloride and sodium sulfate. A chemical equation to describe the reaction is written and balanced like this:

$$BaCl_2(aq) + Na_2SO_4(aq) \rightarrow 2NaCl(aq) + BaSO_4(s)$$

Barium sulfate, $BaSO_4$, is a common precipitate used as an X-ray contrast medium because it is insoluble in water and opaque to X-rays. Typically a patient drinks an aqueous slurry of barium sulfate just before he is X-rayed. The precipitate coats his stomach and intestines. These organs then show up on the X-ray film in vivid contrast, aiding the doctor's diagnosis.

Notice that the reaction that forms $BaSO_4$ is a double-replacement reaction in which the cations and anions of the reactants trade partners to form the products. Also notice that the ratios in which cations and anions combine to form reactants are different from the ratios for products. For example, Na^+ combines with SO_4^{2-} in a ratio of 2:1 in sodium sulfate, Na_2SO_4; whereas Na^+ combines in a ratio of 1:1 in sodium chloride, NaCl. Recall from text Section 5.9 that formulas for ionic compounds must be written so that the net charge of the formula is zero.

Purpose

Lead and silver compounds commonly undergo reactions that form precipitates. Silver bromide, AgBr, for example, is a light-sensitive precipitate used to coat photographic papers. In this lab you will mix solutions of lead and silver compounds with other compounds in solution. You will observe and describe the precipitates that are formed. Finally, you will write and balance complete chemical equations to describe precipitation reactions.

Safety

- Wear your safety glasses.
- Use full small-scale pipets only for the carefully controlled delivery of liquids.

Materials

Small-scale pipets of the following solutions:

lead(II) nitrate ($Pb(NO_3)_2$)   silver nitrate ($AgNO_3$)
potassium iodide (KI)   sodium chloride (NaCl)
sodium hydroxide (NaOH)   iron(III) chloride ($FeCl_3$)
sodium sulfate (Na_2SO_4)   sodium phosphate (Na_3PO_4)
sodium carbonate (Na_2CO_3)   copper(II) sulfate ($CuSO_4$)
calcium chloride ($CaCl_2$)

Equipment

empty pipet for stirring
small-scale reaction surface

Experimental Page

1. Put 1 drop of $AgNO_3$ on each X in the top row.

2. Add 1 drop of the solution at the top of each column. Stir by blowing air.

3. Repeat with $Pb(NO_3)_2$ on the second row and $CaCl_2$ on the bottom row.

4. Record your results in Table 10.1.

	KI	NaCl	NaOH	$FeCl_3$	Na_2SO_4	Na_3PO_4	Na_2CO_3	$CuSO_4$
$AgNO_3$	a X	X	X	b X	X	X	X	X
$Pb(NO_3)_2$	X	c X	X	X	X	d X	X	X
$CaCl_2$	X	X	e X	X	X	X	X	X

Place this side of the Experimental Page facedown. Use the other side under your small-scale reaction surface.

Experimental Data

Record your Experimental Data in Table 10.1 or a table like it in your notebook.

Table 10.1   Experimental Mixings

	KI	NaCl	NaOH	$FeCl_3$	Na_2SO_4	Na_3PO_4	Na_2CO_3	$CuSO_4$
$AgNO_3$	lime green	white	brown	white	NVR	tan	yellow	NVR
$Pb(NO_3)_2$	bright yellow	white	white	white	white	white	white	white
$CaCl_2$	NVR*	NVR	white	NVR	white	white	white	white

*NVR = No Visible Reaction

Cleaning Up

Avoid contamination by cleaning up in a way that protects you and your environment. When you have finished answering the questions, carefully clean the reaction surface by absorbing the contents onto a paper towel. Rinse the reaction surface with a damp paper towel and dry. Dispose of the paper towels in the waste bin.

Questions for Analysis

Use what you learned in this lab to answer the following questions.

1. What is a precipitate? What two cations commonly form precipitates?

A solid that separates from solution. Ca^{2+}, Pb^{2+}, and Ag^+.

2. How can you tell if a precipitate forms when you mix two solutions?

The mixture turns opaque because of the precipitated solid particles

suspended in the solution. Typical adjectives include: milky, grainy, cloudy,

or gelatinous.

3. Which of the mixtures give no visible reaction?

$AgNO_3$ mixed with Na_2SO_4 and with $CuSO_4$; and $CaCl_2$ mixed with KI, NaCl,

$FeCl_3$, and Na_2CO_3.

4. Which solutions react to form precipitates with $CaCl_2$?

NaOH, Na_2SO_4, Na_2CO_3, Na_3PO_4, and $CuSO_4$.

5. What is a double-replacement reaction? What reactions in this experiment are written as double-replacement reactions?

A reaction in which the ions of the reactants switch partners to form

products. Precipitation reactions.

6. Write chemical equations for all the precipitation reactions of $AgNO_3$ you observed. A complete chemical equation for a precipitation reaction can be written as a double-replacement reaction. The cations and anions switch partners. Study the two double-replacement examples from the experiment listed below. Be sure to write formulas where the positive and negative charges are equal before you balance the equations. Notice that the precipitate is designated with an "(s)" to denote that it is a solid.

a. $AgNO_3 + KI \rightarrow AgI(s) + KNO_3$

b. $3AgNO_3 + FeCl_3 \rightarrow 3AgCl(s) + Fe(NO_3)_3$

$AgNO_3 + NaCl \rightarrow AgCl(s) + NaNO_3$

*$AgNO_3 + NaOH \rightarrow AgOH(s) + NaNO_3$

$3AgNO_3 + Na_3PO_4 \rightarrow Ag_3PO_4(s) + 3NaNO_3$

$2AgNO_3 + Na_2CO_3 \rightarrow Ag_2CO_3(s) + 2NaNO_3$

7. Write complete chemical equations for all the precipitation reactions of $Pb(NO_3)_2$ you observed. Study the two double-replacement examples from the experiment listed below.

c. $Pb(NO_3)_2 + 2NaCl \rightarrow PbCl_2(s) + 2NaNO_3$

d. $3Pb(NO_3)_2 + 2Na_3PO_4 \rightarrow Pb_3(PO_4)_2(s) + 6NaNO_3$

$Pb(NO_3)_2 + 2KI \rightarrow PbI_2(s) + 2KNO_3$

$Pb(NO_3)_2 + 2NaOH \rightarrow Pb(OH)_2(s) + 2NaNO_3$

$3Pb(NO_3)_2 + 2FeCl_3 \rightarrow 3PbCl_2(s) + 2Fe(NO_3)_3$

$Pb(NO_3)_2 + Na_2SO_4 \rightarrow PbSO_4(s) + 2NaNO_3$

$Pb(NO_3)_2 + Na_2CO_3 \rightarrow PbCO_3(s) + 2NaNO_3$

$Pb(NO_3)_2 + CuSO_4 \rightarrow PbSO_4(s) + Cu(NO_3)_2$

8. Write complete chemical equations for all the precipitation reactions of $CaCl_2$ you observed. Study the double-replacement example from the experiment listed below.

$$CaCl_2 + 2NaOH \rightarrow Ca(OH)_2(s) + 2NaCl$$

$3CaCl_2 + 2Na_3PO_4 \rightarrow Ca_3(PO_4)_2(s) + 6NaCl$

$CaCl_2 + Na_2SO_4 \rightarrow CaSO_4(s) + 2NaCl$

$CaCl_2 + Na_2CO_3 \rightarrow CaCO_3(s) + 2NaCl$

$CaCl_2 + CuSO_4 \rightarrow CaSO_4(s) + CuCl_2$

*Note to Teacher: This reaction really forms silver oxide, Ag_2O: $2AgNO_3 + 2NaOH \rightarrow Ag_2O(s) + 2NaNO_3 + H_2O$. Write this equation for the students and have the students balance it.

Now It's Your Turn!

1. Design an experiment to find out how iron(III) chloride reacts with all the other chemicals in this lab except potassium iodide. Devise a table in which to record your data and show it below. After you've answered the Questions for Analysis, write the chemical equations for the reactions that took place.

$FeCl_3 + 3NaOH \rightarrow Fe(OH)_3(s) + 3NaCl$

$FeCl_3 + Na_3PO_4 \rightarrow FePO_4(s) + 3NaCl$

$*2FeCl_3 + 3Na_2CO_3 \rightarrow Fe_2(CO_3)_3(s) + 6NaCl$

2. Design an experiment to find out how copper(II) sulfate reacts with all the other chemicals in this lab except potassium iodide. Devise a table in which to record your data and show it below. After you've answered the Questions for Analysis, write the chemical equations for the reactions that took place.

$CuSO_4 + 2NaOH \rightarrow Cu(OH)_2(s) + Na_2SO_4$

$3CuSO_4 + 2Na_3PO_4 \rightarrow Cu_3(PO_4)_2(s) + 3Na_2SO_4$

$CuSO_4 + Na_2CO_3 \rightarrow CuCO_3(s) + Na_2SO_4$

*Because of the relatively high acidity of Fe^{3+}, $Fe_2(CO_3)_3(s)$ does not exist. The overall reaction is better written: $2FeCl_3 + 3Na_2CO_3 + 3H_2O \rightarrow 2Fe(OH)_3(s) + 6NaCl + 3CO_2(g)$. Students will often see the bubbles of $CO_2(g)$. Write this equation for students and have them balance it.

11 Titration: Determining How Much Acid Is in a Solution

Text Section 8.3

For your course planning, you may not want to use this lab until Chapter 19.

Objectives

- **Demonstrate** an understanding of the meaning of each of the following terms: qualitative, quantitative, calibration, titration, equivalence point, end point.

- **Calibrate** pipets by measuring volumes of drops.

- **Measure** the molar concentrations of acid solutions by using the technique of titration.

Introduction

If you read the label on a typical chemical consumer product, you can often find both qualitative and quantitative information. Qualitative information answers the question, "What?" Quantitative information answers the question, "How much?" For example, a typical bottle of toilet bowl cleaner tells you that it contains 9.5% (how much) hydrochloric acid, HCl (what). Hydrochloric acid is the "active ingredient," the ingredient that performs the specific function for which the product is designed. Hydrochloric acid helps dissolve mineral deposits that build up on the inside of the toilet bowl.

A *titration* is a way to measure the number of moles of a substance dissolved in a liter of solution. The resulting quantity is called the molarity of the substance and is expressed in units of moles per liter (mol/L) or simply *M*. An acid–base titration typically uses a known amount of base to measure an unknown amount of acid in a solution. In a typical titration, you slowly add a base with a known concentration, like NaOH, to a measured volume of unknown acid solution, such as HCl. The neutralization reaction occurs:

$$\text{acid + base} \rightarrow \text{salt + water}$$

$$\text{HCl + NaOH} \rightarrow \text{NaCl + HOH}$$

When all the acid is just neutralized by the base, the *equivalence point* has been reached. (The number of moles of base is equivalent to the number of moles of acid at the equivalence point.) You use the volume of base needed to reach the equivalence point to calculate how many moles of acid were neutralized by that volume of base. Because the reactants and products are colorless, it is often necessary to use an indicator to determine the equivalence point of the reaction. Phenolphthalein is an indicator that is colorless in acid solution but bright pink in basic solution. If phenolphthalein is present in the titration mixture, it will remain colorless until 1 drop of base neutralizes the last of the acid and makes the solution very slightly basic. At this point, called the *end point,* a dramatic color change from colorless to pink occurs.

Notice that the end point and the equivalence point are not necessarily the same. In the case of phenolphthalein, the end point occurs when the solution turns just slightly basic, not when the solution is exactly neutral, the equivalence point. Accurate titrations require the use of an indicator that will give an end point that is very close to the equivalence point.

Purpose

In this lab you will use the quantitative technique of titration to determine the concentrations in moles per liter, M, of various acid samples using exactly $0.50M$ sodium hydroxide, NaOH. In a typical experiment, you will deliver a specific number of drops of an acid to a reaction vessel and add an indicator like phenolphthalein. You will then count the number of drops of NaOH that is needed to turn the indicator pink. To find the volume of a drop, you will calibrate pipets by counting the number of drops each pipet delivers to fill the same size volume. You will carry out several experiments to determine what is the best way to calibrate (measure the drop size of) a pipet so that it always delivers the same size drops. Calibration is a way to correct for the different-sized drops delivered by different pipets.

Safety

- Wear your safety glasses.
- Use full small-scale pipets only for the carefully controlled delivery of liquids.

Materials

Small-scale pipets of the following solutions:
hydrochloric acid (HCl)	ethanoic acid (CH_3COOH)
nitric acid (HNO_3)	phenolphthalein (phen)
sulfuric acid (H_2SO_4)	sodium hydroxide (NaOH)

Equipment

well plate
plastic cup
cotton swab

Experimental Procedure

Part A. Calibrating a Small-Scale Pipet: Measuring the Relative Sizes of Drops

1. Perform a series of experiments that will answer the following questions. Work individually, as it is important that you become skilled in calibrations. Record your results in Table 11.1.

   a. How many drops of water from a small-scale pipet are needed to fill a well? Can you repeat this result?

   b. What is the best way to tell exactly when the well is full?

   c. Is it important to expel the air bubble before you begin?

d. Try delivering drops with the pipet vertical, horizontal, and at a 45° angle. At which angle do you obtain the most number of drops? The least? Which angle delivers the smallest drops?

e. What will happen if you do not always hold the pipet at the same angle?

f. Do different pipets give different results at the same angle? Why is it important to calibrate each different pipet you use?

2. Calibrate an HCl pipet and a NaOH pipet. Count the number of drops of each needed to fill a well for each substance. Repeat until your results are reproducible. Record your results in Table 11.2.

Part B. The Titration

3. Carry out a titration of HCl as follows:

a. Holding the pipet vertically, count 20 drops of HCl into a plastic cup. Take care not to touch the ends of the pipet to the cup or to the solution in the cup. Let D_a equal this number of drops.

b. Add one drop of phenolphthalein to the HCl in the cup.

c. Add NaOH slowly, counting the number of drops of NaOH needed to obtain a stable pink end point. As you titrate, swirl the cup gently. Let D_b equal this number of drops.

d. Repeat Steps **a**–**c** in a clean, dry cup until your results are consistent.

4. Titrate HNO_3 and CH_3COOH, each with NaOH in the same way. Here are some tips for accuracy and to avoid contamination. Use a clean cup. Take care not to let the ends of the pipets touch the cup or the solution in the cup. Hold the pipets vertically. As you titrate, swirl gently and count the number of drops of NaOH it takes to get a stable pink color. Clean and dry the cup before each titration. When the pipets are empty, take care to refill them with the proper solutions. Read the labels twice!

Experimental Data

Record the results of your calibrations and titrations in Tables 11.1, 11.2, and 11.3 or tables like them in your notebook.

Table 11.1   Calibration of Small-Scale Pipet

	Trial 1	Drops to fill Trial 2	Trial 3
Vertical	21	21	21
Horizontal	15	16	17
45° angle	18	16	19

Summarize a method that will always accurately *calibrate* or determine the number of drops delivered by any pipet to fill a well.

Hold the pipet vertical, expel the air bubble, and deliver drops slowly with

the tip about 1 cm above the well.

Table 11.2   Calibration of HCl and NaOH Pipets

	Trial 1	Drops to fill Trial 2	Trial 3
HCl	23	22	23
NaOH	19	18	19

Table 11.3   Titrations of Acids

Acid	Drops to fill C_a	Drops NAOH to fill C_b	Drops NaOH to pink D_b	M of acid M_a
HCl	23	19	33	1.0
HCl	23	19	33	1.0
HNO_3	17	19	45	1.0
HNO_3	17	19	45	1.0
CH_3COOH	21	19	29	0.8
CH_3COOH	21	19	29	0.8

Calculate the molar concentration, M_a of HCl and of the other two acids by substituting the following pieces of data into the expression below.

M_b = molar concentration of NaOH (M_b = 0.50 M in this experiment)

D_a = drops of acid used (20 drops in this experiment)

D_b = drops of NaOH to pink end point

C_a = drops of acid needed to fill a well

C_b = drops of NaOH needed to fill a well

$$M_a = \frac{M_b \times D_b}{D_a} \times \frac{C_a}{C_b}$$

$$M_{HCl} = \frac{0.50M \times 33 \text{ drops}}{20 \text{ drops}} \times \frac{23 \text{ drops}}{19 \text{ drops}} = 1.0 \ M$$

$$M_{HNO_3} = \frac{0.50M \times 45 \text{ drops}}{20 \text{ drops}} \times \frac{17 \text{ drops}}{19 \text{ drops}} = 1.0 \ M$$

$$M_{CH_3COOH} = \frac{0.50M \times 29 \text{ drops}}{20 \text{ drops}} \times \frac{21 \text{ drops}}{19 \text{ drops}} = 0.80 \ M$$

Teacher's Note: This equation really calculates normality. Because the stoichiometry is 1:1 in this case, it also calculates molarity.

Cleaning Up

Avoid contamination by cleaning up in a way that protects you and your environment. Carefully clean the plastic cup and well-strip by disposing of the liquid contents in the sink and rinsing them thoroughly with water. Dry both pieces of equipment with a paper towel. Wash your hands thoroughly with soap and water.

Titration: Determining How Much Acid Is in a Solution

Questions for Analysis

Use what you learned in this lab to answer the following questions.

1. What is an acid–base titration? Is titration a qualitative or quantitative method? Explain.

   A method to measure how much acid is in a solution. Quantitative because

   it answers the question, "How much?"

2. What does it mean to calibrate a pipet? Is calibration a qualitative or quantitative method? Explain.

   To measure the size of a drop (in this case in terms of "wells"). Quantitative

   because it tells "how much."

3. Why is it important to calibrate each pipet when measuring the volumes of solutions?

   Each pipet delivers different sized drops.

4. Why is it important to repeat a calibration or a titration until the results are consistent?

   The greater the repeatability of the answer the less doubt there is that it

   is reasonable.

5. Summarize the steps it takes to calibrate a small-scale pipe.

   Hold the pipet vertical, expel the air bubble, and deliver drops slowly with

   the tip about 1 cm above a well.

6. Why do your calculations of acid concentrations include the number of drops of NaOH and HCl needed to fill a well?

   Because the drop sizes for each pipet are different, each pipet needs to be

   calibrated to correct for the different sized drops.

7. Write the chemical equation for each titration reaction you carried out in this experiment.

   NaOH + HCl → NaCl + HOH

   NaOH + HNO$_3$ → NaNO$_3$ + HOH

   NaOH + CH$_3$COOH → CH$_3$COONa + HOH

8. Write the balanced equation for the reaction of sulfuric acid, H$_2$SO$_4$, with sodium hydroxide, NaOH. How is it different from the equations you wrote for the reactions of HCl, HNO$_3$ and CH$_3$COOH with NaOH?

   2NaOH + H$_2$SO$_4$ → Na$_2$SO$_4$ + 2HOH. The mole ratio for base to acid is 2:1

   rather than 1:1.

9. Sulfuric acid, H_2SO_4, is an example of a "diprotic" acid. Explain what this means. Give an example of a "triprotic" acid. Give two examples of monoprotic acids.

An acid that has two acidic hydrogens. H_3PO_4 is triprotic. HCl, HNO_3, and

CH_3COOH are monoprotic.

Now It's Your Turn!

1. Let's explore titration a little further. To carry out a "serial titration," add four drops of HCl^+one drop phen to a 1×12 well plate as shown below.

1	2	3	4	5	6	7	8	9	10	11	12

Then add: 1   2   3   4   5   6   7   8   9   10   11   12   drops of NaOH.

(Add the number of drops of NaOH = to the well number.) Record your results.
a. Which wells have more acid than base? Which have more base than acid?

The colorless ones. The pink ones.

b. The end point is the point at which the indicator changes colors. Which well represents the end point of the titration?

The first pink well, which should be number 8 or number 9.

c. The equivalence point is the point at which enough base is added to just neutralize the acid. (The moles of base are "equal" to the moles of acid.) Which well represents the "equivalence point?"

Somewhere between the last colorless well and the first pink well.

d. How does the equivalence point differ from the end point? By how many drops, at most, is the equivalence point different from the end point?

The equivalence point is where the acid is exactly neutralized by the base.

The end point is where the indicator changes color. 1 drop.

e. What is the absolute error in this experiment?

1 drop.

2. Design titration experiments to determine the molar concentration of H_2SO_4. Be sure to calibrate each pipet you use and run each experiment at least twice so you can be confident of your answers. If you calculate the molar concentration of H_2SO_4 in the same way as the other acids, your result will be off by a factor of two. Where does the factor of 2 go in the molarity calculation?

3. Some toilet bowl cleaners are water solutions containing hydrochloric acid, HCl. Vinegar is a water solution of ethanoic acid, CH_3COOH. Design experiments to determine the molar concentrations of HCl in various household products and of ethanoic acid, CH_3COOH, in vinegar. Be sure to calibrate the pipets you use. Organize your results into a table like Table 11.3 and report your calculations in your laboratory notebook. Note: Because some of the solutions are highly colored, the end point might not be pink. Try using 3 drops phen and look for the end point to be a distinct color change.

12 Weight Titrations: Measuring Molar Concentrations

Text Section 8.5

For your course planning, you may not want to use this lab until Chapter 19.

Objectives

- **Measure** the molar concentration of acids using weight titrations.
- **Compare** the accuracy of weight titrations with that of volumetric titrations.
- **Identify** unknown solutions by applying both qualitative and quantitative analysis.

Introduction

A *weight titration* is a method of finding molar concentration by weighing solutions rather than measuring their volumes. A weight titration is often more accurate than a volumetric titration because a balance is usually a more accurate instrument than a pipet. The result of a weight titration depends only on weights determined directly from the balance and not on volumes determined from pipets.

You can use the balance to determine the volumes of solutions by weighing. You know that the density of water is one gram per cubic centimeter or one milligram per microliter. The densities of dilute aqueous solutions are assumed to be equal to the density of water. This means that if you weigh a solution in milligrams, it has the same numerical volume in microliters.

Purpose

In this lab you will carry out a weight titration. You will weigh a certain amount of acid solution and add an indicator. Then you will determine the weight of NaOH you need to add to reach the end point. To do this using a small-scale balance you will zero your balance with a pipet full of NaOH. There is no need to weigh the pipet as you only need to know the *difference* in weight before and after the titration. Next, you will add NaOH to the acid solution until the indicator changes. Finally, you will determine the weight of the NaOH needed for the titration by placing the pipet back on the small-scale balance and adding weights to make up for the NaOH we used. The total weight you add is the weight of the NaOH that was used in the titration.

Notice that you do not have to count drops. You do not have to hold the pipet at any particular angle. You do not have to be careful to expel any air bubbles.

Safety

- Wear your safety glasses.

- Use full small-scale pipets only for the carefully controlled deliver of liquids.

Materials

Small-scale pipets of the following solutions:

sodium hydroxide (NaOH)
phenolphthalein (phen)
ethanoic acid (CH_3COOH)

hydrochloric acid (HCl)
nitric acid (HNO_3)
sulfuric acid (H_2SO_4)

Equipment

balance
plastic cup

Experimental Procedure

1. Weigh 500 mg of acid solution on your small-scale balance as follows:

    a. Place a 500 mg weight in a clean, dry cup.

    b. Set the balance so the pointer reads zero.

    c. Remove the weight and add acid until the pointer again reads zero.

2. Add 5 drops of phen.

3. Weigh or tare two full NaOH pipets. (If you tare the pipets there is no need to weigh them!)

    a. Place two pipets of NaOH in a second clean, dry cup.

    b. Set the balance so it reads zero. (Use two pipets just to make sure we have enough NaOH.)

4. Titrate the acid solution in the first cup with NaOH from one of the pipets until *1 drop* turns the solution to a stable pink color.

5. Determine the weight of the NaOH used for the titration. Record this weight in Table 12.1.

    a. Return both of the NaOH pipets to the second cup.

    b. Add weights until the balance pointer again reads zero. The sum of the added weights is the weight of the NaOH used in the titration.

6. Repeat Steps 1–5 until you obtain consistent results. (The only way to tell whether your result is reliable is to reproduce it!)

7. Design and carry out weight titrations to determine the molar concentrations of nitric acid, HNO_3; sulfuric acid, H_2SO_4; and ethanoic acid, CH_3COOH. Titrate each acid at least twice.

Experimental Data

Record your results in Table 12.1 or a table like it in your notebook.

Table 12.1   Molarity of Acids

	HCl	HCl	HNO$_3$	HNO$_3$	H$_2$SO$_4$	H$_2$SO$_4$	CH$_3$COOH	CH$_3$COOH
Weight of acid (mg)	500	500	500	500	500	500	500	500
Weight of NaOH (mg)	1000	1000	1000	1000	2000	2000	900	900
Molarity of acid (M)	1.0	1.0	1.0	1.0	1.0	1.0	1.0	1.0

Calculate the molar concentration of HCl in each sample. Record them in Table 12.1. Do the same calculation for the titrations of HNO$_3$, H$_2$SO$_4$, and CH$_3$COOH. Note: When calculating the molar concentration of H$_2$SO$_4$, you must divide your result by 2 because there are 2 moles of acidic hydrogens per mole of sulfuric acid.

$$\text{Molarity of acid} = \frac{(\text{molarity of NaOH}) (\text{weight of NaOH in mg})}{(\text{weight of HCl in mg})}$$

In this experiment the molarity of NaOH is 0.5M.

Teacher's Note: Here we assume that the densities of the solutions are all 1.00 g/mL or (1.00 mg/mL) and that the stoichiometry of the acid–base reactions are all 1:1.

Cleaning Up

Avoid contamination by cleaning up in a way that protects you and your environment. Carefully clean the plastic cup by disposing of the liquid contents, rinsing the cup thoroughly with water, and drying it with a paper towel. Dispose of the paper towels in the waste bin. Wash your hands thoroughly with soap and water.

Questions for Analysis

Use what you learned in this lab to answer the following questions.

1. Why is it that when you weigh a dilute solution, the number of milligrams of solution is equal to the number of microliters of solution?

   The densities of dilute aqueous solutions are assumed to be equal to the

   density of water, 1 mg/mL.

2. When using a small-scale balance, why is it not necessary to weigh the NaOH pipet before you begin titrating?

   You need to know only the weight loss of the NaOH to determine how much

   was used in the titration.

3. Why is it not important to expel the air bubble or hold the pipet at a vertical angle when you titrate?

You are not measuring the volume of drops.

4. Explain how you can determine the weight of the NaOH used in the titration without ever knowing the weight of the pipet or its contents.

The weight loss of the NaOH is the only value you need to determine how

much NaOH was used in the titration. Thus you can tare the balance with

the pipets before the titration, add weights to balance it afterwards, and

sum the amount of added weight to find out how much NaOH you used.

Now It's Your Turn!

1. Your instructor will give you a list of consumer products to titrate. Use the Experimental Procedure in this lab to titrate each consumer product at least twice, or until you obtain consistent results. Substitute the HCl in this experiment for the consumer product containing HCl or another acid. Make a table in which to record your data, and report the name of the product, the weight of the product sample, the weight of NaOH needed to titrate it, and the calculated molar concentration of HCl or other acid in the product.

a. Use your data for the titration of household products to calculate the % HCl in each household product, and record it in a table.

$$\% \text{ HCl} = \frac{\text{g HCl}}{100 \text{ g soln}} = \frac{\text{no. } \cancel{\text{mol HCl}}}{\cancel{\text{L soln}}} \times \frac{36.5 \text{ g HCl}}{\cancel{\text{mol HCl}}} \times \frac{1 \cancel{\text{ L soln}}}{1000 \text{ g soln}} \times 100$$

(The molecular weight of HCl is 36.5 g/mol. The density of each solution is taken to be 1000 g/L.)

b. Read each household product's label and find the % HCl listed. Compare each to your calculated values. Calculate the % error for each.

$$\% \text{ error} = \frac{|\text{calculated value} - \text{product label value}|}{\text{product label value}} \times 100$$

c. Are your values necessarily in error? Explain. What factors might account for the differences?

No. Evaporation or dilution of an older bottle might contribute to the errors.

d. Use your data for the titration of vinegar to calculate the % CH_3COOH in vinegar and record it in a table.

$$\% \text{ } CH_3COOH = \frac{\text{g } CH_3COOH}{100 \text{ g soln}} = \frac{\text{no. } \cancel{\text{mol } CH_3} COOH}{\cancel{\text{L soln}}} \times \frac{60 \text{ g } CH_3COOH}{\cancel{\text{mol } CH_3} COOH} \times \frac{1 \cancel{\text{ L soln}}}{1000 \text{ g soln}} \times 100$$

(The molecular weight of CH_3COOH is 60 g/mol. The density of each solution is taken to be 1000 g/L.)

e. Calculate the percent error of ethanoic acid, CH_3COOH, in vinegar.

2. Now you know how to determine the molar concentration of an acid. This is *quantitative analysis.* Quantitative analysis answers the question, "How much?" However, you also need to know what the acid is. *Qualitative analysis* answers the question, "What is it?"

a. Below is a design for an experiment to study and compare the reactions of various acids. You can use their differences to identify what they are.

Mix 1 drop of each of these compounds in the indicated space.

	BTB	UI	Na_2CO_3	$Pb(NO_3)_2$	$AgNO_3$	$CaCl_2$
HCl	yellow	red	bubbles	white ppt. **X**	white ppt. **X**	NVR **X**
HNO_3	yellow	red	bubbles	NVR **X**	NVR **X**	NVR **X**
H_2SO_4	yellow	red	bubbles	white ppt. **X**	NVR **X**	white ppt. **X**
CH_3COOH	yellow	orange	bubbles	NVR **X**	NVR **X**	NVR **X**

Which reactions are the same for all the acids? Which reactions are different and therefore afford a way to distinguish the acids?

b. Obtain 3 *unknown acids* from your instructor. Design some experiments to identify the acids (qualitative analysis) and to determine their molar concentrations (quantitative analysis). Report your results as instructed.

13 Absorption of Water by Paper Towels: A Consumer Lab

Text Section 9.4

Objectives

- **Measure** the amounts of water absorbed by various commercial paper towels.
- **Measure** the strengths of various brands of paper towels when wet.
- **Measure** the time it takes paper towels to absorb water.
- **Compare** the properties of various brands of paper towels.
- **Determine** the best brand for the money.

Introduction

Each paper-towel manufacturer goes to great lengths to persuade consumers that its brand is better than all the others. Eye-catching packaging and decorator designs compete for your attention on the supermarket shelves. At certain times of the year you can even buy paper towels with holiday themes. Television commercials pitch the various virtues of paper towels: how much moisture they absorb, how fast they do it, and how strong they are when wet. Even microwaveability is touted.

Is one paper towel really better than another? Does price reflect quality? What does it mean to be better? Stronger? Faster? More absorbent?

Purpose

In this lab you will attempt to answer some of these questions and along the way you will formulate even more questions. You will begin by examining several properties of various brands of paper towels. You will weigh a dry paper towel, wet it, and weigh it again to see how much water it picked up. You will test its speed of absorbancy by measuring the time it takes to absorb a certain amount of water. Finally, you will test the wet strength of paper towels to determine how well they hold up to tough jobs. You will then compile your results and compare these results with the price of each product to try to determine the best buy in the paper-towel market.

Safety

- Behave in a way that is consistent with a safe laboratory.

Equipment

several brands of paper towels
  with their labels
a 5 cm × 10 cm card
scissors
balance

1/4-inch office hole punch
plastic cup
clothespins
water (H_2O)
soda straws

Experimental Procedure

Part A. How much water does each towel pick up?

1. Cut a 5 cm × 10 cm piece of paper towel. Use the card as a template to cut the paper towel to the right size. Weigh it dry. Record its weight in Table 13.1.

2. Fold the paper towel in half the long way and wet it thoroughly in a cup half full of water.

3. When removing the towel from the water, skim it across the lip of the cup to remove excess water. Weigh the towel wet.

4. Repeat this procedure for several brands of paper towels.

Part B. How fast does each towel pick up water?

5. Make a straw stand on your balance base to hang paper towels as in Figure 13.1. Hang a 5 cm × 10 cm piece of paper towel from the stand by a clothespin so that 1 cm of the bottom is immersed in a cup of water. Measure the time it takes for the water to travel 2 centimeters. Repeat for the other brands of towels. Record your results in Table 13.2.

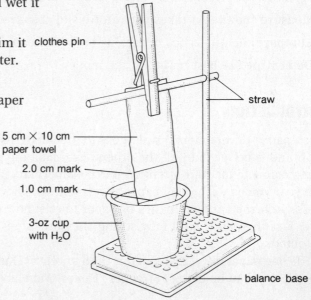

Figure 13.1 *Straw stand for paper towels*

Part C. How strong is each wet towel?

6. Attach 2 clothespins, one to each end of a 1 cm × 10 cm piece of paper towel, and wet the towel in the middle. Be sure the wet part does not touch either clothespin. Hold one clothespin in your hand and attach clothespins, one at a time, to the other clothespin. Count the number of clothespins that are needed to break the wet towel. Record your results in Table 13.3.

Part D. How do the paper towels compare in price?

7. Read the labels on each brand of paper towel you measured. Find the following data and record it in Table 13.4.

  a. The price per roll.

  b. The number of square feet of paper per roll.

  c. The number of square feet you can buy for a penny.

$$x = \frac{\text{square feet}}{\text{penny}} = \frac{\text{number of sq. ft}}{\text{roll}} \times \frac{1 \ \text{roll}}{\text{price pennies}}$$

  d. Calculate the milligrams of water absorbed per penny.

$$x = \frac{\text{mg}}{\text{penny}} = \frac{\text{square feet}}{\text{penny}} \times \frac{929 \ cm^2}{\text{square foot}} \times \frac{\text{no. of mg absorbed}}{50 \ cm^2}$$

Experimental Data

Record your results in Tables 13.1, 13.2, and 13.3 or tables like them in your notebook.

Table 13.1   How much water does each towel pick up?

Brand of towel	A	B	C	D	E
Wet weight (mg)	1677	1863	3135	1045	1977
Dry weight (mg)	287	288	250	215	290
Water weight (mg)	1390	1575	2885	830	1687
Relative water weight	1.67	1.90	3.47	1.00	2.03

What is the wet weight and dry weight of each brand of paper towel, and how many milligrams of water does each pick up? To find the "relative water weight," divide all the "water weights" by the lowest "water weight." This will tell you how many times better each towel is at picking up water compared to the worst one. Record your data in Table 13.1 or a table like it.

Table 13.2   How fast does each towel pick up water?

Brand of towel	A	B	C	D	E
Time to absorb 2 cm. (s)	42	55	15	205	45

Table 13.3   How strong is each wet towel?

Brand of towel	A	B	C	D	E
Number of clothespins	15	12	26	7	16

Table 13.4   How do the paper towels compare in price?

Brand of towel	A	B	C	D	E
Price per roll ($)	0.67	0.69	0.99	0.49	0.79
Square feet per roll	69	85	67	66	63
Square feet per penny	1.0	1.2	0.68	1.3	0.80
mg water absorbed per ¢	26 000	35 000	36 000	20 000	25 000

Cleaning Up

Avoid contamination by cleaning up in a way that protects you and your environment. Please recycle all usable pieces of paper towels. Dispose of unusable scraps in the waste bin.

Questions for Analysis

Use what you learned in this lab to answer the following questions.

1. Which paper towel is the most absorbent? The least?

   The ones with the largest and smallest "water weights," respectively.

2. Which paper towel absorbed moisture faster than all the others? Slower than all the others?

   They vary from several seconds to several minutes.

3. Which is the strongest paper towel? Which is the weakest?

   They vary from 5 to 6 pins to about 20 to 25 pins.

Now It's Your Turn!

1. Why is it important to do the strength test in Step 6 with clothespins touching only dry parts of the towel? Repeat the experiment so the clothespins are touching the wet part.

   If the paper is wet at the clothespin, the towel always breaks at this

   weakest point. This is not a good indication of the wet strength of the paper.

2. What other paper can you try at home?

   Typing paper, computer paper, facial tissue, toilet paper, and napkins.

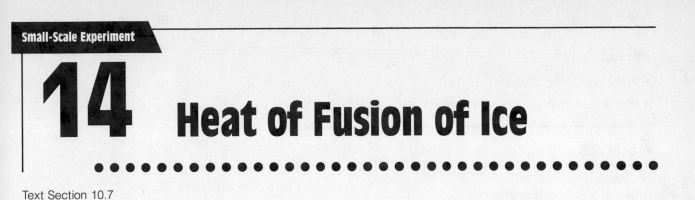

14 Heat of Fusion of Ice

Text Section 10.7

Objectives

- **Measure** temperature changes when ice melts in water.
- **Calculate** heat changes from experimental data.
- **Calculate** the heat of fusion of ice from experimental data.

Introduction

Consider this. You pop the top on the can of your favorite soft drink and pour it over ice. Does the soft drink become cold simply because the ice is cold or is there more to it than that? You know that heat always flows from a warm object to a cooler one. For example, when you place your hand on a cold window your hand gets cold. Heat flows from your hand to the window giving your hand a cooling sensation. Similarly, when you touch a hot stove heat flows from the stove to your hand and your hand feels hot. It makes sense then that when a warm drink comes into contact with cold ice, heat will flow from the drink to the ice and the drink will become cooler.

Something very important also happens: The ice melts! Melting ice is an endothermic process. That is, the melting process absorbs heat from the surroundings causing the surroundings to cool off. It's the melting ice, not its cold temperature, that is most responsible for cooling the drink. The ability of ice to cool objects is largely due to the fact that some of the ice melts when it comes into contact with warm objects.

The heat change associated with melting ice or any other solid can be expressed quantitatively. The amount of heat absorbed from the surroundings when a specific amount of solid melts is called the *heat of fusion*. Heats of fusion are usually expressed in the SI units of kilojoules per mole (kJ/mol). The heat of fusion of ice is also commonly expressed in units of calories per gram (cal/g).

Purpose

In this lab you will use the technique of calorimetry to measure the heat of fusion of ice, the amount of heat absorbed when ice melts. You will place a piece of ice into some hot water and record the temperature change of the system as the ice melts when energy flows from the hot water to the ice. You will first measure the mass and temperature of the hot water. You will also need to know the mass and temperature of the ice but because of possible significant heat losses you will determine these quantities indirectly. Because ice melts at 0°C, it will suffice to assume that the temperature of the ice is 0°C. To minimize heat loss, the best way to measure the mass of the ice is to measure the difference in mass of the hot water before and after you place the ice into it. You will carry out the experiment in an insulated polystyrene coffee cup.

Safety

- Wear your safety glasses.
- Use only small quantities for safety and cost efficiency.

Materials

hot water from the tap
crushed ice

Equipment

alcohol thermometer
one-ounce plastic cup
polystyrene coffee cup
balance

Experimental Procedure

1. Tare a polystyrene coffee cup.

2. Fill a one-ounce plastic cup 1/4 full with hot water from the tap. Transfer it to the tared coffee cup and weigh it. Record the weight in Table 14.1.

3. Measure the temperature of the water and record it in Table 14.1.

4. Place a small ice chip into the water, stir and record in Table 14.1 the lowest temperature reached after the ice melts completely.

5. Reweigh the entire system and record your results in Table 14.1.

6. Work through the calculations on the Experimental Data page and then repeat the experiment until your calculated heat of fusion of ice is consistent.

Experimental Data

Record your results in Tables 14.1 and 14.2 or tables like them in your notebook.

Table 14.1   Experimental Data

Quantity	Trial 1	Trial 2	Trial 3
a. Hot water weight (g)	4.735	5.013	28.129
b. Hot water temperature (°C)	44	49	49
c. Final temperature (°C)	16	23	10
d. Total weight, hot water and ice (g)	6.097	6.138	40.830
e. Ice temperature (°C)	0	0	0

Table 14.2   Calculated Data

Quantity	Calculation:	Trial 1	Trial 2	Trial 3
f. Ice weight (g)	d − a	1.362	1.125	11.674
g. ΔT for hot water (°C)	c − b	−28	−26	−39
h. Heat lost by water (cal)	a × (c − b) × 1	−132.6	−115.3	−1097
i. ΔT for ice (°C)	c − e	16	23	10
j. Heat gained by ice (cal)	f × (c − e) × 1	21.8	25.9	116.7
k. Heat lost + heat gained (cal)	h + j	110.8	−89.4	−980.3
l. Heat of fusion of ice (cal/g)	−k/f	81.4	79.5	83.9

Cleaning Up

Pour the water and ice down the drain. Recycle the cups. Put the thermometer away.

Questions for Analysis

Use what you learned in this lab to answer the following questions.

1. Without first weighing the ice, how can you tell the weight of the ice from your data?

   Weigh the water before and after adding the ice. The difference is the weight of the ice.

2. Why is ΔT for the hot water negative? What does the negative sign mean?

   ΔT is defined as the final temperature minus the initial temperature. The final temperature is lower than the initial temperature, so the sign is negative. The negative sign indicates the direction of the temperature change in the process. The temperature went down.

3. What does the negative sign of the heat lost by the water signify?

   The negative sign indicates the direction of energy flow; heat was lost by the water.

4. Why can you assume the initial temperature of the ice is 0°C?

   The melting point of ice is 0°C. Ice and liquid water are in equilibrium at 0°C.

5. What is the sign of the heat absorbed by the ice? Explain.

   The positive sign means that energy flowed into the ice.

6. The law of conservation of energy requires that the heat gained by the ice should balance the heat lost by the water assuming no losses of energy to the surroundings. Does item **k** in Table 14.2 of the calculated data equal zero? Explain.

   It's not even close. The heat gained by the ice takes into account only the temperature change, not the phase change. The difference is the amount of heat required to melt the ice.

7. Why does the heat required to melt the ice divided by the mass of the ice equal the heat of fusion of ice (heat of fusion = $-k/f$)? Why is the negative sign necessary?

   The units for heat of fusion are calories per gram. The heat we calculated was for a certain mass of ice not equal to one gram so we divided by the mass. The negative sign is necessary to convert the heat lost by the water to heat gained by the ice.

8. Given that one calorie equals 4.18 joules, use your experimental data to calculate the heat of fusion of ice in joules per gram.

   x J/g = 81.4 cal/g × 4.18 J/cal = 340 J/g.

9. Use your experimental data to calculate the molar heat of fusion of ice in kJ/mol.

x J/mol = 340 J/g × 18 g/mol × 1 kJ/1000 J = 6.12 kJ/mol.

10. Find the accepted value for the heat of fusion of ice in your textbook and compare your calculated values with the accepted value. Calculate a % error.
% error = |experimental value − accepted value| × 100/accepted value.

% error = (81.4 − 80.0)(100)/80.0 = 1.75%

Now It's Your Turn!

1. Try doing the experiment using a larger sample of hot water and ice. Use one ounce of hot water and about five times as much ice. Are your results similar? Explain.

There is a larger error presumably because there are more heat losses from

a larger sample.

2. Heat losses to the environment are an obvious source of error in this experiment. For example, significant heat losses can occur between the time you measure the temperature of the hot water and add the ice. Any cooling of the hot water during this period will result in an error. Analyze the experimental procedure and try to identify where it can be improved. Repeat the experiment using a modified method to optimize your results.

15 Synthesis and Qualitative Analysis of Gases

Text Section 11.1

Objectives

- **Carry out** chemical reactions that produce gases.
- **Detect** the aqueous reactions of gases using indicators.
- **Identify** unknown gases by the chemical reactions they undergo.

Introduction

Gases are found everywhere. Open a can or bottle of carbonated soft drink, and carbon dioxide, CO_2, bubbles appear. Balloons are commonly filled with helium, He. The gases that are undoubtedly the most familiar to us make up the atmosphere we breathe. Dry air is composed of approximately 78% nitrogen, N_2; 21% oxygen, O_2; and 1% argon, Ar. Usually air also contains considerable amounts of water vapor along with carbon dioxide and trace quantities of a wide variety of other gases. It is the oxygen in the air that sustains animal life, while carbon dioxide is essential to plant life.

Gases in the atmosphere have varying effects on our environment. Sulfur dioxide, SO_2, is produced from the burning of fuels like coal and oil that contain sulfur. Sulfur dioxide further oxidizes in the atmosphere to form sulfur trioxide, SO_3. Sulfur dioxide and sulfur trioxide are the major air pollutants responsible for acid rain. The oxides of nitrogen are a family of compounds commonly referred to as NO_x (NO_2, NO, N_2O_5, and N_2O). The presence of the NO_x family in the atmosphere is the trigger for photochemical smog. Carbon dioxide, CO_2, and water in the atmosphere are larger contributors to the greenhouse effect, enhanced global warming.

Purpose

In this lab you will investigate a variety of chemical reactions that produce gases. You will make each gas by mixing two aqueous solutions on a small-scale reaction surface. Different chemical reactions will produce different gases. You will cover the mixture with a clear plastic cup while the gas diffuses into an array of indicators placed around the mixture. You will study the color changes imparted to the indicators by the gases and learn to distinguish each gas by those color changes. Finally, you will identify unknown gases by the changes they impart to indicators.

Safety

- Wear your safety glasses.
- Use full small-scale pipets only for the carefully controlled delivery of liquids.

Materials

Small-scale pipets of the following solutions:

sodium hydrogen sulfite ($NaHSO_3$)

sodium nitrite ($NaNO_2$)

potassium permanganate ($KMnO_4$)

sodium hypochlorite ($NaOCl$)

sodium hydroxide ($NaOH$)

potassium iodide (KI)

hydrochloric acid (HCl)

sodium hydrogen carbonate ($NaHCO_3$)

hydrogen peroxide (H_2O_2)

ammonium chloride (NH_4Cl)

bromthymol blue (BTB)

starch

Equipment

2 clear plastic cups

small-scale reaction surface

Experimental Page

1. Place 1 drop of each indicator solution in the squares near the inside edge of each circle. Mix 1 drop of each indicated solution in the center of each circle, and cover the entire circle with a cup. Be sure the cup does not touch any solutions.

2. Observe any changes that take place over several minutes. Also observe the nature of the gas bubbles (if any) produced by the mixing. Gases produced by the mixing of the reactants in the center will cause some of the indicators to change color. Record your results in Table 15.1.

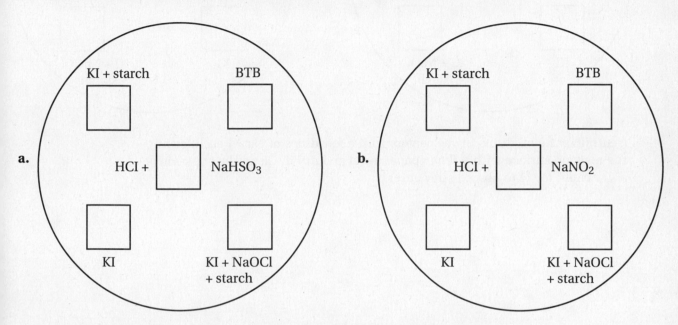

3. Neutralize the mixtures in the centers with a few drops of NaOH each; clean the reaction surface with a *damp* paper towel and dry it. Clean the cups with a *dry* paper towel to absorb stray gases.

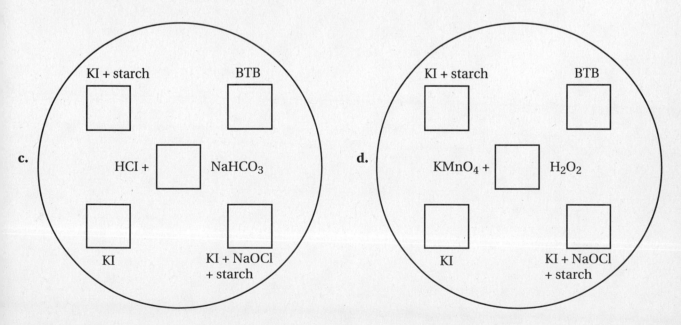

4. Repeat Step 3. Then turn over the Experimental Page and continue with the next mixing.

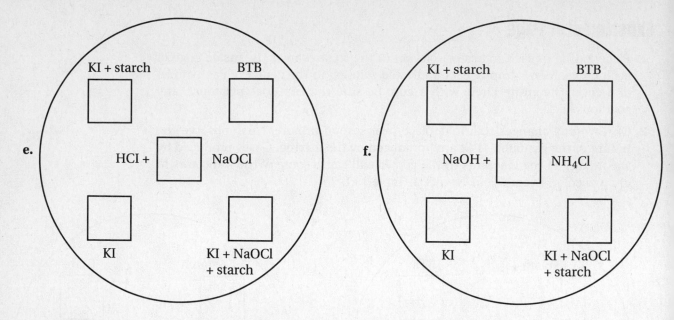

5. Neutralize the mixtures in the centers with a few drops of NaOH each; clean the reaction surface with a *damp* paper towel and dry it. Clean the cups with a *dry* paper towel to absorb stray gases.

Experimental Data

Record your results in Table 15.1 or a table like it in your notebook.

Table 15.1   Observations of Gases

Mixture	Bubbles?	BTB (Green)	KI + Starch (Colorless)	KI + NaOCl + Starch (Black)	KI (Colorless)
a. $NaHSO_3$ + HCl	no	yellow	no change	colorless	no change
b. $NaNO_2$ + HCl	no	yellow	black	no change	yellow
c. $NaHCO_3$ + HCl	yes	no change	no change	no change	no change
d. H_2O_2 + $KMnO_4$	yes	no change	no change	no change	no change
e. NaOCl + HCl	yes	yellow	black	no change	yellow
f. NH_4Cl + NaOH	no	blue	no change	no change	no change

Cleaning Up

Avoid contamination by cleaning up in a way that protects you and your environment. Carefully clean the plastic cups by wiping them with a dry paper towel. Clean the small-scale reaction surface by absorbing the contents onto a paper towel, rinse the the reaction surface with a damp paper towel, and dry it. Dispose of the paper towels in the waste bin. Wash your hands thoroughly with soap and water.

Questions for Analysis

Use your Experimental Data and what you learned in this lab to answer the following questions.

1. What is unique about the way each gas behaved in the presence of indicators?

   Gas a turns I_2 reagent colorless. Gas b does not bubble and turns KI + starch black. Gas c bubbles only. $KMnO_4$ changes from purple to colorless as gas d is formed. Gas e forms bubbles and turns KI + starch black. Gas f turns BTB blue.

2. Gas d was oxygen. What evidence from your procedure might have led you to identify this gas as oxygen or nitrogen?

   Air is composed of mostly nitrogen and oxygen. The indicators didn't change in air, so they shouldn't change in the presence of nitrogen or oxygen.

3. Given the word equations below, write and balance chemical equations to describe the formation of each gas produced in the experiment:

a. Sodium hydrogen sulfite reacts with hydrochloric acid to produce sulfur dioxide gas, water, and sodium chloride.

$NaHSO_3 + HCl \rightarrow SO_2(g) + H_2O + NaCl$

b. Sodium nitrite reacts with hydrochloric acid to produce nitrogen monoxide gas, water, sodium chloride, and sodium nitrate.

$3NaNO_2 + 2HCl \rightarrow 2NO(g) + H_2O + 2NaCl + NaNO_3$

Nitrogen monoxide gas from the above reaction reacts with oxygen gas in the air to produce nitrogen dioxide gas.

$2NO(g) + O_2(g) \rightarrow 2NO_2(g)$

c. Sodium hydrogen carbonate reacts with hydrochloric acid to produce carbon dioxide gas, water, and sodium chloride.

$HCl + NaHCO_3 \rightarrow CO_2(g) + H_2O + NaCl$

d. Hydrogen peroxide reacts with permanganate ion and hydrogen ion to produce oxygen gas, manganese(II) ion, and water.

$5H_2O_2 + 2MnO_4^- + 6H^+ \rightarrow 5O_2(g) + 2Mn^{2+} + 8H_2O$

e. Chlorine gas, water, and sodium chloride are produced when hydrochloric acid is added to sodium hypochlorite, NaOCl.

$NaOCl + 2HCl \rightarrow Cl_2(g) + NaCl + H_2O$

f. Sodium hydroxide reacts with ammonium chloride to produce ammonia gas, water, and sodium chloride.

$NH_4Cl + NaOH \rightarrow NH_3(g) + H_2O + NaCl$

4. Given the word equations below, write and balance chemical equations to describe each reaction of a gas with an indicator or the water in the indicator. In each case explain the change in the indicator. The letter of each word equation corresponds to the letter on the Experimental Page where you saw that reaction.

a. Sulfur dioxide gas reacts with water in the BTB indicator to produce sulfurous acid. (Hint: The formula for sulfurous acid has one fewer oxygen atom than the formula for sulfuric acid.)

$SO_2(g) + H_2O \rightarrow H_2SO_3$. **The sulfurous acid turns BTB yellow.**

Sulfur dioxide gas also reacts with iodine and water to form iodide ion, sulfate ion, and hydrogen ion.

$2H_2O + SO_2(g) + I_2 \rightarrow SO_4^{2-} + 2I^- + 4H^+$. **As I_2 disappears, the black color fades.**

b. Nitrogen dioxide gas reacts with water in the indicator to produce nitric acid and nitrous acid.

$2NO_2(g) + H_2O \rightarrow HNO_2 + HNO_3$. **The acids produced turn BTB yellow.**

c. Chlorine gas reacts with iodide ion to form iodine and chloride ion.

$Cl_2(g) + 2I^- \rightarrow I_2 + 2Cl^-$. **As I₂ forms, its yellow color in aqueous solution**

becomes apparent, and the starch + KI turns black.

Chlorine gas also reacts with water in BTB to form hydrochloric acid and hypochlorous acid.

$Cl_2(g) + H_2O \rightarrow HCl + HOCl$. **The acids produced turn BTB yellow.**

d. Ammonia gas reacts with water in the BTB indicator to produce hydroxide ion and ammonium ion.

$NH_3(g) + HOH \rightarrow NH_4^+ + OH^-$. **The basic solution of hydroxide ions turns**

BTB blue.

Now It's Your Turn!

1. Obtain six unknown solutions from your instructor and apply the technique you used in this experiment to identify the unknown solutions and the gases they produce. Make a table of the number and formula of each solution and each unknown gas it produces.

Look for the distinguishing changes in the indicators as expressed in

Question 1.

2. Acids like ethanoic acid, CH_3COOH, and hydrochloric acid, HCl, are appreciably volatile. That is, they readily evaporate from solution. Design and carry out a way of detecting aqueous solutions of these acids by using this gas detection method. Can your method distinguish these acids from sulfuric and nitric acids? Can it distinguish these acids from one another?

Place 1 drop of acid and 1 drop of BTB next to each other under a cup.

Watch the green BTB turn yellow after time. H_2SO_4 and HNO_3 will not

produce sufficient gases to produce a change in indicators. HCl will

change universal indicator to a much redder color than will ethanoic acid.

3. Besides oxygen, your breath contains carbon dioxide and water vapor. This is because all animals use oxygen to metabolize sugar molecules in a process called cell respiration. The products are CO_2 and H_2O:

$$C_6H_{12}O_6 + 6O_2 \rightarrow 6CO_2 + 6H_2O$$

Carbon dioxide reacts with water to produce carbonic acid, H_2CO_3. Write a balanced equation for this reaction. Using this reaction, devise a way to detect CO_2 in your breath. **Caution:** *Do not touch your mouth to any chemicals or to any apparatus!*

$CO_2 + H_2O \rightarrow H_2CO_3$. Unwrap a sterile soda straw and gently blow on a

drop of phenolphthalein made pink with 0.1M NaOH. The carbonic acid will

neutralize the base.

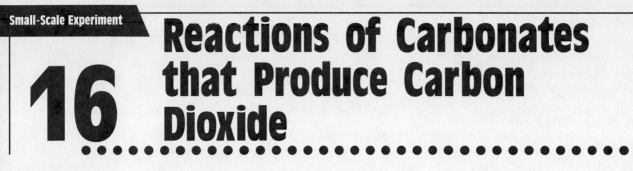

16 Reactions of Carbonates that Produce Carbon Dioxide

Text Section 11.12

Objectives

- **Observe** and **identify** the reactions of carbonates to produce carbon dioxide.
- **Describe** reactions of acids with carbonates by writing complete chemical equations.

Introduction

The usefulness of chemical reactions is in part being able to predict what products result from given reactants. Chemical reactions can be classified into general types, and these general types follow predictable patterns. You have already seen that neutralization reactions are examples of double-replacement reactions where the cations and anions of the reactants trade partners to form products. You have already seen that acids provide hydronium ions, H_3O^+, in aqueous solutions. Hydronium ions give acids their common properties. Acids and bases undergo a number of common chemical reactions that are similarly predictable.

One common property of acids is their reaction with compounds containing the carbonate ion, CO_3^{2-}, to produce carbon dioxide gas, CO_2. Because carbonates react with acids to neutralize them, carbonates can be considered as bases. Familiar antacids commonly employ sodium hydrogen carbonate, $NaHCO_3$, or calcium carbonate, $CaCO_3$, as active ingredients to neutralize stomach acid. Baking soda (sodium hydrogen carbonate) is commonly placed in the refrigerator to keep the refrigerator smelling fresh. Baking soda neutralizes strong food odors caused by acids. Marble and limestone are both mostly calcium carbonate.

Purpose

In this lab you will focus on the reactions that carbonates undergo with acids to produce carbon dioxide gas. You will first make a large number of mixings to observe the macroscopic chemical changes. You will then learn to write chemical equations, using chemical symbols to describe the submicroscopic behavior of matter. Finally, you will explore evidence for these chemical changes.

Safety

- Wear your safety glasses.
- Use full small-scale pipets only for the carefully controlled delivery of liquids.

Materials

Small-scale pipets of the following solutions:

hydrochloric acid (HCl)

nitric acid (HNO$_3$)

sulfuric acid (H$_2$SO$_4$)

sodium hydrogen carbonate (NaHCO$_3$)

sodium carbonate (Na$_2$CO$_3$)

ethanoic acid (CH$_3$COOH)

phosphoric acid (H$_3$PO$_4$)

Solids:

calcium carbonate (CaCO$_3$)

sodium hydrogen carbonate (NaHCO$_3$)

Equipment

empty pipet for stirring

small-scale reaction surface

glass slide

hot plate

Experimental Page

1. Mix each of the following in the indicated square. Record your results in Table 16.1.

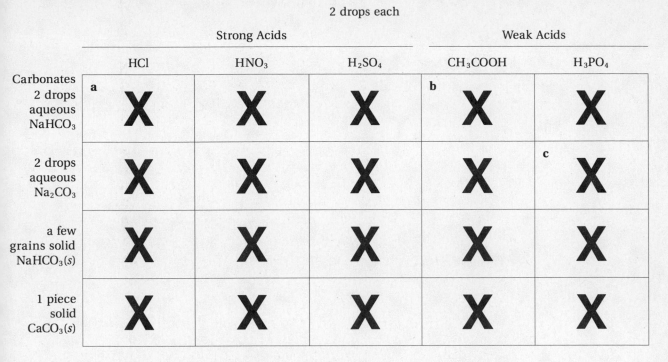

2 drops each

	Strong Acids			Weak Acids	
	HCl	HNO$_3$	H$_2$SO$_4$	CH$_3$COOH	H$_3$PO$_4$
Carbonates 2 drops aqueous NaHCO$_3$	**a** X	X	X	**b** X	X
2 drops aqueous Na$_2$CO$_3$	X	X	X	X	**c** X
a few grains solid NaHCO$_3$(s)	X	X	X	X	X
1 piece solid CaCO$_3$(s)	X	X	X	X	X

2. Mix 2 drops of each substance on a glass slide as shown, and evaporate the liquid on a hot plate. **Caution:** *The glass slides are hot. Handle with plastic spatula.* Record your data in Table 16.2.

HCl + Na$_2$CO$_3$	HNO$_3$ + Na$_2$CO$_3$	H$_2$SO$_4$ + NaCO$_3$	CH$_3$COOH + Na$_2$CO$_3$	H$_3$PO$_4$ + Na$_2$CO$_3$

Place this side of the Experimental Page facedown. Use the other side under your small-scale reaction surface.

Experimental Data

Record your results in Tables 16.1 and 16.2 or tables like them in your notebook.

Table 16.1   Reactions of Carbonates with Acids

Carbonates	Strong Acids			Weak Acids	
	HCl	HNO$_3$	H$_2$SO$_4$	CH$_3$COOH	H$_3$PO$_4$
aqueous NaHCO$_3$	**a** bubbles	bubbles	bubbles	**b** slower bubbles	bubbles
aqueous Na$_2$CO$_3$	bubbles	bubbles	bubbles	slower bubbles	**c** bubbles
solid NaHCO$_3$(s)	bubbles	bubbles	bubbles	slower bubbles	bubbles
solid CaCO$_3$(s)	bubbles	bubbles	bubbles	slower bubbles	bubbles

Table 16.2   Solids from a Carbonate and Acids

	HCl	HNO$_3$	H$_2$SO$_4$	CH$_3$COOH	H$_3$PO$_4$
Na$_2$CO$_3$	**white solid**	**white solid**	**white solid**	**white solid**	**white solid**

Cleaning Up

Avoid contamination by cleaning up in a way that protects you and your environment. Carefully clean the small-scale reaction surface by absorbing the contents onto a paper towel. Rinse the surface with a damp paper towel and dry it. Dispose of the paper towels in the waste bin. Clean the glass slide by rinsing it with water and drying it with a paper towel. Wash your hands thoroughly with soap and water.

Questions for Analysis

Use what you learned in this lab to answer the following questions.

1. What are the gas bubbles you observed in each reaction of an acid with a carbonate?

   Carbon dioxide, CO_2.

2. Below are complete chemical equations for the reactions of acids with carbohydrates and hydrogen carbonates. The letters are keyed to the mixings on the Experimental Page. Notice that in each case a compound containing the carbonate or hydrogen carbonate ion reacts with an acid to produce carbon dioxide, water, and a salt. Study these examples and write complete chemical equations for the other 17 mixings you made on the Experimental Page.

   a. $HCl + NaHCO_3 \rightarrow CO_2(g) + H_2O + NaCl$

   b. $NaHCO_3 + CH_3COOH \rightarrow CO_2(g) + H_2O + CH_3COONa$

   c. $3Na_2CO_3 + 2H_3PO_4 \rightarrow 3CO_2(g) + 3H_2O + 2Na_3PO_4$

   a. $NaHCO_3 + HCl \rightarrow CO_2(g) + H_2O + NaCl$

   $NaHCO_3 + HNO_3 \rightarrow CO_2(g) + H_2O + NaNO_3$

   $2NaHCO_3 + H_2SO_4 \rightarrow 2CO_2(g) + 2H_2O + Na_2SO_4$

   b. $NaHCO_3 + CH_3COOH \rightarrow CO_2(g) + H_2O + CH_3COONa$

   $3NaHCO_3 + H_3PO_4 \rightarrow 3CO_2(g) + 3H_2O + Na_3PO_4$

   $Na_2CO_3 + 2HCl \rightarrow CO_2(g) + H_2O + 2NaCl$

   $Na_2CO_3 + 2HNO_3 \rightarrow CO_2(g) + H_2O + 2NaNO_3$

   $Na_2CO_3 + H_2SO_4 \rightarrow CO_2(g) + H_2O + Na_2SO_4$

   $Na_2CO_3 + 2CH_3COOH \rightarrow CO_2(g) + H_2O + 2CH_3COONa$

   c. $3Na_2CO_3 + 2H_3PO_4 \rightarrow 3CO_2(g) + 3H_2O + 2Na_3PO_4$

   $NaHCO_3(s) + HCl \rightarrow CO_2(g) + H_2O + NaCl$

   $NaHCO_3(s) + HNO_3 \rightarrow CO_2(g) + H_2O + NaNO_3$

   $2NaHCO_3(s) + H_2SO_4 \rightarrow 2CO_2(g) + 2H_2O + Na_2SO_4$

   $NaHCO_3(s) + CH_3COOH \rightarrow CO_2(g) + H_2O + CH_3COONa$

   $3NaHCO_3(s) + H_3PO_4 \rightarrow 3CO_2(g) + 3H_2O + Na_3PO_4$

   $CaCO_3(s) + 2HCl \rightarrow CO_2(g) + H_2O + CaCl_2$

   $CaCO_3(s) + 2HNO_3 \rightarrow CO_2(g) + H_2O + Ca(NO_3)_2$

   $CaCO_3(s) + H_2SO_4 \rightarrow CO_2(g) + H_2O + CaSO_4$

   $CaCO_3(s) + 2CH_3COOH \rightarrow CO_2(g) + H_2O + (CH_3COO)_2Ca$

   $3CaCO_3(s) + 2H_3PO_4 \rightarrow 3CO_2(g) + 3H_2O + Ca_3(PO_4)_2$

3. What are the names and formulas of the residues left after evaporation?

   Sodium chloride, $NaCl$; sodium nitrate, $NaNO_3$; sodium sulfate, Na_2SO_4;

   sodium acetate, CH_3COONa; and sodium phosphate, Na_3PO_4.

4. Study the equations you wrote in Question 2. Are the equations any different if the carbonates are solids or aqueous solutions? How do you know?

No. Notice that the equations for the first and third rows of Table 16.1

are the same, except NaHCO₃ is designated "(s)".

5. What are two compounds (names and formulas) that are always formed by the reaction of an acid with a carbonate?

Carbon dioxide, CO₂, and water, H₂O.

Now It's Your Turn!

1. Design an experiment to isolate other salts by evaporation.

Evaporation of all combinations of acids and carbonates in this experiment

produces white solids.

2. Are NaHCO₃ and Na₂CO₃ acids or bases? Devise an experiment and find out. Tell what you do, what happens, and what it means.

Bases. Add BTB to turn them both blue.

3. Do either NaHCO₃ or Na₂CO₃ neutralize acids? Devise an experiment and find out. Tell what you do and what happens.

Yes. When either is added to a drop of acid and BTB, the BTB turns from

yellow to blue.

4. Suggest a way to test chemically for the carbonate or hydrogen carbonate ion in common materials and consumer products. Try your method on such things as cement, egg shells, sea shells, chalk, antacid tablets, cleaning agents, and various rocks and minerals. Whenever possible, read labels and consult references to try to identify the names or formulas of the carbonates contained in each material you test.

Add acid to a sample and look for bubbles of CO₂. Cement, egg shells,

some rocks and minerals, chalk, and some antacids contain CaCO₃.

5. Baking powder is a mixture of sodium hydrogen carbonate, NaHCO₃ (also called bicarbonate of soda or baking soda), and calcium dihydrogen phosphate, Ca(H₂PO₄)₂. Design an experiment that will give evidence that these two compounds are really there. Tell what you do and explain what happens.

Add some water. Bubbles indicate the presence of NaHCO₃ and Ca(H₂PO₄)₂

because Ca(H₂PO₄)₂ acts as an acid in solution. Teacher's Note: The

equation for this reaction is shown below.

$$12NaHCO_3 + 3Ca(H_2PO_4)_2 \rightarrow 12CO_2(g) + 12H_2O + Ca_3(PO_4)_2 + 4Na_3PO_4$$

6. Cream of tartar is a solid acid also called potassium acid tartrate. Use sodium hydrogen carbonate to prove that cream of tartar is an acid.

Add aqueous NaHCO₃ to a few grains of cream of tartar. Bubbles of CO₂

show that cream of tartar contains an acid (potassium acid tartrate).

17 Design and Construction of a Quantitative Spectroscope

Text Section 12.6

Objectives

- **Design** and **construct** a quantitative spectroscope.
- **Build** a device to calibrate the spectroscope.

Introduction

Chemistry is used to solve problems by identifying materials. Criminologists solve crimes by identifying minute quantities of blood, soil, paint, and other materials that link the criminal with the crime. Radio astronomers identify molecules in outer space. Chemists routinely detect and identify pollutants in our air, water, and soil. Most often these identifications are made by using some form of spectroscopic analysis, or spectroscopy. Spectroscopy is a term that describes a wide range of chemical analyses that probe the interaction of light with matter. Many spectroscopic instruments have been developed to measure different features of light as it interacts with matter.

Perhaps the most obvious feature of visible light is color. When white light from a lamp or the sun travels through a drop of water, it is dispersed into its component colors. This familiar rainbow of colors is known as the visible spectrum. You can produce the same effect by passing light through a prism or diffraction grating. By investigating the visible spectra of various light sources, you can learn about how light interacts with matter.

Purpose

In this lab you will design and build a spectroscope, a device with which you can observe the spectra of various light sources. The body of the spectroscope will be a rectangular box, about 2 cm thick, made from dark-colored poster board. The spectroscope will have a narrow slit at one end to allow light to enter it. A diffraction grating at the other end will disperse white light into a spectrum by bending it at different angles. You should make the box relatively "light-tight" except for the slit and the diffraction grating. Finally, you will build a device to calibrate the spectroscope by taking advantage of a principle called total internal reflection. You will use a plastic rod to "pipe" light into the spectroscope box. A grid scratched on the rod will scatter light and appear to glow inside the box.

Safety

- Behave in a way that is consistent with a safe laboratory.
- Do not look directly at sunlight with your eyes or with the spectroscope. Look at the bright sky away from the sun or at the sun's reflection off snow or a sidewalk.
- Keep all electrical light sources away from water, water faucets, and sinks.

Equipment

teacher-built spectroscope   plastic light rod
poster board   scissors
diffraction grating   3 rubber bands
tape   ruler and 2-cm guide strip
adhesive labels   nail

Experimental Procedure

Part A. The Structure and Function of a Spectroscope

1. Hold a slide-mounted diffraction grating up to your eye and look at a light source. Be careful not to touch the plastic surface of the grating with your fingers. Record what you see.

2. Look at the plastic surface of the grating. Again, don't touch the plastic! Record what you see.

3. Look through the teacher-built spectroscope (without a diffraction grating) at a light source. Record what you see.

4. Place the slide-mounted diffraction grating over the square hole in the teacher-built spectroscope. Hold the grating and spectroscope up to your eye and look through it at a light source. Record what you see.

5. Look through the spectroscope with both your left and right eyes. Record similarities and differences.

Part B. Building Your Own Spectroscope

6. Use a guide strip to draw a 2-cm-wide border around a piece of poster board. Draw a 2-cm-wide center strip as shown in Figure 17.1.

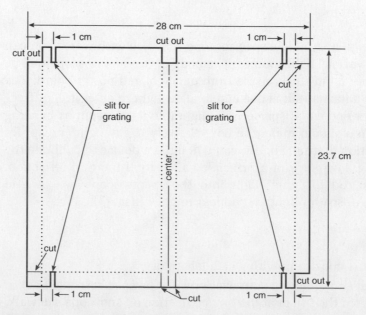

Figure 17.1 *The body of the spectroscope showing folds and cuts*

7. Cut out the diagonal corners entirely as shown. Cut out the four slits 0.5 cm wide and 1 cm from each indicated edge.

8. Use the straight edge of a ruler and fold the poster board along all the lighter lines to form a rectangular box. The slits should line up when the poster board is folded. If they don't, simply cut the poster board so they do. Use rubber bands to hold the folded spectroscope together.

9. Tape a small rectangle of diffraction grating over one slit. Then tape two small pieces of poster board over the other slit to make it 2 mm wide. Take care not to touch the diffraction grating.

10. Place the plastic light rod over the template in Figure 17.2. Use the template as a guide, and a nail to carefully trace a grid onto the light rod. First trace the horizontal scratch and then the evenly spaced parallel scratches onto the light rod.

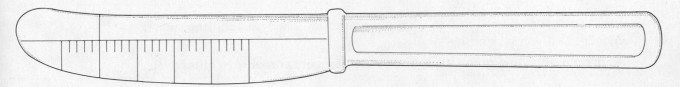

Figure 17.2   *Template for tracing grid onto light rod*

11. Slide the light rod into the end of the spectroscope opposite the diffraction grating (Figure 17.3), and look through it at a white light source. What do you see?

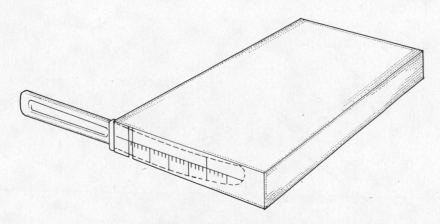

Figure 17.3   *Positioning of the light rod in the spectroscope*

12. When you're sure everything is square and lines up correctly, tape the box together so it's "light tight."

Experimental Data

Part A. Record your data as you examine the spectroscope.

1. What do you see when you hold a slide-mounted diffraction grating up to your eye?

   A rainbow of colors.

2. What do you see on the plastic surface of the grating?

   Many tiny parallel lines.

3. What do you see when you look through the teacher-built spectroscope at a light source?

   White light coming through the slit.

4. What colors do you see and in what order are they when you add the slide-mounted diffraction grating?

   Red, orange, yellow, green, blue, and violet (or reverse order with other eye).

5. Do the colors appear in the same order when you look to the left of the slit as opposed to the right of the slit?

   No, they are in opposite order.

Part B. Building your own spectroscope.

6. Draw a picture of your completed spectroscope.

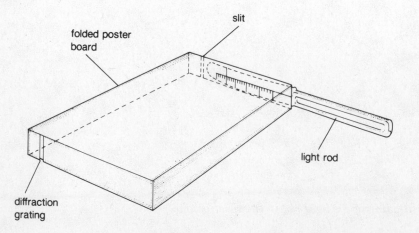

7. What do you see when you look through the completed spectroscope?

   A rainbow with a lighted grid superimposed on it.

Cleaning Up

Avoid contamination by cleaning up in a way that protects you and your environment. Label your spectroscope with your name. Clean up all scraps of paper. Please recycle all usable materials.

Questions for Analysis

Use what you learned in this lab to answer the following questions.

1. What is a spectroscope?

   A device that disperses white light into a spectrum.

2. What is a spectrum?

   A broad range of colors of light.

3. What is white light? How do you know?

   A mixture of all colors. The spectroscope disperses a white light source

   into a rainbow.

4. Which part of the spectroscope separates light into its component colors?

   The diffraction grating.

5. What are the colors of the visible spectrum?

   Red, orange, yellow, green, blue, and violet.

6. How does the light rod work?

   Light travels through it from the outside to the inside of the box. The grid

   scratched on the rod scatters light so it appears to glow.

Now It's Your Turn!

1. Try using various boxes to build spectroscopes. Try a shoe box, a cracker box, a safety-glasses box, a toothpaste box, a pizza box, a cereal box, or any other box available to you. Design each spectroscope so that you can use the same diffraction grating interchangeably.

2. Investigate new ways to calibrate the spectroscope using various light rods.

3. Investigate the effect of changing the size and shape of the slit on your spectroscope.

18 Visible Spectra and the Nature of Light and Color

Text Section 12.6

Objectives

- **Calibrate** a quantitative spectroscope.
- **Compare** visible spectra of common light sources, using a quantitative spectroscope.
- **Plot** graphic representations of various visible spectra.
- **Measure** the wavelength of any colored line in the visible spectrum, and **identify** the range of wavelengths that comprise each color.

Introduction

The diffraction grating in a spectroscope breaks white light into a series of colors called the *visible spectrum.* The visible spectrum is the entire range of colors your eyes can see. A quick look through the spectroscope you built in Small-Scale Experiment 17 will show you that visible white light is a mixture of all colors of the rainbow.

When you look at fluorescent light, three very prominent lines or narrow bands of bright color are superimposed on this continuous rainbow. One line is *violet;* one is *green;* and one is *yellow.* These three lines are caused by the light emission of glowing gaseous mercury atoms in the fluorescent tube. The lines all have characteristic specific positions in the visible spectrum, or *wavelengths,* measured in nanometers (nm):

> violet = 436 nm   green = 546 nm   yellow = 580 nm

Purpose

In this lab you will use the characteristic wavelengths of the prominent spectral lines of mercury to calibrate your spectroscope. The spectroscope contains a plastic light rod that you will use to mark the positions of mercury emission lines. Scratches on the rod appear to glow inside the box. You can use the lighted ruler to mark any place on the visible spectrum. You will move the light rod so that the longest lighted scratch on the ruler is centered over the prominent violet line of the spectrum. You will then note the positions of the other lines on the ruler. These positions are related to the corresponding wavelengths of the prominent lines. Once you have identified the positions of two of the three lines for which you know the wavelength in nanometers, you can calculate the number of nanometers each graduation on the grid represents. The entire process is called *calibration.*

You can then measure any wavelength of visible light in nanometers, represented by the scratches. All you have to do is note the place on the spectrum you wish to know and compare it to the grid you have scratched out on the light rod.

Safety

- Behave in a way that is consistent with a safe laboratory.

- Do not look directly at sunlight with the spectroscope. Look at a bright sky away from the sun or at the sun's reflection off snow or a sidewalk.

- Keep all electrical light sources away from water, water faucets, and sinks.

Equipment

spectroscope
fluorescent and incandescent light sources
graph paper

Experimental Procedure

Part A. Calibrating the Spectroscope

1. View the visible spectrum (rainbow) of fluorescent light through your spectroscope. Identify the three prominent colored lines or narrow bands of brightly colored light superimposed on the rainbow (violet, green, and yellow). Make a rough sketch of the rainbow with its three most prominent bands in your Experimental Data.

2. Move the plastic light rod so that the longest parallel scratch is exactly superimposed over the center of the prominent violet line in the spectrum. Fix the position of the rod with tape, if necessary. The spectroscope is now calibrated.

3. Find the center of the green line relative to the violet line by counting the number of spaces between scratches that separate them. (If this is not a whole number of spaces, estimate the fraction of space.) Repeat for the center of the more diffuse yellow line.

4. Draw in the positions of the green and yellow lines on Figure 18.1 of the Experimental Data section.

Part B. The Visible Spectrum of Fluorescent Light

5. Look through your spectroscope at fluorescent light again.

   a. Note and record the position in spaces from the violet line that marks the *outer edge of the red* region of the spectrum (where red meets black).

   b. Note and record the position of the spectrum where *red meets orange*. This is not very distinct. There is a gradual change from red to orange. Make your own judgment!

   c. Note and record the other places on the spectrum where one color appears to fade into another. Use your judgment!

   d. Use your data to plot a visible spectrum of *fluorescent light* in the Experimental Data section. Find the point on the calibration grid that corresponds to each position of the mark. Read the wavelength that corresponds to that point.

6. Use your spectroscope and the same calibration grid to plot the visible spectrum of *incandescent light* (light from an overhead projector reflected off a white wall or screen, for example).

Experimental Data

Part A. Calibrating a Spectroscope

1. Make a rough sketch of the rainbow produced from fluorescent light, clearly showing the three prominent colored lines or bands of light (violet, green, and yellow).

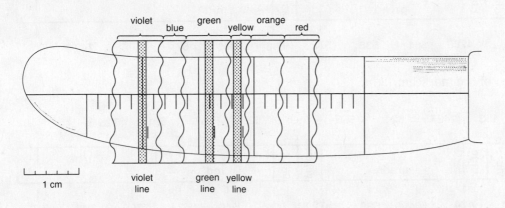

2. Superimpose the light rod on your drawing, showing the approximate positions of the scratches.

3. How many spaces from the violet line is the green line? The yellow line?

   Approximately 6.5 and 8.5 spaces, respectively (assuming the scratches

   are 2 mm apart and the spectroscope was built as in the last lab).

4. The grid shown in Figure 18.1 below is a representation of the grid on the light rod. The violet line is superimposed on the longest scratch.

   a. Draw in the positions of the green and yellow lines with their wavelengths.

   b. Find how many nanometers each small graduation represents by dividing the difference in wavelengths of the green and violet lines (546 − 436 = 110 nm) by the number of spaces between them. Mark the grid in nanometers.

   110/6.5 = 17 nm per graduation.

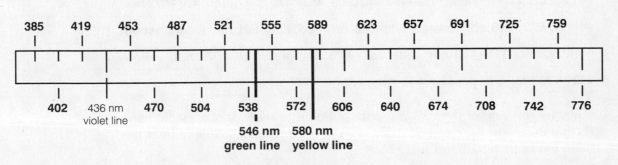

Figure 18.1 *Calibration grid for fluorescent light*

Part B. The Visible Spectrum of Fluorescent Light

5. Plot the spectrum of fluorescent light.

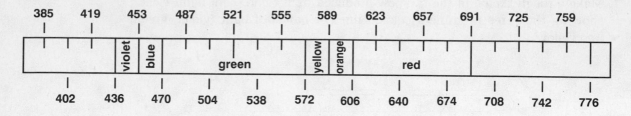

6. Plot the spectrum of incandescent light.

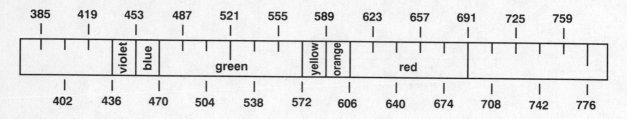

Cleaning Up

Put all the equipment back in its proper place.

Questions for Analysis

1. Explain why the scratched grid on the rod appears to glow.
   Light entering the rod from outside the box reflects off the inside of the

   plastic until it hits an imperfection (a scratch) and is scattered.

2. What part of the spectroscope separates white light into its component colors?
   The diffraction grating.

3. For each of the spectra you plotted, name the colors in the order they appear, and state the wavelengths that border each color.
   Fluorescent light: violet, 419–453 nm; blue, 453–470 nm; green, 470–572 nm;

   yellow, 572–589 nm; orange, 589–606 nm; red, 606–691 nm. Incandescent

   light: violet, 436–453 nm; blue, 453–470 nm; green 470–572 nm; yellow,

   572–589 nm; orange, 589–606 nm; red, 606–708 nm.

4. Compare the plots of the visible spectra of fluorescent and incandescent light. Point out the similarities and differences of each. Which source of light has more red in it? Which has more blue?
   Fluorescent has more violet and less red than incandescent.

5. Which color forms the widest band in each spectrum?
   Green.

6. Why does the incandescent light have the three prominent colored lines in it?

Incandescent light bulbs contain no mercury vapor, as do the fluorescent

lights.

7. Why does each different spectroscope need to be calibrated?

The size of the box and spaces between scratches will affect the results.

Now It's Your Turn!

1. Use your spectroscope and a calibration grid like Figure 18.1 to plot the visible spectra of two other light sources: candlelight and sunlight. Don't look directly at the sunlight! Look away from the sun at a bright sky or at sunlight reflected off snow or a sidewalk. How are sunlight and candlelight the same? How are they different?

Both spectra have all colors of the visible spectrum, ROY G BIV. Sunlight

has more of the blue and violet bands than candlelight.

2. A *reflectance spectrum* is the spectrum of light that is reflected off an opaque object from a source of white light. Use your spectroscope and the same calibration grid to plot the *visible reflection spectra* of various colors of construction paper. What interesting observations do you make?

3. An *absorption spectrum* is the spectrum of light that is transmitted through a translucent material like a colored solution or plastic film. Measure the absorption spectra of several colored plastic films. What can you conclude about the colors your eye perceives and the actual colors of light passing through the films?

4. Measure the absorption spectra of various colored solutions. Use the fluorescent light box to place behind the solutions. What can you conclude about the colors your eye perceives and the actual colors of light passing through the colored solutions?

5. An *atomic emission spectrum* is the spectrum that is emitted from glowing gaseous atoms. Examine the atomic emission spectra of several gas discharge tubes. Make a rough sketch of each in your notebook. What is distinctive about all these atomic emission spectra?

6. Propose how you can make the spectroscope better. Reinvent it. Build another model and test its performance based on various construction parameters.

7. The wavelength of light is the distance between two adjacent peaks of a light wave. The wavelength of visible light is most commonly measured in nanometers (nm). One nanometer is 10^{-9} meters. The frequency of light is the number of waves passing a given point in 1 second. Its units are s^{-1}. The velocity of light in a vacuum is about $3 \times 10^{+8}$ meters/second. The wavelength, frequency, and speed of light are related in terms of the following equation:

$$\text{frequency} = \text{velocity/wavelength} \quad v = c/\lambda$$

Choose any visible spectrum you plotted and use the above equation to convert all the measured wavelengths into frequencies.

8. Mix equal quantities of red, blue, and yellow food dyes in all possible binary combinations (any one with any other one.) What do you conclude?

red + blue = violet; red + yellow = orange; yellow + blue = green. All

colors of the visible spectrum can be generated by mixing the three

primary colors together.

19 Hard and Soft Water

● ●

Text Sections 13.A, 17.B

Objectives

■ **Measure** the total hardness of water in various water samples.

■ **Apply** the ion exchange process to "soften" hard water.

Introduction

Hard water contains dissolved salts, especially those of calcium. Hard water often contains magnesium and iron ions also. Most of the dissolved calcium ions in the natural waters of rivers, lakes, and streams originate from limestone, which is principally calcium carbonate, $CaCO_3$. The limestone is dissolved by rain water or by water contaminated by mining and industrial wastes containing hydrochloric and sulfuric acids.

$$CaCO_3(s) + H^+(aq) \rightarrow Ca^{2+}(aq) + HCO_3^-(aq)$$

The reaction of water with atmospheric carbon dioxide makes rain water naturally slightly acidic. Unnatural acidic rain can result from the reaction of atmospheric water with industrial pollutants like sulfur dioxide and nitrogen dioxide.

$$H_2O + CO_2(g) \rightarrow H_2CO_3(aq)$$

$$H_2O + SO_2(g) \rightarrow H_2SO_3(aq)$$

$$H_2O + 2NO_2(g) \rightarrow HNO_2(aq) + HNO_3(aq)$$

The location of limestone deposits varies throughout the country, as do the amounts of industrial acids exposed to rivers and the acidity of rainfall. Thus, the amount of dissolved calcium ion varies, and so does the resultant hardness of water in various locations.

Calcium ions, while nontoxic, present a number of significant household and industrial problems. For example, calcium ion reacts with the ingredients of many soaps and shampoos to form an insoluble scum that you know as a "bath tub ring." The formation of this precipitate causes the soap to lose its effectiveness.

$$Ca^{2+} + CH_3(CH_2)_{15}COO^- \, Na^+ \rightarrow 2Na^+ + (CH_3(CH_2)_{15}COO^-)_2Ca(s)$$

sodium stearate	calcium stearate
a typical soap	an insoluble scum

Hard water also accounts for the buildup of "boiler scale" on the insides of teapots, water heaters, and industrial boilers. The scale consists mainly of calcium carbonate that has precipitated from hard water upon heating:

$$Ca(HCO_3)_2(aq) + heat \rightarrow CaCO_3(s) + CO_2(g) + H_2O$$

The calcium carbonate scale must be removed periodically because it reduces heating efficiency by acting as an insulator. Calcium carbonate also promotes corrosion and blocks pipes.

Purpose

In this lab you will measure the total amount of calcium and magnesium ions in various water samples around the country and/or from your area. You will add a particular kind of solution, called a buffer, to each water sample which will maintain the pH at about 10.5. You will then titrate each sample with ethylenediamine tetraacetic acid, EDTA, until the indicator Ero-T turns from wine red to sky blue at the end point.

You will report the results as parts per million (ppm) of calcium carbonate, $CaCO_3$, even though some of the hardness may be due to the presence of magnesium ions. A part per million is a milligram of calcium carbonate per liter of water sample. The higher the parts per million of $CaCO_3$, the more calcium ions are in the water and the harder the water is.

Safety

- Wear your safety glasses.
- Use full small-scale pipets only for the carefully controlled delivery of liquids.

Materials

Small-scale pipets of the following solutions:
ethylenediamine tetraacetic acid (EDTA)
deionized water (H_2O)
Solids: eriochrome black T indicator (Ero-T)

ammonia/ammonium chloride (buffer)
various water samples (labeled)

Equipment

small-scale balance with extra pan or other balance

Experimental Procedure

Determine the hardness of each water sample by the following method:

1. Weigh about 2500 mg of water sample in a plastic cup.
   a. Place a 2500 mg weight in your small-scale balance pan, and adjust the balance beam and counterweight until the pointer indicates the zero point.
   b. Remove the weight and drop in enough water sample to return the pointer to the zero point.

2. Add 15 drops of buffer.

3. Add Ero-T indicator until the color is medium to dark wine red.

4. Weigh or tare a full pipet of EDTA.
   a. Place a full pipet in a second small-scale balance pan.
   b. Adjust the small-scale balance to read zero.

5. Titrate the water sample with EDTA until the last tinges of red turn blue.

6. Find the weight loss of EDTA.

   a. Return the used EDTA pipet to the small-scale balance.

   b. Add weights until the pointer again reads zero.

7. Repeat the above steps for each of the other water samples including one from your tap and distilled water. Compare the hardness of water in the various other samples available in your lab.

8. Calculate the parts per million (ppm) of $CaCO_3$ in the water sample. (1 ppm = 1 mg $CaCO_3$/L of water.) Record your results in Table 19.1. To do the calculation you will need the following pieces of information:

   a. The weight loss of EDTA used in the titration in mg.

   b. The weight of the water sample in mg.

   c. The density of EDTA solution = 1 mL/1000 mg.

   d. The density of water = 1000 mg/1 mL.

   e. 1000 mL/1 L.

   f. The concentration of EDTA solution = 0.002 mmol/mL.

   g. The overall stoichiometry of the reaction = 1 mmol $CaCO_3$/1 mmol EDTA.

   h. The formula weight of $CaCO_3$ = 100 mg/mmol.

   $$\text{ppm } CaCO_3 = \text{mg } CaCO_3/L\ H_2O = \frac{a}{b} \times c \times d \times e \times f \times g \times h$$

To be sure you understand the calculation, substitute each quantity (number and units) into the equation and cancel the units. For subsequent calculations, simplify the equation by combining terms that are always constant.

The indicator is red in the presence of Mg^{2+}. EDTA reacts with both Ca^{2+} and Mg^{2+}. The indicator turns blue when all of the Mg^{2+} and Ca^{2+} are combined with EDTA.

Equations:

$$Mg^{2+} + 2In^- = MgIn_2 \qquad EDTA^{2-} + Ca^{2+} \rightarrow CaEDTA$$
$$\text{blue} \qquad\qquad \text{red} \qquad\quad EDTA^{2-} + Mg^{2+} \rightarrow MgEDTA$$

Experimental Data

Record your results in Table 19.1 or a table like it in your notebook.

Table 19.1   Titration Data for Water Samples

Water Sample	Sample Weight (mg)	Weight Loss of EDTA (mg)	ppm CaCO$_3$
_____	2550	600	47
_____	2550	1400	110
_____	2550	2420	190
_____	2550	395	31
_____	2550	2805	220

Cleaning Up

Avoid contamination by cleaning up in a way that protects you and your environment. Carefully clean the plastic balance cup by rinsing the contents down the drain. Rinse the cup and dry it with a paper towel. Dispose of the paper towels in the waste bin. Wash your hands thoroughly with soap and water.

Questions for Analysis

Use what you learned in this lab to answer the following questions.

1. Which sample is the hardest water you titrated? Which is the softest? What does it mean for water to be "hard" or "soft"?

   The hardest water is the one with the highest ppm of CaCO$_3$. The

   softest water is the one with the lowest ppm CaCO$_3$. Hard water contains

   comparatively more calcium ions.

2. What is a part per million?

   One milligram per liter.

3. In the titration, why did you not need to know the weight of the full EDTA pipet?

   I needed to know only how much EDTA I used.

4. Write a balanced equation for the titration of calcium ion with EDTA.

   $EDTA^{2-} + Ca^{2+} \rightarrow CaEDTA$.

5. EDTA is commonly used as an additive in foods such as salad dressings and carbonated soft drinks. The function of the EDTA is to tie up metal cations that may cause clouding of the product. Read some labels at home and find some foods that contain EDTA in some form. List them here.

Some bottled salad dressings and soft drinks.

Now It's Your Turn!

1. When water is passed through an ion exchange buret, it becomes acidic because Ca^+ ions are exchanged for H^+ ions. The equation for the ion exchange reaction follows:

$$Ca^{2+} + H^+H^+ \rightarrow Ca^{2+} + 2H^+$$
$$\setminus \ / \qquad \ \ |$$
$$R \qquad \ \ R \qquad\qquad R = \text{ion exchange "resin"}$$

This principle is used in a practical everyday setting in a home water softener.

a. Recharge an acid resin ion exchanger with a small amount of HCl.

b. Drain it thoroughly and rinse it twice with deionized water. Expel as much of the rinse water as possible.

c. Draw a few drops of hard water into the exchanger and shake gently for 15 seconds. Add 5 drops of this water to 1 drop of BTB and record the color.

   What color does each water sample that was treated in the ion exchanger turn BTB? What ions are present in these samples?

Yellow. Hydrogen ions.

d. Expel 5 more drops from the exchanger, shake in a few grains of Ero-T indicator and add a few drops of buffer. Record the color.

e. Repeat for the other water samples.

   What color does each water sample that was treated with the ion exchanger turn Ero-T? What does this tell you about the presence of calcium ion? Explain.

All turn blue. There is no calcium ion present. The calcium ion was

changed for the hydrogen ion in the ion exchanger.

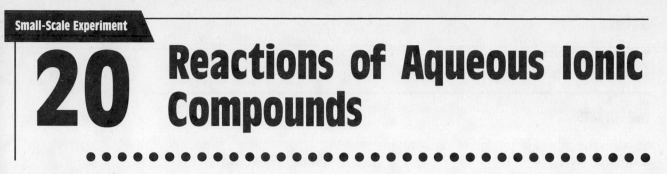

20 Reactions of Aqueous Ionic Compounds

Text Section 14.4

Objectives

- **Observe** a large number of chemical reactions by mixing solutions of ionic compounds.
- **Classify** a large amount of data efficiently, using a matrix.
- **Identify** unknown chemicals by using information in the data matrix.

Introduction

Science progresses through the process of experimentation: *asking questions, finding ways to answer them, and generating more questions.* As a student of chemistry you make many observations in the process of designing and carrying out experiments. You organize your observations in tables so that they are clearly available for answering questions and solving problems. Then you can compare your well-organized data in order to answer questions and solve problems. You consider all of the data so you can make correlations that would not be possible if each observation were considered alone. Your correlations may raise more questions than they answer. But these new questions promote further experimentation which raises more answers and more questions.

All of the steps in the process of experimentation depend on your carefully made observations. The prerequisite to answering any chemical question or to solving any chemical problem is the accumulation of sufficient, accurate, and well-organized observations.

Purpose

In this lab you will solve a chemical logic problem. You will mix 13 solutions of known ionic compounds in all possible binary (two at a time) combinations. You will record your observations in such a way that comparisons of the chemical behavior of the various mixtures can be made easily. You will study the similarities and differences between the reactions of ionic compounds and you will use your record of observations to determine the identity of various unknown solutions. In Small-Scale Experiment 21, you will use the data obtained in this experiment to identify eight unknown solutions chosen at random from the original 13.

Safety

- Wear your safety glasses.

- Use full small-scale pipets only for the carefully controlled delivery of liquids.

Materials

Small-scale pipets of the following solutions:

ammonia (NH_3)

sodium carbonate (Na_2CO_3)

hydrochloric acid (HCl)

silver nitrate ($AgNO_3$)

sodium hydroxide (NaOH)

sodium phosphate (Na_3PO_4)

copper(II) sulfate ($CuSO_4$)

lead(II) nitrate ($Pb(NO_3)_2$)

calcium chloride ($CaCl_2$)

sulfuric acid (H_2SO_4)

nitric acid (HNO_3)

potassium iodide (KI)

iron(III) chloride ($FeCl_3$)

Equipment

small-scale reaction surface

empty pipet for stirring

Experimental Page

Place 1 drop of $Pb(NO_3)_2$ on each × in the first column. Add 1 drop of each of the other solutions to the $Pb(NO_3)_2$. Stir each mixture by blowing air with an empty pipet. Repeat the procedure for each column. Record your results in Table 20.1.

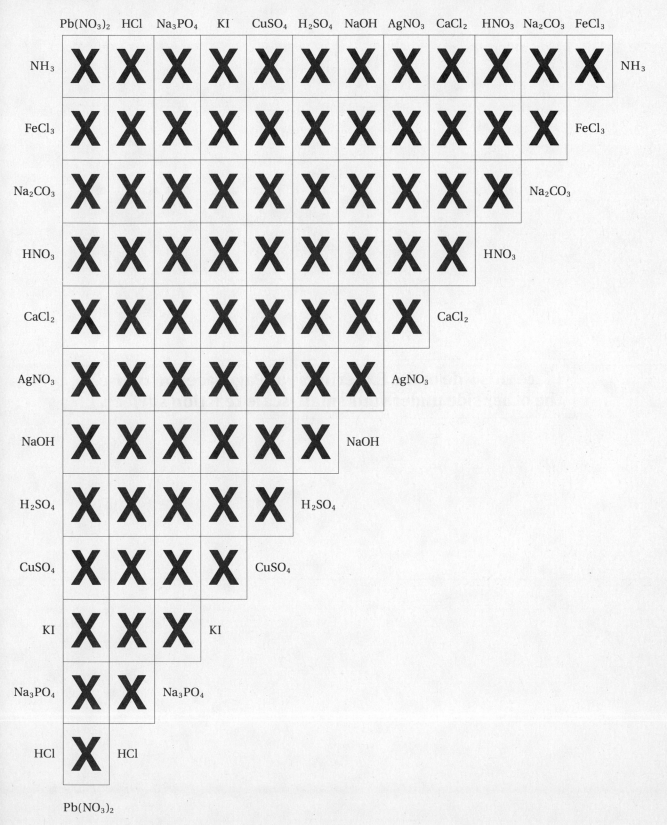

Place this side of the Experimental Page facedown. Use the other side under your small-scale reaction surface.

Experimental Data

Record your results in Table 20.1 or a table like it in your notebook.

Table 20.1   Reactions of Aqueous Ionic Compounds

	Pb(NO$_3$)$_2$	HCl	Na$_3$PO$_4$	KI	CuSO$_4$	H$_2$SO$_4$	NaOH	AgNO$_3$	CaCl$_2$	HNO$_3$	Na$_2$CO$_3$	FeCl$_3$	
NH$_3$	white ppt	NVR	NVR	NVR	blue ppt	NVR	NVR	light white ppt	NVR	NVR	NVR	orange ppt	NH$_3$
FeCl$_3$	white ppt	NVR	orange ppt	amber soln	NVR	NVR	orange ppt	white ppt	NVR	NVR	orange ppt		FeCl$_3$
Na$_2$CO$_3$	white ppt	bubbles	NVR	NVR	blue ppt	bubbles	NVR	tan ppt	white ppt	bubbles	Na$_2$CO$_3$		
HNO$_3$	NVR	NVR	NVR	NVR	NVR	NVR	NVR	NVR	NVR	HNO$_3$			
CaCl$_2$	white ppt	NVR	white ppt	NVR	NVR	slow white ppt	white ppt	white ppt	CaCl$_2$				
AgNO$_3$	NVR	white ppt	tan ppt	light green ppt	NVR	NVR	muddy brown ppt	AgNO$_3$					
NaOH	white ppt	NVR	NVR	NVR	blue ppt	NVR	NaOH						
H$_2$SO$_4$	white ppt	NVR	NVR	NVR	NVR	H$_2$SO$_4$							
CuSO$_4$	white ppt	NVR	blue ppt	brown ppt	CuSO$_4$								
KI	bright yellow ppt	NVR	NVR	KI									
Na$_3$PO$_4$	white ppt	NVR	Na$_3$PO$_4$										
HCl	white ppt	HCl											
	Pb(NO$_3$)$_2$												

Reactions of Aqueous Ionic Compounds   **149**

Cleaning Up

Avoid contamination by cleaning up in a way that protects you and your environment. Carefully clean the small-scale reaction surface by absorbing the contents onto a paper towel. Rinse the reaction surface with a damp paper towel and dry it. Dispose of the paper towels in the waste bin. Wash your hands thoroughly with soap and water.

Questions for Analysis

Use what you learned in this lab to answer the following questions.

1. Write and balance chemical equations for each precipitation reaction you observed for lead(II) nitrate. For example, lead(II) nitrate, $Pb(NO_3)_2$, and potassium iodide, KI, react to form a very bright yellow precipitate:

$$Pb(NO_3)_2 + 2KI \rightarrow PbI_2(s) + 2KNO_3$$

(Hint: Use NH_4OH for NH_3. See Question 2.)

$Pb(NO_3)_2 + 2NH_4OH \rightarrow Pb(OH)_2(s) + 2NH_4NO_3$	$Pb(NO_3)_2 + H_2SO_4 \rightarrow PbSO_4(s) + 2HNO_3$
$3Pb(NO_3)_2 + 2FeCl_3 \rightarrow 3PbCl_2(s) + 2Fe(NO_3)_3$	$Pb(NO_3)_2 + CuSO_4 \rightarrow PbSO_4(s) + 2Cu(NO_3)_2$
$Pb(NO_3)_2 + Na_2CO_3 \rightarrow PbCO_3(s) + 2NaNO_3$	$3Pb(NO_3)_2 + 2Na_3PO_4 \rightarrow Pb_3(PO_4)_2(s) + 6NaNO_3$
$Pb(NO_3)_2 + CaCl_2 \rightarrow PbCl_2(s) + Ca(NO_3)_2$	$Pb(NO_3)_2 + 2HCl \rightarrow PbCl_2(s) + 2HNO_3$
$Pb(NO_3)_2 + 2NaOH \rightarrow Pb(OH)_2(s) + 2NaNO_3$	

2. You may have noticed that some chemicals formed precipitates when mixed with ammonia, NH_3. This is because ammonia reacts with water to produce ammonium hydroxide, NH_4OH:

$$NH_3 + H_2O \rightarrow NH_4OH$$

To write the chemical equations for the precipitations with ammonia, you need to replace NH_3 with NH_4OH. For example,

$$Pb(NO_3)_2 + 2NH_4OH \rightarrow Pb(OH)_2(s) + 2NH_4NO_3$$

Write chemical equations for all the other precipitation reactions you observed with NH_3. In each case, replace NH_3 with NH_4OH.

$CuSO_4 + 2NH_4OH \rightarrow Cu(OH)_2(s) + (NH_4)_2SO_4$

$CaCl_2 + 2NH_4OH \rightarrow Ca(OH)_2(s) + 2NH_4Cl$

$FeCl_3 + 3NH_4OH \rightarrow Fe(OH)_3(s) + 3NH_4Cl$

$AgNO_3 + NH_4OH \rightarrow AgOH(s) + NH_4NO_3$

3. Which reactions gave distinctive bubbles? What chemicals do all these reactions have in common? Write chemical equations to describe all the reactions that produced bubbles.

Na_2CO_3 produces bubbles with the three acids, HCl, HNO_3, and H_2SO_4.

$Na_2CO_3 + 2HCl \rightarrow 2NaCl + CO_2(g) + H_2O$

$Na_2CO_3 + 2HNO_3 \rightarrow 2NaNO_3 + CO_2(g) + H_2O$

$Na_2CO_3 + H_2SO_4 \rightarrow Na_2SO_4 + CO_2(g) + H_2O$

4. Which reactions gave color changes but no precipitate?

$KI + FeCl_3$

5. Which mixings could you have predicted in advance would not result in a reaction?

Any with a common cation or a common anion.

Now It's Your Turn!

1. Investigate further the reaction of $CuSO_4$ with NH_3. Try 1 drop of NH_3 with several drops of $CuSO_4$. Then try 1 drop of $CuSO_4$ with several drops of NH_3. What is distinctive about this reaction?

Excess copper sulfate produces a light blue precipitate that dissolves in

excess ammonia to give a clear dark blue solution.

2. Investigate further the reaction of $AgNO_3$ with NH_3. Try 1 drop of NH_3 with several drops of $AgNO_3$. Then try 1 drop of $AgNO_3$ with several drops of NH_3. What's distinctive about this reaction?

Excess silver nitrate produces a light white precipitate that dissolves in

excess ammonia.

3. Investigate further the reaction of $Pb(NO_3)_2$ with NaOH. Try 1 drop of NaOH with several drops of $Pb(NO_3)_2$. Then try 1 drop of $Pb(NO_3)_2$ with several drops of NaOH. What's distinctive about this reaction?

Excess lead nitrate produces a white precipitate that dissolves in excess

NaOH.

4. A very distinctive precipitate is formed when H_2SO_4 and $CaCl_2$ are mixed. Repeat the reaction between sulfuric acid, H_2SO_4, and calcium chloride, $CaCl_2$. What is so distinctive about this precipitate?

It takes stirring 20 to 30 seconds to form.

5. Challenge a friend. Hide the label and place 1 drop of either the top or bottom solution on your neighbor's grid (below). Ask him or her to identify it by using just 1 drop of any of the 13 chemicals. Repeat for each space.

$AgNO_3$	$CuSO_4$	Na_2CO_3	$FeCl_3$	$NaOH$	HCl	H_2SO_4	HNO_3
X	X	X	X	X	X	X	X
$Pb(NO_3)_2$	$CaCl_2$	Na_3PO_4	KI	NH_3	H_2SO_4	HNO_3	HCl

6. Ask a third person to line up 12 separate drops of any unknown chemical on your acetate. You go first. Add any chemical to the first drop and guess what the unknown is. The second player adds any chemical to the second drop and makes a guess. It's your turn again. Continue until there is a winner. Play this game several times until you can identify the unknown in just a few drops.

7. Choose a chemical and place 1 drop in each of the 11 spaces on a neighbor's grid (below). Challenge him or her to devise a way to uncover its identity in fewer drops than you used to identify his or her unknown.

1	2	3	4	5	6	7	8	9	10	11
X	X	X	X	X	X	X	X	X	X	X

21 Identification of Eight Unknown Solutions

Text Section 14.5

Objective

■ **Identify** eight unknown solutions using known data and logical thinking.

Introduction

The art of logical thinking is essential to mastering chemistry. Although it is important to be familiar with many chemical facts so that you can utilize the language of chemistry effectively, it is even more important to be able to assimilate these facts and organize them in logical ways so they can be used to solve problems. The art of logical thinking is not difficult to acquire but it does require practice. Try out your own ability on the following logic problem.

During a chemistry class, five pairs of students are working on five different experiments at a row of lab stations numbered 1–5 consecutively. From the information given below, can you tell what each student's experiment is, at which lab station he or she is working, and who his or her lab partner is?

Clues:

1. The halogens experiment and all the other experiments are performed by lab partners of the opposite sex. For example, Ann Ion's lab partner is a boy.

2. Milli Liter and Ben Zene work together.

3. Charles Law does not work at lab station #2.

4. Molly Cool and her partner work between station #3 and the station occupied by Barry Um.

5. Phyllis Pipet, building a spectroscope, is not at #4.

6. Milli Liter does not work next to Molly Cool.

7. Earl N. Meyer works at #4.

8. Ionic reactions are being carried out at #5.

9. Hal Ogen is building a small-scale balance.

10. Only one of the Um twins, Francie or Barry, works at station #1 doing an acid–base titration.

Lab Station	Boy	Girl	Experiment
1	Barry Um	Ann Ion	Acid–Base Titration
2	Hal Ogen	Molly Cool	Small-Scale Balance
3	Charles Law	Phyllis Pipet	Spectroscope
4	Earl N. Meyer	Francie Um	Halogens
5	Ben Zene	Milli Liter	Ionic Reactions

Answers:

Purpose

In this lab you will mix eight unknown solutions two at a time just as you did in Small-Scale Experiment 20. The eight unknown solutions have been chosen at random from the original 13. You will compare your results with those you obtained in Small-Scale Experiment 20 and identify the eight unknown solutions through logical reasoning not unlike you used to solve the above problem. A successful conclusion to this lab does not require a Ph.D. in chemistry. It does require good organization, clear logical thinking, and good data.

Safety

- Wear your safety glasses.
- Use full small-scale pipets only for the carefully controlled delivery of liquids.

Materials

Small-scale pipets of the following solutions:

ammonia (NH_3)   lead(II) nitrate ($Pb(NO_3)_2$)
sodium carbonate (Na_2CO_3)   calcium chloride ($CaCl_2$)
hydrochloric acid (HCl)   sulfuric acid (H_2SO_4)
silver nitrate ($AgNO_3$)   nitric acid (HNO_3)
sodium hydroxide (NaOH)   potassium iodide (KI)
sodium phosphate (Na_3PO_4)   iron(III) chloride ($FeCl_3$)
copper(II) sulfate ($CuSO_4$)

Eight small-scale pipets of unknown solutions labeled with different numbers.

Equipment

small-scale reaction surface
empty pipet for stirring

Experimental Page

1. Obtain eight small-scale pipets labeled with numbers from your instructor. The eight pipets contain eight of the original 13 solutions from Small-Scale Experiment 20. Each is different. Write the numbers of the unknowns along the horizontal in Table 21.1 and in reverse order along the vertical. Mix 1 drop of each solution on the indicated X, just as you did in the last experiment. Stir each mixture by blowing air with an empty pipet. Record your results in Table 21.1.

Unknown
Numbers: _____ _____ _____ _____ _____ _____ _____

_____ | X | X | X | X | X | X | X | _____

_____ | X | X | X | X | X | X | _____

_____ | X | X | X | X | X | _____

_____ | X | X | X | X | _____

_____ | X | X | X | _____

_____ | X | X | _____

_____ | X | _____

_____

2. Compare your unknown reactions to those of the 13 solutions in Small-Scale Experiment 20, and see how many unknowns you can identify.

3. Devise a way to use the original 13 solutions to correctly identify your unknowns. To do this you should mix each unknown with several knowns, one at a time.

Place this side of the Experimental Page facedown. Use the other side under your small-scale reaction surface.

Experimental Data

Record your results in Tables 21.1 and 21.2 or tables like them in your notebook.

Table 21.1   Eight Unknowns

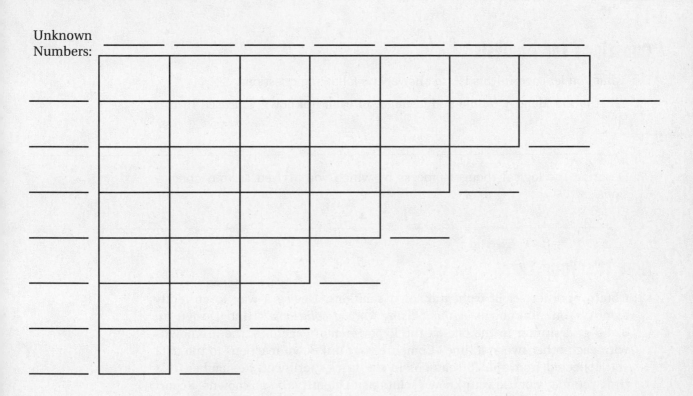

Table 21.2   Numbers, Formulas, and Names of Eight Unknown Solutions

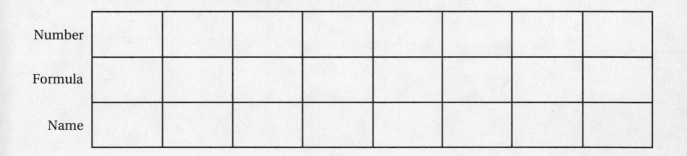

Number								
Formula								
Name								

Identification of Eight Unknown Solutions

Cleaning Up

Avoid contamination by cleaning up in a way that protects you and your environment. Carefully clean the small-scale reaction surface by absorbing the contents onto a paper towel. Rinse the reaction surface with a damp paper towel and dry it. Dispose of the paper towels in the waste bin. Wash your hands thoroughly with soap and water.

Questions for Analysis

Use what you learned in this lab to answer the following questions.

1. What is the identity (name and formula) of each unknown you used in this lab?

   _____

2. Describe the logical thought process by which you arrived at your conclusions.

   _____

Now It's Your Turn!

1. Obtain another set of eight unknown solutions. Devise a way to correctly identify your unknowns *without using known solutions.* (Hint: Design an 8 × 8 grid similar to the one on the Experimental Page. Mix the unknowns with each other two at a time.) Compare your unknown reactions to the data you collected from the 13 solutions in the last experiment. Remember, this time you may not use your known solutions to identify the unknowns. Report the results as you did before. Describe the logical thought process by which you arrived at your conclusions. Check your results with your instructor.

22 Paper Chromatography

Text Section 15.11

Objectives

- **Separate** mixtures of compounds, using the technique of paper chromatography.
- **Identify** compounds contained in some common ink dyes.
- **Compare** formulations of inks in various brands of pens.

Introduction

Chromatography is a technique for separating mixtures of compounds. It is a powerful and versatile method used widely in chemistry and in the biological sciences. Chromatography can also be used to identify unknown substances. All of the several types of chromatography employ two different immiscible phases in contact with each other. One of the phases is moving, *the mobile phase*, and the other is not, *the stationary phase*. In paper chromatography, for example, a solvent moves from one end of a piece of paper to the other end, as the paper absorbs it. The solvent is the mobile phase because it is moving, and the paper is the stationary phase. (In reality, there are water molecules attached to the paper that serve as the stationary phase.)

A mixture of chemicals can be separated using paper chromatography. A small amount of mixture to be separated is placed near the edge of an absorbent paper. That edge of the paper is wetted with solvent. The solvent travels up the paper by capillary action, carrying the mixture with it. Separation occurs because different chemicals in the mixture travel different distances. The physical interaction of each compound in the mixture with the solvent (the mobile phase) and with the water molecules attached to the paper (the stationary phase) determines the distance it travels. Substances that dissolve more readily in the solvent will move farther than substances that have a higher affinity for the water attached to the paper. When the solvent has moved the entire length of the paper, the paper is removed from the solvent and dried. Once developed, the paper, called a *chromatogram*, will contain different chemicals located at different positions on the paper.

The various chemicals visible on the chromatogram can often be identified by their positions and/or their colors. If the mixture contains colored compounds, each different compound will appear on the chromatogram as a colored spot or a streak in a particular place. The color and location of each compound can be used as a basis for identification. The color and location of unknown compounds separated under specific chromatographic conditions can be matched with the color and location of known compounds subjected to the same conditions.

Purpose

In this lab you will use the technique of paper chromatography to separate the colored dyes in a variety of felt-tipped pens. You will then compare the chromatograms of the pens to those of known dyes to identify the dyes used in the pens.

Safety

- Wear your safety glasses.
- Assume that all the colored food and candy in this lab is contaminated with toxic chemicals. Do not eat or even taste anything in the laboratory.

Equipment

template cards	pencil
chromatography paper	stapler
typing paper	2 clear plastic cups
two sets of colored marking pens	solvent
scissors	1 set of FD&C dyes

Experimental Procedure

1. Cut and mark two identical pieces of chromatography paper as follows. Use the cardboard template as a guide. Use *only black pencil* to write on the paper.

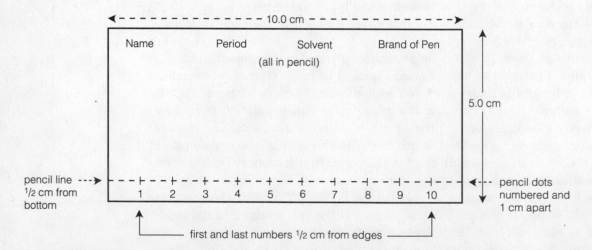

2. Obtain a set of marking pens and draw a small dot of ink from a red pen on the first pencil dot on one piece of chromatography paper. Continue placing colored dots on the pencil dots in the *same order as the visible spectrum:* red, orange, yellow, green, light blue, dark blue, and violet (ROY G BIV). Place other colors such as black, brown, and pink at the end. Record in your notebook the number, color, and brand of the pen.

3. Mark the second piece of chromatography paper with a second set of marker pens (a different brand). Place the colors *in the same order* as on your first chromatogram. Record this data in your notebook.

4. Staple the two papers into cylinders, dot side out, being careful not to allow the edges to touch one another (Figure 22.1).

Figure 22.1

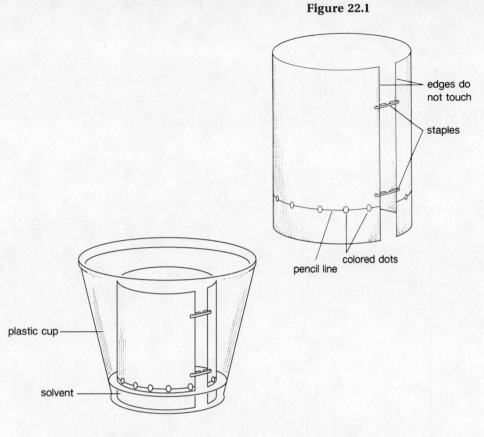

edges do
not touch

staples

pencil line

colored dots

plastic cup

solvent

Figure 22.2

5. Wet the bottom of two plastic cups with solvent and place a paper cylinder in each, colored sides down. Initially, the colored dots should be above the solvent as shown in Figure 22.2.

6. Spot the following FD&C dyes onto a third chromatography paper: red #3, red #40, yellow #5, yellow #6, green #3, blue #1, and blue #2. These dyes will help you to identify the dyes in the marking pens. Use a tiny triangle of *typing paper* to spot these dyes onto the chromatography paper. Cut the triangle and wet one tip in a dye solution. Touch the wet tip lightly to a pencil spot. Use a new triangle for each different dye.

7. While you wait for the solvent to move up the paper or elute (about 10–15 minutes), begin answering the Questions for Analysis.

8. Remove the paper cylinders when the solvent reaches $\frac{1}{2}$–1 cm from the top of the chromatography paper. Mark the highest point the solvent reached with a pencil and allow the paper to dry upright on a paper towel. When the paper is dry, remove the staples. Keep all of the chromatograms obtained from this experiment and attach them to your laboratory notebook or report.

Experimental Data

Tape or staple your dry chromatograms here or in your lab notebook for easy reference.

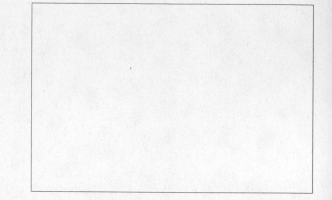

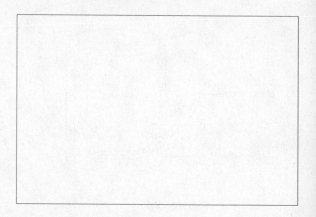

Cleaning Up

Avoid contamination by cleaning up in a way that protects you and your environment. Leave your chromatograms to dry in a place designated by your instructor. Once dry, attach each to your laboratory notebook or report. Dispose of extra solvents down the drain, and rinse and dry the plastic cups. Clean up the area thoroughly, and be sure to recycle usable pieces of paper. Wash your hands thoroughly with soap and water.

Questions for Analysis

Use what you learned in this lab to answer the following questions.

1. What happens to the ink spots as the chromatogram develops? Why?

   Carried by the solvent, they travel up the paper.

2. If one dye moves faster than another, which one dissolves more readily in the moving solvent? Which one dissolves more readily in the water that is attached to the stationary paper?

   The fast ones dissolve more readily in the moving solvent; the slow ones,

   in the stationary phase.

3. Which ink dyes (specify original color) are probably made up of only one compound? How can you tell?

Any that have only one color and one spot or streak.

4. How can you tell which ink dyes are made up of two compounds?

They have two colors and/or two spots or streaks.

5. Which ink dyes are made up of more than two compounds?

Any that have more than two colors and/or two spots or streaks.

6. How can you tell if both brands of pens use the same combination of dyes to make black? Brown? How can you tell?

They are the same only if they have the same pattern of colors and streaks.

7. Compare your two chromatograms of the pens by placing one directly above the other. Which colors of ink use the same compound(s) for both brands?

Any that have the same patterns of colors and spots.

8. Compare your two chromatograms by placing them side by side. By noting the color and position of each spot, tell which pens (color and brand) contain the same (a) light blue dye; (b) red dye; (c) yellow dye.

(Match the colors and positions.)

9. You can identify the ink dyes by their *positions* and *colors* on the chromatogram. Compare the positions and colors of the known FD&C dyes with the positions and colors of the unknown dyes in the pens. Identify as many dyes as you can like this: "The orange brand X pen contains red #40 and yellow #5."

10. Which ink dyes (state the brand name and color) can you *not* identify?

Now It's Your Turn!

1. Design and carry out some experiments to answer one or more of the following questions:

   a. What are the identities of the dyes in other brands of pens? How do they compare to the ones you already tested?

   Make a chromatogram of the brand and compare to the FD&C standards.

   b. What is the effect of the kind of paper you used on your results?

   Coffee filters, unsized (large-pulp) tablet paper, and some paper towels work well.

   c. What is the effect of the solvent you use?

   Try water, rubbing alcohol, and mixtures of these.

2. Use paper chromatography to identify dyes in various consumer food products like soda pop, powdered drinks, instant breakfast drinks, gelatin, candy, and food coloring. You may have to invent ways to extract the dyes from the products.

For example, place a drop of water on a colored candy and use a triangle of

typing paper to extract the dye.

3. In chromatography, the symbol R_f is used to denote the position of a component on a chromatogram relative to the distance the solvent moved. This R_f value is a quantitative reflection of the physical interaction of each component with the mobile phase (the solvent) and stationary phase (the water molecules on the paper).

$$R_f = \frac{\text{distance component moved}}{\text{distance solvent moved}}$$

Measure the distance from the origin to the center of each spot and the distance from the origin to the solvent front. Calculate the R_f values for each spot. The best way to estimate the center of a noncircular spot is to draw the best ellipse around the spot and estimate its center.

4. Water is a very polar solvent that has a particularly strong tendency to form hydrogen bonds. Isopropyl alcohol (rubbing alcohol) is less polar than water and hydrogen bonds less strongly. Because of their differences in polarity and hydrogen bonding, these solvents will interact differently in the chromatographic separation of mixtures.

Generally, if the solvent (mobile phase) is more polar than the stationary phase, the more polar compounds will tend to dissolve more readily and spend more time in the solvent. As a result, they will move farther than the less polar ones. The more polar compounds will appear near the top of the chromatogram, and the less polar compounds will appear near the bottom.

If the solvent (mobile phase) is less polar than the stationary phase, the more polar compounds will spend more time in the stationary phase. As a result, they will move more slowly and appear near the bottom of the chromatogram.

What will happen if you run two chromatograms of pen dyes, one in a very polar solvent like 0.1% aqueous NaCl, and one in a less polar solvent like 70% rubbing alcohol? Try it to see for yourself! Particularly note any differences in the two chromatograms. Explain the differences.

23 Electrolytes

●●

Text Section 16.8

Objectives

- **Observe** and **record** the electrical conductivity of water solutions and solid compounds.
- **Classify** substances as strong electrolytes, weak electrolytes, or nonelectrolytes using conductivity data.
- **Observe** the phenomena of *deliquescence* and *water of hydration*.

Introduction

Electrolytes are compounds that exist as dissolved ions in water solutions. A distinguishing macroscopic property of electrolyte solutions is that they conduct electricity. Molten electrolytes also conduct electricity. The submicroscopic interpretation is that the ions are free to move about in the liquid, and these charged particles carry the electrical current.

Purpose

In this experiment you will investigate water solutions of chemicals by testing them for conductivity. You will then evaporate the water and test them again. You will interpret your results in terms of the submicroscopic behavior of atoms and molecules. Finally, you will test various solutions to determine their relative tendencies to conduct electricity, and again interpret your results in terms of atoms and molecules. You will classify solutions as *strong electrolytes,* those that readily conduct electricity; *weak electrolytes,* those that conduct electricity only weakly; and *nonelectrolytes,* those that do not conduct electricity.

The small-scale conductivity apparatus is shown in Figure 23.1. When the two leads are immersed in a drop of solution or in a solid that conducts electricity, the light emitting diode (LED) will glow.

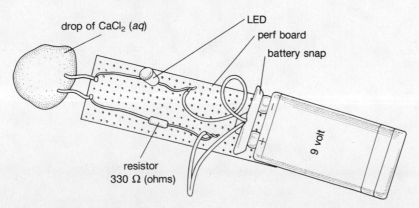

Figure 23.1 *Conductivity apparatus*

Safety

■ Wear your safety glasses.

■ Use full small-scale pipets only for the carefully controlled delivery of liquids.

Materials

Small-scale pipets of the following solutions:

calcium chloride ($CaCl_2$)

sodium hydrogen sulfate ($NaHSO_4$)

sodium hydroxide ($NaOH$)

sodium phosphate (Na_3PO_4)

sodium hydrogen carbonate ($NaHCO_3$)

water (H_2O)

2-propanol ($CH_3CHOHCH_3$)

hydrogen peroxide (H_2O_2)

iron(III) chloride ($FeCl_3$)

copper(II) sulfate ($CuSO_4$)

aluminum chloride ($AlCl_3$)

zinc chloride ($ZnCl_2$)

sodium carbonate (Na_2CO_3)

ethanol (CH_3CH_2OH)

methanol (CH_3OH)

Solids:

sodium chloride ($NaCl$)

potassium iodide (KI)

sodium carbonate (Na_2CO_3)

potassium chloride (KCl)

calcium chloride ($CaCl_2$)

sucrose ($C_{12}H_{22}O_{11}$)

Equipment

small-scale reaction surface

conductivity apparatus

glass slide

hot plate

Experimental Page

Part A. Conductivity of Ionic Compounds

1. Place 1 drop of each indicated chemical solution on a glass slide in the following arrangement, and test each drop for conductivity with the conductivity apparatus. Be sure to *clean and dry* the conductivity leads after each test.

CaCl₂	NaHSO₄	NaOH	Na₃PO₄	NaHCO₃
x	x	x	x	x
x	x	x	x	x
FeCl₃	CuSO₄	AlCl₃	ZnCl₂	Na₂CO₃

The column headers are: $CaCl_2$, $NaHSO_4$, $NaOH$, Na_3PO_4, $NaHCO_3$ (top) and $FeCl_3$, $CuSO_4$, $AlCl_3$, $ZnCl_2$, Na_2CO_3 (bottom).

2. Now evaporate water from the droplets by putting the glass slide on a hot plate. Test for conductivity again. **Caution:** *The glass will be hot. Handle with tongs or a plastic spatula.*

3. Allow the slide to cool and observe any changes over time. Meanwhile, go on to Part B.

Part B. Conductivity of Solids

4. Place 1 grain of each solid (*s*) in the indicated place and test each for conductivity. Then add 1 drop of water to each and test the "wet" mixture for conductivity.

$NaCl(s)$	$KCl(s)$	$KI(s)$	$CaCl_2(s)$	$Na_2CO_3(s)$	$C_{12}H_{22}O_{11}(s)$
salt	"lite" salt	in iodized salt	ice-melter	washing soda	table sugar

Part C. Conductivity of Liquids

5. Place 1 drop of each liquid (*l*) in the indicated place and test each for conductivity. Then add 1 drop of water and test the "wet" mixture for conductivity.

$H_2O(l)$	$CH_3CH_2OH(l)$	$CH_3CHOHCH_3(l)$	$CH_3OH(l)$	$H_2O_2(l)$
water	ethanol grain alcohol	2-propanol rubbing alcohol	methanol wood alcohol	hydrogen peroxide a disinfectant

Place this side of the Experimental Page facedown. Use the other side under your small-scale reaction surface.

Experimental Data

Record your results in Tables 23.1, 23.2, and 23.3 or tables like them in your notebook.

Table 23.1   Conductivity of Ionic Compounds

Compound	Conducts in Solution?	Conducts when Evaporated?	Compound	Conducts in Solution?	Conducts when Evaporated?
$CaCl_2$	Yes	No	$FeCl_3$	Yes	No
$NaHSO_4$	Yes	No	$CuSO_4$	Yes	No
$NaOH$	Yes	No	$AlCl_3$	Yes	No
Na_3PO_4	Yes	No	$ZnCl_2$	Yes	No
$NaHCO_3$	Yes	No	Na_2CO_3	Yes	No

Which of the above solutions seems to be sluggish to evaporate or became wet upon standing in air?

NaOH, NaHSO₄, AlCl₃, ZnCl₂.

Table 23.2   Conductivity of Dry and Wet Solids

Conducts:	$NaCl(s)$	$KCl(s)$	$KI(s)$	$CaCl_2(s)$	$Na_2CO_3(s)$	$C_{12}H_{22}O_{11}(s)$
Dry?	No	No	No	No	No	No
Wet?	Yes	Yes	Yes	Yes	Yes	No

Table 23.3   Conductivity of Dry and Wet Liquids

Conducts:	$H_2O(l)$	$CH_3CH_2OH(l)$	$CH_3CHOHCH_3(l)$	$CH_3OH(l)$	$H_2O_2(l)$
Dry?	No	No	No	No	No
Wet?	No	No	No	No	No

Cleaning Up

Avoid contamination by cleaning up in a way that protects you and your environment. Carefully clean the small-scale reaction surface by absorbing the contents onto a paper towel. Rinse the reaction surface with a damp paper towel and dry it. Dispose of the paper towels in the waste bin. Clean the glass slide by rinsing it with water and drying it with a paper towel. Wash your hands thoroughly with soap and water.

Questions for Analysis

Use what you learned in this lab to answer the following questions.

1. **a.** Do any of the solids in any part of this experiment conduct electricity?
   b. What must be added before a solid will conduct electricity? **c.** Does this work every time? Give an example.

   a. No.   b. Water.   c. No. Table sugar, $C_{12}H_{22}O_{11}$, does not conduct

   when wet.

2. A substance exhibits *deliquescence* when it absorbs enough water from the air to completely dissolve. Which solutions in Part A are deliquescent? (Hint: They seemed sluggish to evaporate or became wet upon standing in air.)

   NaOH, NaHSO₄, AlCl₃, ZnCl₂.

3. Water molecules that are fixed in the lattice of an ionic compound when in the solid form make up the *water of hydration*. Water of hydration will evaporate by strong heating often with a dramatic change in color. Which solids in Part A, Step 2, contain water of hydration?

   $CuSO_4$.

4. You can picture solid sodium chloride as a regular ordered arrangement of atoms called an ionic lattice (Figure 23.2). Solid KCl and KI are similar to NaCl. Draw them and explain the result of the conductivity test in terms of your drawing.

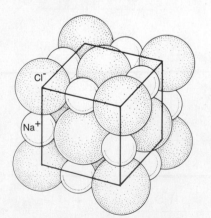

Figure 23.2 *Ionic lattice of NaCl*

The ionic solids do not conduct because their ions are locked in fixed posi

tions in the ionic lattice of the solid.

5. You know that solutions that conduct electricity do so because they contain ions that are free to move about in solution. For example, a solution of aqueous sodium chloride can be pictured as in Figure 23.3. Draw pictures to represent the solutions of KI and KCl. Explain the conductivity test in terms of your pictures.

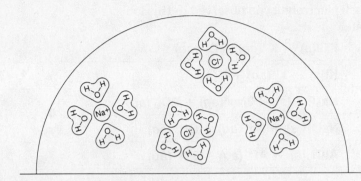

Figure 23.3 *Drop of aqueous NaCl*

The solution process causes the ionic lattice to break apart, freeing the

ions to move and conduct electricity.

6. Which of the liquids in Part C conduct electricity? Which conduct electricity when water is added?

None conduct, with or without water.

7. a. Make a list of electrolytes and another list of nonelectrolytes.

Electrolytes					Nonelectrolytes	
$CaCl_2$	$FeCl_3$	Na_3PO_4	$AlCl_3$	KI	H_2O	CH_3CH_2OH
$NaHSO_4$	$CuSO_4$	$NaHCO_3$	Na_2CO_3		$CH_3CHOHCH_3$	CH_3OH
NaOH	$ZnCl_2$	NaCl	KCl		H_2O_2	$C_{12}H_{22}O_{11}$

b. Pure water is a nonelectrolyte. Predict what will happen if you test tap water for conductivity.

The light will glow dimly. Tap water is a weak electrolyte because it con-

tains ions from dissolved minerals.

8. Study the chemical formulas of the electrolytes and nonelectrolytes. What chemical species do all electrolytes contain? How are the nonelectrolytes different? Draw a conclusion based on your answers to these questions.

Ions. Nonelectrolytes do not contain ions. Aqueous solutions of ionic com-

pounds are electrolytes. Covalent compounds generally are not.

9. You know that when an ionic solid dissolves in water, water molecules attract the ions causing them to come apart or dissociate. The resulting dissolved ions are electrically charged particles that allow the solution to conduct electricity. A chemical equation that represents this phenomenon is written like this:

$$NaCl(s) \rightarrow Na^+(aq) + Cl^-(aq) \rightarrow CaCl_2(s) \rightarrow Ca^{2+}(aq) + 2Cl^-(aq)$$

Write a similar chemical equation for each electrolyte you observed in this lab to show how the ions come apart in water.

$ZnCl_2(s) \rightarrow Zn^{2+}(aq) + 2Cl^-(aq)$　　　　**$KCl(s) \rightarrow K^+(aq) + Cl^-(aq)$**

$CuSO_4(s) \rightarrow Cu^{2+}(aq) + SO_4^{2-}(aq)$　　　　**$KI(s) \rightarrow K^+(aq) + I^-(aq)$**

$FeCl_3(s) \rightarrow Fe^{3+}(aq) + 3Cl^-(aq)$　　　　**$Na_3PO_4(s) \rightarrow 3Na^+(aq) + PO_4^{3-}(aq)$**

$NaHSO_4(s) \rightarrow Na^+(aq) + HSO_4^-(aq)$　　　　**$NaOH(s) \rightarrow Na^+(aq) + OH^-(aq)$**

$NaHCO_3(s) \rightarrow Na^+(aq) + HCO_3^-(aq)$　　　　**$AlCl_3(s) \rightarrow Al^{3+}(aq) + 3Cl^-(aq)$**

$Na_2CO_3(s) \rightarrow 2Na^+(aq) + CO_3^{2-}(aq)$

Now It's Your Turn!

1. Using a soda straw, obtain small samples of these household products: a solid toilet-bowl cleaner, a small piece of seltzer tablet, a baking powder (not soda!). Add a drop of water to each. Test for conductivity. Explain why these substances do not react until water is added.

They all fizz. All solutions conduct. They react only when water breaks the

ionic lattices, thereby freeing the ions.

2. Test these aqueous solutions for conductivity:

1 drop each:	1 drop each:	1 drop each:	1 drop each:
HCl	NaOH	HNO_3	KOH
CH_3COOH	NH_3	H_3PO_4	H_2SO_4

Solutions that cause the LED to glow brightly, with the intensity of the glow not dependent on the distance between the leads, are called *strong electrolytes*. Those that make it glow less brightly, with the glow not dependent on the distance between the leads, are called *weak electrolytes*. Make a list of the strong and weak electrolytes, and propose an explanation for the difference in the brightness of the LED.

Strong: HCl, HNO_3, H_2SO_4, NaOH, KOH. Weak: CH_3COOH, NH_3, H_3PO_4.

Weak electrolytes provide fewer ions in solution and conduct less electric-

ity than strong electrolytes.

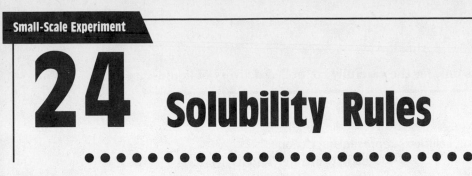

24 Solibility Rules

Text Section 17.1

Objectives

- **Observe** and **record** chemical changes that form precipitates.
- **Derive** general solubility rules from experimental data.
- **Describe** precipitation reactions by writing net ionic equations.

Introduction

In the study of chemical reactions it is helpful to have an idea of which compounds can be expected to form precipitates. A *soluble* compound will dissolve readily in water and, therefore, will *not* form a precipitate. An *insoluble* compound will not dissolve readily in water and, therefore, *will* form a precipitate.

How do we know which ionic compounds form precipitates and which do not? We can make a large number of mixings involving many different cations and anions. By observing the results and correlating them in a logical fashion, we can formulate some general solubility rules based on the formation of precipitates.

These guidelines can be used to describe the behavior of ionic compounds in solution and to determine which compounds form precipitates. For example, if a sodium ion is used as a probe and a large number of observations indicate that no precipitates containing the sodium ion are formed in aqueous solution, one conclusion might be: "All sodium salts are soluble in water. They do not form precipitates." In fact, a large number of such observations have been made, and it is well known that all sodium salts are water-soluble and that there are no common exceptions to this rule.

Purpose

In this lab you will carry out an experiment from whose data you can derive some general solubility guidelines or rules. You will do this by mixing a number of cation solutions and anion solutions two by two. Each anion solution will be used as a probe to determine which cations form precipitates with that anion.

Careful selection of compounds to represent cations and anions is important. For example, the solutions to represent anions are chosen to be compounds of sodium because we know that all sodium compounds are soluble in water, so any precipitate we see will be typical of the anion. Sodium ion, Na^+, will always be a "spectator ion" and will not take part in any chemical reaction.

Keep in mind that you need not perform mixings between solutions having a common ion. For example, it should be obvious that $CuSO_4$ will not react with Na_2SO_4 because both compounds contain the sulfate ion. Thus, with a little planning you can avoid any unnecessary mixings.

Safety

- Wear your safety glasses.
- Use full small-scale pipets only for the carefully controlled delivery of liquids.

Materials

Small-scale pipets containing solutions representing cations:

aluminum chloride ($AlCl_3$)

ammonium chloride (NH_4Cl)

sodium chloride (NaCl)

calcium chloride ($CaCl_2$)

copper(II) sulfate ($CuSO_4$)

iron(III) chloride ($FeCl_3$)

lead(II) nitrate ($Pb(NO_3)_2$)

silver nitrate ($AgNO_3$)

magnesium sulfate ($MgSO_4$)

zinc chloride ($ZnCl_2$)

potassium iodide (KI)

Small-scale pipets containing solutions representing anions:

sodium carbonate (Na_2CO_3)

sodium phosphate (Na_3PO_4)

sodium nitrate ($NaNO_3$)

sodium hydroxide (NaOH)

sodium chloride (NaCl)

sodium sulfate (Na_2SO_4)

Equipment

small-scale reaction surface

empty pipet for stirring

Experimental Page

Mix 1 drop of each. Stir by gently blowing air through a clean, dry pipet.

Anions Cations	Na_2CO_3 (CO_3^{2-})	NaCl (Cl^-)	NaOH (OH^-)	$NaNO_3$ (NO_3^-)	Na_3PO_4 (PO_4^{3-})	Na_2SO_4 (SO_4^{2-})
$AlCl_3$ (Al^{3+})	X	X	X	X	X	X
NH_4Cl (NH_4^+)	X	X	X	X	X	X
$CaCl_2$ (Ca^{2+})	X	X	X	X	X	X
$CuSO_4$ (Cu^{2+})	X	X	X	X	X	X
NaCl (Na^+)	X	X	X	X	X	X
$FeCl_3$ (Fe^{3+})	X	X	X	X	X	X
$Pb(NO_3)_2$ (Pb^{2+})	X	X	X	X	X	X
$MgSO_4$ (Mg^{2+})	X	X	X	X	X	X
KI (K^+)	X	X	X	X	X	X
$AgNO_3$ (Ag^+)	X	X	X	X	X	X
$ZnCl_2$ (Zn^{2+})	X	X	X	X	X	X

Place this side of the Experimental Page facedown. Use the other side under your small-scale reaction surface.

Experimental Data

Record your results in Table 24.1 or a table like it in your notebook.

Table 24.1   Anion–Cation Mixings

Cations	Na_2CO_3 (CO_3^{2-})	NaCl (Cl^-)	NaOH (OH^-)	$NaNO_3$ (NO_3^-)	Na_3PO_4 (PO_4^{3-})	Na_2SO_4 (SO_4^{2-})
$AlCl_3$ (Al^{3+})	white ppt	NVR	white ppt	NVR	white ppt	NVR
NH_4Cl (NH_4^+)	NVR	NVR	NVR	NVR	NVR	NVR
$CaCl_2$ (Ca^{2+})	white ppt	NVR	white ppt	NVR	white ppt	NVR
$CuSO_4$ (Cu^{2+})	blue ppt	NVR	blue ppt	NVR	blue ppt	NVR
NaCl (Na^+)	NVR	NVR	NVR	NVR	NVR	NVR
$FeCl_3$ (Fe^{3+})	orange ppt	NVR	orange ppt	NVR	orange ppt	NVR
$Pb(NO_3)_2$ (Pb^{2+})	white ppt	white ppt	white ppt	NVR	white ppt	white ppt
$MgSO_4$ (Mg^{2+})	white ppt	NVR	white ppt	NVR	white ppt	NVR
KI (K^+)	NVR	NVR	NVR	NVR	NVR	NVR
$AgNO_3$ (Ag^+)	tan ppt	white ppt	brown ppt	NVR	tan ppt	NVR
$ZnCl_2$ (Zn^{2+})	white ppt	NVR	white ppt	NVR	white ppt	NVR

Cleaning Up

Avoid contamination by cleaning up in a way that protects you and your environment. Carefully clean the small-scale reaction surface by absorbing the contents onto a paper towel. Rinse the reaction surface with a damp paper towel and dry it. Dispose of the paper towels in the waste bin. Wash your hands thoroughly with soap and water.

Questions for Analysis

Use what you learned in this lab to answer the following questions.

1. Examine your data for each column of anions. Which anions generally form precipitates? What are the exceptions? Which anions generally do not form precipitates? What are the exceptions?

   Carbonate, hydroxide, and phosphate generally form precipitates, except

   with sodium, potassium, and ammonium. Chloride, nitrate, and sulfate gen-

   erally do not form precipitates, except AgCl(s), PbCl$_2$(s), and PbSO$_4$(s).

2. Examine your data for each row of cations. Which cations generally do not form precipitates?

   Potassium ion, K$^+$, sodium ion, Na$^+$, and ammonium ion, NH$_4^+$.

3. You have seen that precipitation reactions can be written as double-replacement reactions in which the ions of the reactants switch partners to form products. For example, aluminum chloride reacts with sodium hydroxide to form a precipitate of aluminum hydroxide and sodium chloride:

   $$AlCl_3 + 3NaOH \rightarrow Al(OH)_3(s) + 3NaCl$$

   Write and balance complete chemical equations for the other precipitation reactions you observed for aluminum chloride and those you observed for copper sulfate.

   2AlCl$_3$ + 3Na$_2$CO$_3$ $\rightarrow$ Al$_2$(CO$_3$)$_3$(s) + 6NaCl*

   AlCl$_3$ + Na$_3$PO$_4$ $\rightarrow$ AlPO$_4$(s) + 3NaCl

   CuSO$_4$ + 2NaOH $\rightarrow$ Cu(OH)$_2$(s) + Na$_2$SO$_4$

   CuSO$_4$ + Na$_2$CO$_3$ $\rightarrow$ CuCO$_3$(s) + Na$_2$SO$_4$

   3CuSO$_4$ + 2Na$_3$PO$_4$ $\rightarrow$ Cu$_3$(PO$_4$)$_2$(s) + 3Na$_2$SO$_4$

*Teacher's Note: Because of the acidity of Al^{3+} and Fe^{3+}, the carbonates of these cations do not exist. Hydroxides are produced instead.

4. You have seen that ionic compounds are electrolytes in water solution. The reason is that their ionic lattices break apart in water, and the freed ions carry the electric current. For example, AlCl$_3$ exists in water solution as Al^{3+} and Cl$^-$ ions. Similarly, sodium hydroxide exists in water as Na$^+$ and OH$^-$ ions. Therefore, when aqueous aluminum chloride and aqueous sodium hydroxide react, the reactants are really these ions: Al^{3+}, Cl$^-$, Na$^+$, and OH$^-$. The sodium chloride product also exists as ions because it does not precipitate. The ionic equation for the reaction between aluminum chloride and sodium hydroxide is written like this:

   $$Al^{3+} + 3Cl^- + 3Na^+ + 3OH^- \rightarrow Al(OH)_3(s) + 3Na^+ + 3Cl^-$$

   The net ionic equation is obtained by eliminating the ions common to both sides of the equation:

   $$Al^{3+} + 3OH^- \rightarrow Al(OH)_3(s)$$

Write net ionic equations to describe all the reactions you observed that formed precipitates. You may begin by identifying the precipitate and working backwards. The net ionic equations for the three precipitation reactions involving the aluminum ion are written like this:

$$2Al^{3+} + 3CO_3^{2-} \rightarrow Al_2(CO_3)_3(s) \text{ (white)}*$$

$$Al^{3+} + 3OH^- \rightarrow Al(OH)_3(s) \text{ (white)}$$

$$Al^{3+} + PO_4^{3-} \rightarrow AlPO_4(s) \text{ (white)}$$

$Ca^{2+} + CO_3^{2-} \rightarrow CaCO_3(s)$ (white)	$Pb^{2+} + 2Cl^- \rightarrow PbCl_2(s)$
$Ca^{2+} + 2OH^- \rightarrow Ca(OH)_2(s)$ (white)	$Pb^{2+} + SO_4^{2-} \rightarrow PbSO_4(s)$
$3Ca^{2+} + 2PO_4^{3-} \rightarrow Ca_3(PO_4)_2(s)$ (white)	$Mg^{2+} + CO_3^{2-} \rightarrow MgCO_3(s)$
$Cu^{2+} + CO_3^{2-} \rightarrow CuCO_3(s)$	$Mg^{2+} + 2OH^- \rightarrow Mg(OH)_2(s)$
$Cu^{2+} + 2OH^- \rightarrow Cu(OH)_2(s)$	$3Mg^{2+} + 2PO_4^{3-} \rightarrow Mg_3(PO_4)_2(s)$
$3Cu^{2+} + 2PO_4^{3-} \rightarrow Cu_3(PO_4)_2(s)$	$2Ag^+ + CO_3^{2-} \rightarrow Ag_2CO_3(s)$
$2Fe^{3+} + 3CO_3^{2-} \rightarrow Fe_2(CO_3)_3(s)*$	$Ag^+ + OH^- \rightarrow AgOH(s)**$
$Fe^{3+} + 3OH^- \rightarrow Fe(OH)_3(s)$	$3Ag^+ + PO_4^{3-} \rightarrow Ag_3PO_4(s)$
$Fe^{3+} + PO_4^{3-} \rightarrow FePO_4(s)$	$Ag^+ + Cl^- \rightarrow AgCl(s)$
$Pb^{2+} + CO_3^{2-} \rightarrow PbCO_3(s)$	$Zn^{2+} + CO_3^{2-} \rightarrow ZnCO_3(s)$
$Pb^{2+} + 2OH^- \rightarrow Pb(OH)_2(s)$	$Zn^{2+} + 2OH^- \rightarrow Zn(OH)_2(s)$
$3Pb^{2+} + 2PO_4^{3-} \rightarrow Pb_3(PO_4)_2(s)$	$3Zn^{2+} + 2PO_4^{3-} \rightarrow Zn_3(PO_4)_2(s)$

*Teacher's Note: Because of the acidity of Al^{3+} and Fe^{3+}, the carbonates of these cations do not exist. Hydroxides are produced instead.
** Teacher's Note: AgOH(s) does not exist. The reaction is $2Ag^+ + 2OH^- \rightarrow Ag_2O(s) + H_2O$.

Now It's Your Turn!

1. Repeat the reaction between silver nitrate, $AgNO_3$, and sodium hydroxide, NaOH. This mixture produces water, sodium nitrate, and silver oxide rather than silver hydroxide. Write and balance a chemical equation to describe this reaction. What is the distinctive color of silver oxide?

   $2AgNO_3 + 2NaOH \rightarrow Ag_2O(s) + H_2O + 2NaNO_3$. Dark brown.

2. Repeat the reaction between calcium chloride, $CaCl_2$, and sodium sulfate, Na_2SO_4. Write and balance a chemical equation to describe this reaction. What is distinctive about this reaction?

   $CaCl_2 + Na_2SO_4 \rightarrow CaSO_4(s) + 2NaCl$. The precipitate forms slowly.

3. Repeat the reaction between aluminum chloride, $AlCl_3$, and sodium hydroxide, NaOH. Write and balance a chemical equation to describe this reaction. Now add several more drops of NaOH. What is distinctive about this reaction?

   $AlCl_3 + 3NaOH \rightarrow Al(OH)_3(s) + 3NaCl$. The precipitate dissolves in excess

   NaOH.

4. Repeat the reaction between zinc chloride, $ZnCl_2$, and sodium hydroxide, NaOH. Write and balance a chemical equation to describe this reaction. Now add several more drops of NaOH. What is distinctive about this reaction?

$ZnCl_2$ + 2NaOH → $Zn(OH)_2$(s) + 2NaCl. The precipitate dissolves in excess

NaOH.

5. Repeat the reaction between lead(II) nitrate, $Pb(NO_3)_2$, and sodium hydroxide, NaOH. Write and balance a chemical equation to describe this reaction. Now add several more drops of NaOH. What is distinctive about this reaction?

$Pb(NO_3)_2$ + 2NaOH → $Pb(OH)_2$(s) + 2NaNO$_3$. The precipitate dissolves in

excess NaOH.

25 Factors Affecting the Rate of a Chemical Reaction

Text Section 18.2

Objectives

- **Define** rate of reaction in terms of bubble formation.
- **Observe** and **record** the effect of temperature, concentration, and surface area on rate of reaction.

Introduction

You know that energy is required to cook food. The energy may come from boiling water or from the heating elements of a microwave or a conventional oven. Whatever the case, the warmer the temperature, the faster food cooks. On the other hand, in order to preserve food, it's common to place it in a refrigerator or a freezer. The cool temperature in the refrigerator helps to retard spoiling. The warmer the temperature, the faster food spoils. Temperature has an effect on the rate at which food cooks and also on the rate at which it spoils. When food is cooked or when it spoils, many chemical reactions take place. Thus temperature has an effect on how fast chemical reactions take place. But temperature is just one factor that affects the speed at which chemical reactions occur.

If you've ever started a camp fire, you know that small wood shavings are more easily lit than large logs. Given equal volumes of wood in the forms of shavings and a single log, the wood shavings have more exposed surface area than does the log. The wood in the form of shavings makes more surfaces available for ignition. The burning of wood involves several chemical reactions. Increased surface area has an effect on how fast a given chemical reaction occurs.

Fire is a rapid reaction of a fuel with oxygen that gives off a lot of heat. The more oxygen there is available to the reaction, the faster the reaction will go. That is, the greater the concentration of oxygen, the faster the reaction will go. A camp fire burns at a certain rate in air where the concentration of oxygen is only about 20% by volume. If that concentration is cut down by the smothering effect of a fire extinguisher, the fire dies down or goes out; the reaction slows or stops. Thus concentration affects reaction rate.

Purpose

In this lab you will explore these and other factors that affect the rates of chemical reactions. You will examine reactions of hydrochloric acid with magnesium metal, with solid calcium carbonate, and with aqueous sodium hydrogen carbonate. Careful observations will enable you to derive a working definition of *rate of reaction* in terms of the products evolved. You will then examine how temperature, surface area, and concentration affect rate of reaction.

Safety

- Wear your safety glasses.
- Use full small-scale pipets only for the carefully controlled delivery of liquids.

Materials

Small-scale pipets of the following solutions:
hydrochloric acid (HCl)
sodium hydrogen carbonate ($NaHCO_3$)
Solids: magnesium (Mg)
calcium carbonate ($CaCO_3$)

Equipment

small-scale reaction surface
ice
hot water
two plastic cups

Experimental Page

1. What is rate of reaction? Make the following mixings and record your results in Table 25.1.

	1 piece Mg	1 piece CaCO$_3$	1 drop NaHCO$_3$
6 drops HCl			

2. What is the effect of temperature on rate of reaction? Cool one HCl pipet in ice water; warm another in hot water from the tap; and mix the following, one pair at a time. Record your results in Table 25.2.

	1 piece Mg	1 piece CaCO$_3$	1 drop NaHCO$_3$
6 drops cold HCl			
6 drops warm HCl			

3. What is the effect of surface area of Mg or CaCO$_3$ on rate of reaction? Choose two equal-size pieces of Mg, and break or cut one. Repeat for CaCO$_3$. Make the following mixings and record your results in Table 25.3.

	1 piece Mg	Cut or crushed Mg*	1 piece CaCO$_3$	Crushed CaCO$_3$
6 drops HCl				

*Teacher's Note: Cut Mg ribbon or turnings into fine pieces with scissors.

4. What is the effect of concentration of HCl on rate of reaction? Make the following mixings and record your results in Table 25.4.

	1 piece Mg	1 piece CaCO$_3$	1 drop NaHCO$_3$
10 drops HCl			
5 drops HCl + 5 drops HOH			
1 drop HCl + 9 drops HOH			

Place this side of the Experimental Page facedown. Use the other side under your small-scale reaction surface.

Name _____ _____ Class _____ Date _____

Experimental Data

Record your results in Tables 25.1, 25.2, 25.3, and 25.4 or tables like them in your notebook.

Table 25.1 Exploring Rate of Reaction

	1 piece Mg	1 piece CaCO$_3$	1 drop NaHCO$_3$
6 drops HCl	bubbles	bubbles All bubbles start off fast and taper off.	bubbles

Table 25.2 Effect of Temperature

	1 piece Mg	1 piece CaCO$_3$	1 drop NaHCO$_3$
6 drops cold HCl	slow bubbles	slow bubbles	slow bubbles
6 drops warm HCl	fast bubbles	fast bubbles	fast bubbles

Table 25.3 Effect of Surface Area

	1 piece Mg	Cut or crushed Mg	1 piece CaCO$_3$	Crushed CaCO$_3$
6 drops HCl	bubbles	more bubbles	bubbles	more bubbles

Table 25.4 Effect of Concentration

	1 piece Mg	1 piece CaCO$_3$	1 drop NaHCO$_3$
10 drops HCl	fast bubbles	fast bubbles	fast bubbles
5 drops HCl + 5 drops H$_2$O	slower	slower	slower
1 drop HCl + 9 drops H$_2$O	very slow	very slow	very slow

Cleaning Up

Avoid contamination by cleaning up in a way that protects you and your environment. Carefully isolate any unreacted solids and place them in the proper recycling container. Clean the small-scale reaction surface by absorbing the contents onto a paper towel. Rinse the reaction surface with a damp paper towel and dry it. Dispose of the paper towels in the waste bin. Wash your hands thoroughly with soap and water.

Questions for Analysis

Use what you learned in this lab to answer the following questions.

1. Define rate of reaction in terms of bubble formation. How does rate of reaction change with time?

   Rate of reaction is how fast bubbles appear. It slows down with time.

2. What is the effect of temperature on rate of reaction?

   Higher temperature increases rate.

3. What is the effect of the surface area of Mg or $CaCO_3$ on rate of reaction?

   Increasing the surface area speeds up reactions.

4. What is the effect of concentration of HCl on rate of reaction?

   Higher concentrations increase rate.

5. Magnesium reacts with acid to yield hydrogen gas and a salt. Write the balanced chemical equation for the reaction of hydrochloric acid with magnesium.

   $2HCl + Mg \rightarrow H_2(g) + MgCl_2$

6. Recall that an acid reacts with a carbonate or hydrogen carbonate to yield carbon dioxide gas, water, and a salt. Write the balanced chemical equations for the reactions of hydrochloric acid with calcium carbonate and with sodium hydrogen carbonate.

   $2HCl + CaCO_3 \rightarrow CO_2(g) + H_2O + CaCl_2$

   $HCl + NaHCO_3 \rightarrow CO_2(g) + H_2O + NaCl$

Now It's Your Turn!

1. Carry out the following reactions. What happens in each case? Write chemical equations to describe each reaction.

   a. $Pb(NO_3)_2 + KI \rightarrow$ **Immediate bright yellow ppt.**

   $Pb(NO_3)_2 + 2KI \rightarrow PbI_2(s) + 2KNO_3$

   b. $H_2SO_4 + CaCl_2 \rightarrow$ **Slow-forming white ppt.**

   $H_2SO_4 + CaCl_2 \rightarrow CaSO_4(s) + 2HCl$

26 Le Châtelier's Principle and Chemical Equilibrium

Text Section 18.4

Objectives

- **Observe** and **record** how a chemical system at equilibrium responds to changes in concentration of reactants or products.
- **Describe** shifts in equilibrium in terms of Le Châtelier's principle.

Introduction

If you've ever watched a game of football, you know that it has become very specialized. Coaches design special offenses and defenses for various down and distance situations, as well as for positions of the ball on the field, the score, and the time remaining in the game. For example, offensive and defensive strategies are quite different for a third down and one situation than for a first down and ten. As a result, several offensive and defensive players often run on and off the field after each play. One thing remains constant: there are only eleven players per team on the field for any given play. This is an example of a dynamic equilibrium. A dynamic equilibrium is one in which forward reactions (players running on the field) take place at the same rate as reverse reactions (players running off the field). There is no net change in the number of players on the field.

You learned in Section 18.3 that chemical systems often reach a state of dynamic equilibrium. In a system at chemical equilibrium, the rate of the forward reaction equals the rate of the reverse reaction. By adding or taking away reactants and/or products, we can change the balance of reactants and products. The position of the equilibrium is governed by Le Châtelier's principle.

Le Châtelier's principle says that if a system at equilibrium is stressed, the equilibrium balance will shift in a direction that will relieve the stress. For example, if we add a reactant, the equilibrium will shift toward products (to the right) so that there is a different balance of reactants and products. Similarly, if we add products, it will shift toward reactants (to the left).

Purpose

In this lab you will investigate chemical systems at equilibrium. You will disturb them by adding or subtracting reactants or products and observe how the equilibrium system responds. You will attempt to explain those changes in terms of Le Châtelier's principle.

Safety

- Wear your safety glasses.
- Use full small-scale pipets only for the carefully controlled delivery of liquids.

Materials

Small-scale pipets of the following solutions:

hydrochloric acid (HCl)	sodium carbonate (Na_2CO_3)
lead(II) nitrate ($Pb(NO_3)_2$)	bromthymol blue (BTB)
nitric acid (HNO_3)	silver nitrate ($AgNO_3$)
sodium hydroxide (NaOH)	ammonia (NH_3)
copper(II) sulfate ($CuSO_4$)	sodium phosphate (Na_3PO_4)
potassium iodide (KI)	sodium thiosulfate ($Na_2S_2O_3$)

Equipment

small-scale reaction surface
empty pipet for stirring
plastic cup

Experimental Page

Mix the following. Stir each mixture thoroughly by blowing air through a pipet. The chemical equations describe the changes you observe.

1. Mix 1 drop BTB and 1 drop HCl (H^+). Record your observations in Table 26.1. Now add just enough NaOH to induce another change. Alternately add more HCl and NaOH.

$$HBTB \rightleftharpoons H^+ + BTB^-$$
yellow   blue

2. Mix 1 drop BTB and 1 drop NH_3. Record your observations in Table 26.1. Now add just enough HCl (H^+) to effect a change.

$$NH_3 + HOH \rightleftharpoons NH_4^+ + OH^- \qquad NH_3 + H^+ \rightleftharpoons NH_4^+$$

3. Mix 1 drop NH_3 and 2 drops $CuSO_4$ (Cu^{2+}). Record your observations in Table 26.1. Now add with stirring just enough NH_3 to effect a change. Add HCl with stirring until the light blue precipitate returns. Add more HCl until the precipitate disappears. Repeat all this until you are sure of what you see.

$$Cu^{2+} + 2OH^- \rightleftharpoons Cu(OH)_2(s) \text{ (light blue precipitate)}$$
$$Cu^{2+} + 4NH_3 \rightleftharpoons Cu(NH_3)_4^{2+} \text{ (royal blue solution)}$$
$$H^+ + OH^- \rightleftharpoons HOH$$

4. Mix 1 drop $Pb(NO_3)_2$ (Pb^{2+}) and 1 drop KI (I^-). Record your observations in Table 26.1. Now add, with stirring, enough NaOH to effect a change. Now add HNO_3.

$$Pb^{2+} + 2I^- \rightleftharpoons PbI_2(s) \text{ (bright yellow precipitate)}$$
$$Pb^{2+} + 2OH^- \rightleftharpoons Pb(OH)_2(s) \text{ (milky white precipitate)}$$

5. Mix 1 drop $Pb(NO_3)_2$ and 1 drop NaOH with stirring. Record your observations in Table 26.1. Now add more NaOH, drop by drop with stirring, until a change occurs. Finally add nitric acid, HNO_3 (H^+), drop by drop and slowly with stirring until the first change occurs.

$$Pb^{2+} + 2OH^- \rightleftharpoons Pb(OH)_2(s) \qquad Pb^{2+} + 3OH^- \rightleftharpoons Pb(OH)_3^-$$
$$H^+ + OH^- \rightleftharpoons HOH$$

6. Add 2 drops $AgNO_3$ to a plastic cup. Now add one drop of each of the chemicals in the left column, one at a time. Stir and observe after each addition. When a change occurs, record your observations in Table 26.1. Go on to the next chemical. Near the last addition, you may need to add a few more drops of $AgNO_3$.

Add these chemicals in this order.	Equations that account for changes.
a. 1 drop Na_2CO_3	**a.** $2Ag^+ + CO_3^{2-} \rightleftharpoons Ag_2CO_3(s)$
b. HNO_3	**b.** $CO_3^{2-} + 2H^+ \rightleftharpoons HOH + CO_2(g)$
c. NaOH	**c.** $2Ag^+ + 2OH^- \rightleftharpoons Ag_2O(s) + H_2O$
d. HCl	**d.** $H^+ + OH^- \rightleftharpoons HOH$
	$\quad\;\; Ag^+ + Cl^- \rightleftharpoons AgCl$
e. NH_3	**e.** $Ag^+ + 2NH_3 \rightleftharpoons Ag(NH_3)_2^+$
f. KI	**f.** $Ag^+ + I^- \rightleftharpoons AgI(s)$
g. $Na_2S_2O_3$	**g.** $Ag^+ + S_2O_3^{2-} \rightleftharpoons AgS_2O_3^-$
h. Na_3PO_4	**h.** $3Ag^+ + PO_4^{3-} \rightleftharpoons Ag_3PO_4(s)$

Place this side of the Experimental Page facedown. Use the other side under your small-scale reaction surface.

Experimental Data

Record your results in Table 26.1 or a table like it in your notebook.

Table 26.1 Dynamic Equilibria

1. $BTB + HCl$	**green to yellow**		**5.** $Pb(NO_3)_2 + NaOH$	**milky white ppt.**
+ $NaOH$	**yellow to blue**		More $NaOH$	**ppt. dissolves**
	yellow with acid, blue with base		+ HNO_3	**ppt. reappears and dissolves**
2. $BTB + NH_3$	**green to blue**		**6.** $AgNO_3 + Na2CO_3$	**milky white ppt.**
+ HCl:	**blue to yellow**		+ HNO_3	**ppt. dissolves**
3. $NH_3 + CuSO_4$	**clear light blue to milky light blue**		+ $NaOH$	**muddy brown ppt.**
More NH_3	**turns clear to dark blue**		+ HCl	**grainy white ppt.**
+ HCl	**light blue ppt.**		+ NH_3	**ppt. dissolves**
More HCl	**ppt. disappears**		+ KI	**lime green ppt.**
4. $Pb(NO_3)_2 + KI$	**bright yellow ppt.**		+ $Na_2S_2O_3$	**ppt. dissolves**
+ $NaOH$:	**milky white ppt. replaces yellow ppt.**		+ Na_3PO_4	**milky white ppt.**
+ HNO_3	**yellow ppt. reappears**			

Cleaning Up

Avoid contamination by cleaning up in a way that protects you and your environment. Carefully clean the small-scale reaction surface by absorbing the contents
onto a paper towel. Rinse the reaction surface with a damp paper towel and dry it.
Dispose of the paper towels in the waste bin. Wash your hands thoroughly with
soap and water.

Le Châtelier's Principle and Chemical Equilibrium

Questions for Analysis

Use what you learned in this lab to answer the following questions.

1. Bromthymol blue, BTB, is an acid which has a hydrogen ion, H^+, and for the purposes of this question, you will write it HBTB. HBTB ionizes in water to produce hydrogen ion, H^+, and bromthymol blue ion, BTB^-.

$$HBTB \rightleftharpoons H^+ + BTB^-$$
$$\text{yellow} \qquad\qquad \text{blue}$$

   a. What color appeared when you added HCl to BTB? What color is HBTB? Explain the shift in equilibrium in terms of Le Châtelier's principle.

   Yellow. Yellow. The equilibrium shifts to the left to consume some of the

   added hydrogen ion.

   b. What color appeared when you added NaOH to the mixture? What color is BTB^-? Explain the shift in equilibrium in terms of Le Châtelier's principle.

   Blue. Blue. Hydroxide ion neutralizes hydrogen ion, reducing its concentra-

   tion and causing the reaction to shift to the right to replace the hydrogen

   ion. $H^+ + OH^- \rightleftharpoons HOH$.

2. Ammonia reacts with water to produce hydroxide ion. Ammonia is neutralized by hydrogen ion:

$$NH_3 + HOH \rightleftharpoons NH_4^+ + OH^-$$
$$NH_3 + H^+ \rightleftharpoons NH_4^+$$

   a. What color did BTB change in the presence of ammonia, NH_3? Explain the color change in terms of Le Châtelier's principle. Include an equation in your explanation.

   Blue. Ammonia produces hydroxide ion in solution. This hydroxide ion

   neutralizes hydrogen ion, causing the BTB equilibrium to shift to the right

   to replace it. $HBTB \rightleftharpoons H^+ + BTB^-$.

   b. What happened when HCl was added? Explain in terms of Le Châtelier's principle.

   The solution turned yellow. The hydrogen ion from HCl neutralizes the hy-

   droxide ion, causing the BTB equilibrium to shift to the left.

3. Copper ions react differently in the presence of varying amounts of ammonia, NH_3. The hydroxide produced from a small amount of ammonia produces a precipitate. Excess ammonia produces a highly colored solution:

$$Cu^{2+} + 2OH^- \rightleftharpoons Cu(OH)_2(s) \quad \text{(precipitation equilibrium)}$$

$$Cu^{2+} + 4NH_3 \rightleftharpoons Cu(NH_3)_4^{2+} \text{ (complex ion in solution)}$$

a. What color is the *precipitate* when only a little ammonia is added? What color is the *solution* in the presence of excess ammonia?

Light blue. Dark blue.

b. Explain in terms of Le Châtelier's principle the disappearance of the precipitate when excess ammonia is added.

Excess ammonia consumes copper(II) ion from the left side of the precipitation equilibrium, shifting it to the right and causing the precipitate to dissolve.

c. What is the effect of the HCl? Explain in terms of Le Châtelier's principle.

A lesser amount of HCl causes the complex ion to disappear and the precipitate to form again. More HCl dissolves the precipitate. Hydrogen ion from a little HCl neutralizes ammonia, shifting the complex ion equilibrium to the left and causing the dark blue complex ion to disappear. The available copper(II) ions react with hydroxide to form the precipitate. More HCl neutralizes hydroxide and causes the precipitate to dissolve.

4. Lead(II) ion reacts with iodide ion to produce a bright yellow precipitate, and with hydroxide ion to form a milky white precipitate.

$$Pb^{2+} + 2I^- \rightleftharpoons PbI_2(s) \qquad \text{bright yellow}$$

$$Pb^{2+} + 2OH^- \rightleftharpoons Pb(OH)_2(s) \text{ milky white}$$

a. Why does the yellow precipitate disappear when sodium hydroxide is added? Explain in terms of Le Châtelier's principle.

Hydroxide ion uses up lead(II) ion, a reactant in the yellow precipitation equilibrium. This shifts the lead(II) iodide precipitation equilibrium to the left, causing the yellow precipitate to disappear.

b. Why does the yellow precipitate reappear when nitric acid is added?

Nitric acid neutralizes hydroxide ion in the lead(II) hydroxide precipitation equilibrium, driving the equilibrium to the left. This provides more lead ion for the lead(II) iodide precipitation reaction.

5. Lead(II) ion reacts with varying amounts of hydroxide ions in different ways. A small amount of hydroxide produces a precipitate, and excess hydroxide produces a complex ion:

$$Pb^{2+} + 2OH^- \rightleftharpoons Pb(OH)_2(s)$$

$$Pb^{2+} + 3OH^- \rightleftharpoons Pb(OH)_3^- \text{ (complex ion in solution)}$$

a. Why does the precipitate disappear when excess NaOH is added? Explain in terms of Le Châtelier's principle.

Excess hydroxide ion uses up lead(II) ion, a reactant in the precipitation reaction (the first equation.) This shifts the equilibrium to the left, causing the precipitate to dissolve.

b. Why does the precipitate reappear when a little nitric acid is added?

Hydrogen ion from nitric acid neutralizes excess hydroxide ion, causing the complex ion equilibrium to shift to the left. This provides lead(II) ion for the precipitation reaction, causing it to shift to the right.

c. Why does the precipitate disappear when excess nitric acid is added?

More hydrogen ion neutralizes the rest of the hydroxide ion, causing the precipitation reaction to shift to the left.

6. Explain the observations in Step 6 by writing net ionic equations to describe each reaction of silver ion, Ag^+, you observed.

a. $2Ag^+ + CO_3^{2-} \rightleftharpoons Ag_2CO_3(s)$

b. $CO_3^{2-} + 2H^+ \rightleftharpoons H_2O + CO_2(g)$

c. $2Ag^+ + 2OH^- \rightleftharpoons Ag_2O(s) + H_2O$

d. $H^+ + OH^- \rightleftharpoons HOH$ and $Ag^+ + Cl^- \rightleftharpoons AgCl$

e. $Ag^+ + 2NH_3 \rightleftharpoons Ag(NH_3)_2^+$

f. $Ag^+ + I^- \rightleftharpoons AgI(s)$

g. $Ag^+ + S_2O_3^{2-} \rightleftharpoons AgS_2O_3^-$

h. $3Ag^+ + PO_4^{3-} \rightleftharpoons Ag_3PO_4(s)$

7. Explain why BTB is green in neutral water solution. In terms of Le Châtelier's principle, why does it turn yellow when acid is added, and blue when base is added?

It's green because there is a roughly equal amount of both HBTB (yellow) and BTB$^-$ (blue). Hydrogen ion shifts the equilibrium to the left, resulting in more yellow and less blue. Hydroxide ion shifts the equilibrium toward the right, resulting in more blue and less yellow.

Now It's Your Turn!

1. Repeat Step 1 with other indicators like phenolphthalein, HPhen; bromphenyl blue, HBPB; methyl red, HMR; alizarine yellow R, HAYR; and thymol blue, HTB. Explain in terms of Le Châtelier's principle what happens with each when HCl and NaOH are added. Write net ionic equations to describe their reactions in water.

Added HCl drives the equilibrium to the left, with NaOH to the right.

HPhen $\rightleftharpoons$ H$^+$ + Phen$^-$	**HAYR $\rightleftharpoons$ H$^+$ + AYR$^-$**
colorless pink	**yellow red**
HBPB $\rightleftharpoons$ H$^+$ + BPB$^-$	**HTB $\rightleftharpoons$ H$^+$ + TB$^-$**
yellow blue	**pink yellow**
HMR $\rightleftharpoons$ H$^+$ + MR$^-$	
red yellow	

2. Repeat the precipitation reaction of lead nitrate with potassium iodide, as in Step 4. Can you alternately add NaOH and HNO$_3$ to change the precipitates?
Yes. NaOH produces a milky white precipitate, and HNO$_3$ produces a yellow

precipitate.

3. Repeat the precipitation reaction of lead nitrate with sodium hydroxide, as in Step 5. Name two ways you can make the precipitate disappear. Prove your answer by carrying out the experiments. Explain.
Add HNO$_3$. Add NaOH.

4. Perform the following experiment and explain your results in terms of Le Châtelier's principle.

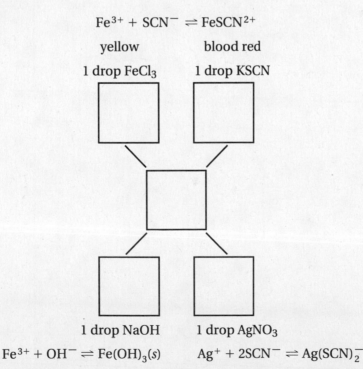

$$Fe^{3+} + SCN^- \rightleftharpoons FeSCN^{2+}$$

yellow   blood red

1 drop FeCl$_3$ 1 drop KSCN

1 drop NaOH   1 drop AgNO$_3$

$Fe^{3+} + OH^- \rightleftharpoons Fe(OH)_3(s)$ $Ag^+ + 2SCN^- \rightleftharpoons Ag(SCN)_2^-$

a. Mix 1 drop $FeCl_3$ with 1 drop KSCN. What happened? Write an equation to explain.

A dark red solution formed. $Fe^{3+} + SCN^- \rightleftharpoons FeSCN^{2+}$

b. Add 10 drops water, separate into 4 parts with a soda straw, and add the indicated solutions. Tell what happens in each case. Explain in terms of the respective equilibria.

c. Upon the addition of $FeCl_3$, the solution also turned darker red, pushing the following equilibrium right, $Fe^{3+} + SCN^- \rightleftharpoons FeSCN^{2+}$.

d. Upon the addition of KSCN, the solution also turned darker red, pushing the following equilibrium right, $Fe^{3+} + SCN^- \rightleftharpoons FeSCN^{2+}$.

e. Upon the addition of NaOH, an orange precipitate was formed, pushing the following equilibrium right, $Fe^{3+} + OH^- \rightleftharpoons Fe(OH)_3(s)$.

f. Upon the addition of $AgNO_3$, the solution turned clear, pushing the following equilibrium right, $Ag^+ + 2SCN^- \rightleftharpoons Ag(SCN)_2^-$.

27 Energy Change and Solution Formation

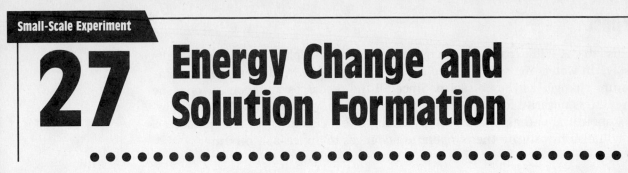

Text Section 18.7

Objectives

- **Measure** and **record** energy changes in the solution process.
- **Describe** and **explain** energy changes in the solution process in terms of changes in entropy and enthalpy.
- **Observe** the change in freezing point upon addition of solute.

Introduction

The two driving forces that favor spontaneous reactions are changes in enthalpy (heat energy of the system) and entropy (randomness or disorder of the system). Chemical and physical changes tend to be spontaneous if there is a decrease in enthalpy, as in exothermic reactions, or an increase in entropy. Often these driving forces oppose one another, and whether a chemical or physical change is spontaneous or not depends on the temperature. Ice, for example, melts spontaneously at temperatures at or above 0°C. Water freezes spontaneously at temperatures at or below 0°C.

The process of melting ice involves absorbing heat, so an endothermic change occurs when there is an increase in enthalpy. The entropy also increases when ice is melted, because liquid water is more random than solid water. The increase in entropy drives this process at temperatures above 0°C. When water freezes, the entropy decreases but the exothermic freezing process drives the reaction at temperatures below 0°C. At 0°C there is a balance between the drive for increasing entropy and the drive for decreasing enthalpy. This balance constitutes a state of equilibrium: both processes occur at the same rate.

This concept can be summarized by the following mathematical expression:

$$\Delta G = \Delta H - T\Delta S$$

ΔG is the change in free energy of the system (see Section 18.11). ΔH is the change in enthalpy of the system, ΔS is the change in entropy of the system, and T is the absolute temperature. Any chemical or physical change is spontaneous when ΔG is negative, and the change in the opposite direction is spontaneous when ΔG is positive. When $\Delta G = 0$, the system is at equilibrium. Consider the case of ice melting:

$$H_2O(s) + \text{heat} \rightarrow H_2O(l)$$

The above process is endothermic, so the sign of ΔH is positive. The liquid phase is more random than the solid phase, so ΔS is positive. In order for the change to be spontaneous, the temperature must be large enough to make the $T\Delta S$ term sufficiently negative to overcome the positive ΔH. At high temperatures (above 0°C) the forward reaction is spontaneous and ice melts. At low temperatures (below 0°C) the reverse reaction is spontaneous and ice freezes.

Purpose

In this lab you will explore the energy changes that take place when various salts dissolve in water. You will dissolve several salts in water and measure the temperature changes as they dissolve. Since all the processes are spontaneous, the sign of ΔG is negative for each. Based on your results, you will draw some conclusions about the enthalpy and entropy changes associated with these processes. You will also investigate the temperature changes in an ice-salt mixture.

Safety

- Wear your safety glasses.
- Use only small quantities of materials for safety and cost efficiency.

Materials

Solids:
rock salt, sodium chloride (NaCl)   ammonium chloride (NH_4Cl)
calcium chloride ($CaCl_2$)   crushed ice (H_2O)

Equipment

small-scale reaction surface
plastic spoon
four 1-ounce plastic cups
alcohol thermometer

Experimental Page

Arrange four plastic cups according to the diagram. Do each experiment one at a time in the following way:

1. Put two level spoonfuls of water in the cup. (Use crushed ice in **d**.)
2. Record the temperature of the water.
3. Add one level spoonful of the indicated solid chemical.
4. Stir gently and record the highest or lowest temperature reached in Table 27.1.

a. NaCl(*s*)

Place one-ounce
plastic cup
here.

b. NH₄Cl(*s*)

Place one-ounce
plastic cup
here.

c. CaCl₂(*s*)

Place one-ounce
plastic cup
here.

d. NaCl(*s*)

Place one-ounce
plastic cup
here.

Place this side of the Experimental Page facedown. Use the other side under your small-scale reaction surface.

Experimental Data

Record your results in Table 27.1 or a table like it in your notebook.

Table 27.1   Temperature Change with Solution Formation

Experimental Mixture	Initial Temperature	Final Temperature	$\Delta T = T_f - T_i$
a. NaCl + $H_2O(l)$	21°C	21°C	0°C
b. NH_4Cl + $H_2O(l)$	21°C	5°C	−16°C
c. $CaCl_2$ + $H_2O(l)$	21°C	53°C	+32°C
d. NaCl + $H_2O(s)$	0°C	−15°C	−15°C

Calculate ΔT for each mixture. Record your results in Table 27.1 above.

ΔT = Change from Initial Temperature to Final Temperature = $T_{final} - T_{initial}$

Cleaning Up

Avoid contamination by cleaning up in a way that protects you and your environment. Carefully clean the plastic cups by pouring their contents down the drain and rinsing them with plenty of water. Rinse the thermometer, and dry everything with a paper towel. Dispose of the paper towels in the waste bin. Wash your hands thoroughly with soap and water.

Questions for Analysis

Use your Experimental Data and what you learned in this lab to answer the following questions.

1. Which mixture(s) did not change much in temperature?

   a
   _____

2. Which mixture(s) cooled off?

   b and d
   _____

3. Which mixture(s) warmed up?

   c
   _____

4. When sodium chloride dissolves in water, the ions "dissociate" or come apart in solution:

$$NaCl(s) \rightarrow Na^+(aq) + Cl^-(aq)$$

Write ionic equations like the one above to show how NH_4Cl and $CaCl_2$ dissociate as they dissolve in water.

$NH_4Cl(s) \rightarrow NH_4^+(aq) + Cl^-(aq)$.
_____

$CaCl_2(s) \rightarrow Ca^{2+}(aq) + 2Cl^-(aq)$.
_____

Energy Change and Solution Formation

5. Is the dissolving of ammonium chloride an exothermic or endothermic process? Explain. Rewrite the ionic equation showing heat as a reactant or product.

Endothermic. The temperature drops; heat is absorbed by the system.

Heat + $NH_4Cl(s) \rightarrow NH_4^+(aq) + Cl^-(aq)$.

6. Is the dissolving of ammonium chloride a spontaneous process? Does it occur with an increase or decrease in entropy? What is the driving force here?

Yes. Entropy increases, which drives the endothermic process.

7. Is the dissolving of calcium chloride an exothermic or endothermic process? Explain. Rewrite the ionic equation showing heat as a reactant or product.

Exothermic. The temperature rises; heat is released by the system.

$CaCl_2(s) \rightarrow Ca^{2+}(aq) + 2Cl^-(aq)$ + Heat.

8. Is the dissolving of calcium chloride a spontaneous process? Does it occur with an increase or decrease in entropy? What is the driving force here?

Yes. Entropy increases. Both increasing entropy and decreasing enthalpy

drive the process.

9. Is the dissolving of sodium chloride an exothermic or endothermic process? Explain. What is the driving force?

Neither. The temperature does not change appreciably. Heat is neither

absorbed nor released by the system. Increasing entropy drives the

solution process.

10. What results do you get when you mix sodium chloride with liquid water and with solid water (ice)?

With liquid water there is no appreciable temperature change, but with

solid water the temperature drops dramatically.

11. The principle behind an ice cream freezer is that when salt is added to the ice, the melting ice absorbs heat from the ice cream, and the ice cream freezes. What drives the spontaneous melting of ice when it is mixed with salt? Explain.

The salt dissolves in the liquid water with an increase in entropy of the

system.

Now It's Your Turn!

1. What is the effect on temperature of dissolving other salts in water? Try potassium chloride, KCl; sodium hydrogen carbonate, $NaHCO_3$; sodium carbonate, Na_2CO_3; and sodium phosphate, Na_3PO_4.

2. What is the effect on temperature of mixing other salts with crushed ice?

28 A Small-Scale Colorimetric pH Meter

Text Section 19.4

Objectives

- **Construct** and **calibrate** a colorimetric pH meter.
- **Measure** and **record** the pH of various household solutions using the colorimetric pH meter.
- **Calculate** pOH from pH and $[H^+]$ and $[OH^-]$ from pH and pOH.

Introduction

pH is a way of expressing how acidic or how basic a solution is. The more acidic a solution is, the lower its pH. The less acidic a solution is, the higher its pH. A pH of 7 represents a neutral solution. A pH lower than 7 is acidic and a pH higher than 7 is basic.

pH is used to express the molar concentration of the acid content of a solution. The relationship between pH and the molar concentration of H^+ or $[H^+]$ is shown below.

pH	$[H^+]$	Solution Acidity/Basicity
14*	10^{-14}	very basic
13	10^{-13}	
12	10^{-12}	
11	10^{-11}	basic
10	10^{-10}	
9	10^{-9}	
8	10^{-8}	slightly basic
7	10^{-7}	neutral
6	10^{-6}	slightly acidic
5	10^{-5}	
4	10^{-4}	
3	10^{-3}	acidic
2	10^{-2}	
1	10^{-1}	
0*	$10^{-0} = 1$	very acidic

*At these pH's, solutions are not ideal and pH $\neq -\log[H^+]$.

In summary: If pH > 7, the solution is basic.

If pH $= 7$, the solution is neutral.

If pH < 7, the solution is acidic.

A pH meter is an instrument used to measure the pH of a solution rapidly and accurately. Most pH meters consist of a pair of electrodes connected to an electronic metering device. A reference electrode has a constant voltage, while a glass electrode changes voltage depending on the pH of the solution being measured. The pH meter compares the difference in voltage between the two electrodes, and this difference is calibrated to read out as a pH. Because pH meters consist of fragile glass electrodes and sensitive electronic parts, they are usually very expensive and often temperamental.

Purpose

In this lab you will make a very reliable *colorimetric pH meter*. The colorimetric pH meter uses a *universal indicator*, one that changes color with pH. You will mix the universal indicator with a series of 12 standard pH solutions called *buffers*. Each buffer solution has an integer pH between 1 and 12. In the presence of 12 different buffers, the universal indicator will change to 12 distinctly different colors. You can use these colors as standards by comparing other solutions to them. To measure the pH of an unknown solution, for example, you can add the universal indicator to the solution and match the resulting color with the color of one of the buffers. The pH of the matching buffer is the pH of the unknown solution.

Safety

- Wear your safety glasses.
- Use full small-scale pipets only for the carefully controlled delivery of liquids.

Materials

Small-scale pipets of the following solutions:
universal indicator (UI)
buffer solutions (pH 1–12)
Household products: baking soda, vinegar, window cleaner, baking powder, lemon juice, tea, a cola soft drink, laundry detergent, milk, orange juice, etc.

Equipment

small-scale reaction surface
empty pipet for stirring

Experimental Page

Part A. Constructing a pH Meter

1. Add 1 drop of UI to each space.

2. Add 5 drops of the buffer corresponding to each pH. Stir. Each integer pH should now have a unique and distinguishing color. If not, add more buffer.

pH 1	pH 2	pH 3	pH 4
pH 8	pH 7	pH 6	pH 5
pH 9	pH 10	pH 11	pH 12

Part B. Measuring pH

3. Measure the pHs of various household solutions by placing 5 drops of each liquid to be tested in 1 drop of UI. Stir, and match the color to one of the pHs above.

4. Measure the pHs of various household solids by adding 5 drops of water and 1 drop of UI to a few grains of each solid. Stir, and match the color to one of the pHs above.

Place this side of the Experimental Page facedown. Use the other side under your small-scale reaction surface.

Name _____ Class _____ Date _____

Experimental Data

Record your results in Tables 28.1 and 28.2 or tables like them in your notebook.

Table 28.1   Colorimetric pH Meter

pH 1	**bright red**	pH 2	**red**	pH 3	**red orange**	pH 4	**orange**
pH 8	**blue green**	pH 7	**green**	pH 6	**yellow green**	pH 5	**yellow**
pH 9	**blue**	pH 10	**dark blue**	pH 11	**blue violet**	pH 12	**violet**

Table 28.2   pHs of Household Products

Household Product	pH	$pH + pOH = 14$ pOH	$[H^+] = 10^{-pH}$ $[H^+]$	$[OH^-] = 10^{-pOH}$ $[OH^-]$
vinegar	4	10	10^{-4}	10^{-10}
window cleaner	9	5	10^{-9}	10^{-5}
cola	3	11	10^{-3}	10^{-11}
baking soda	10	4	10^{-10}	10^{-4}
washing soda	11	3	10^{-11}	10^{-3}

Calculate the pOH, $[H^+]$, and $[OH^-]$ of each household product you tested, and record your results in Table 28.2.

Cleaning Up

Avoid contamination by cleaning up in a way that protects you and your environment. Carefully clean the small-scale reaction surface by absorbing the contents onto a paper towel. Rinse the reaction surface with a damp paper towel and dry it. Dispose of the paper towels in the waste bin. Wash your hands thoroughly with soap and water.

Questions for Analysis

Use what you learned in this lab to answer the following questions.

1. The relationship between pH and pOH is: pH + pOH = 14. List the pOHs of all the household products you tested.

   Subtract pH from 14. Vinegar = 10, window cleaner = 5, cola = 11, baking soda = 4, washing soda = 3.

2. The relationship between pH and [H$^+$] is: [H$^+$] = 10^{-pH}. List the [H$^+$] of each product you tested.

   Place negative pH as an exponent of 10. Vinegar = 10^{-4}, window cleaner = 10^{-9}, cola = 10^{-3}, baking soda = 10^{-10}, washing soda = 10^{-11}.

3. The relationship between pOH and [OH$^-$] is: [OH$^-$] = 10^{-pOH}. List the [OH$^-$] of each product you tested.

   Place negative pOH as an exponent of 10. Vinegar = 10^{-10}, window cleaner = 10^{-5}, cola = 10^{-11}, baking soda = 10^{-4}, washing soda = 10^{-3}.

4. What limitations does your pH meter have?

   It measures pH only to an integer pH unit. Highly colored substances interfere with the measurement of pH.

Now It's Your Turn!

1. Search for any other naturally colored substances that can serve as universal indicators. Try flower petals, grape and berry juices, etc.

2. Design an experiment to determine colors of common indicator solutions at various pHs.

   Add a drop of indicator to 5 drops of each buffer with pH 1 to 12.

29 pH and Indicators

Text Section 19.4

Objectives

- **Observe** and **record** the colors of acid–base indicators at various pH values.
- **Measure** and **record** the pH values at which indicators change colors, and **estimate** their pK_as.
- **Identify** natural substances that act as acid–base indicators.

Introduction

An acid–base indicator is usually a weak acid with a characteristic vivid color. Upon addition of base, this acid is converted into its conjugate base, which is a different color. When the weak acid and its conjugate base exist in solution in approximately equal concentrations, an intermediate color is evident. For example, you are already familiar with the common acid–base indicator bromthymol blue, or BTB. Bromthymol blue is a weak acid that is yellow; its conjugate base is blue. We have used BTB to distinguish between acids and bases because it changes colors around pH 7. At pH 7, approximately equal concentrations of BTB's conjugate acid and conjugate base exist in solution, resulting in a green mixture (blue and yellow make green). This is illustrated by the following chemical equation:

$$HBTB + H_2O \rightleftharpoons BTB^- + H_3O^+$$
$$\text{yellow} \qquad\qquad \text{blue}$$

The acid ionization constant, K_a, for the above reaction is expressed as a ratio of the ionized form of the acid to the form that is not ionized:

$$K_a = \frac{[BTB^-][H_3O^+]}{[HBTB]}$$

When $[BTB^-] = [HBTB]$, then $K_a = [H_3O^+]$, or $pK_a = pH$. In other words, the pH at which the indicator changes color is approximately equal to the pK_a of the acid.

Purpose

In this experiment you will investigate the color changes of various acid–base indicators as a function of pH. To do this you will set up a colorimetric pH meter using universal indicator, and then set up another pH meter using a single indicator. You can then see the color of the single indicator at each of 12 pH units and determine at what pH it changes color. From this data you can approximate the indicator's pK_a.

pH and Indicators **209**

Safety

- Wear your safety glasses.
- Use full small-scale pipets only for the carefully controlled delivery of liquids.

Materials

Small-scale pipets of the following solutions:

universal indicator (UI)
bromthymol blue (BTB)
bromphenol blue (BPB)
thymol blue (TB)

buffer solutions (pH 1–12)
phenolphthalein (phen)
methyl red (MR)

Equipment

small-scale reaction surface
empty pipet for stirring

Experimental Page

1. Add 1 drop of UI first; then add 5 drops buffer:

2. Add 1 drop of each indicator first; then add 1 drop of buffer:

	BTB	Phen	BPB	MR	TB
pH 1					
pH 2					
pH 3					
pH 4					
pH 5					
pH 6					
pH 7					
pH 8					
pH 9					
pH 10					
pH 11					
pH 12					

Place this side of the Experimental Page facedown. Use the other side under your small-scale reaction surface.

Experimental Data

Record your results in Table 29.1 or a table like it in your notebook.

Table 29.1   Various Indicators at Various pHs

	BTB	Phen	BPB	MR	TB
pH 1 bright red	yellow	colorless	yellow	red	pink
red pH 2	yellow	colorless	yellow	red	pink
pH 3 red orange	yellow	colorless	yellow	red	orange
orange pH 4	yellow	colorless	brown	red	yellow
pH 5 yellow	yellow	colorless	blue	orange	yellow
yellow green pH 6	yellow	colorless	blue	yellow	yellow
pH 7 green	green	colorless	blue	yellow	yellow
blue green pH 8	blue	colorless	blue	yellow	yellow
pH 9 blue	blue	light pink	blue	yellow	brown
dark blue pH 10	blue	pink	blue	yellow	blue
pH 11 blue violet	blue	pink	blue	yellow	blue
violet pH 12	blue	pink	blue	yellow	blue

Cleaning Up

Avoid contamination by cleaning up in a way that protects you and your environment. Carefully clean the small-scale reaction surface by absorbing the contents onto a paper towel. Rinse the reaction surface with a damp paper towel and dry it. Dispose of the paper towels in the waste bin. Wash your hands thoroughly with soap and water.

Questions for Analysis

Use what you learned in this lab to answer the following questions.

1. At what pH range does each indicator change? Make a list of the indicators and the pHs at which they change.

BTB = 7, Phen = 9, BPB = 4, MR = 5, TB = 3 and 9.

2. At what pH are the acid and base forms of each indicator in approximately equal concentrations?

BTB = 7, Phen = 9, BPB = 4, MR = 5, TB = 3 and 9.

3. What is the color of the conjugate acid form of each indicator? The conjugate base form?

BTB = yellow, blue; Phen = colorless, pink; BPB = yellow, blue;

MR = red, yellow; TB = red, yellow and yellow, blue.

4. Estimate the pK_a of each indicator. Calculate each corresponding K_a.

BTB = 7, 10^{-7}; Phen = 9, 10^{-9}; BPB = 4, 10^{-4}; MR = 5, 10^{-5}; TB = 3 and 9,

10^{-3} and 10^{-9}.

5. Which indicator is the best for distinguishing all acids from all bases? Why?

BTB. It changes color at pH 7.

Now It's Your Turn!

1. Collect various other indicators and determine how their colors change as a function of pH. What color is the conjugate acid form of each indicator? The conjugate base form? What are the pK_as of the indicators you test?

Do the same experiment with whatever indicators are on hand.

2. Examine the colors of all the individual indicators at various pHs, and try to determine which indicators are responsible for the color changes of the universal indicator. Can you formulate your own universal indicator? Try it!

Mix indicators of various pK_as, and then add 5 drops of each buffer to this

solution to test its use as a universal indicator.

30 Lewis Acids: Electron Pair Acceptors

• •

Text Section 19.9

Objectives

- **Identify** aqueous solutions of metal ions that act as Lewis acids.
- **Determine** which metal ion solutions are the strongest Lewis acids by measuring their pH values.

Introduction

According to Arrhenius's theory, acids are compounds that ionize in aqueous solution to produce hydrogen ions, while bases ionize to yield hydroxide ions in aqueous solution (Section 18.5). The Brønsted–Lowry theory (Section 18.6) defines an acid as a hydrogen–ion donor and a base as a hydrogen–ion acceptor. Both of these theories require that acids contain hydrogen ions, but there are many examples of acidic compounds that do not contain hydrogen ions.

The Lewis definition of acids includes compounds that do not contain hydrogen ions. A Lewis acid is a substance that accepts a pair of electrons; a Lewis base donates a pair of electrons. Metal ions in aqueous solution often act as Lewis acids. They accept unshared pairs of electrons from water molecules that act as Lewis bases. A Lewis acid may or may not contain hydrogen ions.

Purpose

In this lab you will explore the acidic nature of solutions of metal cations to determine which solutions act as Lewis acids. First you will test solutions of metal ions with bromthymol blue and universal indicator to see what colors they produce. Then you will look for evidence of acidic character by mixing these acids with sodium hydrogen carbonate and looking for bubbles. Finally, you will learn to describe the acidic behavior of aqueous metal ions in terms of chemical equations.

Safety

- Wear your safety glasses.
- Use full small-scale pipets only for the carefully controlled delivery of liquids.

Materials

Small-scale pipets of the following solutions:

bromthymol blue (BTB)

sodium hydrogen carbonate (NaHCO$_3$)

tin(IV) chloride (SnCl$_4$)

copper(II) sulfate (CuSO$_4$)

lead(II) nitrate (Pb(NO$_3$)$_2$)

iron(III) chloride (FeCl$_3$)

aluminum chloride (AlCl$_3$)

universal indicator (UI)

sodium chloride (NaCl)

silver nitrate (AgNO$_3$)

calcium chloride (CaCl$_2$)

zinc chloride (ZnCl$_2$)

potassium chloride (KCl)

Equipment

small-scale reaction surface

empty pipet for stirring

Experimental Page

Put 1 drop of each indicated solution in the spaces provided. Observe the color changes in the two indicator solutions, BTB and UI. Watch each $NaHCO_3$ reaction carefully for signs of bubbles. Record your results in Table 30.1.

		BTB	UI	$NaHCO_3$
a.	$AlCl_3$ (Al^{3+})			**X**
b.	$CuSO_4$ (Cu^{2+})			**X**
c.	$CaCl_2$ (Ca^{2+})			**X**
d.	$ZnCl_2$ (Zn^{2+})			**X**
e.	$Pb(NO_3)_2$ (Pb^{2+})			**X**
f.	KCl (K^+)			**X**
g.	$FeCl_3$ (Fe^{3+})			**X**
h.	$AgNO_3$ (Ag^+)			**X**
i.	$NaCl$ (Na^+)			**X**
j.	$SnCl_4$ (Sn^{4+})			**X**

Place this side of the Experimental Page facedown. Use the other side under your small-scale reaction surface.

Experimental Data

Record your results in Table 30.1 or a table like it in your notebook.

Table 30.1   Lewis Acids

	BTB	UI	NaHCO$_3$
a. AlCl$_3$ (Al^{3+})	yellow	orange	white ppt/bub.
b. CuSO$_4$ (Cu^{2+})	yellow	yellow orange	blue ppt/bub.
c. CaCl$_2$ (Ca^{2+})	green	green	white ppt.
d. ZnCl$_2$ (Zn^{2+})	yellow	yellow green	white ppt.
e. Pb(NO$_3$)$_2$ (Pb^{2+})	yellow	yellow orange	white ppt.
f. KCl (K$^+$)	green	green	NVR
g. FeCl$_3$ (Fe^{3+})	yellow	red	orange ppt/bub.
h. AgNO$_3$ (Ag$^+$)	green	green	white ppt.
i. NaCl (Na$^+$)	green	green	NVR
j. SnCl$_4$ (Sn^{4+})	yellow	red	bubbles

Cleaning Up

Avoid contamination by cleaning up in a way that protects you and your environment. Carefully clean the reaction surface by absorbing the contents onto a paper towel. Rinse it with a damp paper towel and dry it. Dispose of the paper towels in the waste bin. Wash your hands thoroughly with soap and water.

Questions for Analysis

Use what you learned in this lab to answer the following questions.

1. Which aqueous solutions are acids? How do you know?

   Al^{3+}, Fe^{3+}, Cu^{2+}, Sn^{4+}, Zn^{2+}, and Pb^{2+}. They turn BTB yellow.

2. Do any of the acids you listed in Question 1 have a hydrogen ion to donate? How then can any of these compounds be acids?

   No. They are Lewis acids, cations that act as electron pair acceptors.

Lewis Acids: Electron Pair Acceptors

3. Lewis acids are electron pair acceptors. Metal cations can attract a lone pair of electrons of a water molecule and form a coordinate covalent bond (Section 15.4). These metal cations are electron pair acceptors. For example, Al^{3+} forms a coordinate covalent bond with water:

$$Al^{3+} + H_2O \rightarrow Al(H_2O)^{3+}$$

The resulting ion can now donate a hydrogen ion which can undergo all the usual reactions of acids:

$$Al(H_2O)^{3+} \rightarrow Al(OH)^{2+} + H^{+*}$$

Write equations like the one above for all the metal cations Lewis acid you observed.

$Fe3^+ + H_2O \rightarrow Fe(H_2O)^{3+}$ **$Fe(H_2O)^{3+} \rightarrow Fe(OH)^{2+} + H^+$**

$Sn^{4+} + H_2O \rightarrow Sn(H_2O)^{4+}$ **$Sn(H_2O)^{4+} \rightarrow Sn(OH)^{3+} + H^+$**

$Zn^{2+} + H_2O \rightarrow Zn(H_2O)^{2+}$ **$Zn(H_2O)^{2+} \rightarrow Zn(OH)^{+} + H^+$**

$Cu^{2+} + H_2O \rightarrow Cu(H_2O)^{2+}$ **$Cu(H_2O)^{2+} \rightarrow Cu(OH)^{+} + H^+$**

$Pb^{2+} + H_2O \rightarrow Pb(H_2O)^{2+}$ **$Pb(H_2O)^{2+} \rightarrow Pb(OH)^{+} + H^+$**

4. The best Lewis acids are the metal cations that can most strongly attract electron pairs. In general, should highly positive cations make stronger acids than cations with lower positive charges? Explain.

   Yes. The higher the positive charge, the greater the ability to attract electrons.

5. Which cations formed bubbles with $NaHCO_3$? Write a net ionic equation to describe each reaction.

   Al^{3+}, Fe^{3+}, Sn^{4+} and Cu^{2+}. $H^+ + HCO_3^- \rightarrow H_2O + CO_2(g)$.

Now It's Your Turn!

1. Set up your colorimetric pH meter from Small-Scale Experiment 28, and determine the pH of each acidic solution to the nearest pH unit. Compare the pH values of these metal cation Lewis acids to the pH values of other acids.

   All metal cation Lewis acids are weak acids.

2. Which of the cations in the original experiment will most likely form bubbles with $NaHCO_3$? Try some experiments to test your answers! Write a net ionic equation to describe these reactions.

   The 3+ and 4+ ions. $2H^+ + CO_3^- \rightarrow H_2O + CO_2(g)$.

*Teacher's note: Al^{3+} and most other cations that are Lewis acids are commonly surrounded by more than one water molecule. For example, aqueous Al^{3+} is often written $Al(H_2O)_6^{3+}$. For simplicity, only one water molecule is shown in these examples.

31 Strong and Weak Acids and Bases

Text Section 19.10

Objectives

- **Identify** and **distinguish between** strong and weak acids and strong and weak bases.
- **Identify** acids and bases as hydrogen–ion acceptors and hydrogen–ion donors.
- **Identify** conjugate acid–base pairs in acid–base reactions.
- **Describe** acid–base reactions by using hydrogen–ion transfer equations.
- **Explain** the differences between strong and weak acids and bases by using equilibrium principles.

Introduction

You have seen that acids are substances that react with water to produce H_3O^+ ions in solution. Similarly, bases are chemicals that react with water to produce OH^- ions. For example, you have already seen that when an acid like HCl dissolves in water, it reacts by transferring a hydrogen ion to water according to the following equation:

$$HCl + H_2O \rightarrow H_3O^+ + Cl^-$$

To what degree does this reaction proceed? Do all the molecules of HCl react, or do only some of them transfer hydrogen ions while others remain intact?

Purpose

In this lab you will take a new look at acids and bases and classify them according to the Brønsted–Lowry theory. You have already acquired working definitions of acids and bases. Acids turn BTB yellow and produce hydrogen ions in solution. Bases turn BTB blue and produce hydroxide ions in solution. You will use BTB (bromthymol blue) and UI (universal indicator) as probes to classify solutions as acids and bases. You will review how to write net ionic equations to show how each substance transfers a hydrogen ion to or from water. You will learn to identify the acid–base conjugate pairs in hydrogen–ion transfer equations. You will then use the hydrogen carbonate ion, HCO_3^-, to investigate acid–base reactions and group acid solutions according to relative strengths. You will use your data to formulate the concept that acids and bases can be classified as both strong and weak, depending on their behavior.

Safety

▪ Wear your safety glasses.

▪ Use full small-scale pipets only for the carefully controlled delivery of liquids.

Materials

Small-scale pipets of the following solutions:

sodium hydrogen sulfate ($NaHSO_4$)

sodium hydrogen carbonate ($NaHCO_3$)

sodium hydroxide (NaOH)

sodium dihydrogen phosphate (NaH_2PO_4)

sodium monohydrogen phosphate (Na_2HPO_4)

sodium ethanoate (CH_3COONa)

hydrochloric acid (HCl)

bromthymol blue (BTB)

calcium hydroxide ($Ca(OH)_2$)

nitric acid (HNO_3)

ethanoic acid (CH_3COOH)

sodium carbonate (Na_2CO_3)

sodium hydrogen sulfite ($NaHSO_3$)

sodium phosphate (Na_3PO_4)

boric acid (H_3BO_3)

citric acid ($C_6H_8O_7$)

ammonium chloride (NH_4Cl)

ammonia (NH_3)

universal indicator (UI)

sulfuric acid (H_2SO_4)

potassium hydroxide (KOH)

Equipment

small-scale reaction surface

conductivity apparatus

empty pipet for stirring

Experimental Page

Part A. Acids and Indicators

1. Mix 1 drop of each indicated solution. Look carefully for similarities and differences to distinguish from strong and weak acids.

2. Test each acid for conductivity. Be sure to rinse the leads of the conductivity apparatus between tests. Record your results in Table 31.1.

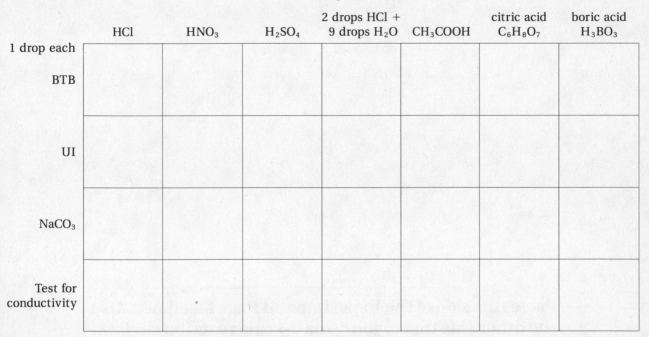

	1 drop of each acid						
1 drop each	HCl	HNO₃	H₂SO₄	2 drops HCl + 9 drops H₂O	CH₃COOH	citric acid C₆H₈O₇	boric acid H₃BO₃
BTB							
UI							
NaCO₃							
Test for conductivity							

Part B. Acids, Bases, and Indicators

3. Mix 1 drop of indicator with 5 drops of each of the indicated solutions. Record your results in Table 31.2.

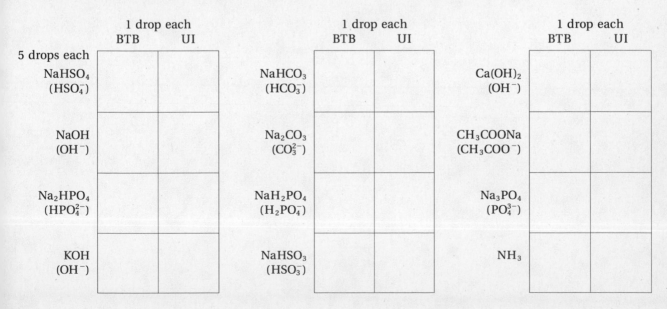

5 drops each	BTB	UI		BTB	UI		BTB	UI
NaHSO₄ (HSO₄⁻)			NaHCO₃ (HCO₃⁻)			Ca(OH)₂ (OH⁻)		
NaOH (OH⁻)			Na₂CO₃ (CO₃²⁻)			CH₃COONa (CH₃COO⁻)		
Na₂HPO₄ (HPO₄²⁻)			NaH₂PO₄ (H₂PO₄⁻)			Na₃PO₄ (PO₄³⁻)		
KOH (OH⁻)			NaHSO₃ (HSO₃⁻)			NH₃		

Place this side of the Experimental Page facedown. Use the other side under your small-scale reaction surface.

Experimental Data

Record your results in Tables 31.1 and 31.2 or tables like them in your notebook.

Table 31.1   Acids and Indicators

	HCl	HNO₃	H₂SO₄	1 drop HCl + 9 drops H₂O	CH₃COOH	C₆H₈O₇	H₃BO₃
BTB	yellow	yellow	yellow	yellow	yellow	yellow	yellow
UI	red	red	red	red	orange	yellow	yellow
Na₂CO₃	bubbles	bubbles	bubbles	slow bubbles	slow bubbles	slow bubbles	slow bubbles
Test for conductivity	bright light	bright light	bright light	dim light	dim light	dim light	dim light

Table 31.2   Acids, Bases, and Indicators

	1 drop each			1 drop each			1 drop each	
	BTB	UI		BTB	UI		BTB	UI
NaHSO₄ (HSO₄⁻)	yellow	red	NaHCO₃ (HCO₃⁻)	blue	blue	Ca(OH)₂ (OH⁻)	blue	violet
NaOH (OH⁻)	blue	violet	Na₂CO₃ (CO₃²⁻)	blue	blue	CH₃COONa (CH₃COO⁻)	blue	blue green
Na₂HPO₄ (HPO₄²⁻)	blue	blue	NaH₂PO₄ (H₂PO₄⁻)	yellow	yellow	Na₃PO₄ (PO₄³⁻)	blue	blue
KOH (OH⁻)	blue	violet	NaHSO₃ (HSO₃⁻)	yellow	orange	NH₃	blue	blue

Cleaning Up

Avoid contamination by cleaning up in a way that protects you and your environment. Carefully clean the small-scale reaction surface by absorbing the contents onto a paper towel, wipe the reaction surface with a damp paper towel, and dry it. Dispose of the paper towels in the waste bin. Wash your hands thoroughly with soap and water.

Questions for Analysis

Use what you learned in this lab to answer the following questions.

1. What does BTB indicate that all solutions in Part A can be classified as?
   Acids.

2. What is the chemical behavior of all the solutions with Na_2CO_3? Is this typical of acids or bases?
   They all form bubbles of $CO_2(g)$. Acids.

3. Suggest a reason that the acids give different colors with universal indicator.
   HCl, HNO_3, and H_2SO_4 are red with UI, thus showing they have lower pHs

   than the other acids. These acids deliver more hydrogen ions to solution

   than do the other acids.

4. Which HCl reaction does the ethanoic acid reaction more closely resemble? Why does the undiluted HCl seem to be a "stronger" acid than ethanoic acid?
   The diluted one. The undiluted HCl has a lower pH and reacts faster than

   ethanoic acid.

5. To account for the different rates of reaction with Na_2CO_3, predict which acid, HCl or ethanoic, probably has the greater amount of hydrogen ions present in solution. Do both acids transfer hydrogen ions to water to the same degree? Which ionizes to the greater degree?
   HCl. No. HCl.

6. Classify each solution in Part B as an acid or a base. Estimate the pH of each solution and classify each as strong or weak. For all the weak acids and bases, write a net ionic equation to describe the hydrogen–ion transfer reaction of each acid or base with water. (Show each acid as a hydrogen–ion donor and each base as a hydrogen–ion acceptor.)
   For example:

   An acid is a *hydrogen–ion donor:* $CH_3COOH + HOH \rightleftharpoons H_3O^+ + CH_3COO^-$

   A base is a *hydrogen–ion acceptor:* $NH_3 + HOH \rightleftharpoons NH_4^+ + OH^-$

Notice that water acts as a base in the first equation and as an acid in the second. Water is said to be *amphoteric* because it can act as an acid or base, depending on the conditions. As always, when writing net ionic equations, you can ignore Na^+ ions because they are spectator ions.

weak acid: $HSO_4^- + H_2O \rightleftharpoons SO_4^{2-} + H_3O^+$

strong base: $Ca(OH)_2$

weak base: $CO_3^{2-} + HOH \rightleftharpoons HCO_3^- + OH^-$

weak base: $HPO_4^{2-} + HOH \rightleftharpoons H_2PO_4^- + OH^-$

weak base: $PO_4^{3-} + HOH \rightleftharpoons HPO_4^{2-} + OH^-$

weak acid: $HSO_3^- + HOH \rightleftharpoons SO_3^{2-} + H_3O^+$

weak base: $HCO_3^- + HOH \rightleftharpoons H_2CO_3 + OH^-$

strong base: $NaOH$

weak base: $CH_3COO^- + HOH \rightleftharpoons CH_3COOH + OH^-$

weak acid: $H_2PO_4^- + HOH \rightleftharpoons HPO_4^{2-} + H_3O^+$

strong base: KOH

weak base: $NH_3 + HOH \rightleftharpoons NH_4^+ + OH^-$

7. Identify each pair of species in your net ionic equations (both reactants and products) as a conjugate acid–base pair. For example:

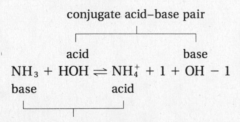

The first reactant and the second product listed above are conjugate acid–

base pairs. The second reactant and the first product are also conjugate

acid–base pairs.

Now It's Your Turn!

1. Investigate the common chemical solutions in this lab for use in a colorimetric pH meter in place of pH buffer standards. Set up the pH meter as in Small-Scale Experiment 28, and match the colors various solutions produce with UI.

2. Design an experiment to use hydrogen carbonate ion, HCO_3^-, as a probe for weak acids. For example, you have seen that carbonates react with acids to produce carbon dioxide and water:

$$CO_3^{2-} + 2H^+ \rightleftharpoons CO_2(g) + H_2O$$

Notice that the stoichiometry of the reaction requires 2 moles of hydrogen ions for every 1 mole of carbonate. If the amount of available hydrogen ion were limited, say, by the presence of a weak acid, the reaction might produce hydrogen carbonate ion rather than carbon dioxide:

$$CO_3^{2-} + H^+ \rightleftharpoons HCO_3^-$$

An additional equivalent of hydrogen ion is needed to carry the reaction to completion:

$$HCO_3^- + H^+ \rightleftharpoons CO_2(g) + H_2O$$

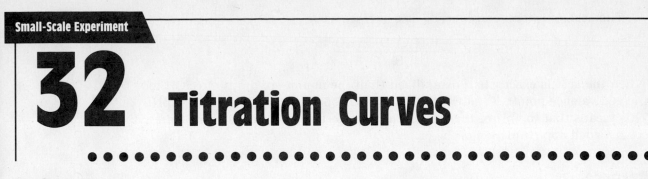

32 Titration Curves

Text Section 20.2

Objectives

- **Observe** and **record** pH changes during various acid–base titrations.
- **Construct** titration curves from experimental data for these titrations.
- **Interpret** titration curves and identify suitable indicators for the titrations.
- **Estimate** the pKs of various weak acids and bases.

Introduction

You have already learned that acid–base indicators are weak acids or bases that change color near their pKs. Because the accuracy of a titration depends in part on how closely the end point coincides with the equivalence point, the indicator used should change color very near the equivalence point. Phenolphthalein changes from colorless to pink in basic solution at about pH 9, yet we used this indicator to detect the end points of acid–base titrations that have equivalence points at exactly pH 7. How can you tell if phenolphthalein is a suitable indicator for the titrations of strong acids with strong bases? You can answer this question by examining the nature of titration curves.

A *titration curve* is a graph showing how the pH changes as a function of the amount of added titrant in a titration. You obtain data for a titration curve by titrating a solution and measuring the pH after every drop of added titrant. For example, you can construct a titration curve for the titration of hydrochloric acid with sodium hydroxide, NaOH, by measuring the pH after every drop of NaOH. A plot of the pH on the *y*-axis versus drops of NaOH on the *x*-axis will tell us how the pH changes as the titration proceeds.

A titration curve gives you a lot of information about a titration. For example, you can use the curve to identify the pH of the *equivalence point* of the titration. The equivalence point is the point on the titration curve where the moles of acid equal the moles of base. The midpoint of the steepest part of the curve (the most abrupt change in pH) is a good approximation of the equivalence point.

You can use knowledge of the equivalence point to choose a suitable indicator for a given titration. The indicator must change color at a pH that corresponds to the equivalence point. Because all titrations of weak acids and bases are different, it is important to construct titration curves and choose suitable indicators before you try to determine the concentrations of weak acids and bases.

Finally, you can use your titration curves to approximate the pKs of various weak acids and bases. Ethanoic acid, for example, ionizes in water to a small extent according to the following equation:

$$CH_3COOH + H_2O \rightleftharpoons CH_3COO^- + H_3O^+$$

The acid ionization constant, K_a, is expressed as:

$$K_a = \frac{[CH_3COO^-][H_3O^+]}{[CH_3COOH]}$$

When the acid is exactly half neutralized (half the number of drops of NaOH to the equivalence point), $[CH_3COOH] = [CH_3COO^-]$. So $K_a = [H_3O^+]$ or $pK_a = pH$. This means that the pH of the solution halfway to the equivalence point represents a good approximation of the pK_a.

Purpose

In this lab you will use your colorimetric pH meter from Small-Scale Experiment 28 to generate data to construct the titration curves for various acid–base titrations. You will use the information obtained from the graphs to estimate the pKs of various weak acids and bases and to choose the appropriate indicator for each titration.

Safety

- Wear your safety glasses.
- Use full small-scale pipets only for the carefully controlled delivery of liquids.

Materials

Small-scale pipets of the following solutions:
buffer solutions (pH 1–12)
universal indicator (UI)
hydrochloric acid (HCl)
sodium hydroxide (NaOH)
ethanoic acid (CH₃COOH)

Equipment

plastic cups
small-scale reaction surface
empty pipet for stirring

Experimental Page

1. Construct a pH meter for use in this experiment: Place 1 drop of UI in each space below, then add 5 drops of each indicated pH solution. Record your data in Table 32.1.

pH 1	pH 2	pH3	pH4
pH 8	pH 7	pH 6	pH 5
pH 9	pH 10	pH 11	pH 12

2. Add 1 drop of UI and 4 drops of HCl to each of the following spaces. Then add the indicated number of drops of NaOH while stirring. Record the pH of each mixture in Table 32.2.

1 drop NaOH	2 drops NaOH	3 drops NaOH	4 drops NaOH
8 drops NaOH	7 drops NaOH	6 drops NaOH	5 drops NaOH
9 drops NaOH	10 drops NaOH	11 drops NaOH	12 drops NaOH

3. Repeat Step 2 on a larger scale in a cup. Add 1 drop of UI and 10 drops of HCl to a clean, dry cup. Add NaOH drop by drop, and record the pH after each drop in Table 32.1. Continue for 25 to 30 drops of NaOH.

4. Repeat Step 3, using CH_3COOH. Add 1 drop of UI and 10 drops of CH_3COOH to a clean, dry cup. Add NaOH drop by drop, and record the pH after each drop in Table 32.1. Continue for 25 to 30 drops of NaOH.

Place this side of the Experimental Page facedown. Use the other side under your small-scale reaction surface.

Experimental Data

Record your results in Tables 32.1 and 32.2 or in tables like them in your notebook.

Table 32.1   Colorimetric pH Meter

pH 1 **bright red**	pH 2 **red**	pH 3 **red orange**	pH 4 **orange**
pH 8 **blue green**	pH 7 **green**	pH 6 **yellow green**	pH 5 **yellow**
pH 9 **blue**	pH 10 **dark blue**	pH 11 **blue violet**	pH 12 **violet**

Table 32.2   Titration

Drops of NaOH and corresponding pHs

HCl/NaOH Drops (reaction surface)	1	2	3	4	5	6	7	8	9	10	11	12
pH	1	1	1	1	1	1	1	1	2	7	10	12

	1	2	3	4	5	6	7	8	9	10	11	12
Drops												
pH	1	1	1	1	1	1	1	1	1	1	1	1
HCl/NaOH Drops (cup)	13	14	15	16	17	18	19	20	21	22	23	24
pH	1	1	1	1	1	1	3	7	10	12	12	12
Drops	25	26	27	28	29	30						
pH	12	12	12	12	12	12						

	1	2	3	4	5	6	7	8	9	10	11	12
Drops												
pH	3	4	4	4	4	4	5	5	5	5	5	5
CH₃COOH/NaOH Drops (cup)	13	14	15	16	17	18	19	20	21	22	23	24
pH	6	6	6	6	6	7	8	9	10	11	12	12
Drops	25	26	27	28	29	30						
pH	12	12	12	12	12	12						

Use graph paper to construct a titration curve for both titrations, HCl and CH$_3$COOH, by plotting the pH (y-axis) versus the number of drops of NaOH added (x-axis). Connect the points with a smooth "S" curve.

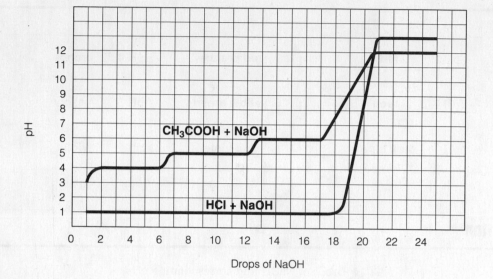

Drops of NaOH

Cleaning Up

Avoid contamination by cleaning up in a way that protects you and your environment. Carefully clean the reaction surface by absorbing the contents onto a paper towel, wipe it with a damp paper towel, and dry it. Clean the plastic cup by disposing of the liquid contents and rinsing it thoroughly with water. Dry it with a paper towel. Dispose of the paper towels in the waste bin. Wash your hands thoroughly with soap and water.

Questions for Analysis

Use what you learned in this lab to answer the following questions.

1. Write and balance a chemical equation to describe the reaction between HCl and NaOH. What is the mole ratio between HCl and NaOH?

   HCl + NaOH → HOH + NaCl. 1:1 ratio.

2. Write and balance a chemical equation to describe the reaction between CH$_3$COOH and NaOH. What is the mole ratio between CH$_3$COOH and NaOH?

   CH$_3$COOH + NaOH → HOH + CH$_3$COONa. 1:1 ratio.

3. The equivalence point is the point on the titration curve where the moles of acid equal the moles of base. The pH of the equivalence point of the titration can be approximated by finding the midpoint of the steepest part of the graph (where the pH changes most rapidly). Examine your titration curve for the titration of HCl with NaOH in the cup. What is the pH at the equivalence point for the titration?

   About 7.

4. Examine your titration curve for the titration of CH_3COOH with NaOH. What is the pH at the equivalence point for the titration?

About 9.

5. You can use your knowledge of the equivalence point to choose a suitable indicator for any acid–base titration. The indicator must change color at a pH that is at the steepest part of the titration curve. Examine your titration curve of HCl with NaOH, and explain why a large number of indicators would be suitable for this titration.

In one or two drops the pH jumps from about 3 to about 11. Any indicator

that changes color between about 4 and 10 would be suitable.

6. Choose suitable indicators for this titration from your data in Small-Scale Experiment 31.

Bromcresol green, methyl red, bromthymol blue, phenolphthalein.

7. Choose a suitable indicator for the titration of CH_3COOH with NaOH from your data in Small-Scale Experiment 31.

Phenolphthalein.

8. Compare the general shape of the curve for the weak acid (CH_3COOH) with the one for the strong acid (HCl).

   a. Which curve has a higher initial pH?

   Ethanoic acid.

   b. Which curve rises faster near the equivalence point?

   HCl.

   c. Is the pH at the equivalence point the same for both?

   No.

   d. Will the same group of indicators detect both equivalence points?

   No. Only phenolphthalein will detect both.

9. You can use your titration curve to approximate the pK_a of ethanoic acid (CH_3COOH). Ethanoic acid ionizes in water to a small extent, according to the following equation:

$$CH_3COOH + H_2O \rightleftharpoons CH_3COO^- + H_3O^+$$

The acid ionization constant, K_a, is expressed as:

$$K_a = \frac{[CH_3COO^-][H_3O^+]}{[CH_3COOH]}$$

When the acid is exactly half-neutralized (half the number of drops of NaOH to the equivalence point), then half of the ethanoic acid has been converted to acetate ion. This means that the amount of ethanoic acid left equals the amount of acetate ion produced, or $[CH_3COOH] = [CH_3COO^-]$. These values cancel in the above expression, resulting in $K_a = [H_3O^+]$ or $pK_a = pH$. This means that the pH of the solution halfway to the equivalence point represents a good approximation of the pK_a. At the equivalence point, how many drops of NaOH are required?

About 15 to 19.

10. What is the pH of the solution when half that many drops have been added? Estimate the pK_a of ethanoic acid.

pH = 4.5, pK_a = 4.5.

11. If NaOH is 0.5M, use your titration data to calculate the approximate molar concentration of HCl and CH_3COOH. Assume that the drop sizes are the same and that they are proportional to liters.

$$x \frac{\text{mol HCl}}{\text{L}} = \frac{20 \text{ L NaOH}}{10 \text{ L HCl}} \times \frac{0.5 \text{ mol NaOH}}{\text{L}} \times \frac{1 \text{ mol HCl}}{1 \text{ mol NaOH}} = 1.0M \text{ HCl}$$

$$x \frac{\text{mol } CH_3COOH}{\text{L}} \times \frac{16 \text{ L NaOH}}{10 \text{ L } CH_3COOH} \times \frac{0.5 \text{ mol NaOH}}{\text{L}} \times \frac{1 \text{ mol } CH_3COOH}{1 \text{ mol NaOH}} = 0.8M \text{ } CH_3COOH$$

Now It's Your Turn!

1. Repeat Step 3 on the Experimental Page, using HNO_3 instead of HCl. Add 1 drop of UI and 10 drops of HNO_3 to a clean, dry cup. Add NaOH drop by drop, and record the pH after each drop. Continue for 25 to 30 drops of NaOH. Record your observations. Construct a titration curve.

2. Design experiments to construct titration curves for the titrations of the following: H_2SO_4 with NaOH, H_3PO_4 with NaOH, Na_2CO_3 with HCl, and NH_3 with HCl.

3. Repeat all four titrations, but this time do them "backwards." For HCl, HNO_3, and CH_3COOH, add 20 drops of NaOH first and then titrate with the acid. Record the pH after each drop, and construct titration curves. For NH_3, add 10 drops of HCl and titrate with NH_3.

33 Buffers

• •

Text Section 20.6

Objectives

■ **Measure** and **record** the pHs of various buffer solutions.

■ **Determine** the resistance of various buffers to changes in pH.

Introduction

A buffer solution is a solution that resists a change in pH when small amounts of acid or base are added to it. Buffer solutions are usually composed of a conjugate acid–base pair—either a weak acid and the salt of its conjugate base or a weak base and the salt of its conjugate acid. For example, a buffer that maintains a pH of about 4.5 can be prepared by making a solution of ethanoic acid and sodium acetate.

$$CH_3COOH + H_2O \rightleftharpoons H_3O^+ + CH_3COO^-$$

acid   base

                                   (from sodium acetate)

$$CH_3COO^- + H_2O \rightleftharpoons CH_3COOH + OH^-$$

base   acid

(from sodium acetate)

Such a mixture resists a change in pH because the weak acid, CH_3COOH, will react with any added base. Similarly, the base, CH_3COO^-, will react with added acid.

A buffer can also be made of a weak base and the salt of its conjugate acid. Ammonia and ammonium chloride, for example, make up a buffer that maintains a pH of about 10.

$$NH_3 + H_2O \rightleftharpoons NH_4^+ + OH^-$$

base   acid

This buffer also has an acid and a base that are capable of reacting with added hydronium or hydroxide ions to maintain the pH at a nearly constant value.

Purpose

In this lab you will prepare several buffer solutions. You will add small amounts of both acid and base to each buffer to test their resistance to change in pH. You will then design other buffer solutions from weak acids and weak bases and test their behavior toward added acid and base.

Safety

■ Wear your safety glasses.

■ Use full small-scale pipets only for the carefully controlled delivery of liquids.

Materials

Small-scale pipets of the following solutions:

sodium hydroxide (NaOH)	hydrochloric acid (HCl)
ethanoic acid (CH_3COOH)	sodium ethanoate (CH_3COONa)
ammonia (NH_3)	ammonium chloride (NH_4Cl)
sodium carbonate (Na_2CO_3)	sodium hydrogen carbonate ($NaHCO_3$)
phosphoric acid (H_3PO_4)	sodium dihydrogen phosphate (NaH_2PO_4)
sodium chloride (NaCl)	sodium nitrate ($NaNO_3$)
potassium iodide (KI)	sodium sulfate (Na_2SO_4)
water (H_2O)	universal indicator (UI)
buffer solution (pH 1–12)	

Equipment

3 plastic cups
small-scale reaction surface

Experimental Page

1. Construct a pH meter for use in this experiment: Place 1 drop of UI in each space below, then 5 drops of each indicated pH solution.

pH 1	pH 2	pH 3	pH 4
pH 8	pH 7	pH 6	pH 5
pH 9	pH 10	pH 11	pH 12

2. Place 3 cups in the designated places, and add 1 drop of UI and 10 drops of distilled H_2O to each.

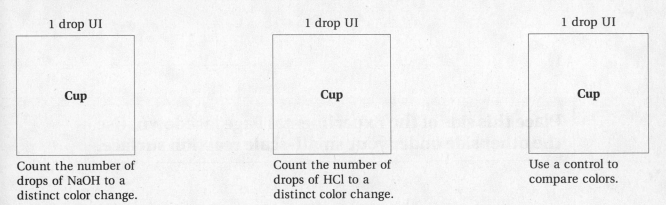

1 drop UI

Cup

Count the number of drops of NaOH to a distinct color change.

1 drop UI

Cup

Count the number of drops of HCl to a distinct color change.

1 drop UI

Cup

Use a control to compare colors.

3. Place 3 cups in the designated places and add 1 drop of UI, 10 drops of CH_3COOH, and 10 drops of CH_3COONa to each.

1 drop UI

Cup

Count the number of drops of NaOH to a distinct color change.

1 drop UI

Cup

Count the number of drops of HCl to a distinct color change.

1 drop UI

Cup

Use a control to compare colors.

4. Repeat Step 3, replacing the CH_3COOH and CH_3COONa, in turn, with the following combinations.

a. $H_3PO_4 + NaH_2PO_4$ **b.** $NaHCO_3 + Na_2CO_3$ **c.** $NH_4Cl + NH_3$

d. $NaCl + NaNO_3$ **e.** $Na_2SO_4 + KI$ **f.** $H_3PO_4 + NaOH$

g. Try mixing various combinations and test their buffer capacities.

Place this side of the Experimental Page facedown. Use the other side under your small-scale reaction surface.

Experimental Data

Record your results in Tables 33.1 and 33.2 or tables like them in your notebook.

Table 33.1   Colorimetric pH Meter

pH 1 **bright red**	pH 2 **red**	pH 3 **red orange**	pH 4 **orange**
pH 8 **blue green**	pH 7 **green**	pH 6 **yellow green**	pH 5 **yellow**
pH 9 **blue**	pH 10 **dark blue**	pH 11 **blue violet**	pH 12 **violet**

Table 33.2   Buffers

Mixture	Initial pH	Drops HCl to change	Drops NaOH to change
HOH	1	1	1
$CH_3COOH + CH_3COONa$	5	10–20	10–20
$H_3PO_4 + NaH_2PO_4$	4	10–20	10–20
$NaHCO_3 + Na_2CO_3$	9	10–20	10–20
$NH_4Cl + NH_3$	9	10–20	10–20
$NaCl + NaNO_3$	7	1–2	1–2
$Na_2SO_4 + KI$	7	1–2	1–2
$H_3PO_4 + NaOH$	5	10–20	10–20

Cleaning Up

Avoid contamination by cleaning up in a way that protects you and your environment. Carefully clean the reaction surface by absorbing the contents onto a paper towel, wipe it with a damp paper towel, and dry it. Clean the plastic cups by disposing of the liquid contents and rinsing them thoroughly with water. Dry them with a paper towel. Dispose of the paper towels in the waste bin. Wash your hands thoroughly with soap and water.

Questions for Analysis

Use what you learned in this lab to answer the following questions.

1. What is a buffer?

   A solution that resists change in pH.

2. How do you know which mixtures are buffers?

   They do not change pH with small amounts of added acid or base.

3. How do you know which mixtures are not buffers?

   They change pH immediately upon addition of acid or base.

4. Buffer capacity is a measure of the amount of acid or base a buffer will absorb before it changes pH significantly. A crude measure of buffer capacity is the number of drops of acid or base that is added before a pH change is shown by an indicator color change. What is the buffer capacity of each solution you measured in this experiment?

   In each case, equal to the number of drops of acid or base added before the

   pH changed significantly.

Now It's Your Turn!

1. Use the chemicals in this lab to explore other possible buffer combinations. Mix 10 drops each of various solutions, two at a time, and test the buffer capacity of each resulting solution. Tell what you mix and what happens in each case.

   Carry out Step 3 of the experiment with different combinations of the

   chemicals available in this lab.

2. Buffers are mixtures of weak acids and bases. Because of their formulations, some common household products are potential buffers. Design and carry out experiments to test household products for buffer capacity. Tell what you do and what the results are. Whenever possible, read the label of each product to try to determine the chemicals that give the substance its buffer capacity.

   Try Alka-Seltzer, baking soda, baking powder, cream of tartar, aspirin,

   vitamin C formula (a mixture of ascorbic acid and sodium ascorbate), liquid

   and solid antacids, and other household items. Students may have to dilute

   the acids and bases depending on the sample size they use. Note: Do not

   make available to students bleach and ammonia, as these solutions are

   incompatible.

34 Reactions of Acids with Metals

Text Section 21.2

Objectives

- **Observe** and **record** the oxidation–reduction reactions between metals and acids.
- **Describe** electron transfer in oxidation–reduction reactions by writing half-reactions and chemical equations.
- **Identify** half-reactions as oxidations or reductions by observing changes in oxidation numbers.
- **Derive** an activity series (Section 7.5) for the oxidation of metals from experimental data.

Introduction

The chemical changes that occur when electrons are transferred between reactants are called oxidation–reduction reactions, or redox reactions. When a metal reacts with an acid, there is a transfer of electrons from the metal to the acid, and the products are hydrogen gas and a salt. Magnesium, for example, reacts with nitric acid to produce magnesium nitrate and hydrogen gas. The complete and net ionic equations are written like this:

$$Mg(s) + 2HNO_3 \rightarrow Mg(NO_3)_2 + H_2(g)$$

$$Mg(s) + 2H^+ \rightarrow Mg^{2+} + H_2(g)$$

Assigning oxidation numbers to each atom in each formula results in the following equation:

$$Mg(s) + 2H^+ \rightarrow Mg^{2+} + H_2(g)$$

Oxidation numbers: $Mg(s) = 0$ $H^+ = +1$ $Mg^{2+} = +2$ $H_2 = 0$

Notice that both the magnesium and hydrogen atoms change oxidation numbers as they change from reactants to products. This reaction can be expressed in terms of two half-reactions, one showing a loss of electrons (oxidation) and the other showing a gain of electrons (reduction). Notice that we can add the half-reactions to create the original equation:

Oxidation $Mg(s) \rightarrow Mg^{2+} + 2e^-$
Reduction $2H^+ + 2e^- \rightarrow H_2(g)$

Net Ionic $Mg(s) + 2H^+ \rightarrow Mg^{2+} + H_2(g)$

Purpose

In this lab you will investigate the reactions of various metals toward acids. You will learn which metals react with acids and which do not. You will learn how to write complete and net ionic equations to describe these reactions. You will learn how to describe these reactions in terms of half-reactions and how to identify the half-reactions as oxidations or reductions. You will also examine how those same metals behave in the presence of copper(II) ions in aqueous solution and explain your results in terms of half-reactions.

Safety

- Wear your safety glasses.
- Use full small-scale pipets only for the carefully controlled delivery of liquids.

Materials

Small-scale pipets of the following solutions:

hydrochloric acid (HCl)   nitric acid (HNO_3)
sulfuric acid (H_2SO_4)   phosphoric acid (H_3PO_4)
ethanoic acid (CH_3COOH)   copper(II) sulfate ($CuSO_4$)

Five pieces of each of the following solid metals:

zinc (Zn)   iron (Fe)
magnesium (Mg)   copper (Cu)

Equipment

small-scale reaction surface
glass slide
hot plate

Experimental Page

1. Add 4 drops of each acid to 1 piece of each metal in the spaces below.

4 drops each

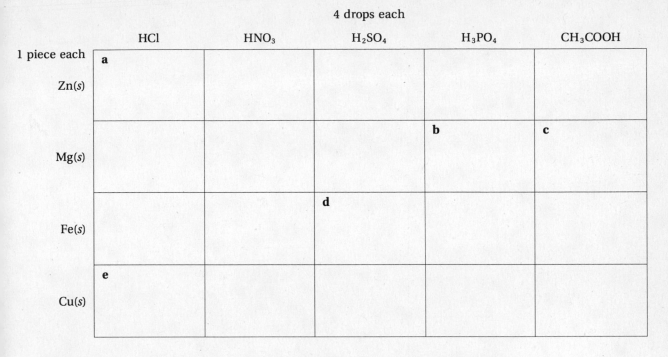

1 piece each	HCl	HNO₃	H₂SO₄	H₃PO₄	CH₃COOH
Zn(s)	a				
Mg(s)				b	c
Fe(s)			d		
Cu(s)	e				

2. To isolate the salts formed in the reactions of acids with metals, make the indicated mixings on a glass slide. Allow each mixture to react for a few minutes, remove the metals, and then evaporate the liquid on a hot plate. **Caution:** *The glass will be hot. Handle with tongs.*

Mg	Mg	Zn	Zn	Mg
+	+	+	+	+
HCl	HNO₃	HCl	HNO₃	H₂SO₄

3. Add 4 drops of CuSO₄ to one piece of each metal.

1 piece each

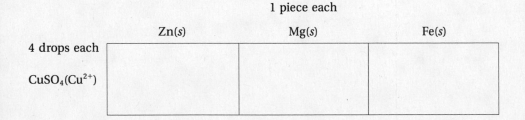

4 drops each	Zn(s)	Mg(s)	Fe(s)
CuSO₄(Cu²⁺)			

Place this side of the Experimental Page facedown. Use the other side under your small-scale reaction surface.

Experimental Data

Record your results in Tables 34.1–34.3 or tables like them in your notebook.

Table 34.1   Reactions of Metals with Acids

	HCl	HNO$_3$	H$_2$SO$_4$	H$_3$PO$_4$	CH$_3$COOH
Zn(s)	medium bubbles	medium bubbles	medium bubbles	medium bubbles	medium bubbles
Mg(s)	fast bubbles	fast bubbles	fast bubbles	fast bubbles	fast bubbles
Fe(s)	slow bubbles	slow bubbles	slow bubbles	slow bubbles	slow bubbles
Cu(s)	NVR	NVR	NVR	NVR	NVR

Table 34.2   Salts from Reactions of Metals with Acids

Mg + HCl	Mg + HNO$_3$	Zn + HCl	Zn + HNO$_3$	Mg + H$_2$SO$_4$
white solid	white solid	white solid	white solid	white solid

Table 34.3   Reactions of Metals and CuSO$_4$

	Zn(s)	Mg(s)	Fe(s)
CuSO$_4$(Cu^{2+})	black	black	black

Cleaning Up

Avoid contamination by cleaning up in a way that protects yourself and your environment. Recycle the leftover pieces of metals by carefully drying each on a paper towel and placing them in the appropriate recycling containers. Clean the reaction surface by absorbing the contents onto a paper towel, wipe it with a damp paper towel, and dry it. Clean and dry the glass slide. Dispose of the paper towels in the waste bin. Wash your hands thoroughly with soap and water.

Questions for Analysis

Use what you learned in this lab to answer the following questions.

1. An active metal is one that produces a visible reaction with acids. Which of the metals you tested are *active metals*?

Mg, Zn, and Fe.

2. Based on your observations, which metal seems to be the most reactive? Which is the least reactive?

Mg is most reactive, Cu is least reactive.

3. Make a list of the metals in decreasing order of reactivity (most reactive first). This is called an activity series.

Mg > Zn > Fe > Cu.

4. What is the name and chemical formula for the gas bubbles formed when acids react with metals?

Hydrogen, H_2.

5. The following equations are keyed to the experiment. Study them to find the common pattern, and then write complete chemical equations for each of the other reactions you observed. Notice that in each case hydrogen gas and a salt are formed when a metal replaces the hydrogen cation of an acid. What kind of reactions are these? (Hint: See Section 7.5.)

Single-replacement.

  a. $2HCl + Zn(s) \rightarrow H_2(g) + ZnCl_2$

  b. $3Mg(s) + 2H_3PO_4 \rightarrow 3H_2(g) + Mg_3(PO_4)_2$

  c. $Mg(s) + 2CH_3COOH \rightarrow H_2(g) + (CH_3COO)_2Mg$

  d. $Fe(s) + H_2SO_4 \rightarrow H_2(g) + FeSO_4$

  e. No visible reaction. Copper metal is not reactive.

$2HCl + Mg(s) \rightarrow H_2(g) + MgCl_2$

$2HCl + Fe(s) \rightarrow H_2(g) + FeCl_2$

$2HNO_3 + Mg(s) \rightarrow H_2(g) + Mg(NO_3)_2$

$2HNO_3 + Fe(s) \rightarrow H_2(g) + Fe(NO_3)_2$

$2HNO_3 + Zn(s) \rightarrow H_2(g) + Zn(NO_3)_2$

$H_2SO_4 + Mg(s) \rightarrow H_2(g) + MgSO_4$

$H_2SO_4 + Zn(s) \rightarrow H_2(g) + ZnSO_4$

$2H_3PO_4 + 3Zn(s) \rightarrow 3H_2(g) + Zn_3(PO_4)_2$

$2H_3PO_4 + 3Fe(s) \rightarrow 3H_2(g) + Fe_3(PO_4)_2$

$2CH_3COOH + Zn(s) \rightarrow H_2(g) + (CH_3COO)_2Zn$

$2CH_3COOH + Fe(s) \rightarrow H_2(g) + (CH_3COO)_2Fe$

6. Write a general statement that describes the reactions of acids with metals.

An active metal reacts with an acid to produce hydrogen gas and a salt.

7. What is the name and chemical formula of each solid (other than the remaining metal) that remains after evaporating the mixtures?

Magnesium chloride, $MgCl_2$; magnesium nitrate, $Mg(NO_3)_2$; zinc chloride,

$ZnCl_2$; zinc nitrate, $Zn(NO_3)_2$; magnesium sulfate, $MgSO_4$.

8. Examine the equations you wrote in Question 5. Do the oxidation numbers of any elements change from reactants to products? Do oxidation numbers generally change in acid–base reactions or precipitation reactions?

Yes. No.

9. What must an atom gain or lose in order for its oxidation number to change? How does your answer explain both an increase in oxidation number and a decrease in oxidation number?

Electrons. Loss of electrons results in an increase in oxidation number.

Gain of electrons results in a decrease in oxidation number.

10. Which metals reacted with $CuSO_4$?

All of them.

11. Below are half-reactions that describe the observed reaction between $CuSO_4$ and the other metals. Identify which are oxidation and which are reduction. Add the half-reactions to obtain the net ionic equation. (Hint: Each metal loses 2 electrons.)

$Cu^{2+} + 2e^- \rightarrow Cu^0$ **Reduction.**

$Mg(s) \rightarrow Mg^{2+} + 2e^-$ **Oxidation.**

$Mg(s) + Cu^{2+} \rightarrow Mg^{2+} + Cu(s)$

$Cu^{2+} + 2e^- \rightarrow Cu^0$ **Reduction.**

$Zn(s) \rightarrow Zn^{2+} + 2e^-$ **Oxidation.**

$Zn(s) + Cu^{2+} \rightarrow Zn^{2+} + Cu(s)$

$Fe(s) \rightarrow Fe^{2+} + 2e^-$ **Oxidation.**

$Cu^{2+} + 2e^- \rightarrow Cu^0$ **Reduction.**

$Fe(s) + Cu^{2+} \rightarrow Fe^{2+} + Cu(s)$

Now It's Your Turn!

1. Pennies minted after 1982 are made of zinc with a thin copper coating. Find a penny that has been damaged so that a portion of the zinc shows through. Carry out some experiments to compare the reactivity of the zinc and the copper toward various acids. What are your results?

One drop of acid to exposed zinc on a penny results in bubbling.

2. We have already learned that many household products, such as toilet-bowl cleaners and vinegar, contain acids. Design and carry out experiments to find out if these products also dissolve metals. When using these household products in your home, what precautions should you take?

Keep acid-containing toilet-bowl cleaners and vinegar away from items

made from active metals.

3. Besides their reactivity with acids, some metals react with strong bases like NaOH and KOH. Design and carry out an experiment to find out which of the metals react with these bases. What kinds of household products contain strong base? What precautions should you heed in using them at home?

Zn and Al bubble with sodium or potassium hydroxide. Drain cleaners usu-

ally contain strong base, so keep them away from zinc and aluminum items.

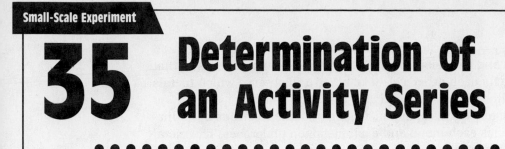

35 Determination of an Activity Series

Text Section 21.5

Objectives

- **Derive** an activity series from experimental data.
- **Describe** oxidation–reduction reactions by writing net ionic equations and half-reactions.
- **Formulate** a functional definition for "oxidation" and "reduction."

Introduction

You have seen that magnesium reacts with HCl much more readily than does zinc. Copper appears not to react at all with hydrochloric acid. The half-reactions that describe these processes reveal that electrons are lost by the metals and gained by the hydrogen ions. For example, the half-reactions for the reaction of magnesium with hydrochloric acid are

$$2H^+ + 2e^- \rightarrow H_2(g) \qquad \text{reduction}$$
$$Mg(s) \rightarrow Mg^{2+} + 2e^- \qquad \text{oxidation}$$

The relative ease with which a metal loses electrons is called its *oxidation potential*. You have seen, for example, that magnesium is more reactive toward acids than is zinc. This means that magnesium loses electrons more readily than zinc does. In other words, magnesium has a higher oxidation potential.

Conversely, the relative ease with which a metal cation gains electrons is called its *reduction potential*. For example, we have seen that copper ions react with zinc metal according to the following half-reactions and net ionic equation:

Reduction	$Cu^{2+} + 2e^- \rightarrow Cu(s)$
Oxidation	$Zn(s) \rightarrow Zn^{2+} + 2e^-$
Net ionic	$Cu^{2+} + Zn(s) \rightarrow Cu(s) + Zn^{2+}$

Because copper ions react with zinc metal by taking away its electrons, we can say that copper has the greater reduction potential and zinc has the greater oxidation potential.

Purpose

In this lab you will carry out a series of reactions in which electrons are gained and lost between metals and metal ions. You will organize the experiments so that metals actually compete for each other's electrons. You will observe which metals lose electrons more readily and which metal ions gain electrons more readily. You can compare the relative tendencies of metals to gain and lose electrons by counting the number of reactions each metal and each metal ion undergoes. The metal involved in the most reactions is the one that loses electrons (is oxidized) the most readily. It has the highest oxidation potential. The metal involved in the least number of reactions loses electrons the least readily. It has the lowest oxidation potential. A list of metals ranging from those most easily oxidized to those least easily oxidized is called an activity series. From this data you will derive an activity series for common metals.

Safety

- Wear your safety glasses.

- Use full small-scale pipets only for the carefully controlled delivery of liquids.

Materials

Small-scale pipets of the following solutions:

silver nitrate ($AgNO_3$)   copper(II) sulfate ($CuSO_4$)
iron(II) sulfate ($FeSO_4$)   magnesium sulfate ($MgSO_4$)
zinc chloride ($ZnCl_2$)

Four pieces each of the following solid metals:

zinc (Zn)   iron (Fe)
magnesium (Mg)   silver (Ag)
copper (Cu)

Equipment

small-scale reaction surface

©Addison-Wesley Publishing Company, Inc.

Experimental Page

Add 2 drops of each salt solution to one piece of each of the indicated metals.

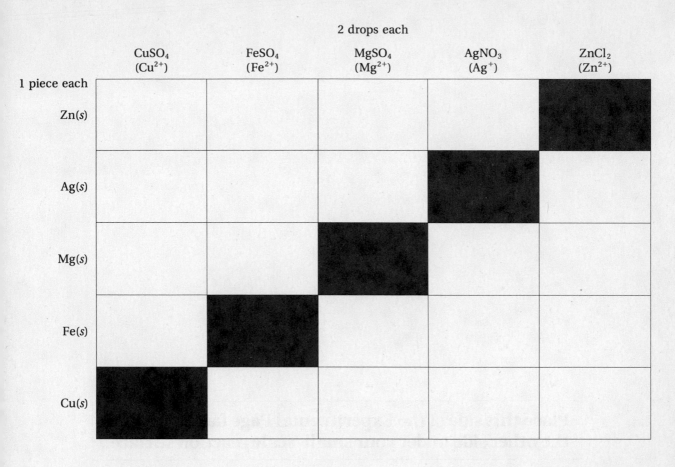

2 drops each

	CuSO₄ (Cu²⁺)	FeSO₄ (Fe²⁺)	MgSO₄ (Mg²⁺)	AgNO₃ (Ag⁺)	ZnCl₂ (Zn²⁺)
1 piece each Zn(s)					■
Ag(s)				■	
Mg(s)			■		
Fe(s)		■			
Cu(s)	■				

Place this side of the Experimental Page facedown. Use the other side under your small-scale reaction surface.

Experimental Data

Record your results in Table 35.1 or a table like it in your notebook.

Table 35.1 Metal Activity

	CuSO$_4$ (Cu^{2+})	FeSO$_4$ (Fe^{2+})	MgSO$_4$ (Mg^{2+})	AgNO$_3$ (Ag$^+$)	ZnCl$_2$ (Zn^{2+})	
Zn(s)	Rxn	Rxn	NVR	Rxn	■	Zn(s) → Zn^{2+} + 2e$^-$ Zn^{2+} + 2e$^-$ → Zn(s)
Ag(s)	NVR	NVR	NVR	■	NVR	Ag(s) → Ag$^+$ + e$^-$ Ag$^+$ + e$^-$ → Ag(s)
Mg(s)	Rxn	Rxn	■	Rxn	Rxn	Mg(s) → Mg^{2+} + 2e$^-$ Mg^{2+} + 2e$^-$ → Mg(s)
Fe(s)	Rxn	■	NVR	Rxn	NVR	Fe(s) → Fe^{2+} + 2e$^-$ Fe^{2+} + 2e$^-$ → Fe(s)
Cu(s)	■	NVR	NVR	Rxn	NVR	Cu(s) → Cu^{2+} + 2e$^-$ Cu^{2+} + 2e$^-$ → Cu(s)

Write oxidation and reduction half-reactions for each metal in the spaces provided next to the table.

Cleaning Up

Avoid contamination by cleaning up in a way that protects you and your environment. Carefully clean and dry each piece of leftover metal and place it in the appropriate recycling container. Clean the reaction surface by absorbing the contents onto a paper towel, rinse it with a damp paper towel, and dry it. Dispose of the paper towels in the waste bin. Wash your hands thoroughly with soap and water.

Questions for Analysis

Use what you learned in this lab to answer the following questions.

1. Read across each row of Table 35.1. Count the number of reactions that each metal undergoes with the metal salts. Order them according to reactivity. This order is called an activity series.

   Mg > Zn > Fe > Cu > Ag.

2. Reading down the rows of Table 35.1, count the number of reactions that each metal ion undergoes. Order them according to reactivity.

   $Ag^+ > Cu^{2+} > Fe^{2+} > Zn^{2+} > Mg^{2+}$.

3. Compare the reactivity of the metal ions to that of the metals. What are the similarities and differences?

   The activity series for the metal ions is in the reverse order of that of

   the metals.

4. For each reaction you observe, a metal is oxidized; that is, it gives away its electrons. In doing so, the metal becomes a metal ion. Write an oxidation half-reaction for each reaction you observed. Write them in order of reactivity, with the most reactive first.

   Oxidations: $Mg(s) \rightarrow Mg^{2+} + 2e^-$

   $Zn(s) \rightarrow Zn^{2+} + 2e^-$

   $Fe(s) \rightarrow Fe^{2+} + 2e^-$

   $Cu(s) \rightarrow Cu^{2+} + 2e^-$

   $Ag(s) \rightarrow Ag^+ + e^-$

5. For each reaction you observe, a metal ion is reduced; that is, the metal ion gains electrons. In doing so, the metal ion becomes a metal atom. Write a reduction half-reaction for each reaction you observed. Write them in order of reactivity, with the most reactive first.

   Reductions: $Ag^+ + 1e^- \rightarrow Ag(s)$

   $Cu^{2+} + 2e^- \rightarrow Cu(s)$

   $Fe^{2+} + 2e^- \rightarrow Fe(s)$

   $Zn^{2+} + 2e^- \rightarrow Zn(s)$

   $Mg^{2+} + 2e^- \rightarrow Mg(s)$

6. Examine your two lists of half-reactions and describe how each list can be used to predict whether a reaction will occur between a metal and a metal ion.

   Each metal on the list will react with a metal ion below it but not above it.

   Likewise, each metal ion on the list will react with a metal below it but not

   above it.

7. Add the half-reactions to obtain the net ionic equations for each of the reactions you observed. Use either list and choose two half-reactions. Reverse the one lower on the list and add them together. Make sure the number of electrons gained equals the number of electrons lost. For example,

Oxidation $\quad\quad\quad\quad Mg^0(s) \rightarrow Mg^{2+} + 2e^-$

Reduction $\quad\quad\quad\quad 2\,[Ag^+ + 1e^- \rightarrow Ag^0(s)]$

Net Ionic Equation $\quad\quad Mg^0(s) + 2Ag^+ \rightarrow Mg^{2+} + 2Ag^0(s)$

Notice that silver metal does not give its electrons to a zinc ion:

$Ag^0(s) + Zn^{2+} \rightarrow$ No Visible Reaction

$Zn(s) + 2Ag^+ \rightarrow Zn^{2+} + 2Ag(s)$

$Fe(s) + 2Ag^+ \rightarrow Fe^{2+} + 2Ag(s)$

$Cu(s) + 2Ag^+ \rightarrow Cu^{2+} + 2Ag(s)$

$Mg(s) + Cu^{2+} \rightarrow Mg^{2+} + Cu(s)$

$Zn(s) + Cu^{2+} \rightarrow Zn^{2+} + Cu(s)$

$Fe(s) + Cu^{2+} \rightarrow Fe^{2+} + Cu(s)$

$Zn(s) + Fe^{2+} \rightarrow Zn^{2+} + Fe(s)$

$Mg(s) + Fe^{2+} \rightarrow Mg^{2+} + Fe(s)$

$Mg(s) + Zn^{2+} \rightarrow Mg^{2+} + Zn(s)$

Now It's Your Turn!

1. Repeat the experiment, using common household objects in place of the metals. For example, use galvanized nails or zinc-plated washers for zinc, silverware for silver, staples for iron, and pennies for copper. How do your results compare with the original experiment?

They are about the same.

36 Oxidation–Reduction Reactions

● ●

Text Section 21.7

Objectives

- **Observe** and **record** oxidation–reduction reactions between aqueous ions.
- **Describe** oxidation and reduction processes by writing half-reactions.
- **Write** and balance redox equations by balancing half-reactions.
- **Identify** reactants as oxidizing agents and reducing agents.

Introduction

You saw in the last two labs that oxidation–reduction reactions commonly occur when metals react with either acids or metal ions. Redox reactions also occur between ions, one ion being oxidized and the other being reduced. For example, permanganate ions, MnO_4, undergo a redox reaction with iodide ions, I^-, in the presence of acid:

$$16H^+ + 2MnO_4^- + 10I^- \rightarrow 2Mn^{2+} + 5I_2 + 8H_2O$$

This reaction is easily seen in the laboratory because permanganate has a distinctive purple color that disappears upon formation of the nearly colorless Mn^{2+} ion. Similarly, the colorless iodide ion reacts to form the iodine molecule, which appears yellow in aqueous solution. The reaction mixture turns from purple to yellow as the reaction proceeds.

In this reaction, permanganate is reduced and iodide is oxidized. In other words, manganese gains electrons and iodine loses electrons. Because permanganate accepts electrons from iodide and causes iodide to be oxidized, permanganate, the reduced reactant, is also called the oxidizing agent. Similarly, because iodide donates electrons to permanganate and causes permanganate to be reduced, iodide, the oxidized reactant, is also called a reducing agent.

Purpose

In this lab you will carry out a number of redox reactions involving ions in aqueous solution and write balanced equations to describe the reactions. You will also identify the oxidizing and reducing agents in each case and become familiar with which substances usually act as oxidizing agents and which are most often reducing agents.

Safety

- Wear your safety glasses.
- Use full small-scale pipets only for the carefully controlled delivery of liquids.

Materials

Small-scale pipets of the following solutions:

potassium iodide (KI)

potassium permanganate (KMnO$_4$)

hydrogen peroxide (H$_2$O$_2$)

sodium nitrite (NaNO$_2$)

copper(II) sulfate (CuSO$_4$)

hydrochloric acid (HCl)

sodium hydrogen sulfate (NaHSO$_4$)

sodium hypochlorite (NaOCl)

potassium iodate (KIO$_3$)

sodium hydrogen sulfite (NaHSO$_3$)

potassium dichromate (K$_2$Cr$_2$O$_7$)

iron(III) chloride (FeCl$_3$)

starch solution

sodium thiosulfate (Na$_2$S$_2$O$_3$)

Equipment

small-scale reaction surface

Experimental Page

1. Mix 1 drop each of the indicated solutions in the spaces below. If no reaction is visible, add starch, an indicator for I_2. If no reaction occurs still, add HCl. Record your results in Table 36.1.

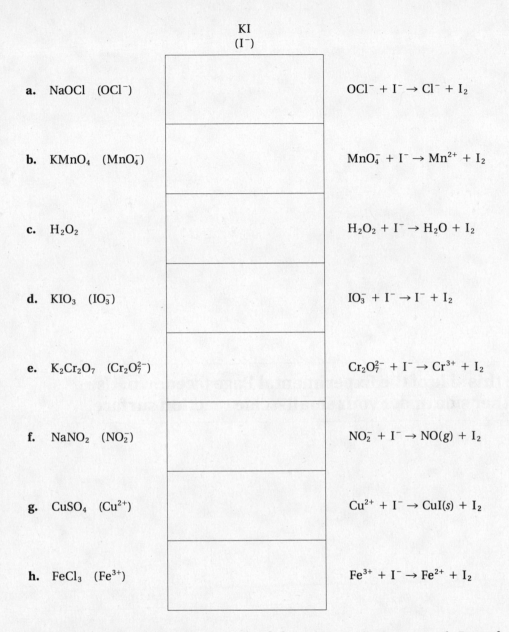

KI
(I^-)

a. NaOCl (OCl^-) $OCl^- + I^- \rightarrow Cl^- + I_2$

b. $KMnO_4$ (MnO_4^-) $MnO_4^- + I^- \rightarrow Mn^{2+} + I_2$

c. H_2O_2 $H_2O_2 + I^- \rightarrow H_2O + I_2$

d. KIO_3 (IO_3^-) $IO_3^- + I^- \rightarrow I^- + I_2$

e. $K_2Cr_2O_7$ ($Cr_2O_7^{2-}$) $Cr_2O_7^{2-} + I^- \rightarrow Cr^{3+} + I_2$

f. $NaNO_2$ (NO_2^-) $NO_2^- + I^- \rightarrow NO(g) + I_2$

g. $CuSO_4$ (Cu^{2+}) $Cu^{2+} + I^- \rightarrow CuI(s) + I_2$

h. $FeCl_3$ (Fe^{3+}) $Fe^{3+} + I^- \rightarrow Fe^{2+} + I_2$

2. Add a few drops of $NaHSO_3$ to each of the mixtures in Step 1, a–d. Record your results in Table 36.1.

$$HSO_3^- + I_2 \rightarrow SO_4^{2-} + I^-$$

3. Add a few drops of $Na_2S_2O_3$ to each of the mixtures in Step 1, e–h. Record your results in Table 36.1.

$$S_2O_3^{2-} + I_2 \rightarrow S_4O_6^{2-} + I^-$$

Place this side of the Experimental Page facedown. Use the other side under your small-scale reaction surface.

Name _____ Class _____ Date _____

Experimental Data

Record your results in Table 36.1 or a table like it in your notebook.

Table 36.1 Redox Reactions and Indicators

		KI	Starch	HCl	NaHSO₃	Na₂S₂O₃
a.	Cl_2	yellow	NA	NA	colorless	NA
b.	$KMnO_4$	pink to yellow	NA	NA	colorless	NA
c.	H_2O_2	NVR	NVR	black	colorless	NA
d.	KIO_3	NVR	NVR	black	colorless	NA
e.	$K_2Cr_2O_7$	NVR	NVR	black	NA	colorless
f.	$NaNO_2$	NVR	NVR	black	NA	colorless
g.	$CuSO_4$	brown	NA	NA	NA	colorless
h.	$FeCl_3$	dark orange	NA	NA	NA	light yellow

*NA = Not Applicable

Cleaning Up

Avoid contamination by cleaning up in a way that protects you and your environment. Carefully clean the reaction surface by absorbing the contents onto a paper towel, wipe it with a damp paper towel, and dry it. Dispose of the paper towels in the waste bin. Wash your hands thoroughly with soap and water.

Questions for Analysis

Use what you learned in this lab to answer the following questions.

1. What color is aqueous I_2? What color is I_2 in the presence of starch?

   Yellow. Black.

2. Listed below are the reactants and products for each mixing. Assign oxidation numbers to each chemical species that changes oxidation number and then write half reactions for each reaction.

   a. $\overset{+1}{OCl^-} + \overset{-1}{I^-} \rightarrow \overset{-1}{Cl^-} + \overset{0}{I_2}$

      $OCl^- + 2e^- \rightarrow Cl^-$

      $2I^- \rightarrow I_2 + 2e^-$

   b. $\overset{+7}{MnO_4^-} + \overset{-1}{I^-} \rightarrow \overset{+2}{Mn^{2+}} + \overset{0}{I_2}$

      $MnO_4^- + 5e^- \rightarrow Mn^{2+}$

      $2I^- \rightarrow I_2 + 2e^-$

   c. $\overset{-1}{H_2O_2} + \overset{-1}{I^-} \rightarrow \overset{-2}{H_2O} + \overset{0}{I_2}$

      $H_2O_2 + 2e^- \rightarrow H_2O$

      $2I^- \rightarrow I_2 + 2e^-$

   d. $\overset{+5}{IO_3^-} + \overset{-1}{I^-} \rightarrow \overset{-1}{I^-} + \overset{0}{I_2}$

      $IO_3^- + 6e^- \rightarrow I^-$

      $2I^- \rightarrow I_2 + 2e^-$

   e. $\overset{+6}{Cr_2O_7^{2-}} + \overset{-1}{I^-} \rightarrow \overset{+3}{Cr^{3+}} + \overset{0}{I_2}$

      $Cr_2O_7^{2-} + 6e^- \rightarrow 2Cr^{3+}$

      $2I^- \rightarrow I_2 + 2e^-$

   f. $\overset{+3}{NO_2^-} + \overset{-1}{I^-} \rightarrow \overset{+2}{NO(g)} + \overset{0}{I_2}$

      $NO_2^- + e^- \rightarrow NO(g)$

      $2I^- \rightarrow I_2 + 2e^-$

   g. $\overset{+2}{Cu^{2+}} + \overset{-1}{I^-} \rightarrow \overset{+1}{CuI(s)} + \overset{0}{I_2}$

      $Cu^{2+} + 1e^- \rightarrow CuI(s)$

      $2I^- \rightarrow I_2 + 2e^-$

   h. $\overset{+3}{Fe^{3+}} + \overset{-1}{I^-} \rightarrow \overset{+2}{Fe^{2+}} + \overset{0}{I_2}$

      $Fe^{3+} + 1e^- \rightarrow Fe^{2+}$

      $2I^- \rightarrow I_2 + 2e^-$

(*Remember:* Half-reactions must be balanced only for the chemical species that gains or loses electrons.)

3. What color did the mixtures turn upon addition of $NaHSO_3$? $Na_2S_2O_3$? What does each indicate?

   All turned back to the original color or colorless, indicating the

   disappearance of I_2.

4. Given the reactants and products for Steps 2 and 3, write half-reactions for each:

   $HSO_3^- + I_2 \rightarrow SO_4^{2-} + I^-$

   $HSO_3^- \rightarrow SO_4^{2-} + 2e^-$

   $I_2 + 2e^- \rightarrow 2I^-$

   $S_2O_3^{2-} + I_2 \rightarrow S_4O_6^{2-} + I^-$

   $2S_2O_3^{2-} \rightarrow S_4O_6^{2-} + 2e^-$

   $I_2 + 2e^- \rightarrow 2I^-$

5. Fill in the table below with all of the oxidizing agents and reducing agents that you observed in this experiment.

Oxidizing agents	Reducing agents	Oxidizing agents	Reducing agents
Cl_2	I^-	$Cr_2O_7^{2-}$	I^-
MnO_4^-	I^-	NO_2^-	I^-
H_2O_2	I^-	Cu^{2+}	I^-
IO_3^-	I^-	Fe^{3+}	I^-
I_2	HSO_3^-	I_2	$S_2O_3^{2-}$

6. Complete and balance redox equations for each reaction you observed. Multiply each half-reaction by coefficients that balance the electrons gained and lost, and add the half-reactions. For example,

$$2 [MnO_4^- + 5e^- \rightarrow Mn^{2+}]$$
$$5 [2I^- \rightarrow I_2 + 2e^-]$$
$$\overline{2MnO_4^- + 10I^- \rightarrow 2Mn^{2+} + 5I_2}$$

Add water to one side of the equation to balance the oxygens, and add H^+ to the other side to balance the hydrogens:

$$16H^+ + 2MnO_4^- + 10I^- \rightarrow 2Mn^{2+} + 5I_2 + 8H_2O$$

Check to see that all atoms are balanced and that the total charge is balanced.

a. $2H^+ + OCl^- + 2I^- \rightarrow Cl^- + I_2 + H_2O$

b. $16H^+ + 2MnO_4^- + 10I^- \rightarrow 2Mn^{2+} + 5I_2 + 8H_2O$

c. $2H^+ + H_2O_2 + 2I^- \rightarrow 2H_2O + I_2$

d. $6H^+ + IO_3^- + 5I^- \rightarrow 3I_2 + 3H_2O$

e. $14H^+ + Cr_2O_7^{2-} + 6I^- \rightarrow Cr^{3+} + 3I_2 + 7H_2O$

f. $4H^+ + 2NO_2^- + 2I^- \rightarrow 2NO(g) + I_2 + 2H_2O$

g. $2Cu^{2+} + 4I^- \rightarrow 2CuI(s) + I_2$

h. $2Fe^{3+} + 2I^- \rightarrow 2Fe^{2+} + I_2$

Now It's Your Turn!

1. Recall that an *oxidizing agent* is a chemical that causes another chemical to be oxidized, and in the process the oxidizing agent is reduced (gains electrons). Similarly, a *reducing agent* is a chemical that causes another chemical to be reduced, and in the process the reducing agent is oxidized (loses electrons.) For example, in this lab you observed that OCl^- is an oxidizing agent because each Cl atom is reduced from an oxidation number of +1 to −1. Also, I^- is a reducing agent because each I atom is oxidized from an oxidation number of −1 to 0.

$$OCl^- + 2e^- \rightarrow Cl^- \qquad 2I^- \rightarrow I_2 + 2e^-$$

Add one drop of each solution to the indicated space. Add HCl if no reaction occurs. Then write half-reactions and a redox equation, and identify the oxidizing agent and the reducing agent for each. If no reaction occurs, write "NVR."

	$MnO_4^- \rightarrow Mn^{2+}$ $KMnO_4$	$Cr_2O_7^{2-} \rightarrow Cr^{3+}$ $K_2Cr_2O_7$	$I_2 \rightarrow I^-$ KI + Starch + NaOCl	$Fe^{3+} \rightarrow Fe^{2+}$ $FeCl_3$
NaHSO$_3$ $HSO_3^- \rightarrow SO_4^{2-}$	colorless	NVR	colorless	colorless
H$_2$O$_2$ $H_2O_2 \rightarrow O_2$	colorless, bubbles	black to blue to green, bubbles	NVR	colorless, bubbles
Na$_2$S$_2$O$_3$ *$S_2O_3^{2-} \rightarrow SO_4^{2-}$	colorless	green	colorless	colorless
NaNO$_2$ **NO(g) $\rightarrow$ NO(g) + NO$_3^-$	colorless	NVR	NVR	NVR

What gas produces the bubbles you saw? In which mixtures did you see bubbles?

O$_2$ gas. H$_2$O$_2$ + KMnO$_4$, H$_2$O$_2$ + K$_2$Cr$_2$O$_7$, and H$_2$O$_2$ + Fe^{3+}.

Describe what happens with each mixing. Make a table of your results.

*In the presence of I$_2$, thiosulfate reacts to form $S_2O_3^{2-} + I_2 \rightarrow S_4O_6^{2-} + I^-$
**In the presence of acid, the nitrite ion reacts to form nitrogen oxide gas: $3NO_2^- + 2H^+ \rightarrow 2NO(g) + H_2O + NO_3^-$

37 Small-Scale Voltaic Cells

Text Section 22.3

Objectives

- **Build** and **test** simple voltaic cells.
- **Measure** and **compare** the voltages of commercial cells with the ones you build.
- **Describe** the chemistry of voltaic cells by writing half-reactions.
- **Construct** an electrochemical series from experimental data.

Introduction

Americans own some 900 million battery-operated devices and spend 2.5 billion dollars a year feeding them batteries. Batteries (voltaic dry cells) are simple devices that transform chemical energy into electrical energy. They operate on the principle of oxidation–reduction chemistry. One chemical inside the battery is a reducing agent and gives up electrons. Another chemical is an oxidizing agent and accepts the electrons given up by the former. The flow of electrons from one chemical to another constitutes an electric current. The device is designed to tap the electric current that flows from reducing agent to oxidizing agent. As the chemical reaction progresses, less and less current is produced. Eventually the current diminishes to the extent that the battery is essentially "dead." At this point we usually throw it away and replace it with a new one.

Which materials make the best batteries? In previous labs you discovered that some metals lose electrons more readily than others. The metal cations that are formed as a result do not gain electrons as readily as do metal cations formed from less reactive metals.

The following list of half-reactions shows the reduction of metal ions to metal atoms. The reverse of each half-reaction is the oxidation half-reaction of the metal. Any metal on the list will react only with a metal ion that is below it in the list. For example, magnesium metal, $Mg(s)$, will react with all of the other metal ions in the list. Iron, $Fe(s)$, will react only with Cu^{2+} and Ag^+. Silver, $Ag(s)$, will not react with any of the metal ions in the list.

$$Mg^{2+} + 2e^- \rightarrow Mg(s)$$

$$Zn^{2+} + 2e^- \rightarrow Zn(s)$$

$$Fe^{3+} + 3e^- \rightarrow Fe(s)$$

$$Cu^{2+} + 2e^- \rightarrow Cu(s)$$

$$Ag^+ + 1e^- \rightarrow Ag(s)$$

Purpose

In this lab you will build some small-scale batteries (voltaic cells) from metals and solutions of metal ions. You will use a volt meter to measure and compare the voltages they produce. You will relate this information to the redox chemistry involved and to the activity series you developed in Small-Scale Experiment 35.

Safety

- Wear your safety glasses.
- Use full small-scale pipets only for the carefully controlled delivery of liquids.

Materials

Small-scale pipets of the following solutions:

silver nitrate ($AgNO_3$) copper(II) sulfate ($CuSO_4$)
magnesium sulfate ($MgSO_4$) lead(II) nitrate ($Pb(NO_3)_2$)
zinc chloride ($ZnCl_2$) sodium nitrate ($NaNO_3$)

Solids:

silver (Ag) lead (Pb)
copper (Cu) zinc (Zn)
magnesium (Mg)

Equipment

small-scale reaction surface volt meter
9-centimeter filter paper various commercial batteries
scissors (dry cells)

Experimental Page

1. Measure the voltage of these commercial cells: standard carbon, heavy duty, alkaline, rechargeable. (A positive meter reading means the electrons flow into the meter at the connector labeled "−".) Reverse the leads and measure the voltage again. Record your results in Table 37.1.

2. Test copper and zinc in the spaces below. Record your results in Table 37.2.

   a. Mix 2 drops of each of the indicated solutions with one piece of each metal.

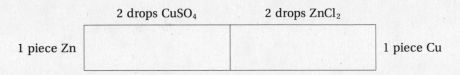

	2 drops CuSO₄	2 drops ZnCl₂	
1 piece Zn			1 piece Cu

   b. Cut and place a rectangular piece of filter paper on the template below, and add 3 drops of each solution so the center solution barely overlaps the other two solutions. Then add one piece of each metal and measure the positive (+) voltage of the cell you just made. Reverse the leads and measure it again. Record your results in Table 37.2.

CuSO₄	NaNO₃	ZnCl₂
Cu(s)		Zn(s)

3. Cut a piece of filter paper as shown below, and add a few drops of each solution so that each "arm" is wet. The NaNO₃ solution should touch the other solutions. Place a piece of the indicated metal on each arm and measure the voltages of each lead (Pb) cell with the black, negative (−) connector on "Pb." Press firmly. Record the voltages in Table 37.3.

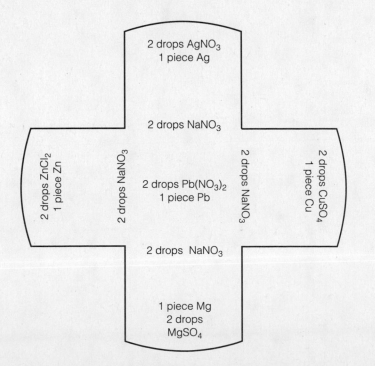

Place this side of the Experimental Page facedown. Use the other side under your small-scale reaction surface.

Experimental Data

Record your results in Tables 37.1–37.3 or tables like them in your notebook.

Table 37.1 Commercial Dry Cell Voltages

Name of commercial cell	Voltage	Voltage (with leads reversed)
standard carbon	1.5	−1.5
heavy duty	1.5	−1.5
alkaline	1.5	−1.5
rechargeable	1.25	−1.25

Values may be lower if "dead" batteries are used.

Table 37.2 Copper-Zinc Cell

a. $CuSO_4 + Zn(s)$	$ZnCl_2 + Cu(s)$	**b.** Voltage of Cu–Zn cell
Black ppt.	**NVR**	**+0.95**

Table 37.3 Lead Cells

Ag	Cu	Mg	Zn	Pb
0.84	0.42	−1.25	−0.53	0

Electrons flow away from:				
Pb	Pb	Mg	Zn	

Cleaning Up

Avoid contamination by cleaning up in a way that protects you and your environment. Carefully clean and dry the pieces of metal and place them in the proper recycling containers. Clean the reaction surface by absorbing the contents onto a paper towel, wipe it with a damp paper towel, and dry it. Dispose of the paper towels in the waste bin. Wash your hands thoroughly with soap and water.

Questions for Analysis

Use what you learned in this lab to answer the following questions.

1. When measuring voltages, what happens when you reverse the red, positive (+) and black, negative (−) leads of the volt meter?

   The sign of the voltage changes but the absolute value does not.

2. When the meter reads a positive voltage, into which connector do the electrons flow?

   The black, negative (−) one.

3. Which reaction occurs in Step 2a? Write half-reactions for the reaction.

   Zinc reacts with copper sulfate: $Zn(s) \rightarrow Zn^{2+} + 2e^-$. $Cu^{2+} + 2e^- \rightarrow Cu(s)$.

4. Based on the sign of the voltage, which metal loses electrons, Cu or Zn? Explain.

   Zn. The voltage is positive when black (−) connector is on zinc. Electrons flow from Zn into the meter.

5. Write the half-reactions for the Cu–Zn cell you constructed in Step **2b**. How do these compare to those you wrote for Step **2a**?

   $Zn(s) \rightarrow Zn^{2+} + 2e^-$. $Cu^{2+} + 2e^- \rightarrow Cu(s)$. They are the same.

6. Construct a set of reduction potentials by writing *reduction* half-reactions for all five metals, including lead, from Step **3**. Assign 0.00 volts to Pb, and list the half-reactions in order of increasing voltages (most negative value first).

Half-reaction	Voltage
$Mg^{2+} + 2e^- \rightarrow Mg(s)$	−1.25
$Zn^{2+} + 2e^- \rightarrow Zn(s)$	−0.53
$Pb^{2+} + 2e^- \rightarrow Pb(s)$	0.00
$Cu^{2+} + 2e^- \rightarrow Cu(s)$	+0.42
$Ag^+ + 1e^- \rightarrow Ag(s)$	+0.84

7. Compare your ordered list of half-reactions to the activity series you developed in Small-Scale Experiment 35. What conclusions can you draw?

   It's similar but lead is in place of iron.

8. Draw a simple cross-sectional diagram of the Zn–Cu cell you made showing the direction of electron flow. Mark the cathode, the anode, and the salt bridge.

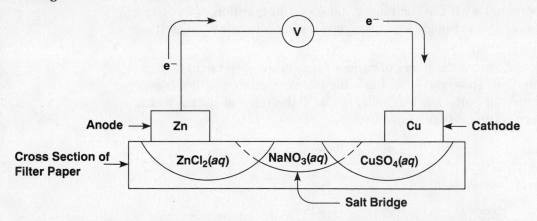

9. The table of reduction potentials you constructed above can be used to predict the voltages of a cell made from any two metals on the table. Simply find the difference between the two voltages in question. For example, the voltage of an Ag–Zn cell will probably be about 1.37 volts ($0.84 - -0.53 = 1.37$). Use your reduction potential table above to predict the voltages of the following cells: Ag–Cu, Ag–Zn, Ag–Mg, Cu–Zn, Cu–Mg, Zn–Mg.

0.42, 1.37, 2.1, 0.95, 1.7, 0.72.

Now It's Your Turn!

1. Design an experiment to measure the cell voltages of each cell for which you predicted values in Question 9, and compare your results with your predicted values.

	Red (+) connector on:				
	Ag	**Cu**	**Pb**	**Zn**	**Pb**
Ag		−0.40	−0.86	−1.42	−2.13
Cu	+0.40		−0.42	−0.98	−1.75
Pb	+0.89	+0.42		−0.53	−1.25
Zn	+1.40	+0.96	+0.56		−0.59
Mg	+2.17	+1.75	+1.30	+0.61	

Black (−) connector on:

2. Make a good guess as to what the metals are in such common metal objects as nickels, dimes, food cans, soda cans, nails, washers, galvanized nails, etc. Test each of your predictions by replacing one of the metal electrodes in Step 3 of the experiment with the common metal object in question. What common metal is each object made from? Are your results conclusive? Suggest an explanation.

3. Go shopping and record the prices of various types of the same sizes of commercial voltaic cells (batteries). The following table compares the lifetimes of various commercial batteries. Use your data and the table to decide which type of battery is the most cost-effective.

Type of cell	Expected lifetime (hours)*	Price
General purpose (zinc-carbon)	1–7	_____
Heavy duty (zinc-chloride)	1.5–15	_____
Alkaline	5–27	_____
Rechargeable (nickel-cadmium)**	2–7	_____

*The expected lifetime varies with the size of the battery, the device in which it is used, and whether it is used continuously or intermittently.
**Can be recharged up to 1,000 times with a recharger.

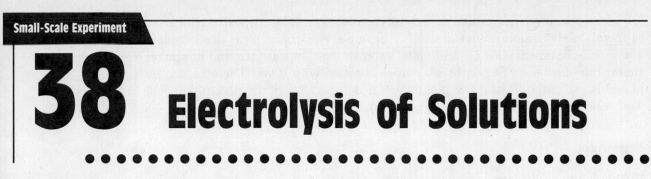

38 Electrolysis of Solutions

Text Section 22.9

Objectives

■ **Observe** the electrolysis of aqueous solutions and identify the reaction products at the cathode and anode.

■ **Describe** electrolysis reactions by writing half-reactions and net ionic equations for electrolysis reactions.

Introduction

You have already learned that aqueous solutions of ionic compounds are electrolytes. They conduct electricity because water causes the ions to dissociate or break apart. The positive and negative ions are free to move about in solution, thus enabling them to carry an electric current.

You may have noticed that some of the solutions reacted chemically when you tested them for conductivity in Small-Scale Experiment 23. The ions in solution not only conducted electrons, they also gained and lost them. In other words, the ions were oxidized or reduced.

Electrolysis is the process by which an electric current causes a chemical reaction to take place. An electrolytic cell is a vessel in which electrolysis reactions occur. An electrolytic cell consists of two electrodes, a positive electrode called an anode, and a negative electrode called a cathode. When a voltage is applied to the cell, an electrolysis reaction takes place as shown in Figure 38.1.

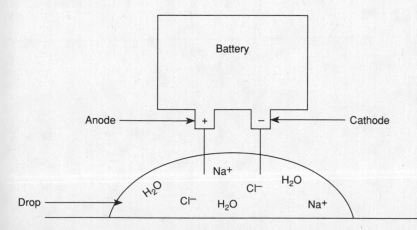

Figure 38.1 *A drop as an electrolytic cell*

Electrolysis of Solutions **275**

Electroplating is an industrial electrolytic process used to deposit a thin layer of metal "plate" onto another metal. For example, electroplating is used to plate automobile bumpers with chromium to improve their appearance and to protect them from corrosion. Similarly, silverware is plated with silver. The object to be plated is the cathode, and the plating metal is the anode of an electrolytic cell. The aqueous solution contains ions of the plating metal.

Purpose

In this lab you will investigate electrolysis of various aqueous solutions and use indicators to identify the reaction products at the cathode and anode. You will electroplate metals onto other metals and identify them.

Safety

- Wear your safety glasses.
- Use small-scale pipets only for the carefully controlled delivery of liquids.

Materials

Small-scale pipets of the following solutions:
water (H_2O)   sodium sulfate (Na_2SO_4)
bromthymol blue (BTB)   potassium iodide (KI)
starch   sodium chloride (NaCl)
potassium bromide (KBr)   copper(II) sulfate ($CuSO_4$)

Equipment

small-scale reaction surface
electrolysis apparatus

Experimental Page

Place one drop of each solution in the indicated place, and apply the leads of the electrolysis apparatus. Be sure to clean the leads between each experiment. Look carefully at the cathode (negative lead) and the anode (positive lead), and record your observations for each electrode in Table 38.1.

a. H_2O

b. Na_2SO_4

$$2H_2O + 2e^- \rightarrow H_2(g) + 2OH^-$$
$$H_2O \rightarrow \tfrac{1}{2}O_2(g) + 2H^+ + 2e^-$$

c. Na_2SO_4 + BTB

d. KI

$$2\ H_2O + 2e^- \rightarrow H_2(g) + 2OH^-$$
$$2I^- \rightarrow I_2(aq) + 2e^-$$

e. KI + starch

f. KI + BTB

g. NaCl

$$2H_2O + 2e^- \rightarrow H_2(g) + 2OH^-$$
$$2Cl^- \rightarrow Cl_2(g) + 2e^-$$

h. NaCl + BTB

i. KBr

$$2H_2O + 2e^- \rightarrow H_2(g) + 2OH^-$$
$$2Br^- \rightarrow Br_2(aq) + 2e^-$$

j. KBr + BTB

k. $CuSO_4$

$$Cu^{2+} + 2e^- \rightarrow Cu(s)$$
$$H_2O \rightarrow \tfrac{1}{2}O_2(g) + 2H^+ + 2e^-$$

Place this side of the Experimental Page facedown. Use the other side under your small-scale reaction surface.

Experimental Data

Record your results in Table 38.1 or a table like it in your notebook. Assign each given half-reaction as occurring at the anode or the cathode.

Table 38.1   Electrolysis of Solutions

		Cathode	Anode	Half-Reactions
a.	H_2O	NVR	NVR	
b.	Na_2SO_4	bubbles	bubbles	$2H_2O + 2e^- \rightarrow H_2(g) + 2OH^-$ **Cathode** $H_2O \rightarrow \frac{1}{2}O_2(g) + 2H^+ + 2e^-$ **Anode**
c.	Na_2SO_4 + BTB	blue	yellow	
d.	KI	bubbles	yellow	$2H_2O + 2e^- \rightarrow H_2(g) + 2OH^-$ **Cathode** $2I^- \rightarrow I_2(aq) + 2e^-$ **Anode**
e.	KI + starch	bubbles	black	
f.	KI + BTB	blue	yellow	
g.	NaCl	bubbles	bubbles	$2H_2O + 2e^- \rightarrow H_2(g) + 2OH^-$ **Cathode** $2Cl^- \rightarrow Cl_2(g) + 2e^-$ **Anode**
h.	NaCl + BTB	blue	yellow	
i.	KBr	bubbles	brown	$2H_2O + 2e^- \rightarrow H_2(g) + 2OH^-$ **Cathode** $2Br^- \rightarrow Br_2(aq) + 2e^-$ **Anode**
j.	KBr + BTB	blue	yellow	
k.	$CuSO_4$	brown	bubbles	$Cu^{2+} + 2e^- \rightarrow Cu(s)$ **Cathode** $H_2O \rightarrow \frac{1}{2}O_2(g) + 2H^+ + 2e^-$ **Anode**

Cleaning Up

Avoid contamination by cleaning up in a way that protects you and your environment. Carefully rinse and dry the leads of the electrolysis apparatus. Clean the reaction surface by absorbing the contents onto a paper towel, wipe it with a damp paper towel, and dry it. Dispose of the paper towels in the waste bin. Wash your hands thoroughly with soap and water.

Name _____ Class _____ Date _____

Questions for Analysis

Use what you learned in this lab to answer the following questions.

1. Explain how you know that pure water does not conduct electricity and why it does not undergo electrolysis.

   Nothing happens when the electrolysis apparatus is applied. There are no

   significant amounts of ions present in pure water.

2. What do you observe when you apply the electrolysis apparatus to the water + sodium sulfate, Na_2SO_4? Why do experiments **a** and **b** give different results?

   Bubbles at the electrodes. Experiment b contains ions that can carry the

   electric current.

3. Which reaction of the half-reactions below is the oxidation? Which is the reduction? Which is the cathode reaction? Which is the anode reaction?

   $$2H_2O + 2e^- \rightarrow H_2(g) + 2OH^-$$

   $$H_2O \rightarrow \tfrac{1}{2}O_2(g) + 2H^+ + 2e^-$$

   Gain of electrons is reduction at the cathode. Loss of electrons is oxidation

   at the anode.

4. What do you observe when you electrolyze $H_2O + Na_2SO_4 + BTB$? Given the electrode half-reactions in Question 3, what must be one product at the cathode (negative electrode)? What must be one product at the anode (positive electrode)?

   BTB turns yellow at one electrode and blue at the other. Hydroxide ion at

   the negative and hydronium ion at the positive.

5. Add the half-reactions in Question 3 to obtain the net ionic equation. Simplify the result by adding together the OH^- and H^+ to get HOH, and then cancel out anything that appears on both sides of the equation.

   $$H_2O \rightarrow H_2(g) + \tfrac{1}{2}O_2(g)$$

6. What do you observe when you electrolyze $H_2O + KI$? How do the given half-reactions explain your observations? Add the half-reactions below to obtain the net ionic equation.

   $$2H_2O + 2e^- \rightarrow H_2(g) + 2OH^-$$

   $$2I^- \rightarrow I_2(g) + 2e^-$$

   A yellow solution forms at the anode. The oxidation half-reaction produces

   I_2 which is yellow. $2H_2O + 2I^- \rightarrow H_2(g) + 2OH^- + I_2(g)$

7. What is the effect of the starch added to the $H_2O + KI$? What chemical species does starch detect?

   A black substance is produced at the anode. I_2.

8. Recalling that Cl and I are in the same family, predict the half-reactions that occur when H_2O + NaCl is electrolyzed. Cite evidence from your experiments that supports your theory. Repeat this for KBr.

$2H_2O + 2e^- \rightarrow H_2(g) + 2OH^-$ **Bubbles appear at both electrodes.**

$2Cl^- \rightarrow Cl_2(g) + 2e^-$

$2H_2O + 2e^- \rightarrow H_2(g) + 2OH^-$ **Bubbles appear at the cathode, and a**

brown substance appears at the anode.

9. What happened to the color of the cathode as you electrolyzed $CuSO_4$? What did you observe at the anode? Write half-reactions to explain.

The cathode turned brownish black and bubbles formed at the anode.

$Cu^{2+} + 2e^- \rightarrow Cu(s) \cdot H_2O \rightarrow H_2(g) + \frac{1}{2}O_2(g)$

Now It's Your Turn!

1. Design an experiment to use a penny and a nickel as electrodes, and to plate copper metal onto the nickel. Explain the procedure you plan to use and how you would carry it out.

Place the nickel and penny about two millimeters apart. Add a drop of cop-

per sulfate so both are wet. Apply the negative electrode of the electrolysis

apparatus to the penny and the positive electrode to the nickel. Wait a few

seconds as the nickel is plated with brown copper metal.

2. Place a small piece of filter paper on a square of aluminum foil. Wet the paper with a drop of $NaNO_3$. Place a penny on the wet paper. Apply the negative electrode of the electrolysis apparatus to the penny and the positive electrode to the aluminum, and wait five seconds. Take the filter paper and add a few drops of NH_3. Tell what you see and explain what happened.

The filter paper turned blue indicating the presence of Cu^{2+} ions. Copper

metal was oxidized to copper(II) ions. The ions migrated into the filter pa-

per and formed the familiar blue $Cu(NH_3)_4^{2+}$ ion.

39 Amphoterism and the Formation of Complex Ions with Hydroxide

Text Section 23.3

Objectives

- **Observe** the behavior of amphoteric hydroxides in the presence of acid and base.
- **Describe** amphoteric behavior by writing net ionic equations.

Introduction

An **amphoteric** compound behaves as a **base** under some conditions and as an **acid** under other conditions (Section 18.6). For example, water behaves as a Brønsted base in the presence of hydrochloric acid because it accepts a hydrogen ion. In the presence of ammonia, water is a Brønsted acid because it donates a hydrogen ion to ammonia:

$$HCl + HOH \rightleftharpoons H_3O^+ + Cl^- \quad NH_3 + HOH \rightleftharpoons NH_4^+ + OH^-$$

Some insoluble hydroxides are also amphoteric because they react with both acids and bases. For example, aluminum hydroxide, $Al(OH)_3$, is a Brønsted base because it neutralizes acids:

$$Al(OH)_3(s) + 3H^+ \rightarrow Al^{3+} + 3H_2O$$

Aluminum hydroxide also behaves as an acid because it reacts with excess hydroxide ion to form a complex ion. A *complex* ion is an ion containing one or more molecules or ions bonded to a central metal ion.

$$Al(OH)_3(s) + OH^- \rightarrow Al(OH)_4^-$$

Another way to describe this complex-ion-forming reaction is in terms of competing equilibria. In the presence of water an aluminum hydroxide precipitate is in equilibrium with its ions, and the reaction lies far to the left favoring the formation of $Al(OH)_3(s)$:

$$Al(OH)_3(s) \rightleftharpoons Al^{3+} + 3OH^-$$

When excess hydroxide is introduced to the equilibrium system, the following equilibrium is established which lies far to the right:

$$Al^{3+} + 4OH^- \rightleftharpoons Al(OH)_4^-$$

Both equilibria involve the Al^{3+} ion, and therefore both equilibria compete for this ion. Because the second equilibrium lies far to the right, it consumes Al^{3+} ions at the expense of the first equilibrium. The first system, obeying Le Châtelier's principle, shifts to the right. You observe that the aluminum hydroxide precipitate in the first equilibrium system dissolves as the complex ion in the second equilibrium system is formed.

Purpose

In this lab you will use a small amount of hydroxide ion to precipitate various metal cations as hydroxides. You will then use excess hydroxide ion as a probe to determine which of these precipitates dissolve. You can conclude that dissolution of a hydroxide precipitate in the presence of excess hydroxide ion is evidence for the formation of a complex ion. You will also observe the amphoteric nature of these compounds by combining them with acid.

Safety

- Wear your safety glasses.

- Use full small-scale pipets only for the carefully controlled delivery of liquids.

Materials

Small-scale pipets of the following solutions:

copper(II) sulfate ($CuSO_4$)	sodium hydroxide (NaOH)
silver nitrate ($AgNO_3$)	nitric acid (HNO_3)
aluminum chloride ($AlCl_3$)	lead(II) nitrate ($Pb(NO_3)_2$)
zinc chloride ($ZnCl_2$)	calcium chloride ($CaCl_2$)
iron(III) chloride ($FeCl_3$)	magnesium sulfate ($MgSO_4$)
potassium hydroxide (KOH)	

Equipment

small-scale reaction surface
empty pipet for stirring

Experimental Page

1. Place one drop of KOH on each X below. Add 1 drop of each indicated metal ion solution to the KOH. Stir each mixture by blowing air through an empty pipet.

2. To each mixture in the second column, stir in enough HNO_3 to dissolve the precipitate.

3. To each mixture in the third column, add several drops of NaOH and stir. Record your results in Table 39.1.

1 drop each	KOH	KOH + HNO_3	KOH + NaOH
a. $CuSO_4$ (Cu^{2+})	X	X	X
b. $CaCl_2$ (Ca^{2+})	X	X	X
c. $AlCl_3$ (Al^{3+})	X	X	X
d. $FeCl_3$ (Fe^{3+})	X	X	X
e. $ZnCl_2$ (Zn^{2+})	X	X	X
f. $Pb(NO_3)_2$ (Pb^{2+})	X	X	X
g. $AgNO_3$ (Ag^+)	X	X	X
h. $MgSO_4$ (Mg^{2+})	X	X	X

Place this side of the Experimental Page facedown. Use the other side under your small-scale reaction surface.

Experimental Data

Record your results in Table 39.1 or a table like it in your notebook.

Table 39.1　Formation of Complex Ions

	KOH	KOH + HNO$_3$	KOH + NaOH
a. CuSO$_4$ (Cu^{2+})	blue ppt.	blue ppt. dissolves.	blue ppt. no change.
b. CaCl$_2$ (Ca^{2+})	white ppt.	white ppt. dissolves.	white ppt. no change.
c. AlCl$_3$ (Al^{3+})	white ppt.	white ppt. dissolves.	white ppt. dissolves.
d. FeCl$_3$ (Fe^{3+})	orange ppt.	orange ppt. dissolves.	orange ppt. no change.
e. ZnCl$_2$ (Zn^{2+})	white ppt.	white ppt. dissolves.	white ppt. dissolves.
f. Pb(NO$_3$)$_2$ (Pb^{2+})	white ppt.	white ppt. dissolves.	white ppt. dissolves.
g. AgNO$_3$ (Ag$^+$)	brown ppt.	brown ppt. dissolves.	brown ppt. no change.
h. MgSO$_4$ (Mg^{2+})	white ppt.	white ppt. dissolves.	white ppt. no change.

Cleaning Up

Avoid contamination by cleaning up in a way that protects you and your environment. Carefully clean the reaction surface by absorbing the contents onto a paper towel, wipe it with a damp paper towel, and dry it. Dispose of the paper towels in the waste bin. Wash your hands thoroughly with soap and water.

Questions for Analysis

Use what you learned in this lab to answer the following questions.

1. Hydroxide ions commonly form precipitates with metal ions. For example, copper(II) ion reacts with hydroxide ion to produce copper(II) hydroxide:

$$Cu^{2+} + 2OH^- \rightarrow Cu(OH)_2(s)$$

Write net ionic equations to describe each precipitation reaction you observed.

$Al^{3+} + 3OH^- \rightarrow Al(OH)_3(s)$ $Zn^{2+} + 2OH^- \rightarrow Zn(OH)_2(s)$

$Pb^{2+} + 2OH^- \rightarrow Pb(OH)_2(s)$ $Fe^{3+} + 3OH^- \rightarrow Fe(OH)_3(s)$

$Ag^+ + 2OH^- \rightarrow Ag(OH)_2(s)*$ $Mg^{2+} + 2OH^- \rightarrow Mg(OH)_2(s)$

*Although students will write this, it is the oxide rather than the hydroxide that forms: $2Ag^+ + 2OH^- \rightarrow Ag_2O(s) + H_2O$

2. Hydroxide precipitates dissolve readily in acid solution. For example, copper(II) hydroxide reacts with acid to form copper(II) ions and water.

$$Cu(OH)_2(s) + 2H^+ \rightarrow Cu^{2+} + 2H_2O$$

Which other precipitates dissolved in acid? Write net ionic equations to describe each neutralization reaction you observed.

$Ca(OH)_2(s) + 2H^+ \rightarrow Ca^{2+} + 2H_2O$ $Zn(OH)_2(s) + 2H^+ \rightarrow Zn^{2+} + 2H_2O$

$Al(OH)_3(s) + 3H^+ \rightarrow Al^{3+} + 3H_2O$ $Fe(OH)_3(s) + 3H^+ \rightarrow Fe^{3+} + 3H_2O$

$Pb(OH)_2(s) + 2H^+ \rightarrow Pb^{2+} + 2H_2O$ $Ag_2O(s) + 2H^+ \rightarrow 2Ag^+ + H_2O$

$Mg(OH)_2(s) + 2H^+ \rightarrow Mg^{2+} + 2H_2O$

3. When hydrogen ions are added, do the hydroxide precipitates act as bases or acids? Explain.

Bases. They are neutralized by acid.

4. Some hydroxide precipitates dissolve in excess NaOH. For example, aluminum hydroxide reacts with excess hydroxide ions to produce an aluminum hydroxide complex ion.

$$Al(OH)_3(s) + OH^- \rightarrow Al(OH)_4^-$$

Write similar equations for the other hydroxide precipitates that reacted with excess sodium hydroxide.

$Zn(OH)_2$ and $Pb(OH)_2$.   **$Pb(OH)_2(s) + OH^- \rightarrow Pb(OH)_3^-$**

5. When a base is added in excess, do the hydroxide precipitates act as acids or bases? Explain.

Acids. They react with bases.

6. Which hydroxide precipitates are amphoteric? (That is, which act as both acids and bases?)

$Al(OH)_3$, $Zn(OH)_2$ and $Pb(OH)_2$.

Now It's Your Turn!

1. Several metal ions form complexes with thiocyanate ion, SCN^-, and thiosulfate ion, $S_2O_3^{2-}$. Design some experiments to find out which ions form complexes with these ions.

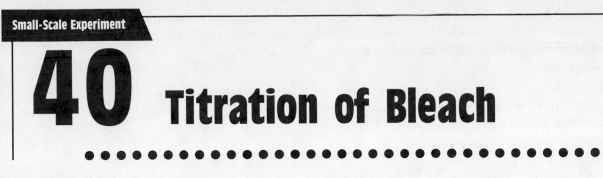

40 Titration of Bleach

Text Section 23.6

Objective

- **Measure** and **record** the amount of sodium hypochlorite in household bleach.

Introduction

Sodium hypochlorite, NaOCl, is a common chemical that has many household applications. Sodium hypochlorite is the active ingredient in household bleach, liquid drain openers, powdered cleansers, and automatic dish washing liquids. The hypochlorite ion, OCl^-, is useful in these cleaners because it is a powerful oxidizing agent. Hypochlorite ion as an oxidizing agent is able to whiten, brighten, or otherwise remove the color from all sorts of materials. For example, manufacturers of paper and textiles often use some sort of bleach to whiten their products and prepare them to be dyed.

The hypochlorite ion is also useful as a disinfectant. Hypochlorous acid, HOCl, is very toxic to bacteria. A very small concentration of about one part per million (1 ppm) is required to kill bacteria. The small OCl^- ion easily penetrates the cell of a bacterium. Once inside, its strong oxidizing effect destroys the bacterium protein.

Swimming pools are typically treated with hypochlorite ion to disinfect the water and keep it sanitary. One pool sanitizer is calcium hypochlorite, $Ca(OCl)_2$, which introduces hypochlorite ion directly into the water. Larger pools commonly contain chlorine gas, which reacts with water to produce hypochlorous acid:

$$Cl_2(g) + H_2O \rightarrow HOCl + H^+ + Cl^-$$

Another kind of bleach is an "oxygen bleach." Examples of oxygen bleaches are hydrogen peroxide, H_2O_2, and sodium perborate, Na_3BO_4. Many laundry detergents advertise that they contain "color safe" bleach, meaning that the active ingredient is sodium perborate. Sodium perborate, an oxygen bleach, is much milder than sodium hypochlorite, the active ingredient in "chlorine bleach." In fact, sodium hypochlorite is so powerful it can fray or discolor fabric, and dissolve stitching. Even so, consumer tests have shown repeatedly that chlorine bleach (containing sodium hypochlorite) is superior to oxygen bleaches (containing hydrogen peroxide or sodium perborate) at removing stains and brightening fabrics.

The use of all products that contain sodium hypochlorite can be dangerous. Sodium hypochlorite reacts with hydrochloric acid to produce toxic chlorine gas:

$$NaOCl + 2HCl \rightarrow NaCl + H_2O + Cl_2(g)$$

For this reason one should avoid mixing household bleach or any other product containing sodium hypochlorite with other household products such as toilet-bowl cleaners that contain acid. Warning labels on bottles of household bleach are very clear about this:

Warning! Do not mix with other chemicals, such as toilet-bowl cleaners, rust removers, acid or ammonia containing products. To do so will release hazardous gases.

Purpose

In this lab you will use sodium thiosulfate, $Na_2S_2O_3$, to determine the amount of sodium hypochlorite, NaOCl, in household bleach. Your method will be iodometric titration. That is, you will add starch, ethanoic acid, CH_3COOH, and iodide ion (KI) to a dilute solution of bleach, NaOCl. This will cause a reaction producing iodine. The starch acts as an indicator, turning the mixture blue-black in color. You will then titrate the iodine with thiosulfate. In the titration, you will measure the amount of sodium thiosulfate it takes to change the mixture from blue-black to colorless at the end point. The measured amount of $Na_2S_2O_3$ is directly proportional to the amount of NaOCl in the bleach.

You will begin by examining the chemistry of the titration and then apply it to the analysis of a bleach sample. Finally, you will design and carry out experiments to find out how much sodium hypochlorite there is in other consumer products.

Safety

- Wear your safety glasses.
- Use full small-scale pipets only for the carefully controlled delivery of liquids.

Materials

Small-scale pipets of the following solutions:

sodium hypochlorite (NaOCl)   sodium thiosulfate ($Na_2S_2O_3$)
ethanoic acid (CH_3COOH)   potassium iodide (KI)
starch   diluted household bleach

Equipment

small-scale reaction surface
plastic cup
12-well strip

Experimental Procedure

Part A. Some Chemistry of NaOCl

1. Place one drop of NaOCl on a small-scale reaction surface and add the solutions mentioned in the following steps. Stir each mixture and record your results in Table 40.1.

a. Add 1 drop of KI and 1 drop of CH_3COOH to the drop of NaOCl in Step 1. In acid solution, hypochlorite ion oxidizes iodide ion to iodine:

$$OCl^- + 2I^- + 2H^+ \rightarrow Cl^- + H_2O + I_2$$

b. Add a few more drops of KI to the mixture. Excess iodide ion reacts with iodine to form triiodide ion: $I^- + I_2 \rightarrow I_3^-$

c. Now add a drop of starch. Starch reacts with triiodide ion to form a starch-iodine complex: $I_3^- + starch \rightarrow$ starch-iodine complex.

d. Now add several drops of $Na_2S_2O_3$ until the reaction mixture turns colorless. Thiosulfate ion reduces triiodide to iodide ion:

$$I_3^- + 2S_2O_3^{2-} \rightarrow 3I^- + S_4O_6^{2-}$$

Part B. Titration of Sodium Hypochlorite in Bleach with Sodium Thiosulfate

2. Carry out the following procedure for the titration of bleach.

a. Calibrate a $Na_2S_2O_3$ pipet. (Count the number of drops to fill a well.)

b. Calibrate a NaOCl (bleach) pipet. (Count the number of drops to fill a well.)

c. Using the same pipet, add the same number of drops of NaOCl it took to fill a well to a clean, dry cup.

d. Add in order: 3 drops starch, 25 drops KI, and 20 drops CH_3COOH.

e. Titrate the NaOCl with $Na_2S_2O_3$ to a colorless end point. (Count the number of drops of $Na_2S_2O_3$ it takes to change the mixture from black to colorless.)

f. Repeat the experiment until your results are consistent.

Experimental Data

Record your results in Tables 40.1 and 40.2 or tables like them in your notebook.

Table 40.1   Chemistry of NaOCl

	NaOCl	KI + CH$_3$COOH	Excess KI	Starch	Na$_2$S$_2$O$_3$
Color	Colorless	Yellow	Dark yellow	Black	Colorless

Table 40.2   Titration of Bleach

NaOCl Sample	Drops Na$_2$S$_2$O$_3$ to fill	Drops NaOCl to fill	Drops NaOCl in cup	Drops Na$_2$S$_2$O$_3$ to end point	NaOCl conc. mol/L
1	19	21	21	48	0.13
2	19	21	21	48	0.12
3	19	21	21	48	0.13

Calculate the concentration in mol NaOCl/L of sodium hypochlorite in the bleach samples you titrated. Record your results in Table 40.2. To do the calculation, you will need the following pieces of information:

a. The drops of Na$_2$S$_2$O$_3$ used to obtain a colorless end point in the titration.

b. The drops of NaOCl added to the cup.

c. The drops of NaOCl needed to fill a well in drops/well.

d. The drops of Na$_2$S$_2$O$_3$ needed to fill a well in drops/well.

e. The concentration of Na$_2$S$_2$O$_3$ = 0.1 M.

f. The overall stoichiometry = 1 mol NaOCl/2 mol Na$_2$S$_2$O$_3$.

$$\frac{x \text{ mol NaOCl}}{\text{L NaOCl}} = \frac{a}{b} \times \frac{c}{d} \times e \times f$$

To be sure you understand the calculation, substitute each quantity (number and unit) into the equation and cancel the units. For subsequent calculations, simplify the equation by combining terms that are always constant. For example, in this experiment, the number of drops of NaOCl added to the cup is equal to the number of drops of NaOCl it took to fill a well, so **b = c** and they cancel.

$$xM \text{ NaOCl} = \frac{a}{1} \times \frac{1}{d} \times e \times f = \frac{aef}{d}$$

Cleaning Up

Avoid contamination by cleaning up in a way that protects you and your environment. Carefully clean the reaction surface by absorbing the contents onto a dry paper towel, wipe it with a damp paper towel, and dry it. Rinse out the cup, wipe it with a damp paper towel, and dry it. Dispose of the towels in the waste bin. Wash your hands thoroughly with soap and water.

Questions for Analysis

Use what you learned in this lab to answer the following questions.

1. What happens when you add NaOCl to KI and CH_3COOH? What is the colored product? Write the net ionic equation (see Experimental Procedure).

   The solution turns yellow. I_2. $OCl^- + 2I^- + 2H^+ \rightarrow Cl^- + H_2O + I_2$.

2. A few more drops of KI produces what change? Write the net ionic equation for the reaction of excess potassium iodide with iodine (see Experimental Page).

   The yellow color darkens. $I^- + I_2 \rightarrow I_3^-$.

3. What happens when you add starch? Write the equation for the reaction between triiodide and starch.

   The solution turns black. I_3^- + starch $\rightarrow$ starch-iodine complex.

4. What color is the final mixture after you add sodium thiosulfate? Write the net ionic equation for the reaction between triiodide and sodium thiosulfate.

   Colorless. $I_3^- + 2S_2O_3^{2-} \rightarrow 3I^- + S_4O_6^{2-}$.

5. Explain how starch acts as an indicator for the presence or absence of triiodide.

   It turns black when I_3^- is present.

6. Calculate the percent of NaOCl in the bleach, using the number of moles of NaOCl per liter that you calculated from your Experimental Data.

   $$\% \text{ NaOCl} = \frac{g \text{ NaOCl}}{100 \text{ g soln}} = \frac{\textbf{0.13} \text{ moles NaOCl}}{\text{L soln}} \times \frac{74.5 \text{ g NaOCl}}{\text{mol NaOCl}} \times \frac{1 \text{ L soln}}{1000 \text{ g soln}} \times 100 = \textbf{0.97\%}$$

7. Multiply the percent of NaOCl in bleach from Question 6 by 5 (the bleach sample you titrated was diluted by a factor of 5), and compare your result to the percent of NaOCl listed on the bleach bottle's label by calculating the percent error and suggesting possible sources of error.

$$\% \text{ error} = \frac{5 \times \text{your result} - \% \text{ on label}}{\% \text{ on label}} \times 100 = \frac{(5 \times 0.97) - 5.25}{5.25} \times 100 = 7.6\% \text{ error}$$

As bleach gets older, the NaOCl loses chlorine in the form of chlorine gas.

Thus, it is reasonable that the experimentally determined percent of NaOCl

would be lower than the percent on the bottle. Also, adding ethanoic acid

to the bleach accelerates the loss of chlorine.

Now It's Your Turn!

1. Design and carry out some weight titration experiments, using your small-scale balance or other balance to determine the molar concentration of NaOCl in bleach. Compare your results to your volumetric titrations.

   Weigh about 500 mg of bleach. Add 3 drops of starch, 25 drops of KI, and 20

   drops of ethanoic acid. Balance a pipet full of $Na_2S_2O_3$, and titrate the

   bleach to colorless. Find the weight loss of $Na_2S_2O_3$. Mol/L of NaOCl =

   wt. of bleach/(wt. loss of $Na_2S_2O_3$)(20).

2. The labels of many household products say they contain sodium hypochlorite. Dish-washing-machine liquids often contain NaOCl. Design and carry out some experiments to determine the molar concentration of NaOCl in some household dish-washing-machine liquids.

3. Design some experiments to show that sodium hypochlorite is not "color-safe."

   Add NaOCl to food dyes, colored paper, and colors made from marker

   pens on paper.

41 Halogen Ions in Solution

Text Section 23.7

Objectives

- **Observe** the chemical properties of halide ions in aqueous solution.
- **Identify** halide ions by noting the differences in their chemical properties.
- **Describe** the chemical reactions of halide ions by writing and balancing chemical and net ionic equations.

Introduction

Halogens is the name given to the family of elements that comprise Group 17 (VIIA), on the periodic table. The individual elements are fluorine, chlorine, bromine, iodine, and astatine. All but astatine are relatively common elements. Because they are chemically reactive, the halogens never occur as single, free atoms in nature. The halogens form a large number of compounds and have many uses. In the elemental form, halogens are most stable as diatomic molecules whose formulas are written F_2, Cl_2, Br_2, and I_2.

The reactivity of the halogens and their similar properties are due to their very similar electron configurations. All halogens have seven valence (outer orbital) electrons, and each halogen readily gains one electron to form an anion with a single negative charge:

$$X + e^- \rightarrow X^- \qquad \text{where } X = F, Cl, Br, I$$

These halogen anions are called halide ions. Their individual names are derived from their element names: F^- = fluoride, Cl^- = chloride, Br^- = bromide, and I^- = iodide.

Purpose

In this lab you will examine some of the chemical reactions of the halide ions, derived from the halogen elements. You will learn to write chemical equations to describe their reactions. You will learn to use these chemical reactions to distinguish one halide ion from another.

Safety

- Wear your safety glasses.
- Use full small-scale pipets only for the carefully controlled delivery of liquids.

Materials

Small-scale pipets of the following solutions:

calcium chloride ($CaCl_2$)

lead(II) nitrate ($Pb(NO_3)_2$)

silver nitrate ($AgNO_3$)

sodium hypochlorite (NaOCl)

ammonia (NH_3)

starch

hydrochloric acid (HCl)

FD&C blue #1 (blue dye)

iron(III) chloride ($FeCl_3$)

potassium fluoride (KF)

potassium chloride (KCl)

potassium bromide (KBr)

potassium iodide (KI)

sodium thiosulfate ($Na_2S_2O_3$)

bromthymol blue (BTB)

copper(II) sulfate ($CuSO_4$)

hydrogen peroxide (H_2O_2)

Equipment

small-scale reaction surface

empty pipet for stirring

clear plastic cup

Experimental Page

Part A. Chemistry of the Halide Ions

1. Add 1 drop of each of the indicated solutions on the **X**. Stir each mixture by blowing air with an empty small-scale pipet. Record your results in Table 41.1.

		KF (F$^-$)	KCl (Cl$^-$)	KBr (Br$^-$)	KI (I$^-$)	
a.	CaCl$_2$ (Ca^{2+})	X	X	X	X	
b.	Pb(NO$_3$)$_2$ (Pb^{2+})	X	X	X	X	
c.	AgNO$_3$ (Ag$^+$)	X	X	X	X	Now add 5–10 drops NH$_3$ to each and stir. Look for a change.
d.	AgNO$_3$ (Ag$^+$)	X	X	X	X	Now add 5–10 drops Na$_2$S$_2$O$_3$ to each and stir. Look for a change.
e.	NaOCl (OCl$^-$)	X	X	X	X	Now add 1 drop of starch and 1 drop of HCl to each and stir.

Part B. Chemistry of Chlorine Gas, Cl$_2$(g)

2. Place 1 drop of each solution in the indicated space. Add 1 drop of NaOCl to the HCl and cover the entire array with a cup. Observe the drops for any change over time, about 10 minutes. After you record your results in Table 41.2, turn this page over and continue the experiment.

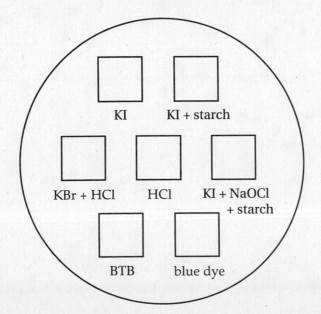

Part C. Chemistry of the Iodide Ion

3. Mix 1 drop of each of the following solutions on the **X**'s. Record your results in Table 41.3.

	NaOCl	CuSO₄	FeCl₃	H₂O₂
KI	**X**	**X**	**X**	**X**

Now add 1 drop of starch to each mixture, then 1 drop of HCl.

Experimental Data

Record your results in Tables 41.1, 41.2, and 41.3 or tables like them in your notebook.

Table 41.1   Chemistry of the Halide Ions

	KF (F$^-$)	KCl (Cl$^-$)	KBr (Br$^-$)	KI (I$^-$)	
a. CaCl$_2$ (Ca^{2+})	light white ppt.	NVR	NVR	NVR	
b. Pb(NO$_3$)$_2$ (Pb^{2+})	white ppt.	NVR	white ppt.	bright yellow ppt.	
c. AgNO$_3$ (Ag$^+$)	NVR	white ppt.	white ppt.	lime green ppt.	Ppts. dissolve or lighten with NH$_3$.
d. AgNO$_3$ (Ag$^+$)	NVR	white ppt.	white ppt.	lime green ppt.	Ppts. dissolve or lighten with Na$_2$S$_2$O$_3$.
e. NaOCl (OCl$^-$)	NVR	NVR	NVR, brown	yellow soln., black with starch	

Table 41.2   Chemistry of Chlorine Gas, Cl$_2$(g)

	KI colorless	KBr + HCl colorless	BTB green	KI + starch colorless	blue dye blue	Starch + KI + NaOCl black
HCl + NaOCl	yellow	brown	yellow	black	gray	no change

Table 41.3   Chemistry of Iodide Ion

	NaOCl	CuSO$_4$	FeCl$_3$	H$_2$O$_2$
KI	yellow soln. black with starch	yellow ppt black with starch	orange soln. black with starch	NVR black with starch + HCl

Cleaning Up

Avoid contamination by cleaning up in a way that protects you and your environment. Carefully clean the reaction surface by absorbing the contents onto a paper towel. Rinse the reaction surface with a damp paper towel and dry it. Clean the plastic cup by wiping it with a dry paper towel. Dispose of the paper towels in the waste bin. Wash your hands thoroughly with soap and water.

Questions for Analysis

Use what you learned in this lab to answer the following questions.

1. What similarities did you observe in the reactions of halogens in Part A?

All of the ions but F$^-$ formed precipitates with the Ag$^+$ and Pb^{2+} ions.

2. Describe how the four halide ions—F$^-$, Cl$^-$, Br$^-$, and I$^-$—can be distinguished from one another. (That is, what chemical solutions undergo reactions that are unique to each ion?)

Only F$^-$ precipitates with Ca^{2+}. I$^-$ is bright yellow with Pb^{2+}. AgCl dissolves

in NH$_3$ and Na$_2$S$_2$O$_3$. Only Br$^-$ turns brown with NaOCl and HCl.

3. Lead(II) ion reacts with iodide ion to produce a lead(II) iodide precipitate:

$$Pb^{2+} + 2I^- \rightarrow PbI_2(s)$$

Write similar net ionic equations to describe the other precipitation reactions you observed.

Pb^{2+} + 2Br$^-$ → PbBr$_2$(s)	**Pb^{2+} + 2Cl$^-$ → PbCl$_2$(s)**
Ca^{2+} + 2F$^-$ → CaF$_2$(s)	**Ag$^+$ + Cl$^-$ → AgCl(s)**
Ag$^+$ + Br$^-$ → AgBr(s)	**Ag$^+$ + I$^-$ → AgI(s)**

4. Would you get different results if you used aqueous solutions of sodium halides rather than potassium halides? Explain.

No. The chemistry is due to the halide ions. Na$^+$ would be a spectator ion

like K$^+$.

5. Silver forms a *complex* ion with ammonia:

$$AgX(s) + 2NH_3 \rightarrow Ag(NH_3)_2^+ + X^-$$

In the equation above, X represents a halide ion. Write equations for the reactions of ammonia for the silver halides that dissolve in ammonia by replacing X with each halide ion that dissolves.

AgCl(s) + 2NH$_3$ → Ag(NH$_3$)$_2^+$ + Cl$^-$

AgBr(s) + 2NH$_3$ → Ag(NH$_3$)$_2^+$ + Br$^-$

6. Silver halide precipitates also dissolve in excess thiosulfate, $S_2O_3^{2-}$, to form the complex ion $Ag(S_2O_3)_2^{3-}$.

$$AgX(s) + 2S_2O_3^{2-} \rightarrow Ag(S_2O_3)_2^{3-} + X^-$$

Write equations for each reaction you observed with thiosulfate.

$AgCl(s) + 2S_2O_3^{2-} \rightarrow Ag(S_2O_3)_2^{3-} + Cl^-$

$AgBr(s) + 2S_2O_3^{2-} \rightarrow Ag(S_2O_3)_2^{3-} + Br^-$

7. The reaction of iodide ion, I^-, with NaOCl can be described by the following equation:

$$OCl^- + 2H^+ + 2I^- \rightarrow Cl^- + I_2 + HOH$$

Write an equation for the reaction of bromide ion with NaOCl.

$OCl^- + 2H^+ + 2Br^- \rightarrow Cl^- + Br_2 + HOH$

8. Which chemical product in the sample equation in Question 7 is responsible for the formation of the black color with starch?

I_2.

9. Describe in your own words what must have happened under the cup to cause reactions in the solutions without mixing them with any other solution.

A gas that formed in the center diffused to the other drops and reacted

with them.

10. Sodium hypochlorite, NaOCl, reacts with hydrochloric acid to yield chlorine gas, sodium chloride, and water. Write the chemical equation.

$NaOCl + 2HCl \rightarrow Cl_2(g) + NaCl + H_2O$

11. Given the word equation, write a balanced chemical equation to describe each reaction between chlorine gas and the indicated reagent. In each case, explain the change in the reagent.

a. Chlorine gas reacts with water to produce hydrochloric acid and hypochlorous acid, HOCl.

$Cl_2 + H_2O \rightarrow HCl + HOCl$. BTB turns yellow indicating the presence of

acid.

b. Chlorine reacts with iodide ion to form iodine and chloride ion.

$Cl_2 + 2I^- \rightarrow I_2 + 2Cl^-$. I_2 turns black with starch. As I_2 forms, its character-

istic yellow color appears in aqueous solution.

c. Chlorine reacts similarly with bromide ion.

$Cl_2 + 2Br^- \rightarrow Br_2 + 2Cl^-$. The characteristic brown color of Br_2 appears.

12. What color do all the reaction mixtures in Part C have in common? What chemical species is indicated by this color?

Black. I_2.

---

13. Write and balance chemical equations for all the reactions you observed in Part C. Here are some hints:

$Cl_2 + I^- \rightarrow Cl^- + ?$ | $Cl_2 + 2I^- \rightarrow 2Cl^- + I_2$

$Cu^{2+} + I^- \rightarrow CuI(s) + ?$ | $2Cu^{2+} + 4I^- \rightarrow 2CuI(s) + I_2$

$Fe^{3+} + I^- \rightarrow Fe^{2+} + ?$ | $2Fe^{3+} + 2I^- \rightarrow 2Fe^{2+} + I_2$

$H_2O_2 + I^- + H^+ \rightarrow H_2O + ?$ | $H_2O_2 + 2I^- + 2H^+ \rightarrow 2H_2O + I_2$

Now It's Your Turn!

1. Study the chemistry of bromine, Br_2, by setting up KI, KI + starch, and BTB indicators like those in Part B. Instead of using NaOCl and HCl in the center, use 1 drop each of the following: KBr, KIO_3, and HCl. The reaction is

$$6Br^- + IO_3^- + 6H^+ \rightarrow 3Br_2 + I^- + 3H_2O$$

Report the results of each mixing. Complete and balance the following chemical equations. (Hint: They are like the reactions of Cl_2.)

$Br_2 + I^- \rightarrow$ $Br_2 + H_2O \rightarrow$

$Br_2 + 2I^- \rightarrow 2Br^- + I_2$ **$Br_2 + H_2O \rightarrow HBr + HOBr$**

	KI colorless	KI + starch colorless	BTB green
HCl + KBr + KIO_3	**yellow**	**black**	**yellow**

2. Both I_2 and Br_2 are nonpolar molecules. This means that they are more soluble in nonpolar solvents like baby oil than they are in polar solvents like water. On the other hand, I^- and Br^- are water-soluble ions. Use aqueous solutions of I^- and Br^- to generate some I_2 and Br_2, and watch them dissolve in a nonpolar solvent like baby oil.

On a glass slide, mix 1 drop of each of the following:

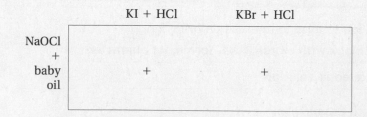

Observe over time. Write chemical equations for each reaction. What color does each halogen appear to be in the baby oil?

$Cl^- + OCl^- + 2H^+ \rightarrow Cl_2 + H_2O$ $Cl_2 + 2Br^- \rightarrow Br_2 + 2Cl^-$

$Cl_2 + 2I^- \rightarrow I_2 + 2Cl^-$ **(brown)**

        (violet)

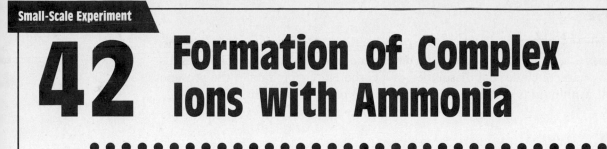

42 Formation of Complex Ions with Ammonia

Text Section 23.10

Objectives

- **Observe** the formation of complex ions when various cations react with ammonia.
- **Identify** metal cations that form complex ions with ammonia.
- **Describe** the formation of complex ions by writing net ionic equations.

Introduction

You have seen in previous labs that ammonia, NH_3, is a base because it reacts with water to produce hydroxide ions in solution:

$$NH_3 + H_2O \rightleftharpoons NH_4^+ + OH^-$$

Ammonia also reacts with a variety of metal cations in aqueous solution to form complex ions. A *complex* ion is an ion containing one or more molecules bonded to a central metal ion. For example, you are already familiar with the royal blue color that results from mixing a copper ion (Cu^{2+}) with ammonia. This reaction produces the highly colored, distinctive complex ion, $Cu(NH_3)_4^{2+}$, called the tetrammonium copper(II) ion.

$$Cu^{2+} + 4NH_3 = Cu(NH_3)_4^{2+}$$
$$\text{royal blue}$$

This reaction is an example of a Lewis acid–base reaction. Copper(II) acts as a Lewis acid because it accepts an electron pair from ammonia. Ammonia is a Lewis base, because it donates an electron pair. The bond between ammonia and copper(II) is a coordinate covalent bond because both electrons come from the ammonia.

While many complex ions are highly colored species, others show only subtle colors or none at all. Hence, color is a limited tool in detecting complex ion formation. In this lab you will detect the formation of colorless complex ions by probing the solubility of certain precipitates in the presence of excess ammonia. Dissolution of the precipitate suggests the formation of a complex ion with ammonia. For example, silver ion will react with carbonate ion to produce silver carbonate:

$$2Ag^+ + CO_3^{2-} = Ag_2CO_3(s)$$

Silver ion also reacts with ammonia to produce a colorless complex ion:

$$Ag^+ + 2NH_3 \rightleftharpoons Ag(NH_3)_2^+$$

When you add ammonia to an aqueous mixture of solid silver carbonate, you will find that the precipitate dissolves. Both of the above equilibria compete for the silver ion, and the formation of the complex ion predominates. That is, the complex-ion reaction lies farther to the right than does the precipitation reaction. Le Châtelier's principle predicts that the first reaction will shift to the left as the second reaction consumes silver ions. Thus, the precipitate will disappear.

Purpose

In this lab you will precipitate various metal cations as carbonates. You will then use excess ammonia ion as a probe to determine which of these precipitates dissolve. You can conclude that dissolution of a carbonate precipitate in the presence of excess ammonia is evidence for the formation of a complex ion.

Safety

- Wear your safety glasses.
- Use full small-scale pipets only for the carefully controlled delivery of liquids.

Materials

Small-scale pipets of the following aqueous solutions:

copper(II) sulfate ($CuSO_4$)   sodium hydrogen carbonate ($NaHCO_3$)
silver nitrate ($AgNO_3$)   3 M ammonia (NH_3)
aluminum chloride ($AlCl_3$)   lead(II) nitrate ($Pb(NO_3)_2$)
zinc chloride ($ZnCl_2$)   calcium chloride ($CaCl_2$)
iron(III) chloride ($FeCl_3$)   magnesium sulfate ($MgSO_4$)
tin(IV) chloride ($SnCl_4$)   sodium chloride ($NaCl$)

Equipment

small-scale reaction surface
empty pipet for stirring

Experimental Page

On each **X** below, mix 1 drop of $NaHCO_3$ with 2 drops of each indicated solution.
Stir by blowing air through an empty pipet. Then add several drops of NH_3 and stir.

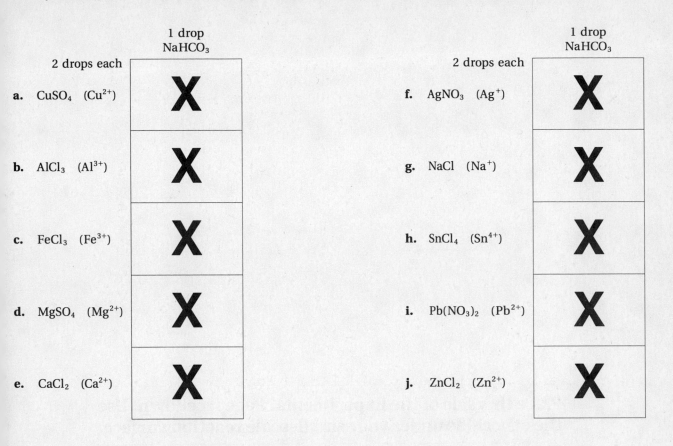

1 drop
$NaHCO_3$

2 drops each

a. $CuSO_4$ (Cu^{2+})

b. $AlCl_3$ (Al^{3+})

c. $FeCl_3$ (Fe^{3+})

d. $MgSO_4$ (Mg^{2+})

e. $CaCl_2$ (Ca^{2+})

1 drop
$NaHCO_3$

2 drops each

f. $AgNO_3$ (Ag^+)

g. $NaCl$ (Na^+)

h. $SnCl_4$ (Sn^{4+})

i. $Pb(NO_3)_2$ (Pb^{2+})

j. $ZnCl_2$ (Zn^{2+})

Place this side of the Experimental Page facedown. Use the other side under your small-scale reaction surface.

Experimental Data

Record your results in Table 42.1 or a table like it in your notebook.

Table 42.1   Complex Ions with Ammonia

a. $CuSO_4$ (Cu^{2+})	blue ppt. **Dissolves** with NH_3.	**f.** $AgNO_3$ (Ag^+) — white ppt. **Dissolves** with NH_3.
b. $AlCl_3$ (Al^{3+})	white ppt. **No change** with NH_3.	**g.** $NaCl$ (Na^+) — **NVR**
c. $FeCl_3$ (Fe^{3+})	orange ppt. **No change** with NH_3.	**h.** $SnCl_4$ (Sn^{4+}) — bubbles. **No change** with NH_3.
d. $MgSO_4$ (Mg^{2+})	white ppt. **No change** with NH_3.	**i.** $Pb(NO_3)_2$ (Pb^{2+}) — white ppt. **No change** with NH_3.
e. $CaCl_2$ (Ca^{2+})	white ppt. **No change** with NH_3.	**j.** $ZnCl_2$ (Zn^{2+}) — white ppt. **Dissolves** with NH_3.

Cleaning Up

Avoid contamination by cleaning up in a way that protects you and your environment. Carefully clean the reaction surface by absorbing the contents onto a paper towel, wipe it with a damp paper towel, and dry it. Dispose of the paper towels in the waste bin. Wash your hands thoroughly with soap and water.

Questions for Analysis

Use what you learned in this lab to answer the following questions.

1. Write net ionic equations for each precipitation reaction you observed.

$Cu^{2+} + CO_3^{2-} \rightarrow CuCO_3(s)$ _____ $2Ag^+ + CO_3^{2-} \rightarrow Ag_2CO_3(s)$

*$2Al^{3+} + 3CO_3^{2-} \rightarrow Al_2(CO_3)_3(s)$ _____ $Zn^{2+} + CO_3^{2-} \rightarrow ZnCO_3(s)$

*$2Fe^{3+} + 3CO_3^{2-} \rightarrow Fe_2(CO_3)_3(s)$ _____ $Pb^{2+} + CO_3^{2-} \rightarrow PbCO_3(s)$

$Mg^{2+} + CO_3^{2-} \rightarrow MgCO_3(s)$ _____ $Ca^{2+} + CO_3^{2-} \rightarrow CaCO_3(s)$

*Although students will write these equations, Al^{3+} and Fe^{3+} are sufficiently strong Lewis acids to react with CO_3^{2-} to form $CO_2(g)$ and water. Do your students observe bubbles?

2. Precipitates of cations that dissolve upon addition of excess ammonia form complex ions with ammonia. Which cations form complex ions with ammonia? Ask your instructor for the formulas of each complex ion.

Cu^{2+}, Zn^{2+}, Ag^+. $Cu(NH_3)_4^{2+}$, $Zn(NH_3)_4^{2+}$, $Ag(NH_3)_2^+$.

3. Write net ionic equations to describe the formation of each complex ion. Identify each Lewis acid and Lewis base.

Lewis acid	Lewis base	
Cu^{2+} +	$4NH_3 \rightarrow$	$Cu(NH_3)_4^{2+}$
Zn^{2+} +	$4NH_3 \rightarrow$	$Zn(NH_3)_4^{2+}$
Ag^+ +	$2NH_3 \rightarrow$	$Ag(NH_3)_2^+$

4. What are the colors of the complex ions?

$Cu(NH_3)_4^{2+}$ is royal blue, $Zn(NH_3)_4^{2+}$ and $Ag(NH_3)_2^+$ are colorless.

Now It's Your Turn!

1. Devise an experiment to determine the cations that form complex ions with ammonia by employing a different precipitate. How do your results compare with this lab? Try forming the initial precipitates with sodium phosphate and sodium hydroxide.

2. Devise an experiment to determine the cations that form complex ions with ammonia using an excess of cation and only a small amount of ammonia as a source of hydroxide to bring down the original precipitates as hydroxides. For example, add 1 drop of ammonia, NH_3, to two drops of copper(II) sulfate, $CuSO_4$. Because ammonia is a weak base it is a source of hydroxide ions:

$$NH_3 + H_2O \rightarrow NH_4^+ + OH^-$$

A small amount of ammonia added to an excess of copper ions will produce a light blue copper(II) hydroxide precipitate:

$$Cu^{2+} + 2OH^- \rightarrow Cu(OH)_2(s)$$

Now add several more drops of ammonia and stir. Excess ammonia will cause copper ions to react to form the royal blue complex ion, $Cu(NH_3)_4^{2+}$:

$$Cu^{2+} + 4NH_3 \rightarrow Cu(NH_3)_4^{2+} \text{ (royal blue solution)}$$

Try adding a little ammonia to an excess of the other cations in this experiment. Then add excess ammonia and see what happens. How do your results compare to the original experiments?

They are the same except that ammonia usually causes the silver ion to go

directly to the complex ion, $Ag(NH_3)_2^+$. No precipitate is usually observed.

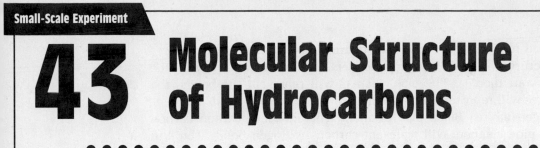

43 Molecular Structure of Hydrocarbons

Text Section 24.5

Objectives

- **Construct** models of hydrocarbon molecules.
- **Compare** the structures of hydrocarbons with their chemical formulas.
- **Compare** the structures of alkanes, alkenes, and alkynes.

Introduction

Chemical formulas give you information about the compositions of substances as well as their structures. Organic chemistry uses many different kinds of formulas and models to describe the compositions and structures of molecules.

A *molecular formula* gives limited information about a compound. Only the actual number and kinds of atoms present in a molecule of a compound are shown. A *structural formula* is more useful for studying organic compounds because it shows the arrangement of each atom and each bond in a molecule. Different structural arrangements of the same molecular formula are called isomers. An *expanded structural formula* actually shows each atom and each bond. A *condensed structural formula* is a shorthand method for writing a structural formula. A *line-angle formula* for a hydrocarbon uses straight lines to represent each carbon-carbon bond. Carbon atoms are understood to be at the ends of each line. Hydrogen atoms are not shown at all. Instead, it is understood that there are enough hydrogen atoms for each carbon atom to have 4 bonds. A *ball-and-stick diagram* of a molecule shows the three-dimensional arrangement of each atom and each bond. Finally, a *space-filling model* gives a clearer picture of the relative sizes of atoms and the distances between them.

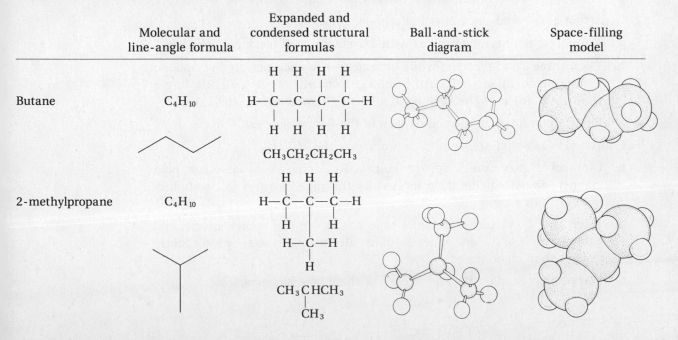

	Molecular and line-angle formula	Expanded and condensed structural formulas	Ball-and-stick diagram	Space-filling model
Butane	C_4H_{10}			
2-methylpropane	C_4H_{10}			

Purpose

In this lab you will make models of various hydrocarbons to study their three-dimensional structures. You will use pipe cleaners, pop beads, and polystyrene spheres to make your models. The pipe cleaners will represent the bonds; the polystyrene spheres will represent the carbon atoms; and the pop beads will represent the hydrogen atoms. Black pipe cleaners will represent carbon-carbon bonds and white pipe cleaners will represent carbon-hydrogen bonds. You will bend the pipe cleaners into angles to better represent the three-dimensional geometry of molecules.

Safety

■ Behave in a way that is consistent with a safe laboratory.

Equipment

6 one-inch polystyrene spheres
12 pop beads
3 black and 3 white pipe cleaners
scissors
ruler

Experimental Procedure

Make a model of each hydrocarbon indicated on Table 43.2, and use the information to fill in Table 43.2 or a table like it.

1. Construct a ball-and-stick model of methane, CH_4.

   a. Place four 2-cm pieces of white pipe cleaner in a polystyrene sphere, arranging them so they form a tetrahedron with angles slightly larger than right angles. (The ideal bond angles in methane are all 109.5°.)

   b. Place a pop bead on the end of each of the 4 pipe cleaners.

2. Construct a ball-and-stick model of ethane, CH_3CH_3.

   a. Connect 2 polystyrene spheres with a 5-cm piece of black pipe cleaner.

   b. Place three 2-cm pieces of white pipe cleaner in each polystyrene sphere, arranging them so they form a tetrahedron with angles slightly larger than right angles. (The ideal bond angles in ethane are all 109.5°.)

   c. Place a pop bead on the end of each of the 6 pipe cleaners.

3. Construct a ball-and-stick model of propane, $CH_3CH_2CH_3$.

   a. Connect 3 polystyrene spheres with two 5-cm pieces of black pipe cleaner, adjusting the angle formed by the pipe cleaners to be slightly greater than a right angle.

   b. Place two 2-cm pieces of white pipe cleaner in the center sphere and three in each of the end spheres. Adjust all the angles so they are slightly greater than right angles.

   c. Place a pop bead on the end of each of the 8 pipe cleaners.

4. Use the same techniques to construct models of the following hydrocarbons. Be sure each carbon has 4 bonds.

    a. butane, $CH_3CH_2CH_2CH_3$ (See p. 309.)

    b. 3-methylbutane (See p. 309.)

    c. pentane, $CH_3CH_2CH_2CH_2CH_3$

5. Ethene is an alkene. All 6 atoms lie in the same plane with bond angles of 120°.

    a. Construct a model of ethene, $CH_2 = CH_2$.

    b. Construct a model of propene, $CH_3CH = CH_2$.

6. Ethyne is an alkyne. All 4 atoms lie in a straight line.

    a. Construct a model of ethyne, $CH \equiv CH$.

    b. Construct a model of propyne, $CH_3C \equiv CH$.

Experimental Data

Record your results in Table 43.1 or a table like it in your notebook.

Table 43.1 Models of Hydrocarbons

Name	Molecular Formula	Structural Formula	Ball-and-Stick Diagram	Bond Angles
1. methane	CH_4	CH_4		109°
2. ethane	C_2H_6	CH_3CH_3		109°
3. propane	C_3H_3	$CH_3CH_2CH_3$		109°
4a. butane	C_4H_{10}	$CH_3CH_2CH_2CH_3$		109°
b. 3-methyl-butane	C_4H_{10}	CH_3CHCH_3 | CH_3		109°
c. pentane	C_5H_{12}	$CH_3CH_2CH_2CH_2CH_3$		109°
5a. ethene	C_2H_4	$CH_2{=}CH_2$		120°
b. propene	C_3H_6	$CH_3CH{=}CH_2$		109° and 120°
6a. ethyne	C_2H_2	$CH{\equiv}CH$		180°
b. propyne	C_3H_4	$CH_3C{\equiv}CH$		180° and 109°

Cleaning Up

When you finish, take apart your models, straighten out each piece of pipe cleaner, and put them away.

Questions for Analysis

Use what you learned in this lab to answer the following questions.

1. What information does a molecular formula give? Give an example.

   It shows the number of each kind of atom in a compound. C_2H_6, ethane.

2. What information does a structural formula give? Give an example.

   It shows the arrangement of each bond and each atom in a formula.

   CH_3CH_3, ethane.

3. What's the difference between an expanded structural formula and a condensed structural formula?

   The expanded structural formula shows each atom and each bond,

   whereas the condensed structural formula shows only the atoms.

4. What's the difference between a ball-and-stick model and a space-filling model? Which is more representative of the true structure of a molecule?

   The ball-and-stick model greatly exaggerates bond lengths. The space-

   filling model is more representative.

5. The atoms around a carbon-carbon single bond exhibit what bond angles?

   109.5°.

6. The atoms around a carbon-carbon double bond exhibit what bond angles?

   120°.

7. The atoms around a carbon-carbon triple bond exhibit what bond angles?

   180°.

Now It's Your Turn!

1. Construct models of the following cyclic hydrocarbons that contain hydrocarbon rings.

   a. cyclopropane (Hint: Attach the black ends of your propane model.)

   b. cyclobutane

2. Longer chain alkenes have *cis* and *trans* geometric isomers (text Section 24.6). Construct models of 1-butene ($CH_2 = CHCH_2CH_3$) and 2-butene ($CH_3CH = CHCH_3$). Which has geometric isomers? Construct models of each geometric isomer.

   2-butene has geometric isomers, *cis* and *trans*.

3. Construct models of 1-butyne, $C \equiv CCH_2CH_3$, and 2-butyne, $CH_3C \equiv CCH_3$. Use them to determine if either of these alkynes have geometric isomers.

Alkynes have no geometric isomers because each of the carbons on either

side of the triple bond are bonded to only one other atom and have 180°

bond angles.

4. Benzene, C_6H_6, is an aromatic hydrocarbon (text Section 24.8). All 12 of its atoms lie in the same plane. Its 6 carbon atoms lie in a flat ring. Construct a model of benzene.

5. Construct a model of methane, CH_4, without using spheres as atoms. Compare it to your ball-and-stick model.

   a. Fold two 4-cm pieces of white pipe cleaner in half, making a bend at each center.

   b. Interlock the pipe cleaners and pinch them together at the bends.

   c. Unfold the 4 ends so they make angles slightly larger than right angles.

6. Construct a line-angle model of ethane, CH_3CH_3, without using spheres as atoms. Compare it to your ball-and-stick model.

   a. Make another model of methane.

   b. Cut a 5-cm piece of black pipe cleaner and bend a small hook at each end.

   c. Attach a methane molecule to each end of the black pipe cleaner by pinching a hook around each methane's center. (How many bonds does each carbon have in your model?)

   d. Eliminate a hydrogen from each end by twisting together any two of the white pipe cleaners.

   e. Arrange all the angles so they are slightly larger than right angles.

7. Construct a model of propane, $CH_3CH_2CH_3$.

   a. Cut a 10-cm piece of black pipe cleaner and fold it in half.

   b. Fold a 4-cm piece of white pipe cleaner in half, and pinch together the black and white pipe cleaners at their folds.

   c. Attach a methane molecule to each end, as with ethane, and twist together two hydrogens and each end.

   d. Make all the angles slightly larger than right angles.

44 Vitamin C in Tablets

Text Section 25.10

Objectives

- **Determine** the vitamin C content of commercial vitamin C tablets by iodometric titration.
- **Observe** the oxidation of vitamin C in aqueous solution.

Introduction

Vitamins are chemical compounds that are essential to human health. These compounds regulate biochemical reactions that take place within living cells. The human body requires vitamins only in tiny amounts. For a compound to be classified as a vitamin, its absence in the diet must cause a specific disease that is cured when the vitamin is resupplied. Vitamin C deficiency, for example, causes scurvy, a disease common to seamen until the latter part of the eighteenth century. Scurvy is cured by increasing the intake of vitamin C.

Purpose

In this lab you will use an iodometric titration to measure the amount of vitamin C in various commercially available vitamin supplements. This method takes advantage of the fact that vitamin C is a water-soluble organic compound that is easily oxidized and is therefore a good reducing agent. Iodine oxidizes vitamin C according to the following equation:

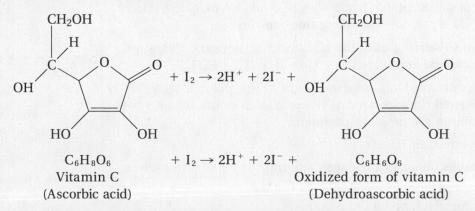

$$C_6H_8O_6 + I_2 \rightarrow 2H^+ + 2I^- + C_6H_6O_6$$

Vitamin C (Ascorbic acid)   Oxidized form of vitamin C (Dehydroascorbic acid)

Because aqueous iodine solutions are unstable and inconvenient to work with, you will titrate vitamin C samples in this lab with potassium iodate, KIO_3, in the presence of an acidic iodide solution. The iodate ion oxidizes iodide to iodine:

$$IO_3^- + 5I^- + 6H^+ \rightleftharpoons 3I_2 + 3H_2O$$

Notice that an equilibrium is established between reactants and products. To insure that the reaction goes to completion (far to the right), it is necessary to use excess iodide and to make the solution acidic.

The iodine formed in this reaction immediately oxidizes the vitamin C according to the previous equation. Once all the vitamin C is oxidized, there will be an excess of I_2 that will react with starch to form the distinctive blue-black complex. This change serves as a good end point.

Safety

- Wear your safety glasses.

- Use full small-scale pipets only for the carefully controlled delivery of liquids.

Materials

Small-scale pipets of the following solutions:

$0.1M$ potassium iodate (KIO_3)   potassium iodide (KI)
vitamin C (ascorbic acid)   hydrochloric acid (HCl)
starch   various vitamin C tablets (100 mg)

Equipment

plastic cup, small-scale reaction surface, balance

Experimental Procedure

Part A. The Chemistry of the Titration

1. Place 2 drops of KIO_3 on a small-scale reaction surface, and add the following solutions. Stir each mixture and record your results in Table 44.1.

   a. Add 2 drops of KI and 2 drops of HCl. In acid solution, iodate ion oxidizes iodide ion to iodine: $IO_3^- + 5I^- + 6H^+ \rightleftharpoons 3I_2 + 3H_2O$

   b. Add a few more drops of KI to the above mixture. Excess iodide ion reacts with iodine to form triiodide ion: $I^- + I_2 \rightarrow I_3^-$

   c. Now add 1 drop of starch. Starch reacts with triiodide ion to form a starch iodine complex: $I_3^- + starch \rightarrow starch\text{-}iodine\ complex$

   d. Now add vitamin C, stirring until the black color disappears. Vitamin C reduces iodine to iodide ion: $C_6H_8O_6 + I_2 \rightarrow 2H^+\ 2I^- + C_6H_6O_6$

   e. Finally, add KIO_3 until the black color reappears. At this point, all the vitamin C has reacted and the excess iodate reacts to form iodine, which gives the black end point in the presence of starch.

Part B. Titration of Vitamin C in Tablets

2. Crush a vitamin C tablet on a piece of paper, and transfer *all* of it to a clean, dry cup.

3. Add 10 drops KI, 2 drops HCl, and 3 drops starch.

4. Tare or weigh a full KIO_3 pipet.

   a. Place a full KIO_3 pipet in a clean dry small-scale balance pan.

   b. Adjust the beam until the small-scale pointer indicates the zero point.

5. Titrate the vitamin C with KIO_3 to a jet black end point.
6. Determine the weight loss of the KIO_3. Record your findings in Table 44.2.
   a. Replace the pipet on the small-scale balance.
   b. Add weights to zero the small-scale balance again. The sum of the added weights is the weight loss of the KIO_3.
7. Repeat until your results are consistent.

Experimental Data

Record your results in Tables 44.1 and 44.2 or tables like them in your notebook.

Table 44.1   The Chemistry of the Titration

	KIO_3	KI + HCl	Excess KI	Starch	Vitamin C	KIO_3
Color	Colorless	Yellow	Dark yellow	Black	Colorless	Black

Table 44.2   Titration of Vitamin C in Tablets

Tablet	1	2	3	4
Weight loss of KIO_3 (mg)	1932	1855		
Vitamin C per tablet (mg)	102	98		

Calculate the milligrams of vitamin C in each tablet you titrated. Record your results in Table 44.2. To do the calculation you will need the following pieces of information:

a. The weight loss of KIO_3 used in the titration in mg.
b. The density of the KIO_3 solution = 1 mL/1000 mg.
c. The concentration of KIO_3 = 0.1 mmol/mL.
d. Overall stoichiometry = 3 mmol vitamin C/1 mmol of KIO_3.
e. The molecular weight of vitamin C = 176 mg/mmol.
   mg Vitamin C = $\mathbf{a} \times \mathbf{b} \times \mathbf{c} \times \mathbf{d} \times \mathbf{e}$

To be sure you understand the calculation, substitute each quantity (number and units) into the equation and cancel the units. For subsequent calculations, simplify the equation by combining terms that are always constant.

Cleaning Up

Avoid contamination by cleaning up in a way that protects you and your environment. Carefully clean the plastic cup by pouring the liquid contents down the drain and rinsing it thoroughly with water. Dry it with a paper towel. Clean the reaction surface by absorbing the contents onto a paper towel, wipe it with a damp paper towel, and dry it. Dispose of the paper towels in the waste bin. Wash your hands thoroughly with soap and water.

Questions for Analysis

Use what you learned in this lab to answer the following questions.

1. When you mix KI, KIO_3, and HCl, what is produced? How can you tell? Write the net ionic equation.

   I_2. Starch turns black. $IO_3^- + 5I^- + 6H^+ \rightleftharpoons 3I_2 + 3H_2O$.

2. When you add vitamin C to the black I_2 mixture, why does the color disappear? Write a net ionic equation.

   Vitamin C reduces I_2 to I^-. $C_6H_8O_6 + I_2 \rightarrow 2H^+ \ 2I^- + C_6H_6O_6$.

3. Compare the values for the amount of vitamin C you calculated with the values you find on the product label by calculating the absolute error and the relative error.

   absolute error = |mg measured experimentally − mg on label|

   |102 mg measured − 100 mg on label| = 2 mg absolute error
   |98 mg measured − 100 mg on label| = 2 mg absolute error

   relative (%) error = $\dfrac{\text{absolute error}}{\text{mg on label}} \times 100$

   $\dfrac{2 \text{ mg}}{100 \text{ mg}} \times 100$ = 2% relative error

4. Why can the density of the KIO_3 solution be taken as 1000 mg/mL?

   Dilute aqueous solutions have very nearly the same density as pure water.

Now It's Your Turn!

1. Design and carry out an experiment to determine the amount of vitamin C in tablets containing amounts of vitamin C larger than 100 mg. Tell what you do, what your results are, and what they mean.

   The major problem is the sample size. Either students must use fractions

   of tablets and account for the differences, or they must use more concen-

   trated KIO_3.

2. Design an experiment to measure the amount of vitamin C in a tablet by using volumetric techniques. Compare your results to those obtained from the weight titration in this lab. (Hint: Dissolve the vitamin C tablet in a known amount of water, and titrate a measured amount of the resulting solution. You will have to calibrate your pipets by using a balance or a well strip.)

3. Dissolve a vitamin C tablet in water, and design an experiment to measure the amount of vitamin C that remains as a function of time. How does temperature affect your results?

45 Vitamin C in Drinks

Text Section 25.10

Objective

■ **Measure** and **compare** the amounts of vitamin C in various kinds of fruit juices and fruit-drink mixes.

Introduction

If you have decided to obtain your vitamin C from a well-balanced diet, you may be wondering, "What is the best source of vitamin C, and how much of it do I need to eat or drink?" Orange juice is well-known for its vitamin C content, but many other foods, especially fresh fruits and vegetables, provide substantial amounts of the nutrient. Most noteworthy are other citrus fruits like lemons, tangerines, and grapefruits. Other good sources of vitamin C are asparagus, broccoli, Brussels sprouts, cauliflower, cabbage, cantaloupe, green peppers, parsley, spinach, rutabagas, and turnip greens. However, prolonged cooking of fresh vegetables in water destroys much of the existing vitamin C.

Purpose

In this lab you will use the iodometric titration technique you learned in Small-Scale Experiment 44 to determine the vitamin C content of various foods. You will compare the vitamin C content of fresh-squeezed orange juice, frozen orange juice concentrate, and grapefruit juice. You will also measure and compare the vitamin C content of other juices and fruit-drink mixes.

Safety

■ Wear your safety glasses.

■ Use full small-scale pipets only for the carefully controlled delivery of liquids.

■ Consider all foods used in this lab to be contaminated. Do not taste any samples or eat or drink anything in the laboratory.

Materials

Small-scale pipets of the following solutions:
0.01M potassium iodate (KIO$_3$)   potassium iodide (KI)
starch   hydrochloric acid (HCl)
various samples of fruit
    juices and fruit drinks

Equipment

plastic cup

Experimental Procedure

1. Weigh approximately 5000 mg of juice. Record the weight in Table 45.1.

   a. Place a nickel (or 2 pennies) of known weight in the balance pan.

   b. Adjust the balance to zero.

   c. Remove the nickel, and add juice until the balance again reads zero.

2. Add 10 drops of KI, 20 drops of HCl, and 5 drops of starch to the juice.

3. Weigh or tare a full KIO$_3$ pipet.

   a. Place a full KIO$_3$ pipet in a second clean, dry balance plan.

   b. Adjust the beam until the pinter indicates the zero point.

4. Titrate the juice with KIO$_3$ to a jet black end point.

5. Determine the weight loss of the KIO$_3$. Record your results in Table 45.1.

   a. Replace the KIO$_3$ pipet in the balance.

   b. Add weights to zero the balance. The sum of the added weights is the weight loss of KIO$_3$.

6. Repeat until your results are consistent.

7. Repeat for several other juice samples as directed by your instructor.

Experimental Data

Record your results in Table 45.1 or a table like it in your notebook.

Table 45.1   Vitamin C in Drinks

	Wt. of juice (mg)	Wt. loss of KIO_3 (mg)	Vitamin C per 6-oz glass (mg)
Fresh orange juice	5000	305	57
Frozen orange juice	5000	250	47
Fresh grapefruit juice	5000	150	28

Calculate the milligrams of vitamin C in a 6-ounce glass for each sample you titrated. Record your results in Table 45.1. To do the calcuation you will need the folowing pieces of information:

a. The weight loss of the KIO_3 you used in the titration in mg.

b. The weight of the juice you used in the titration in mg.

c. Density of juice = 1000 mg/mL

d. Density of KIO_3 solution = 1000 mg/mL

e. Concentration of KIO_3 = 0.01 mmol/mL

f. Molecular weight of vitamin C = 176 mg/mmol

g. Overall stoichiometry: 3 mmol vitamin C/1 mmol KIO_3.

h. 29.6 mL/1 oz.

i. 6 oz/1 glass.

$$\frac{x \text{ mg vitamin C}}{1 \text{ glass}} = \frac{\mathbf{a}}{\mathbf{b}} \times \frac{\mathbf{c}}{\mathbf{d}} \times \mathbf{e} \times \mathbf{f} \times \mathbf{g} \times \mathbf{h} \times \mathbf{i}$$

To be sure you understand the calculation, substitute each quantity (number and units) into the equation and cancel the units. For subsequent calculations, simplify the equation by combining terms that are always constant.

Cleaning Up

Avoid contamination by cleaning up in a way that protects you and your environment. Carefully clean the plastic balance pan by pouring the liquid contents down the drain and rinsing it thoroughly with water. Dry it with a paper towel. Dispose of the paper towels in the waste bin. Wash your hands thoroughly with soap and water.

Questions for Analysis

Use your Experimental Data and what you learned in this lab to answer the following questions.

1. Write a net ionic equation for the reaction of iodate ion with iodide ion in the presence of acid. (See Small-Scale Experiment 44.)

$$IO_3^- + 5I^- + 6H^+ \rightleftharpoons 3I_2 + 3H_2O$$

2. Given the two half-reactions for the reaction of Vitamin C with iodine, identify the oxidation and the reduction, and write and balance an equation in acid solution:

   oxidation: $C_6H_8O_6 \rightarrow C_6H_6O_6 + 2e^-$

   reduction: $I_2 + 2e^- \rightarrow 2I^-$

   net ionic: $C_6H_8O_6 + I_2 \rightarrow 2H^+ + 2I^- + C_6H_6O_6$

3. The recommended dietary allowance (RDA) is the amount of any vitamin or mineral your daily diet should supply to maintain a general standard of good health. The RDA of vitamin C is 60 milligrams. Calculate how many ounces of each of the various fruit juices you need to consume to receive the RDA of vitamin C.

   $$\text{oz. of juice} = 60 \text{ mg} \times \frac{6 \text{ oz of juice}}{\text{mg vitamin C}}$$

   Fresh orange juice = 60 × 6/57 = 6.3 oz, frozen orange juice = 60 × 6/47 = 7.7 oz, fresh grapefruit juice = 60 × 6/28 = 12.9 oz.

4. Go on a shopping trip and record the prices of the various sources of vitamin C you titrated (orange juice, grapefruit juice, fruit drinks, and tablets). Determine the cost of 60 milligrams of vitamin C from each source. Which source is least expensive? Which source is most expensive?

Now It's Your Turn!

1. Design and carry out experiments that will give you data to compare the amount of vitamin C in various packages of orange juice (cartons, cans, fresh-squeezed).

2. Design and carry out experiments to determine the amount of vitamin C in powdered flavored fruit drinks.

   Use a 200 mg sample of the powder and titrate with 0.01M KIO₃. Read the label on the powdered product to determine what fraction 200 milligrams is of the total contents. Use this fraction to calculate the total amount of vitamin C in the original package.

3. Determine the amount of vitamin C in the water used to boil a fresh vegetable that is known to be high in vitamin C.

   Boil the vegetable and titrate a sample of the water.

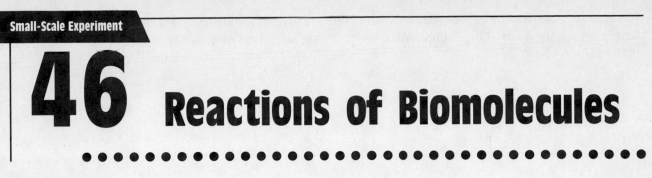

46 Reactions of Biomolecules

Text Section 25.13

Objectives

- **Observe** and **record** reactions of important classes of biological molecules.
- **Identify** classes of biological compounds in foods from experimental data.

Introduction

The food you eat can be classified into five different chemical categories: carbohydrates, proteins, fats, vitamins, and minerals. Carbohydrates are monomers and polymers of aldehydes and ketones with numerous hydroxyl groups attached. One of the simplest carbohydrates is glucose, a monosaccharide, or simple sugar. The chemical structure of glucose looks like this:

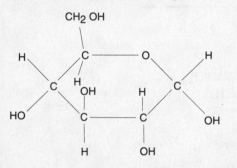

Starch is a polysaccharide composed of many repeating glucose subunits. Its structure looks like this:

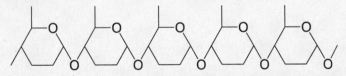

Proteins are long, continuous chains of simpler molecules called amino acids. Amino acids are compounds containing amino ($-NH_2$) and carboxylic acid ($-COOH$) groups in the same molecule. Linked together, two or more amino acids constitute a peptide. A peptide with more than 100 amino acids is called a protein.

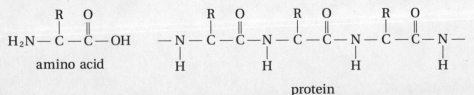

Fats are long-chain carboxylic acids, or esters. Triglycerides are triesters of long-chain fatty acids. The R-groups represent a long saturated or unsaturated hydrocarbon chain.

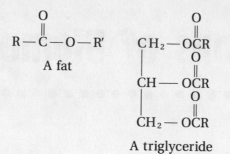

A fat

A triglyceride

Purpose

In this lab you will test various foods for the presence of starch, protein, and fat. You will do this by carrying out some common chemical tests for these kinds of molecules.

Safety

- Wear your safety glasses.
- Use full small-scale pipets only for the carefully controlled delivery of liquids.

Materials

Small-scale pipets of the following solutions:
potassium iodide (KI)
starch
copper(II) sulfate ($CuSO_4$)
Sudan III

sodium hypochlorite (NaOCl)
sodium hydroxide (NaOH)
water (H_2O)

Small samples of various foods including: dry cereal, milk, powdered milk, pasta, sugar, potato chips, crackers, peanut butter, margarine, corn oil, yeast, gelatin, and flour.

Equipment

small-scale reaction surface
scissors
toothpick
white paper

Experimental Page

1. To test for starch, mix 1 drop each of KI and NaOCl in each square below with a small sample of the indicated substance. Record your results in Table 46.1.

starch	pasta	cracker	bread	cereal	flour

2. To test for protein, mix 1 drop each of $CuSO_4$ and NaOH in each square below with a small sample of the indicated substance. Record your results in Table 46.2.

milk	powdered milk	yeast	gelatin	bread	water

3. To test for fat, place a small white scrap of paper over each square below, and use a toothpick to stir 1 drop of Sudan III thoroughly with a small sample of the indicated substance. Record your results in Table 46.3.

corn oil	margarine	peanut butter	milk	flour	water

Place this side of the Experimental Page facedown. Use the other side under your small-scale reaction surface.

Name _____ Class _____ Date _____

Experimental Data

Record your results in Tables 46.1–46.3 or tables like them in your notebook.

Table 46.1   Test for Starch

starch	pasta	cracker	bread	cereal	flour
black	black	black	black	black	black

Table 46.2   Test for Protein

milk	powdered milk	yeast	gelatin	bread	water
blue violet	blue violet	blue violet	blue violet	no change	no change

Table 46.3   Test for Fat

corn oil	margarine	peanut butter	milk	flour	water
dark red	dark red	dark red	dark red	no change	no change

Cleaning Up

Avoid contamination by cleaning up in a way that protects you and your environment. Carefully clean the small-scale reaction surface by absorbing the contents onto a paper towel, wipe it with a damp paper towel, and dry it. Dispose of the paper towels, scraps of paper and toothpicks in the waste bin. Wash your hands thoroughly with soap and water.

Questions for Analysis

Use what you learned in this lab to answer the following questions.

1. Describe a positive test for starch. Which samples gave a positive test for starch?

   KI + NaOCl added to the sample produces a blue black color. Pasta, crackers, bread, cereal, and flour.

2. Describe a positive test for protein. Which samples gave positive tests?

   $CuSO_4$ + NaOH added to the sample produces a blue violet color. Milk, powdered milk, yeast, and gelatin.

3. Describe a positive test for fat. Which samples gave positive tests?
Sudan III mixed into the sample with a toothpick causes the red color to

intensify as it is absorbed into the sample. Corn oil, margarine, peanut

butter, and milk.

4. Which substance contained more than one classification of food?
Milk.

5. The positive test for starch works because potassium iodide reacts with sodium hypochlorite to produce I_2. The presence of iodine is detected by starch, which turns blue black according to the following unbalanced chemical equations:

$$\underline{1}\ OCl^- + \underline{2}\ I^- + \underline{2}\ H^+ \rightarrow \underline{1}\ I_2 + \underline{1}\ H_2O + \underline{1}\ Cl^-$$

I_2 + starch → blue black starch-iodine complex.

a. Balance the first equation above.

b. Write half-reactions to show the oxidation and the reduction for the first equation above.

$OCl^- + 2e^- \rightarrow Cl^-$
reduction

$2I^- \rightarrow I_2 + 2e^-$
oxidation

6. Sodium hydroxide breaks protein chains into individual amino acids, which bond to copper(II) ions to form a distinguishing deep blue violet color. Draw the structural formula of an amino acid.

7. Sudan III is a fat-soluble dye that imparts a red orange stain to the long-chain fat molecules. Do you expect Sudan III to be very soluble in water? Why?
No. Fat-soluble dyes dissolve in non-polar molecules. Water is very polar.

("Like dissolves like.")

8. Why do you suppose the dye color of Sudan III intensifies when it is mixed with fats?
As Sudan III is absorbed into the fat, it becomes more concentrated.

Now It's Your Turn!

1. Try testing the various foods in this lab for all three classes of biological molecules—starch, protein, and fat.

Name _____ Class _____ Date _____

2. So-called "reducing sugars" have structural properties that will give electrons to copper(II) ion and reduce it.

$$Cu^{2+} + 1e^- \rightarrow Cu^+$$

Reducing sugars can be identified by using Benedict's solution, which contains copper(II) ions, or Cu^{2+}. When heated, a mixture of Benedict's solution and a reducing sugar turns from blue to green or yellow.

Carry out a positive Benedict's test for reducing sugars in the following way:

a. Combine the chemicals below on a glass slide as shown.

b. Place the glass slide on a hot plate. **Caution:** *The glass will be hot. Handle with a plastic spatula.*

c. Note the change with time. A distinct color change indicates a reducing sugar.

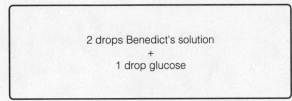

2 drops Benedict's solution
+
1 drop glucose

3. Test 1 drop of various other samples with 2 drops of Benedict's solution. Try HOH, galactose, milk, honey, etc.

4. Add a drop of HCl to sucrose, a non-reducing sugar. What happens when you add Benedict's solution? What can you conclude?

The solution turns from blue to green or yellow. HCl has hydrolyzed the

sucrose to produce glucose, a reducing sugar.

47 Half-Lives and Reaction Rates

Text Section 26.4

Objectives

- **Measure** and **record** the rate at which hydrochloric acid, HCl, reacts with magnesium, Mg.
- **Identify** the half-life of the reaction by interpreting a graph of the experimental data.
- **Determine** the order of the reaction by plotting the experimental data.

Introduction

A half-life is the time required for one half of the atoms of a radioisotope to emit radiation and to decay to products. After one half-life, half of the radioactive atoms have decayed into atoms of another element. After another half-life, only a quarter of the original sample remains. After another half-life, only an eighth remains, and so on.

Because the concept of half-life is probably unfamiliar to you, you may conclude intuitively that if it takes one hour for half of a radioactive sample to decay, then it should take only another hour for the other half to decay. This conclusion is based on the false assumption that the rate of decay is linear (constant over time). In fact, radioisotopes decay in a nonlinear fashion. The rate of decay slows over time so that the more time has elapsed, the more slowly the decay proceeds. The reactants of many chemical reactions that involve no radioactivity at all react to form products at an easily measurable half-life.

Purpose

In this lab you will make a quantitative study of the rate of reaction between hydrochloric acid and magnesium and determine the half-life of the reaction.

$$2HCl + Mg \rightarrow MgCl_2 + H_2(g)$$

As time progresses, the reactants will be consumed. You will stop the reaction after various time intervals by removing the magnesium. You will then measure the amount of HCl consumed in reacting with Mg by titrating the unreacted HCl with potassium hydroxide, KOH. The number of drops of KOH required in the titration is proportional to the amount of HCl consumed by the magnesium.

You will then begin the reaction again, stop it after a longer period of time, and titrate the HCl again. By doing this several times, you will have measured the number of drops of KOH required for the titration at various times during the reaction. The same piece of magnesium can be used because the thin ribbon has nearly the same surface area exposed in each run. For this reason the amount of magnesium exposed to the acid in each run will not change. This is important because you will be measuring the disappearance of HCl over time, and you do not want it to be affected by the different sizes of magnesium pieces. Finally, after several runs, the ribbon will become so thin that it will no longer be useful, and you can stop the experiment. You will determine the half-life of the reaction by plotting the drops of KOH used in the titration versus time.

Safety

- Wear your safety glasses.

- Use full small-scale pipets only for the carefully controlled delivery of liquids.

Materials

Small-scale pipets of the following solutions:
hydrochloric acid (HCl)   potassium hydroxide (KOH)
phenolphthalein (phen)   water (H$_2$O)
Solid: magnesium ribbon.

Equipment

watch or clock

Experimental Procedure

1. Add 10 drops of HCl to a clean, dry one-ounce plastic cup.

2. Add 1 drop of phenolphthalein and titrate with KOH, counting the drops to the pink end point. Record your results in Table 47.1 or a table like it. Clean and dry the cup for the next run. Note: This run for time 0 is a titration of the HCl before any magnesium is added.

3. Add 10 more drops of HCl to a clean, dry cup.

4. Cut 3 cm of Mg ribbon. Dip the piece of Mg in a few drops of HCl for a few seconds to dissolve the tarnish. Dry the ribbon.

5. Tilt the cup at an angle and dip the piece of Mg into the HCl for 10 seconds. Hold the Mg ribbon vertically, moving it constantly to dislodge the forming gas bubbles. Keep the magnesium submerged at a constant depth. At the end of 10 seconds, remove the Mg and wash it quickly with water, making sure the wash water enters the HCl in the cup. Dry the Mg for the next run.

6. Add one drop of phenolphthalein and titrate and record your data in Step 2.

7. Repeat Steps 5 and 6 for time intervals of 20, 30, 40, 50, 60, and 70 seconds or until all the magnesium is used up. Record your results in Table 47.1 or a table like it.

Experimental Data

Record your results in Table 47.1 or a table like it in your notebook.

Table 47.1   Reaction-Rate Data

Run	0	1	2	3	4	5	6	7
Drops of HCl	10	10	10	10	10	10	10	10
Time (s)	0	10	20	30	40	50	60	70
Drops of KOH to pink	43	25	15	7	5	4	Mg depleted	Mg depleted
1/drops of KOH	0.023	0.040	0.067	0.14	0.10	0.25	—	—
Log drops of KOH	1.6	1.4	1.2	0.85	0.70	0.60	—	—

1. Calculate the reciprocal of the number of drops of KOH (1/drops of KOH) for each time you measured. Record your results in Table 47.1 above.

2. Calculate the log of the number of drops of KOH, log (drops of KOH), for each time you measured. Record your results in Table 47.1.

3. Make a plot of drops of KOH (*y*-axis) vs. time in seconds (*x*-axis).
   Drops of KOH vs. time

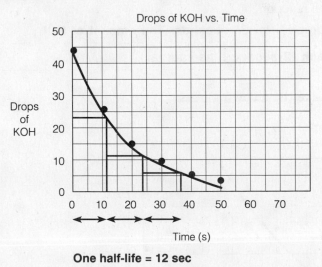

One half-life = 12 sec

Cleaning Up

Avoid contamination by cleaning up in a way that protects you and your environment. Carefully clean the plastic cup by flooding it with water and rinsing its contents down the drain. Shake excess water out, and allow it to dry upside down on a paper towel. Dispose of any remaining magnesium by placing it in the appropriate recycling container. Wash your hands thoroughly with soap and water.

Questions for Analysis

Use what you learned in this lab to answer the following questions.

1. What do you see when Mg reacts with HCl? Write a complete chemical equation and a net ionic equation for the reaction between Mg and HCl.

   Bubbles. $2HCl + Mg(s) \rightarrow MgCl_2 + H_2(g)$. $2H^+ + Mg(s) \rightarrow Mg^{2+} + H_2(g)$.

2. Look at your plot of drops KOH vs. time. What happens to the rate of reaction as time progresses? Why?

   It slows down because the concentration of the HCl decreases over time.

3. How many drops of KOH were required to titrate the HCl after 0 seconds? What is half this value?

   43. 21.5.

4. Using your plot of drops KOH vs. time, determine the half-life of the reaction. To do this, find the time required for the HCl to drop to half its value by finding the time that corresponds to half the number of drops of KOH in Question 3.

   Approximately 12 seconds.

5. Find the time required for the number of drops to fall to one-fourth of the original value and one-eighth of the original value. Explain how these values also represent the half-life of the reaction.

   11 drops after 24 seconds, 6 drops after 36 seconds. The amount of HCl

   falls to half of its value after each 12-second time interval.

6. Use your data in Table 47.1 to make the following plots:

   a. 1/drops of KOH vs. time in seconds

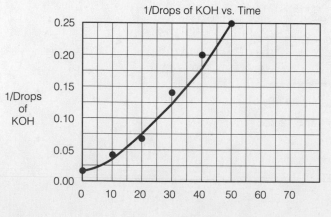

1/Drops of KOH vs. Time

b. log (drops KOH) vs. time in seconds.

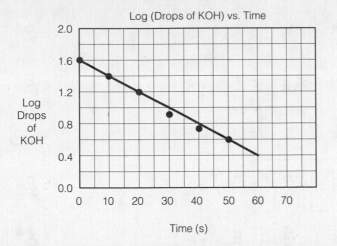

Log (Drops of KOH) vs. Time

7. The "order" of the reaction gives us information about the number of hydrogen ions involved up to and including the rate-determining step. The rate of a zero-order reaction is independent of the concentration of HCl. In a first-order reaction, the rate varies directly with the concentration of HCl. The rate of a second-order reaction varies with the square of the concentration of HCl. The order with of the reaction of HCl and Mg (respect to the HCl concentration) can be determined from the plot that most closely resembles a straight line.

Straight-Line Plot	Order of Reaction
drops KOH vs. time	zero order
log (drops KOH) vs. time	first order
1/drops KOH vs. time	second order

What is the "order" of the reaction with respect to the HCl concentration? How do you know?

First order. The plot of log (drops KOH) vs. time is a straight line.

8. The rate law for the reaction takes the form: rate = $k[HCl]^n$ where n = the order of the reaction. What is the rate law for this reaction?

Rate = $k[HCl]^1$.

Now It's Your Turn!

1. Design and carry out a similar experiment for the reaction of $CaCO_3(s)$ + HCl.

2. Design and carry out an experiment to measure the rate of reaction in a different way. For example, measure the amount of hydrogen gas produced over time or the weight loss of magnesium over time.

Periodic Table of the Elements

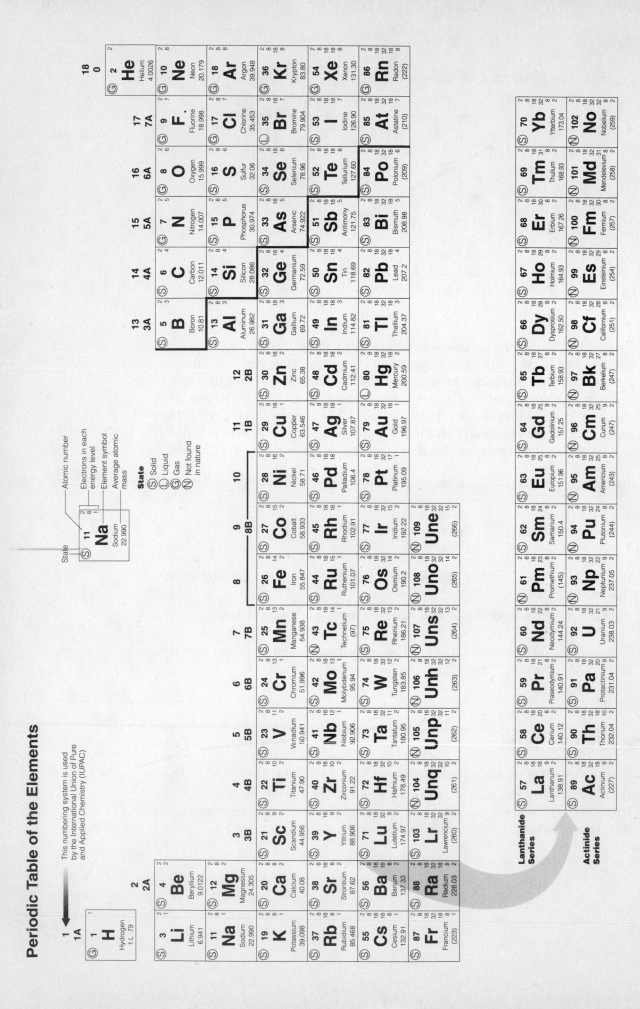